HANDTOOLS
OF ARTS AND CRAFTS

HANDTOOLS
OF ARTS AND CRAFTS
The Encyclopedia of the Fine, Decorative and Applied Arts

the Diagram Group

St. Martin's Press
New York

The Diagram Group

Managing editor	Ruth Midgley
Editor	Gail Lawther
Copy editor	Maureen Cartwright
Researchers	Hope Cohen, Enid Moore, Linda Proud, Marita Westberg
Indexer	Mary Ling
Art director	Kathleen McDougall
Art editor	Mark Evans
Artists	Stephen Clark, Brian Hewson, Richard Hummerstone, Susan Kinsey, Janos Marffy, Graham Rosewarne
Art assistants	Richard Colville, Neil Connell, Paul Fowke, Alan Harris, Richard Prideaux, Andrew Riley, Ray Stevens, John Woodcock

Foreword

The visitor to Florence, Pompeii, Cairo, Mexico City or any of the art capitals of the world cannot but be impressed by the buildings, sculptures, paintings, furnishings and objets d'art which bear testament to the skills of earlier artists. Television programs and museum exhibitions present artefacts from every culture and age to an ever widening audience. Unfortunately the artist of today is becoming the rare custodian of vanishing human skills. 20th century technology is replacing individual artistry with repetitive and mechanical techniques. We are losing the knowledge of how to make paper, carve stone, weave fabric, or even use a pen and ink to produce clear, beautiful letterforms.

As each new labor-saving device is introduced, the existence of traditional tools is threatened. Unlike the works of art, the tools that created them are seldom preserved for their intrinsic value. All too often, as the need for the tool is reduced, the ability to use it is lost, until finally it becomes rare and mysterious—its original function is no longer known. So although the appreciation of art objects is expanding among the public, how they were—and are—made is becoming a secret known only by a few. How many people now would know how to make jewelry like that in the tomb of Tutankhamen, mix colors like those of the Mona Lisa, inlay pearl shell in tabletops, bind a book, or even make the simplest thrown pot?

The editors of HANDTOOLS have gathered together examples of the tools for over 150 specialized fine and applied arts, involving the use of over 2000 tools. Each skill is illustrated by an example of the art form, or by a documentary illustration of the artist at work. Where possible, examples of early tools, now rare museum pieces, are placed alongside present-day tools to show development and continuity within artistic activities. The implements are presented in the order in which they are used by the artist, with step-by-step diagrams of the tools in use.

Working from actual artefacts, manufacturers' catalogs, museum exhibits and historical documents, it has been necessary for the editors to revive one of the basic skills of the artist: the ability to draw objects accurately and in detail. They hope that this study of handtools will help stimulate and renew general interest in this fascinating subject, and in this way further extend the appreciation of all the fine and applied arts.

Contents

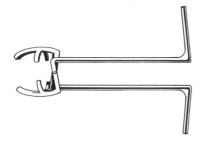

1 Writing and drawing

This chapter illustrates writing and drawing instruments, the tools of the autographic artist. Both writing and drawing have existed since ancient times, and both have developed in all parts of the world.

The implements that have been used for writing through the ages have depended on a variety of factors. Convenience dictated some of the developments, such as the use of small portable wax tablets (and therefore writing styli) for informal tasks in Roman times, instead of the more cumbersome papyrus roll and reed pen that were used for legal and documentary work. In some areas the tool dictated the letter-form, for instance in the development of the cuneiform "alphabet" from pictures drawn with a wedge-shaped reed. In other cases the tool had to be adapted to the changes in writing styles; when

the Japanese pictorial characters became symbolic representations in which every line was important, the wide-bodied, fine-tipped Sumi brushes were developed to reproduce the necessary detail.

The process of refining and developing writing and drawing instruments still continues. The necessity for accuracy in technical illustration in modern times has led to the production of pens that will draw lines of constant thicknesses. New materials and new requirements are continuing to provide fresh challenges and fresh opportunities for the autographic artist.

This stone frieze depicts Egyptian scribes at work, and dates from the 4th Dynasty (2650-2500 BC). The hieroglyphics above the scribes describe the work that is being done.

Writing on bone and stone

As language evolved, man began to seek more permanent ways of recording information; the smooth surfaces of bone and stone were ideal trial grounds. Simple pictures had been made on cave walls for thousands of years, and it was a logical refinement to make these into pictograms conveying specific information—the forerunners of writing as we know it.

The Rosetta stone (right) is one of the most famous examples of ancient writing on stone. Dating from c. 200BC, it was found in Egypt in 1799 and is now in the British Museum. It shows three scripts: Egyptian hieroglyphic, Egyptian demotic, and Greek.

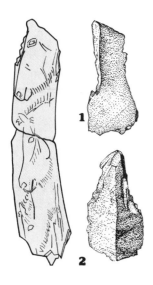

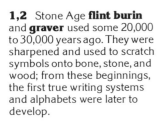

1,2 Stone Age **flint burin** and **graver** used some 20,000 to 30,000 years ago. They were sharpened and used to scratch symbols onto bone, stone, and wood; from these beginnings, the first true writing systems and alphabets were later to develop.

Above is a fragment of a Roman inscription from the area of Regium Lepidum in Northern Italy. Horizontal and vertical guidelines have been marked first, and compasses have been used to trace the curved letters. On the right are tools of the kind used by the Roman stonecutter.
3 Round-ended scalprum (chisel).
4 Sharp-ended scalprum.
5 Malleus (hammer) used for guiding the chisels.
6 Calipers for taking accurate measurements.
7 Square with **plumbline.**
8 Square.

The finest examples of Roman lettering were cut with two equal slices of the **chisel,** making a V-shaped incision (right). Strong shadows in the grooves made some strokes of the letter appear thick and others thin, and these characteristics survive in modern "roman" alphabets.

Writing on clay and wax

Once written communication had begun, man experimented with more convenient writing surfaces. Clay and wax were readily available, and could be shaped into portable tablets; they were soft, and therefore easier to mark than bone and stone, and mistakes could simply be smoothed over. Gradually, writing systems became more and more sophisticated.

Illustrated (right) are two examples of Sumerian writing in clay. The first, dating from c. 2900BC, is essentially pictorial in character. The second, from the city of Nippur, shows a more developed Sumerian script with symbols made up mainly of triangles.

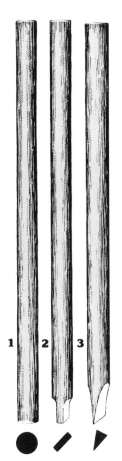

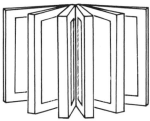

Clay tablets were often very small, perhaps to allow scribes to hold them in one hand while they were writing (as shown above). While the clay was still soft it was marked with a shaped **reed;** on the left are shown three possible end shapes.

1 Blunt reed for making dots.

2 Chisel-ended reed for drawing lines.

3 Pointed reed suitable for making the triangular shapes of developed cuneiform writing. The completed tablets were often baked to make them more durable, and indeed many of them have survived to the present day.

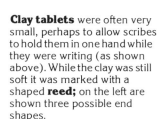

Many civilizations have used forms of **wax tablets** as writing surfaces; they could be marked with a variety of sharp instruments, and then the wax smoothed over when the writing was no longer needed. Shown above are some implements for writing on wax.

4 Wooden tablet; the frame made by the raised edges was filled with soft wax.

5,6,7 Styli used for marking the wax.

The tablets were sometimes made into elementary "books" by making holes in the edge of each tablet and tying them together with thongs, as shown on the left.

Development of the pen 1

The first implements developed specifically for writing with liquids were the reed pens used in ancient Egypt, Greece and Rome. These were superseded by the more durable quill pen used in medieval times; the quill was to remain virtually unchallenged until the development of the steel pen in the 1840s.

The section of a frieze on the left comes from an Egyptian tomb. The center hieroglyph is the symbol for "writing" or "scribe," and consists of a pen, a water pot, and a palette. The detail shown on the right is part of the Decretum Gratiani, a 13th century Czechoslovakian manuscript of canon law.

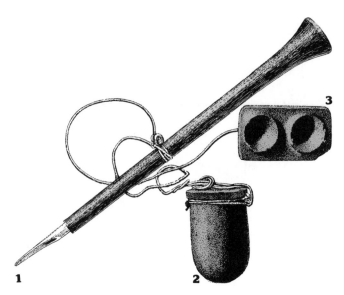

1 Illustration of a typical Egyptian **reed pen.**
2 **Water container,** attached to the pen; the water was used for mixing pigments.
3 **Palette** with two circular hollows, used for holding two different colors of ink or pigment.

4 **Half-moon knife,** used for removing blemishes or mistakes from vellum and parchment.
5 **Quill pen**—an early, unsophisticated form.
6 **Horn inkwell,** with compass-drawn ornaments.

On the right is an Egyptian stone relief from the 4th dynasty (2650-2500BC). The figure is that of a scribe, kneeling in the customary writing pose of the time; spare **pens** are kept behind his ears, and he holds the **palette** of pigments in his left hand.

The 15th century woodcut on the right is of Saint Augustine writing in his cell. He is using a **quill pen,** and around him are various medieval writing accessories such as the **inkpot, inkstand, pounce container** and **candleholder.**

Very few old quill pens have survived intact, but contemporary sources provide a good deal of information about their use; handwriting and craft manuals have detailed instructions and illustrations on the selection and preparation of quills and all their accessories. The print (right), published in 1540, shows every possible writing aid that might have been required for the production of fine script—all the accessories are keyed individually in the list on the right.

1 Straight-edge **ruler.**
2 **Square.**
3 **Pounce container.**
4 **Hour glass.**
5 **Ink container.**
6 **Quill pen.**
7 **Sealing wax.**
8 **Tweezers.**
9 **Thread.**
10 **Pen knife.**
11 **Shears.**
12 **Dividers.**
13 Hooded **candleholder.**
14 **Hare's foot** for spreading pounce.
15 **Mirror.**
16 **Pounce shaker.**
17 **Seal.**
18 **Inkstand.**
19 **Stylus** for ruling lines.
20 **Thimble.**
21 **Candle snuffer.**

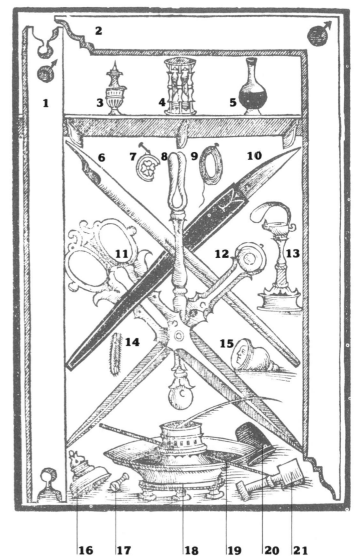

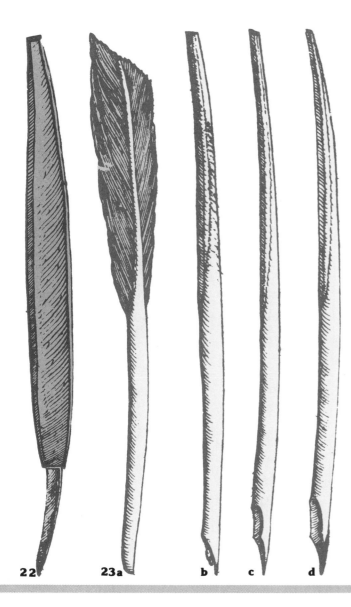

22 23a b c d

22 Pen-knife used for scraping the quill barrel and for cutting the nib.
23a,b,c,d Quill pen in the various stages of its preparation; the feathers are removed, the barrel hardened and clarified, then the nib is shaped and slit.

The illustration above is from a book produced in 1544 by Johann Neudorfer; it is demonstrating the correct way of holding a quill in order to produce well-formed handwriting.

Development of the pen 2

Quill pens required tedious preparation, but their flexibility and adaptability were hard to match. Many years of experimentation took place before the steel pen was marketed in the 1820s, but once the breakthrough had been made ways were soon found of improving the flexibility of the nib and of lowering the cost through mass production.

The print reproduced on the right is a detail from a Sears Roebuck catalog produced at the turn of the century. The pen is made of solid gold, with an iridium point, and its filling system is typical of that time.

PRESS THE BUTTON
FILLED IN A FLASH

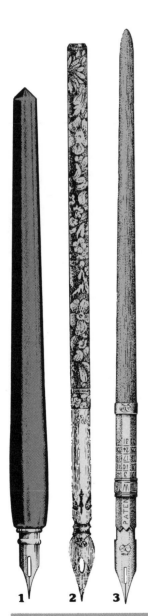

As a greater variety of steel nibs became available, manufacturers devised large ranges of attractive penholders. Pens for very special gifts could be made out of ivory, ebony, silver or gold, but even at the cheaper end of the market the choice was wide. On the left are three fairly cheap wooden penholders of the 1880s.

1 Plain penholder; the thick shaft would have been easy for a child to grip.
2 Decorated penholder.
3 Penholder with calendar; the monthly calendar is made of stamped metal and molded round the shaft.
4 Blotter.

Originally ink was dried by sprinkling it with sand or with powdered chalk or mica. In the 18th century it was discovered that a very absorbent paper would "blot" extremely well, and this blotting paper was often made into shaped **blotters** such as the one below.

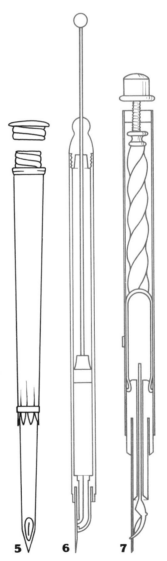

With **quill** and **steel pens** alike, the problem remained of supplying a constant flow of ink; the need to dip the pen every few words made it difficult to produce an even and consistent line. Small reservoirs were produced that could be fixed onto nibs, but again the flow was not easily controlled. A logical progression was to the hollow shaft; this was filled with ink which then flowed into the nib, but it was messy to fill and very liable to leak. The idea was further refined to produce hollow shafts filled by means of a plunger or a screw, and eventually the fountain pen as we know it was developed when the expanding ink sac became a separate part of the pen, inside the rigid shaft.
The first ink sacs were made from animal intestines, but the advantages of rubber were soon realized. Shown on the left are three early fountain pens.
5 Screw-top pen with hollow shaft.
6 Plunger-operated fountain pen.
7 Screw-operated fountain pen with enclosed ink sac.

1   2   3   4   5   6   7

Modern Western calligraphy

The revival of interest in the art of calligraphy, perhaps as a reaction to the mass-produced book, has meant that the quill pen and steel nib have not disappeared entirely from the market. Although the fountain pen and the ball-point have come into general use, craftsmen still prefer the traditional tools for executing specialized lettering.

An example of modern Western calligraphy is illustrated on the right. The capital letters are based on Roman lettering, and the lower-case letters are in the style of a half-uncial alphabet.

ABCD abcdefg EFGH

The Western world uses **pens** and **quills** rather than brushes for its calligraphy, but the choice of nib shape or quill cut depends very much on personal taste and on the lettering to be done. Steel nibs are usually inserted into wood or plastic **holders,** and can be interchanged. Two common styles of holder are illustrated on the left.
1 Plastic penholder with a "crow quill" type steel nib.
2 Wood penholder with a slightly broader nib and a slip-on **reservoir** to hold the ink against the nib.
3 Copperplate nib.

Broad nibs are used to produce contrasting thick and thin lines, varying with the angle of the nib and the way in which the pen is held. Below are shown three nib variations.
4 Straight nib.
5 Left oblique nib.
6 Right oblique nib.

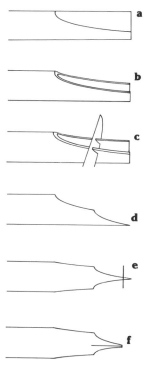

a
b
c
d
e
f
g

Cutting the nib is the most important part of the preparation of a quill for lettering. The illustrations on the left show the main stages in the process.
a The line to be cut first on the quill is gauged by eye.
b The first shallow cut is made with one slice of the **knife** from the top edge of the quill to the tip.
c A further downward slice is made nearer the tip.
d This results in a point and forms the basic nib shape.
e The tip of the nib can be cut off either straight, as shown, or at an oblique angle.
f A slit is made in the center of the nib to carry the ink to the tip.
g A spring made of metal can be inserted into the nib to act as a reservoir if required.

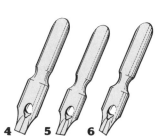

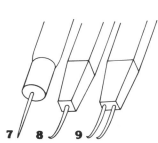

Accurate margins and lines for lettering can be marked out with these tools.
7 Awl, used to prick marks through several pages at once.
8 Ruling stylus, curved to prevent it from tearing the paper.
9 Double ruling stylus.

1   2   3   4   5   6   7   8   9

© DIAGRAM

Modern pens

Considerable ingenuity has been devoted to the development of modern pens. Fountain pens now combine efficient filling systems with hard-wearing nibs. Ball-points became serious rivals following the work of L.J. Biro in the 1930s, and since their development in the 1950s fiber-tips have won widespread popularity. Technical drawing pens have also been developed.

The drawing on the right shows an illustrator using a technical drawing pen for fine work. Each nib for the pen draws a line of predictable and consistent thickness, which is a major asset in technical illustration.

1 Fountain pen of modern design, with barrel and cap made of plastic. In many of the early examples, ink was held directly within the barrel. Diagrams show the most usual modern systems: ink is held in a rubber sac, or in a plastic cartridge.
2 Ink cartridge.

If a **fountain pen** has an interior rubber sac it is filled by immersing the nib in ink and then using a side lever (**a**) or an end plunger (**b**) to compress and release the sac until it fills by suction. Other pens (**c**) are fitted with a new ink-holding cartridge.

3 Ball-point pen with push-button retractable point. Other types have a non-retractable point with a cap for protection. The ink is contained in a plastic tube. Cheap pens are usually thrown away when the ink is finished.
4 Refill for ball-point pen.
5 Felt-tip pen is part way between a pen and a brush. Ink is contained in the barrel (see left), and the pen thrown away when empty. Different types of fiber-tip pen are designed for specific uses.
6 Marking pen, with chunky barrel and broad felt tip.

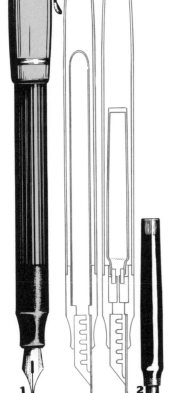

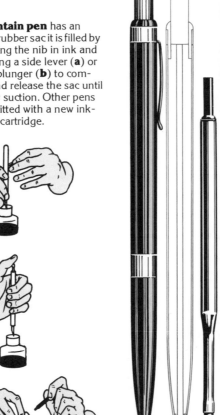

a

b

c

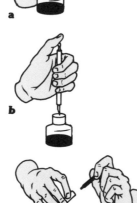

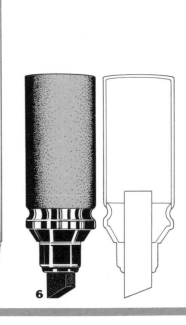

1   2   3   4   5   6

These diagrams show the ink-flow systems for different kinds of pen.

a Fountain pen: pressure on the nib in writing causes more ink to flow down into the nib.

b Ball-point pen: the ball-bearing rotates in use to pick up the greasy ink from the capillary tube.

c Felt-tip pen: ink from the barrel of the pen soaks down through the fiber tip.

d Reservoir-nib pen: this is similar to a fountain pen, with the ink contained in a reservoir behind the nib.

e Stencil-type pen: a tiny piston controls the ink flow from the cartridge; to work, it must be held vertically.

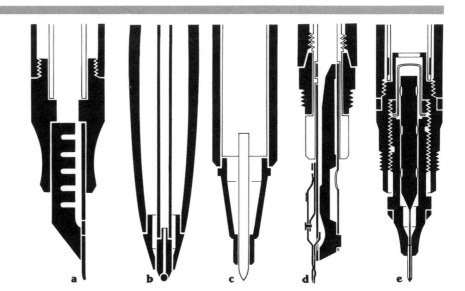

a   b   c   d   e

1 Reservoir-nib pen is used by technical artists. Nibs are clipped over an ink reservoir screwed into the holder.

2 Examples of **nibs** are shown below: fine and broad ruling nibs, nib for sketching, stencil nib, round nib, oblique nib.

Ink for use in **technical drawing pens** is often obtained in plastic bottles with nozzle ends. A **reservoir-nib pen** is filled by squeezing the bottle so that drops of ink enter the reservoir. A **dropper** can be used to transfer ink from a bottle.

3 Stencil-type drawing pen is an extremely useful technical drawing pen. As shown left, an ink-holding cartridge fits into the holder.

4 Screw-in **nibs** are illustrated below, ranging from a .13mm (very fine) to a 3.0mm (broad).

To fill a **stencil-type pen,** the artist either replaces the ink cartridge with a new one, or tops up the old cartridge from a nozzle-ended bottle of special ink. To allow room for the screw-in nib, the cartridge should only be two-thirds full of ink.

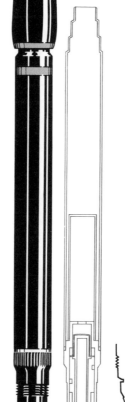

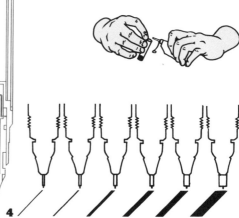

Pencils, chalks, crayons

Various solid-substance writing implements are now in common use. Pencils are designed to meet many different needs; artists' charcoal, chalks, pastels, and wax crayons all have their particular uses. In some instances the marking material is fitted into a holder or protective casing. Erasers and sharpening tools are valuable accessories.

Illustrated (left) is an early **pencil** fitted with a graphite "lead."
On the right is a pencil self portrait by Henry Fuseli (in the National Gallery, London). The drawing demonstrates the wide variety of tonal and line effects that can be achieved with pencil.

Pencils may have been used in the 13th century, but the earliest known text reference to what we call a pencil dates from 1565. Modern pencil manufacture is based on a process developed in 1795 by N.J. Conté: graphite is ground with clay, pressed into sticks, and fired in a kiln. A hard lead contains more clay than a soft lead.

1 Typical modern pencil with juniper wood casing and graphite and clay lead. Pencils range from 9H (very hard) through HB (medium) to 6B (very soft). The range is illustrated here by the pencils' different ends and the types of line produced.

2 Propelling pencil with screw mechanism to draw the lead through the holder.

3 Clutch pencil with a button-operated clutch device to hold the lead in position. Pressing the button releases the lead.

4 Box of leads.

5 Engineer's pencil, a type of propelling pencil with a broad, flat lead.

6 Lithographer's pencil has removable paper strips over a thick, waxy "lead."

7 Colored pencil with lead made from clay, waxes, gum tragacanth and coloring.

8 Wax pencil with soft lead for use on smooth surfaces, eg china or film.

9 Promotional pencil with rubber.

9H
8H
7H
6H
5H
4H
3H
2H
H
HB
B
2B
3B
4B
5B
6B

1   2   3   4   5   6   7   8   9

Solid-substance writing implements call for a variety of accessories.

1 Blackboard eraser for removing chalk has a thick felt pad in a wood handle.

2 Dual-purpose eraser with white soft rubber for erasing pencil and colored hard rubber for use on ink.

3 Putty eraser is soft and pliable. Dabbed on pencil or charcoal it reduces tonal value without smudging.

4 Pen-knife may be used for sharpening pencils.

5 Hand pencil sharpener with screwed-in blade.

6 Desk pencil sharpener, operated by turning the handle. Holes take pencils of different sizes.

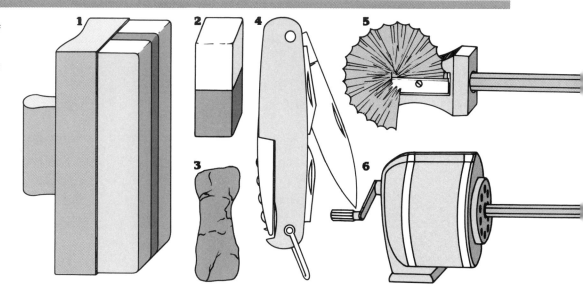

Shown left and below is a selection of other solid-substance writing tools.

7 Charcoal pencil with "lead" of finely ground, highly compacted charcoal. Less messy, but not as versatile as stick charcoal.

8 Charcoal stick, usually willow, beech, or vine, is an extremely responsive artist's drawing tool.

9 Graphite pencil, a squat propelling pencil with thick graphite lead giving a smooth, shiny line.

10 Graphite stick for larger areas of tone.

11 Blackboard chalk made from natural chalk (also called whiting) or from artificially prepared calcium carbonate. Usually white but may be colored.

12 Chalk holder with clutch grip. Keeps chalk off hands.

13 Kindergarten chalk, thick sticks of chalk available in various bright colors.

14 Pastel made of finely ground pigments and a non-greasy binder. Blended on the paper, pastels give a wide range of shades and tints.

15 Conté crayon is a type of crayon produced in black, white, grays, sepia, and sanguine (blood red) colors.

16 Wax crayon made in many colors by combining dyes or pigments in wax. Paper-wrapped to keep hands clean.

17 Oil pastel.

18 Triangular wax crayon designed for young children.

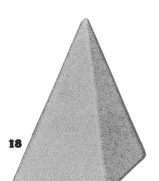

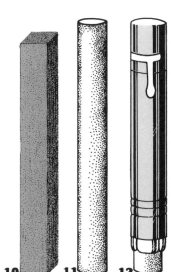

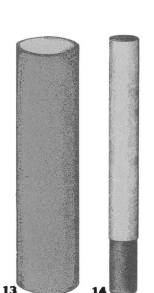

Technical drawing 1

Accuracy and clarity are essential in all technical drawing work, and various precision instruments have been developed to meet these needs. The technical drawing pen developed from the fountain pen and is described on page 19. A selection of other technical drawing instruments is included here.

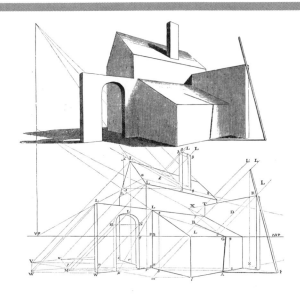

Taken from Charles Hayter's "Perspective, Practical Geometry, Drawing and Painting" of 1845, the illustration shows a skilled use of technical drawing instruments.

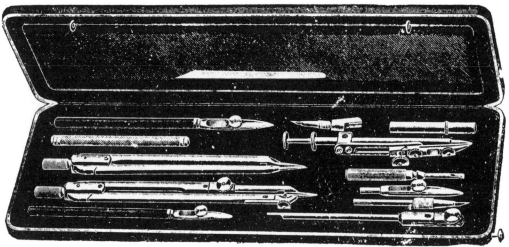

The **set of technical drawing instruments** (left) appeared in a 1912 German catalog. It includes ruling pens, dividers, compasses, and various attachments and accessories. Very similar instruments are used by technical artists today.

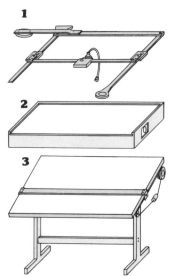

1 Pantograph, a device for marking larger or smaller copies of an illustration.
2 Light box; light shining through the white translucent lid allows the artist to trace from a transparency.
3 Drafting table, with parallel-motion fitting. The rule is moved manually up and down to indicate parallel straight lines.

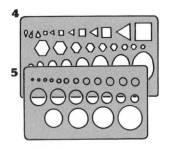

Templates, usually made of metal or plastic, help the technical artist to draw a great variety of shapes with accuracy and speed. Several examples are shown here.
4 Multishape template.
5 Circle template.
6 30° ellipse template.

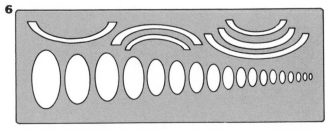

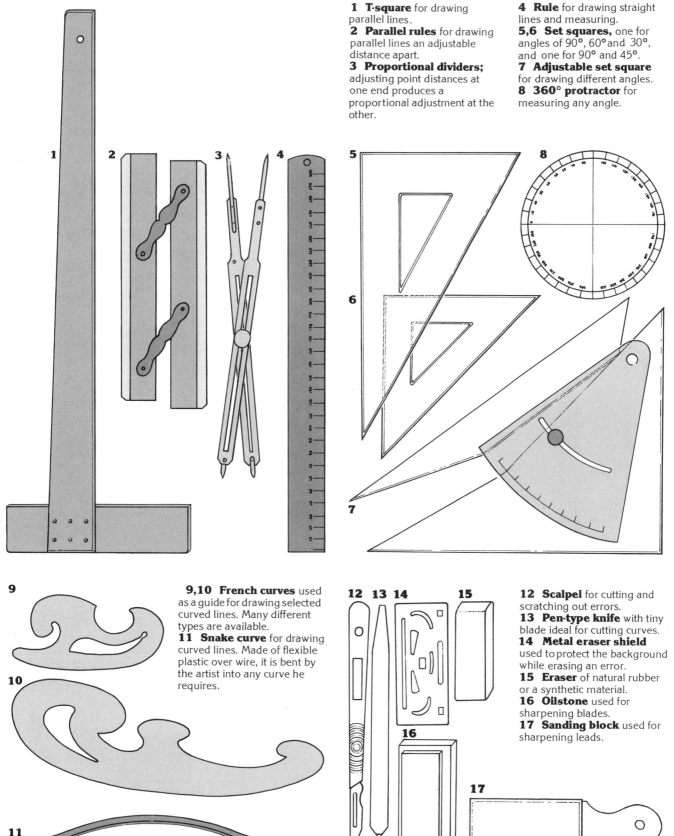

1 T-square for drawing parallel lines.
2 Parallel rules for drawing parallel lines an adjustable distance apart.
3 Proportional dividers; adjusting point distances at one end produces a proportional adjustment at the other.

4 Rule for drawing straight lines and measuring.
5,6 Set squares, one for angles of 90°, 60° and 30°, and one for 90° and 45°.
7 Adjustable set square for drawing different angles.
8 360° protractor for measuring any angle.

9,10 French curves used as a guide for drawing selected curved lines. Many different types are available.
11 Snake curve for drawing curved lines. Made of flexible plastic over wire, it is bent by the artist into any curve he requires.

12 Scalpel for cutting and scratching out errors.
13 Pen-type knife with tiny blade ideal for cutting curves.
14 Metal eraser shield used to protect the background while erasing an error.
15 Eraser of natural rubber or a synthetic material.
16 Oilstone used for sharpening blades.
17 Sanding block used for sharpening leads.

©DIAGRAM

Technical drawing 2

The ruling pen is among the most useful of all the technical artist's tools. Although less versatile than the artist's drawing pen, it can not be bettered when drawing lines. Fitted to a compass it produces neat and accurate arcs and circles. The scriber is an easily used lettering tool.

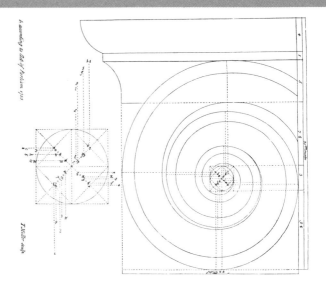

Instructions for drawing a spiral with a compass were included with the detail (right) from Thomas Chippendale's "Gentleman and Cabinet-maker's Director" published in 1754.

1 Ruling pen for ruling lines. Two metal blades form a "nib." Line width depends on blade distance, controlled by a screw.
2 Double ruling pen rules two lines at once. Screws control line thicknesses and distance between lines.

3 Pipette used to fill a **ruling pen** with Indian ink. Ink is drawn into the pipette by suction, and then released onto the insides of the pen blades, as shown below. Alternatively, pens may be filled with a **brush.**

A **scriber lettering set** may consist of the following.
4 Alphabet template.
5 Pencil attachment.
6 Pen attachment.
7 Scriber.

The **scriber** is used as shown below. A **pen** or **pencil attachment** is fitted into place, then the artist uses the scriber's **metal point** to trace a letter from the **template;** the **writing attachment** duplicates the letter onto the paper.

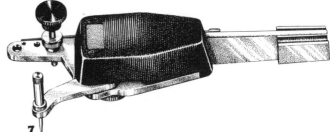

1 Dotting wheel is used to rule a stippled line of dots, dashes, or both. The pattern of the line is determined by the small **cog.**
2 Cogs of different patterns for the dotting wheel. The cog drives a bar ending in a **ruling pen.**

As shown below, the artist uses the **dotting wheel** by drawing it alongside a **rule,** with the **cog** resting on the top of the rule. The notches on the cog cause the **ruling pen** to move up and down to produce patterned lines such as those illustrated.

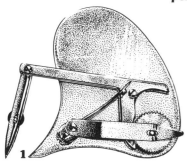

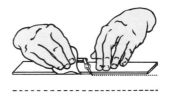

3 Beam compass with an **extension bar** and **accessories.**
4 Springbow compass and **accessories,** used for drawing small, precise circles. A screw adjusts and fixes the distance between its legs.

5 Half-set compass and **attachments;** this compass has leg screws enabling the artist to adjust the angle between the **writing attachment** and the paper.
6 Center tack is used to avoid central compass holes.

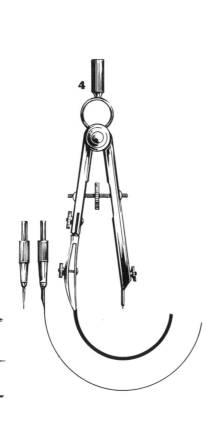

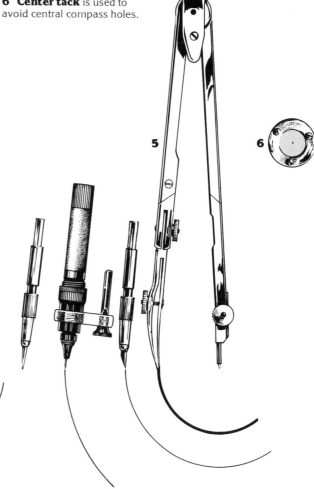

Oriental calligraphy

Since ancient times, calligraphy has been a major art form in China and elsewhere in the Orient. The calligrapher uses the structural and rhythmic qualities of the traditional characters to produce works of great abstract beauty. The basic tools—brush, brush holder, ink, and inkstone—are known in China as the Four Treasures of the Scholar's Room.

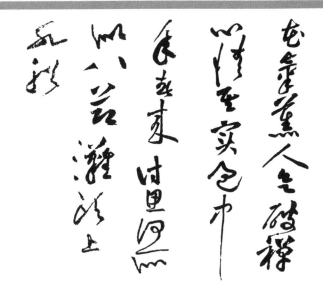

The example of Chinese calligraphy (right) is a poem by Huang Ting Chien, a poet and calligrapher of the Sung dynasty (960-1279). As with all traditional Chinese calligraphy it is read vertically, starting at the top right.

A selection of Oriental **writing brushes** is illustrated (left). Most types have a hollow reed or bamboo handle into which is fitted a tied bunch of animal hair. Brushes are stiffer than western watercolor brushes, and end in a fine point. Types of hair used include: sheep, deer, pony, sable, rabbit, and mouse.

1,2,3 Oriental writing brushes from a US catalog.
4 Writing brush from the Ch'ing dynasty (1644-1912) with a protective cap.
5 Tou brush used for writing large characters.
6 Brush holder of green jade, Ch'ing dynasty. (Items 4,5 and 6 are in the National Palace Museum, Taipei, Taiwan.)

The Chinese calligrapher holds his **writing brush** perpendicular. The illustration below shows the Five Character Method of brush-holding: the brush is held by the thumb and first three fingers, with the little finger used in support.

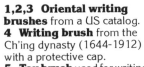

1 2 3 4 5 6

The Oriental calligrapher works with his paper flat on a **table** or **desk.** If he sits, his waist should be just below the level of the table. It is usual to stand for large works.

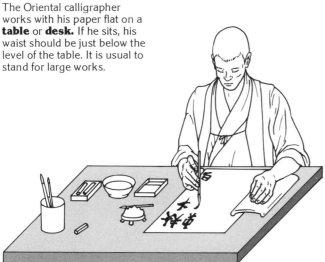

The basic items for Oriental calligraphy can be obtained in a **portable set** such as the one shown below. It contains a choice of **brushes, ink-stick, inkstone,** and **water container.** The box lid folds to make a useful **brush holder.**

Included below and right is a selection of special accessories and inks used in Chinese calligraphy.

1 Inkstone on which the calligrapher mixes his ink. This example is from the Sung dynasty (960-1279).
2 Inkstick rest.
3,4,5 Inksticks made from soot or colored pigments combined with gum. Many are beautifully patterned.
6 Calligrapher's seal used to "sign" a work.
7 Armrest of white jade, carved to be a source of poetic inspiration, Ming dynasty (1368-1644). (Items 1 and 7 are in the National Palace Museum, Taipei, Taiwan.)

To prepare ink the calligrapher grinds an **inkstick** on his **inkstone,** holding the inkstick vertical as shown below. A little water is then mixed with the ground ink; the inkstone has a deeper depression at one end to take any surplus water.

3   4

6

1

2

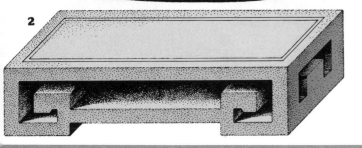

5

7

2 Printing

The tools in this chapter are those of the printer and printmaker. The basis of printing is the preparation of an original, which can then be used to produce many copies by using it with a medium that transfers the image onto the surface to be printed.

The tools of the printmaker vary according to the nature of the following requirements: the original, the medium, and the receptive surface. Some originals, such as the metal for engraving or the wood for woodcuts, are hard and therefore require sharp, strong tools to shape them. Other originals are prepared by cutting stencils, as in silkscreen, or by casting them, as with metal type. In marbling the material used for the original is water, and the medium is simply floated on it. The printing media are frequently liquid, and so require tools for mixing and spreading them, but in photography the medium that transfers the image is a carefully directed light beam.

With the plastic and metal technology of the present day, techniques have been developed for printing onto steel, acetate and other previously problematic surfaces, but in all this progress the fine art of printing has not been lost. Craftsmen are more concerned than ever before that the ancient printing techniques, with their particular qualities and unique tools, should not fall into disuse.

The print reproduced here illustrates an engraving works, and shows the metal plates at various stages in the engraving process. Workmen can be seen engraving, warming, inking and printing the plates, and drying the finished prints.

Ioan. Stradanus inuent.

19.

Sculptor noua arte, brac

SCVLPTVRA IN ÆS.

a in lamina   *Scalpit figuras, atque prælis imprimit.*

Relief printing

Relief printing involves taking an impression from a raised surface coated with pigment. In principle relief is the most straightforward of the printing processes, and was probably the earliest; the technique of impressing a blind design, without pigment, into pottery or leather, was the ancestor of relief printing as we now know it.

This print is from Jost Amman's "Ständebuch," or "Book of Trades," and illustrates a block cutter at work preparing wood blocks for relief printing. Wood blocks were the first means of reproducing both pictures and text.

The following steps in relief printing are basic principles that apply, in modified forms, to any relief process.

a The reversed design is transferred either manually or mechanically onto the surface that is to be used for making the print.

b The spaces around and between all parts of the design are cut away with a sharp tool, so that only the design itself remains raised. All parts to be printed are left at the same height so that they will print evenly.

c The surface is inked, either by hand or machine, with some kind of **roller;** this means that ink is transferred onto the raised parts of the **block** but not into the valleys between them.

d Paper (or any other medium that is to be printed upon) is placed against the inked block and pressure is applied to ensure that the ink is transferred. The pressure can come either from a **press** or from a hand-held **burnisher.**

e When the paper has been removed with the design transferred onto it, the block can be inked again and the printing repeated.

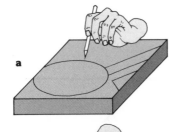
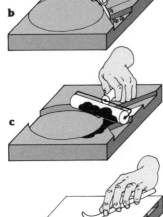
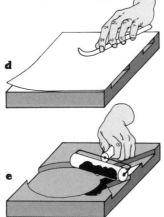

There are three main methods of ensuring that the paper to be printed comes firmly into contact with the relief block.

a A **scraper** can be drawn across the paper as it lies on the block.

b Pressure can be applied to the entire block from above.

c A **roller** can be run across the paper.

All these methods help to produce prints that are of an even quality throughout, since equal pressure has been applied to each part of the paper.

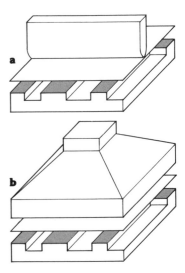
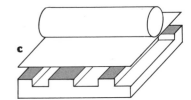

Kindergarten blocks (right) are hand-held wood sticks cut into a simple shape in cross section. The ends can be dipped into ink or paint so that the child can use them to produce elementary prints on paper or fabric.

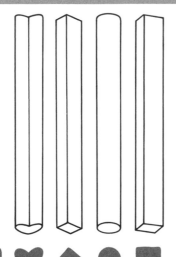

Cheap, simple but surprisingly attractive prints can be obtained from all kinds of everyday objects. Feathers, leaves, flowers, shells, fossils, heavily textured fabrics, wood grains etc, can all be used to produce prints; the Japanese even have an art called gyotaku, which involves making prints from fish (right). A little experimenting will reveal those inks or paints that produce the most successful prints from different objects.
The chosen article is brushed with the medium, then pressed onto paper to transfer the pattern.

Shown below is a 19th century hand-operated American **printing press.**

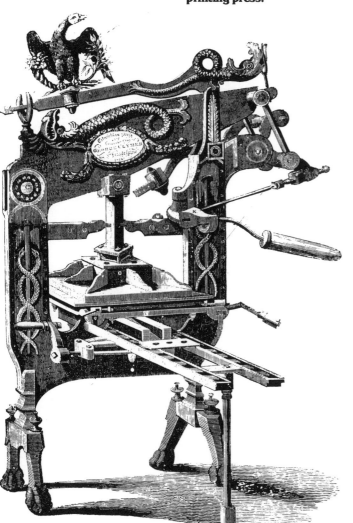

Potato printing is one of the simplest methods of relief printmaking. It lends itself to bold, simple designs, rather than fine detail, since the quality of the prints is not very high!

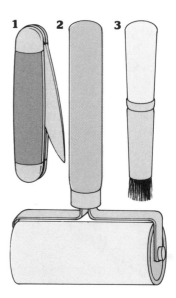

Tools for potato printing are elementary.
1 Pen-knife for cutting out the design.
2 Roller, which can be used for applying the paint or ink.
3 Stencil brush (or any other firm brush) can be used instead of the roller.

Firm, medium-sized potatoes are the most successful for use in potato printing.
a The potato is halved, ideally with one stroke of the **knife** as this produces the most even surface.
b The potato on one cut face is carved away around the chosen shape; this produces a simple relief block.
c The raised shape is coated with ink or paint; the block can then be held in the hand and pressed onto paper to print the design.

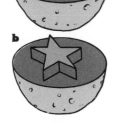

Linocuts and wood engraving

Lino is a fairly soft medium that can readily be cut to produce a relief printing block. When many prints are to be made, for instance when printing fabric, the lino can be mounted onto a block of wood for easier handling.

On the right is a modern linocut portrait, illustrating the typical wide deep strokes that characterize most work in this medium.

Wood is considerably harder than lino, and therefore more difficult to cut, but it is also more durable and better able to survive long runs of printing. Sharp tools are used to cut a relief printing block from the wood.

The illustration on the right shows a detail from a wood engraving portrait by W. J. Linton. Linton eschewed stale systems of engraving tone in formalized lines, and used the tools to make free, expressive marks on the wood.

Lino tends to require a heavy coating of ink, and produces quite a coarse print. Since very fine lines are easily flooded with ink, the cutting tools used are relatively broad; as a result, this technique is better suited to bold design than to fine detail.

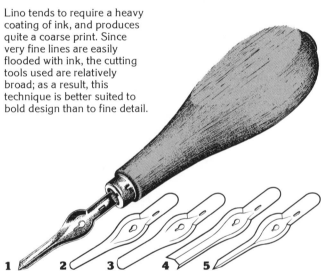

Wood engraving is done on the end grain of the wood, that is on a piece cut across the tree rather than along its length. Very sharp tools can be used to produce extremely fine detail in this process.

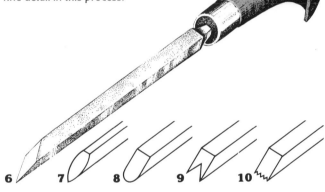

Lino is a much softer medium than wood, and is therefore much easier to work upon. The tools are known as **cutters** or **gravers. Cutting blades** of different thicknesses can be fitted into a common handle. The cutter is held pointing away from the body, and is pushed into the lino to cut away the surface, leaving a raised design which can then be printed as a relief block. The lino is inked with a **roller,** using an oil-based ink, and the block is printed either by hand or in a **press.**

1 Wood-handled **cutter. 2,3,4,5** Selection of interchangeable **cutting blades** that can be fitted into the cutter's handle; each blade produces a different kind of line.

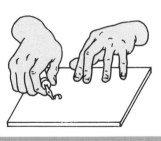

A wood block that is to be engraved is placed on a **pad** so that it can easily be turned during the work. The engraver either pushes the **burin** through the wood, for instance when cutting straight lines or small details, or he may hold the burin still and move the block against it when cutting pronounced curves. The depth of the line can be altered by changing the angle of the burin against the wood.

6 Burin or **graver** with shaped wood handle. **7,8,9,10** Some of the diverse shapes in which gravers can be made. The shape and size of the cutting point determine the quality of the line produced by the tool.

Woodcuts

Woodcuts are made on the side, or plank, grain of the wood. Woodcutting was the first method of book printing, with both illustration and type incorporated in one relief block. After the introduction of movable metal type, woodcut illustrations were cut in a block the same height as the type to allow both to be printed together.

Shown on the right is a detail of a woodcut portrait of the playwright Ibsen. The treatment of the subject is broad and stylized, and yet the result is a sensitive and faithful portrait.

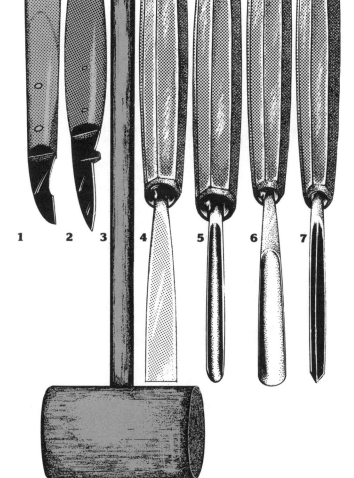

1,2 Knives; these must be kept extremely sharp in order to cut the wood cleanly.
3 Mallet for striking the gouges.
4 Scorper with square, chisel-shaped edge, used for clearing large areas of wood from the block.
5,6 Round gouges in two different widths; these produce U-shaped channels in the wood.
7 V-shaped gouge or **parting tool** for incising very sharp lines.

The woodcutting **knife** is held with the forefinger at the top of the blade and the other fingers to the side of the knife. The forefinger is then used to exert the required amount of pressure on the blade as it cuts (below).

The **gouges** are generally used with a **mallet** to drive them through the wood, as shown below. The gouge is pointed away from the body and guided with one hand, while the other hand uses the mallet to strike the flat handle of the tool.

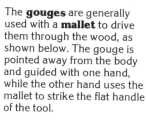

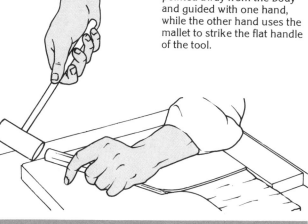

© DIAGRAM

Oriental woodcuts

Woodcuts are the main form of printmaking in the East, and the art has a long and highly respected tradition in Oriental countries. Subjects for prints are often taken from nature, court, stage and commercial life. Technique varies widely with the country and with the individual artist; these pages describe moku hanga, Japanese woodcuts.

The Japanese master Hokusai (1760-1849) made the wood-cut from which the detail on the right is taken; it depicts a print seller's shop. Hokusai was an artist of the Ukiyoe school, and his woodcuts are among the finest ever to emerge from the Orient.

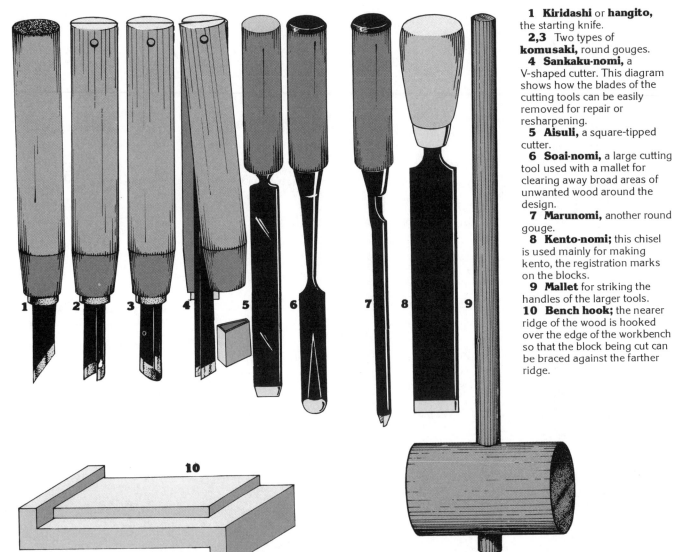

1 **Kiridashi** or **hangito,** the starting knife.
2,3 Two types of **komusaki,** round gouges.
4 **Sankaku-nomi,** a V-shaped cutter. This diagram shows how the blades of the cutting tools can be easily removed for repair or resharpening.
5 **Aisuli,** a square-tipped cutter.
6 **Soai-nomi,** a large cutting tool used with a mallet for clearing away broad areas of unwanted wood around the design.
7 **Marunomi,** another round gouge.
8 **Kento-nomi;** this chisel is used mainly for making kento, the registration marks on the blocks.
9 **Mallet** for striking the handles of the larger tools.
10 **Bench hook;** the nearer ridge of the wood is hooked over the edge of the workbench so that the block being cut can be braced against the farther ridge.

The basic process of making one-color Oriental prints is as follows.

a The block is smoothed and prepared, and the design is transferred onto it. The surface is then cut with the appropriate **small tools** to mark out the main lines and details of the design.

b The areas of unwanted wood around the design are cleared away by cutting them out with the **larger tools.** A **mallet** is used to strike the handles of the tools in order to drive the cutters through the wood.

c The finished relief block is washed free of wood chippings and dried very thoroughly. It is then colored with a water-based ink until all the surfaces have been evenly coated.

d Hand-made paper is laid onto the block and rubbed with a **barén** to ensure that all parts of the design receive equal pressure. The print is lifted from the wood block, and left to dry between sheets of newsprint, weighted on top so that the paper does not wrinkle.

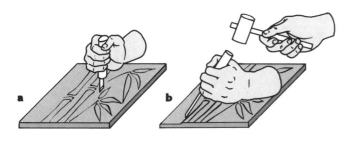

1,2,3 Haké, soft brushes used for applying the ink to the blocks. They are usually made of horsehair, and the tips are softened by brushing them on sharkskin.

4 Cloth **bag,** used for dabbing ink onto the block.

5 Dish for mixing ink to the correct consistency.

6 Barén, used to rub the paper onto the inked block. This barén is covered with the fiber that protects bamboo shoots, and is held in one hand.

7 Barén made of bunches of reeds. This kind of barén can be held in two hands; it is used mainly in China and Korea.

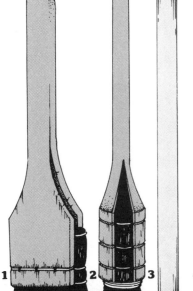
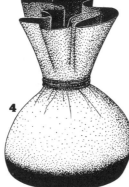
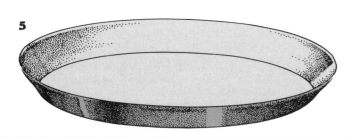
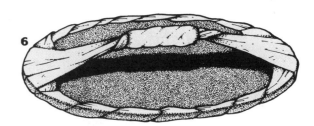
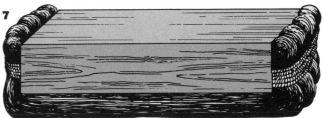

Printing type

The invention of movable metal type by Johann Gutenberg in 1450 was so successful that many of the basic processes have survived almost unchanged. Although the development of mechanization has introduced greater speed and efficiency into printing, the hand setting of type is carried out today much as it was in Gutenberg's time.

Reproduced (right) is a detail from Gutenberg's 42-line Bible, printed in 1455. The book is an excellent example of the transition from manuscript to printing; the type is printed, but the illuminations are still done by hand.

Type characters were originally cut individually by hand, but a system of matrices (right) was soon developed to allow many types to be molded from one original.

a A **punch** is cut by hand from a detailed drawing of the typeface; the punch is made from a long, thin block of steel.

b The letter appears reversed and in relief on the end of the punch.

c The hardened punch is forcibly struck into the face of an oblong of copper. This produces an impression of the character, the correct way round, and now forms the **matrix** from which the type will be cast.

d The matrix can be held in position in a **hand mold,** which is then filled with molten type metal—an alloy of lead, antimony and tin. Metal is forced into all parts of the matrix, and the character is turned out when the metal has cooled.

e The character now appears reversed and in relief on the end of the molded type; this means that it will print the correct way round. Numerous types of the same character can be molded from one matrix; mechanical type casting systems are also available, and work on the same principle.

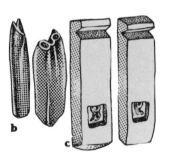

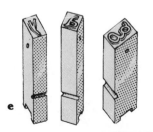

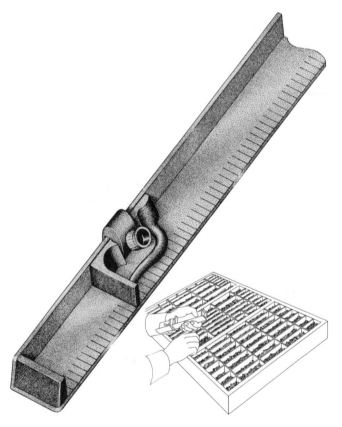

A **composing stick** is used by the compositor to assemble the type in exactly measured lines; the measure is determined by an adjustable slide that can be secured in place for each job. The lines of type are composed and corrected individually within the stick, as above.

The characters used for printing are stored in a **type case** (above), a wooden tray divided into numerous compartments. The frequency of use of each character determines its place in the case and the size of its compartment, and there are also spaces for punctuation.

Shown (right) is part of the interior of a 17th century printing shop. One of the men in the foreground is inking the type, using two inking balls; in the background can be seen other men composing type.

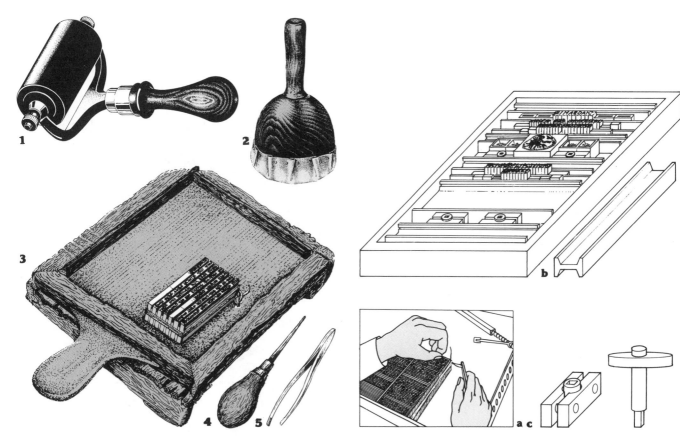

1 Composition roller for applying ink to prepared type.
2 Inking ball of the sort used until the 19th century.
3 Old galley for storing **type** or taking proofs (trial prints).
4,5 Bodkin and **tweezers** for moving or correcting lines of type.

Type is prepared for the press in the following way.
a When the lines of **type** have been composed they are transferred to a perfectly flat surface, and each block of type is temporarily secured by tying twine around it.
b When sufficient type has been prepared, the **chase** (a metal frame) is placed around it and the twine is removed. The spacing of the type is adjusted in the frame with **furniture**— pieces of wood or metal that are lower than the height of the type so that they will not print. When the spacing is correct, **quoins** are inserted.

c A **quoin** consists of a metal block in two sections; when the **quoin key** is inserted and turned the two sections move apart, exerting pressure on both sides, and so holding the type and furniture firmly in place.

©DIAGRAM

Intaglio printing

An intaglio printing process is one in which the ink is drawn onto the paper from an incision below the surface of the printing plate; intaglio processes include engravings on wood and metal, and almost all types of etching. Great pressure is applied to the paper during printing to force the ink from the plate onto the paper.

The intaglio print illustrated (right) is a detail from an etched self-portrait by Rembrandt van Rijn; his wife Saskia is depicted in the background. This detail is reproduced actual size.

In order to make a good print by an intaglio printing process, the surface of the plate must be free from all blemishes, since the tiniest indentation will hold ink and therefore mark the paper.

a The design is drawn or traced onto the **plate.**

b The lines are incised with a **burin,** or **graver,** a steel tool with a lozenge-shaped point; this produces a very sharp-edged cut that is V-shaped in section.

c The entire surface is inked with a **roller;** ink is pressed into the lines with a **dabber.**

d The entire surface of the plate is wiped clean so that ink remains only in the incised lines.

e Paper is placed over the plate, and pressure applied by hand with a **burnisher** or by a **press** to ensure that the paper comes into contact with the ink. The deeper the lines are, the more ink they will hold and the darker they will print; similarly, the more pressure is applied to the plate, the darker the final print will be.

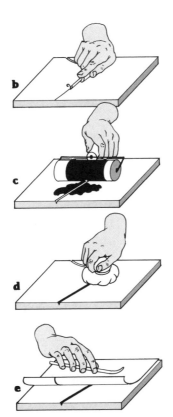

The print below is from Bosse's "Traicte des manières de graver en taille douce . . ." published in Paris in 1645. It illustrates a 17th century etching or engraving press.

Engraving

Engraving has been tried on many metals, but copper has proved the most successful because it is relatively soft and easy to work on. Since the surface of a copper plate tends to wear away quickly under the pressure of printing, plates are sometimes faced with steel to prolong their lives.

On the right is a steel engraving of Edward Fitzgerald, made by the firm of Richard Bentley & Son in 1895. The engraving was taken from a photograph, and the very sharp point used for the process has reproduced all the fine photographic detail.

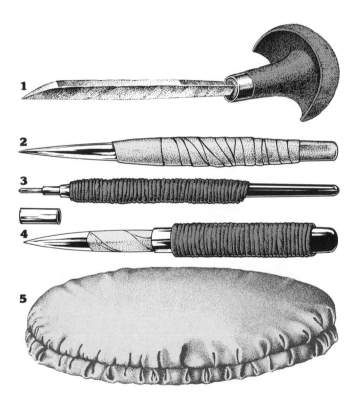

1 Burin or **graver.**
2 Burnisher for smoothing the surface of the plate to correct mistakes.
3 Engraving needle with its own cap to protect the point.

4 Scraper for erasing large mistakes on the plate; the edge of the blade is drawn sideways across the area to be corrected.
5 Leather bag filled with sand. The plate being engraved is rested on the bag so that it can be turned easily.

The process of engraving falls into four basic stages.
a The **plate** to be engraved is polished smooth and then rested on a pad so that it can easily be turned; a sharp-pointed **burin,** or **graver,** is used to cut the lines into the plate. Sometimes the burin can be held still while the plate is moved and turned against its pressure; this helps to create a clear, flowing line. The depth and width of the lines can be altered by changing the pressure of the burin. The raised "burr" of metal produced around the lines by the burin is removed with a **scraper** to level the surface of the plate.
b The engraved surface is inked thoroughly and evenly with a **roller.**
c Ink is pressed into the engraved lines with a firm **dabber** to ensure that every line is loaded with ink; any excess is wiped off with **rags,** so that the surface is entirely clean.
d Paper, often dampened to make it pick up the ink more readily, is laid across the inked plate. Great pressure is applied in order to force the ink from the lines onto the paper.

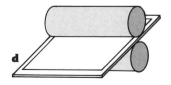

© DIAGRAM

Etching

The name etching comes from the Dutch etsen, meaning to eat, and refers to the biting of acid into scratched lines on a metal plate; this makes them deep enough to hold ink, so that prints can be taken from them. The first etching plates, in the 16th century, were of iron, but these were very soon replaced by the smoother surfaces of copper and zinc.

The detail on the right is part of an etching of a young man made in 1822. The crisscross marks (known as cross-hatching) made by the engraving needle can be clearly seen around the cheekbone and the eyebrow.

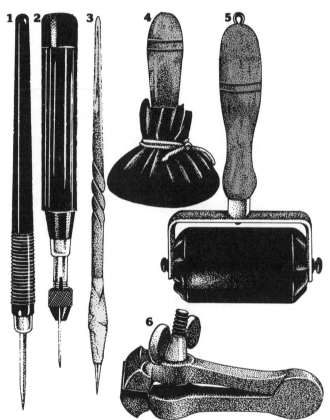

1,2,3 Etching needles of various types.
4 Silk bag containing the mixture for the etching ground.
5 Roller for inking the finished plate.
6 Clamp used for gripping the plate when it is being blackened over the flame.

Before etching begins, the plate is polished with fine abrasives to prepare the surface.
a A **silk bag** containing an acid-resistant mixture of waxes, resins and gums is applied to the heated **plate** until the etching surface is coated with the mixture.
b Smoke is used to blacken the plate so that any lines etched on it will be clearly visible.
c The edges and back of the plate are coated with an acid-resistant varnish to protect
d The design is drawn in reverse onto the plate with a sharp, strong **etching needle.**
e The plate is dipped in a **bath** of acid to etch out the exposed lines; any bubbles collecting are dispersed with the tip of a **feather.** The more times the plate is dipped in the acid, the deeper the lines will become; lines that are intended to be fine can be "stopped" with varnish in the early stages to prevent them from becoming too deep.
f The plate is dried, the ground is removed, and then the entire surface is inked with a **roller.**
g Excess ink is wiped off with **rags;** the plate can then be printed on a flatbed **press.**

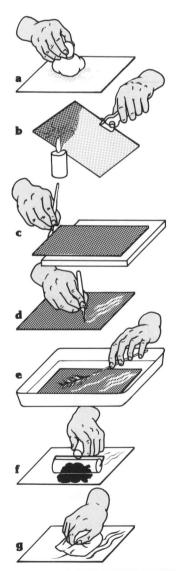

The reproduction of tonal values is always a challenge in engraving and etching. The most successful methods involve texturing the plate with tiny dots or fine lines; tone can be achieved by varying the spacing, size and depth of the marks.

On the right are examples of three tonal variations of etching. From left to right they are: aquatint, producing effects similar to watercolor; mezzotint, characterized by burnished highlights; soft ground etching, imitative of pencil work.

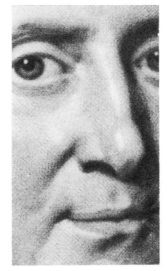

Aquatint is named after the acid (aqua fortis) used to etch away the prepared surface; it produces well-defined areas of almost flat tone, and is particularly effective for simulating watercolor work. Powdered resin is either blown onto the surface and fixed by heat, or it is mixed with spirit and painted on. When dry it forms fine cracks that can be etched out with acid; the areas to remain light are "stopped" with varnish (as explained under etching) and the rest become deeper with each dip in the acid. The deep lines will hold the most ink and so print darkly.

Stipple engraving is a combination of engraving and etching. The etching ground is laid on the plate as usual, and the drawing to be reproduced is placed across the surface. The main lines and shadows of the drawing are pricked through the paper onto the ground, either by dotting them with an **etching needle,** or by using a specially spiked wheel known as a **roulette.** The plate is dipped in acid to etch the main lines, then tone is created by making dots of varying sizes and depths with a curved **graver.** The plate is then cleaned, inked and printed in the normal fashion.

Mezzotint is the reverse of most engraving processes, since the areas that are most worked upon produce the lightest tones. The surface to be worked is roughened with a **mezzotint rocker,** a curved tool with a serrated edge; this covers the ground with numerous indentations, each one having a "burr" of displaced metal around it. If printed at this stage, the entire plate would print dark because the burr holds a great deal of ink. Lighter tones are produced by scraping the burr away to different levels; pure white highlights are made by burnishing the surface until it is completely smooth.

Soft ground etching was developed to reproduce the effects of pencil or chalk drawing. The "soft ground" referred to is the usual etching ground of wax, resin and gum, with tallow added to soften it. Thin paper, often with a texture or grain, is laid over the ground, and the design is drawn onto it with a **lead pencil;** the soft ground adheres to the paper where the pencil has pressed, and comes away from the plate when the paper is removed. The plate is then dipped in acid as usual, and the design that appears has all the texture of the pencil lead and the grained paper.

1 **Multiple-pointed stippler.**
2,3 Gravers with several points; these produce many lines with one stroke.
4 Roulette covered with jagged teeth.
5 Rocker for laying the ground on mezzotint plates.

Inking and correcting intaglio plates

The inking and correcting of intaglio plates are specialized processes that require their own particular tools. Because the impression from an intaglio plate is taken from ink in grooves below the surface, the inking process has to be very precise, and any mistakes in the engraving must be totally erased and the plate restored to a completely level surface.

Inking tools are shown in the illustration (right).
1 Gelatin roller.
2 Dabber made from rolled canvas.
3 Spatula for mixing the ink before it is applied to the plate.

The most common **correcting tools** are shown (below).
4 Scraper with a triangular cross-section.
5 Burnisher.
6 Calipers used for locating the position of a mistake on the reverse side of the plate.
7 Correcting hammer.

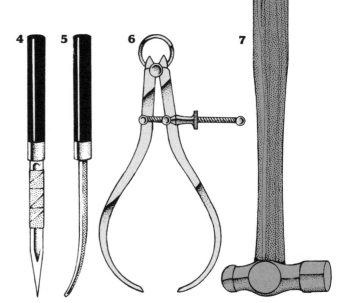

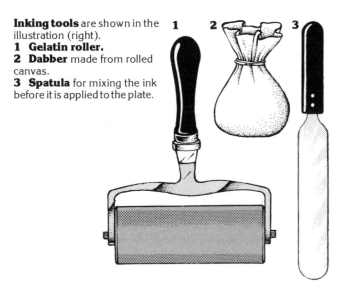

The procedure for inking an intaglio plate is shown in the sequence (right).
a The intaglio plate is warmed slightly by holding it over a heated box. This is done so that the ink will flow more readily into the lines.
b The ink is applied to the plate, usually with a **roller,** and then rubbed into the lines with a **dabber.**
c Excess ink is wiped off the plate with rags, and then with the palm of the hand, leaving ink only in the lines.
d The plate is then warmed again, and printed in a press.

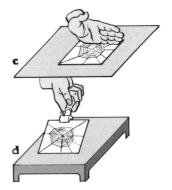

Mistakes on engraved plates are corrected in the following way.
a The error is removed by paring down the surface of the plate with a three-sided **scraper.**
b The surface of the plate is then smoothed again by rubbing it with a **burnisher.**
c One foot of a pair of **calipers** is placed on the error so that the other foot will locate the position of the error on the reverse side of the plate.
d The surface is then restored to flatness by hammering the plate from the reverse side over an **anvil**.

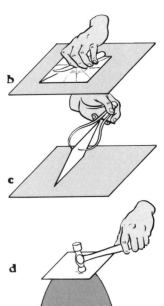

Marbling

Marbling is a simple printing technique that was once very popular for decorating the end-papers of books. Depending on the repelling of oil-based inks or paints by water, the technique can be used to produce extremely attractive abstract designs in one or more colors. Marbling requires few tools, all of which can be easily improvised in the home.

The sheet of paper shown (right) was decorated by the marbling method, and illustrates the typical swirling and flowing patterns made by the inks floating on the surface of the water.

Possible tools for marbling include the following.
1 Stick, straight or forked.
2 Comb, such as a wide-toothed pet's comb.
3 Brush, flat or round.
4 Photographic bath or some other kind of shallow container is needed to contain water and the inks or paints used to produce marble-patterned prints.

The marbling process falls into the following stages.
a The **bath** is part-filled with water. Oil-based colored inks or paints, made fairly thin by diluting with turpentine, are then gently poured or dripped onto the water so that they float.

b As the colors spread over the water's surface, they can be formed into swirling patterns by gently stirring with tools such as a **stick, comb,** or **brush.** Overstirring is likely to spoil the effect or to cause the colors to sink and mix with the water.

c A sheet of paper is then carefully lowered onto the liquid's surface, and left for a moment. The area where marbling will occur can be influenced to some extent by pressing the paper under the water in a number of places.

d The printed paper is removed from the bath and placed on newspaper or blotting paper to dry. The tendency of diluted oil-based colors to dull on drying can be countered by applying a clear screen ink varnish when the print is dry.

Lithography

Lithography is a printing process invented in Munich in the 1790s by Alois Senefelder. A greasy drawing on a special stone slab or metal plate attracts printing ink, while the remainder of the surface repels ink if wetted with water. The process has great potential for artists since it allows a whole range of tonal values as well as lines of any thickness.

The lithograph on the right was made by Franz Hanfstaengl in 1834; it depicts Alois Senefelder, the inventor of lithography. The technique became very popular in the early 19th century for reproducing portraits and for printing music.

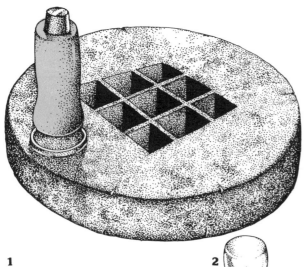

1

2

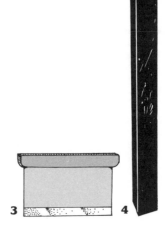

3   **4**

A **lithographic stone** is prepared with these tools.
1 Levigator, an iron disk with a handle and holes in the center (see below for method of use).
2 Muller, a glass or steel tool used with pumice for finer grinding.

The lithographer draws the image to be printed onto a prepared **litho stone** or onto a commercially available **metal litho plate,** usually made of zinc or aluminum. A stone gives a better print, but plates are bought ready for use and are easily portable.

A strong abrasive such as silicon carbide sand is applied to the wetted stone. The lithographer then holds the **levigator** by the handle and rotates it rapidly over the stone's surface (see right). More sand can be applied through the holes in the levigator.

The drawing is made on the dry **stone** or **plate,** using a special greasy ink or a greasy **litho crayon** or **pencil.** Printing ink adheres to the greasy areas, making them appear on the print; non-greasy areas will be white on the print.

5   **6**   **7**   **8**   **9**   **10**

3 Razor blade for scratching and correcting.
4 Lithographic crayon.
5 Crayon holder.
6 Lithographic pencil with greasy "lead."
7 Brush for applying tusche (greasy litho ink).
8 Pen for applying tusche.
9,10 Engraving tools.

Illustrated (right) are stages in making a litho print.
a The **stone** is prepared.
b The drawing is made with a greasy **litho crayon.**
c Talcum is dusted over.
d A **brush** is used to apply gum etch, which is gently hosed off some hours later.
e A nitric acid solution is applied, and washed off after a few seconds. This process is repeated, and then more gum etch applied.
f The greasy drawing is washed out with turpentine.
g The stone is blackened with asphaltum, to make the design reappear, and then washed.
h The stone is inked.
i Paper is laid on and the stone printed in a **press.**

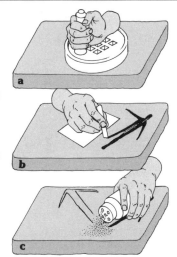
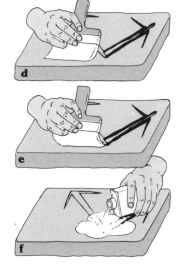
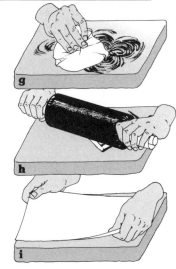

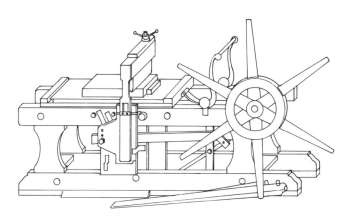

1 Brush with wide, flat head may be used to apply etch (gum arabic, water, and nitric acid). The etch makes the greased areas receptive to the printing ink and helps to keep ink off the rest.
2 Flag dryer makes gum arabic dry more quickly.
3 Roller is used to apply printing ink to the **stone** or **plate.** The example shown is made of wood covered with felt and calfskin. Rubber rollers are also used.
4 Leather handle grips are put onto the roller to make rolling easier.

5 Scraping tool may be used to clean a leather roller. Made of metal, the scraping tool is shaped to fit over the roller. The lithographer draws it toward him over the roller as shown below. Alternatively, he may use the back of a **knife.**

A **hand press** such as the French star press (above) is used for high-quality art prints. As shown below, a leather-covered **scraper** applies pressure from above as the stone, with the paper on it, is drawn through the press on the movable **bed.**

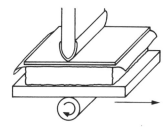

©DIAGRAM

Silkscreen

Silkscreening was first done by the Chinese, using a paper stencil attached to a loose mesh of very fine silk threads; for modern use, the screen has been refined to a fine, evenly woven mesh of silk or synthetic fiber. Ink is spread across a stenciled screen, and only passes through the areas of the mesh that are not blocked by the stencil.

The detail on the right is from a silkscreened Indian poster for birth control. The free, loosely defined areas of flat tone are a characteristic feature of this technique, but the fine screening of the writing demonstrates the accuracy that is also possible.

Stencils can be applied to the screen in many different ways; some of the basic methods are described here.

a) A stencil is cut from paper or card and placed against the screen during printing.

b) A liquid blocking-out medium is painted onto the screen to cover the areas that are not to be printed; this dries into a solid stencil that is incorporated into the mesh of the screen and cannot be displaced.

c) A stencil film is cut, and applied to the screen by heat; this stencil also is firmly fixed.

d) Greasy **lithographic crayons** or liquid **wax** can be used to produce a stencil with soft outlines.

e) The stencil is transferred to the screen by photography. The image is exposed onto soft gelatin painted onto the mesh; this hardens the areas exposed to light. The remaining soft gelatin is washed away, leaving a stencil on the screen.

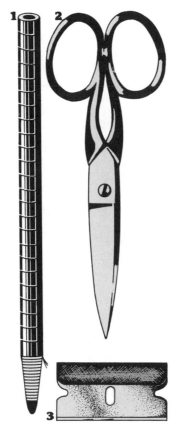

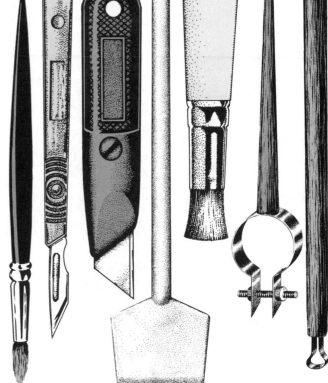

1 Lithographic crayon; this is greasy, and produces a soft-edged mark on the screen.
2 Scissors.
3 Razor blade.
4 Paintbrush for applying liquid blocking-out medium.

5 Scalpel.
6 Craft knife.
7 Spreader for coating the screen with gelatin, blocking medium etc.
8 Stencil brush with short, firm bristles.

9,10 Cutter and **marker** for use with wax stencils; these tools can be used to scrape away the unwanted areas of wax.

The basic stages of silkscreen printing are as follows.
a The image is applied to the **screen** by any of the stenciling methods.
b The paper to be printed is placed on a flat surface and the screen is locked into place above it. Ink is spread across the mesh with a **squeegee;** this ensures an even deposit of ink over the entire print.
c The screen is lifted, and the print is removed and allowed to dry.

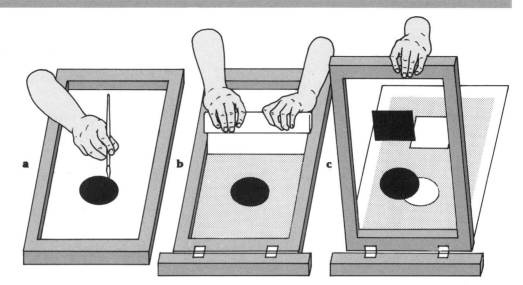

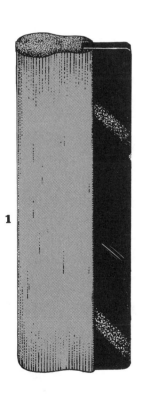

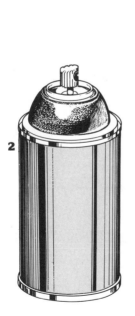

1 Squeegee, used to spread the ink across the screen in an even film.
2 Spray can; the ink or paint may be sprayed through the stencil for particular effects.

The **frame** for screen printing, illustrated above, is generally made from four battens of wood fixed together rigidly. The frame is then covered with stretched muslin or nylon—or any fabric with a very fine thread and open weave—which forms the screen.

Photography 1

The camera has been described as the marriage between art and science—success in photography depends on a combination of technical advances and the skill and instinct of the user. Photography consists of recording the pattern of light in the scene photographed onto a sensitive film so that it can later be faithfully reproduced.

The photograph reproduced (right) is demonstrating the process of taking a picture with a single lens reflex camera. The subject is steadying the camera while adjusting the focus dial before taking the photograph.

The chart below illustrates the development of the camera from the ancient camera obscura to the sophisticated and specialized cameras of today. The camera obscura, on which the photographic camera is based, was known to Aristotle; if an image in a strong light is placed in front of a darkened box with a pinhole in one wall, the rays of light will shine through the pinhole and project the image, upside down and laterally reversed, onto the rear wall of the box. It was not until 1824 that it was discovered, by Nicéphore Niêpce, that if the wall was replaced by a light-sensitive plate the image could be made semi-permanent. His associate Daguerre discovered how to produce positive images, and William Henry Fox Talbot worked on producing a latent image for later development. From this idea of negative/positive photography the modern cameras evolved; film is exposed in the camera and later developed to form a negative. The positive print is then processed and printed.

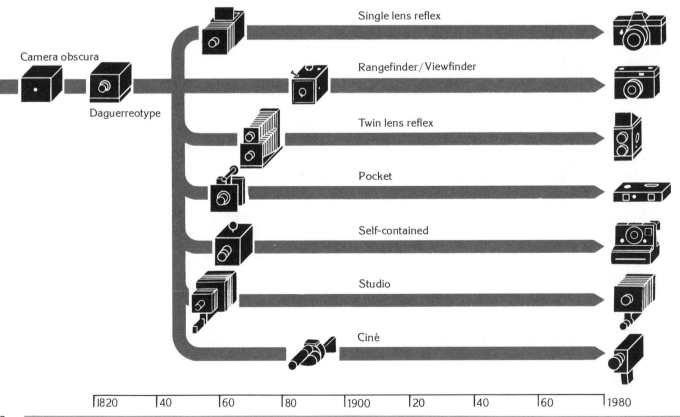

Camera obscura

Daguerreotype

Single lens reflex

Rangefinder/Viewfinder

Twin lens reflex

Pocket

Self-contained

Studio

Ciné

1820   40   60   80   1900   20   40   60   1980

The characteristics common to all cameras are illustrated (right).

1 Lens focuses the image and refracts the rays of light so that the image emerges upside down and laterally reversed on the film.

2 Diaphragm controls the amount of light reaching the film.

3 Shutter controls exposure time; the shutter illustrated slides up, but the design varies with camera type.

4 Film, light-sensitive so that the image appears with dark and light tones reversed.

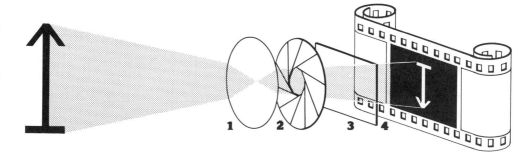

In black and white photography the exposed film is taken from the camera and processed to obtain a negative image of the subject. Light subject areas will tend toward black on the negative, and dark areas will record as clear film. In the **enlarger,** light is projected through the negative onto light-sensitive paper. This paper is similar to film in its reaction to light. Dark parts of the negative will not allow light to strike the paper, so it remains white after it is developed. Clear negative areas let the light pass through onto the paper, eventually producing a dark image. The result is a black and white positive image of the original subject.

Two types of film are used in color photography. Negative film is used in the same way as black and white film, except that colors as well as tones are reversed. So a blue subject will appear yellow, and a green subject magenta. This negative is enlarged onto a color printing paper which has the same characteristics—changing yellow back to blue, and so on.

Color transparency film is a similar material, but undergoes a totally different development process. A blue subject, for example, records directly as blue on the transparency. This original piece of film from the camera is then mounted and viewed by means of a **hand viewer** or a **slide projector.**

Black and white film records the various levels of intensity in the light reflected off a subject. The film comprises a light-sensitive emulsion thinly coated on a flexible plastic base. At the moment of exposure, the silver halides suspended in this emulsion begin to blacken under the

action of light, forming metallic silver. This "latent" image is invisible until development begins. The developer amplifies the effect of the light, producing a dense black in the most brightly lit areas of the subject. Halides exposed to the shadow areas of the subject are not activated, and

are subsequently rendered colorless by the fixer.

5 Black and white cylinder to be photographed.

6 Lens focusing and inverting the image.

7 Black and white film.

8 Black and white negative, with the light and dark tones reversed.

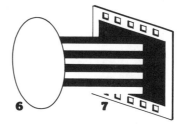

Color photography is more complex than black and white. The lens projects the inverted rays of light onto color negative film. The film is made up of three different color-sensitive emulsions on a plastic base, each of which reacts to and halts the progress of light of one color but allows the others to

pass through. Just as black and white film reverses black to white and vice versa, color emulsions reverse each color to its complementary.

9 Colored cylinder.

10 Lens.

11 Blue-sensitive emulsion (producing complementary yellow).

12 Green-sensitive emulsion (producing complementary magenta).

13 Red-sensitive emulsion (producing complementary cyan).

14 Color negative.

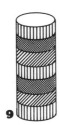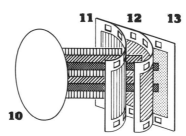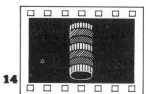

©DIAGRAM

Photography 2

Camera accessories are extra pieces of equipment that are added to the camera or used with it for specific effects.

1 **Lens cap** used to protect the lens from dirt and abrasion.
2 **Standard lens.**
3 **Wide-angle lens.**
4 **Fish-eye lens.**
5 **Telephoto lens.**
6 **Zoom lens.**
7 **Lens hood.**
8 **Lens brush.**
9 **Filters** of various kinds.
10 **Light meter.**
11 **Light-diffusing dome.**
12 **Electronic flash gun.**
13 **Flash cube.**
14 **Cable release.**
15 **Tripod.**

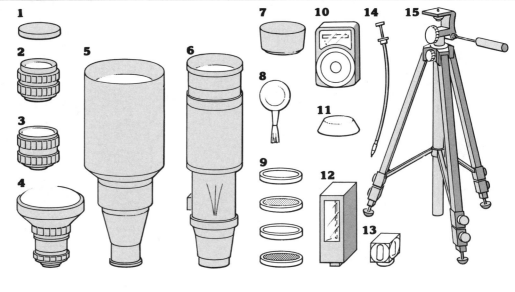

Processing equipment is used for converting the film into developed negatives or transparencies.

16 **Spiral insert** for the developing tank.
17 **Developing tank.**
18 **Developing timer.**
19 **Measuring cylinder.**
20 Film washing **hose.**
21 Glass **stirring rod.**
22 **Bottle** for chemicals.
23 **Clips** for holding the film while it is drying.
24 **Funnel** to aid in pouring the chemicals.
25 Heated **drying cabinet.**

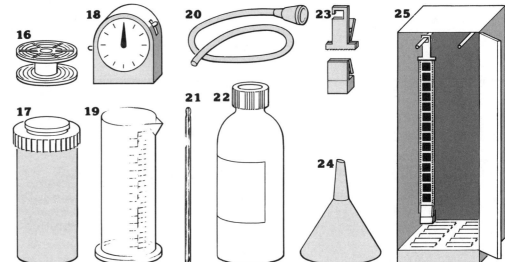

Printing equipment is used to convert negatives into positive images.

26 **Print enlarger.**
27 **Negative carrier** fits into the enlarger lens.
28 **Masking frame** used to determine the shape of the final image.
29 **Dodger,** a tool for masking a small area.
30 **Safelight,** a dim light that will not fog the paper.
31 **Scissors.**
32 **Tongs.**
33 **Thermometer.**
34 **Measuring cylinder.**
35 **Automatic timer.**
36 **Trays** for chemicals and water.
37 **Print washer.**
38 **Print dryer.**

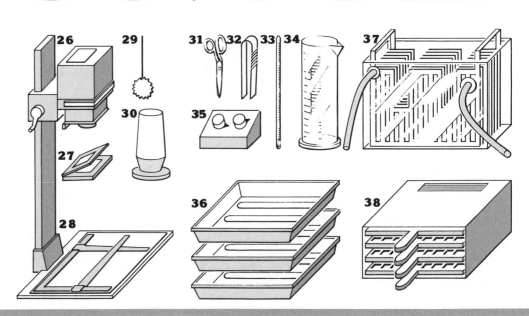

Taking pictures with any **camera** involves these four steps.
a The camera is loaded with the film or plate that will receive the initial image.

b The correct **lens** for the proposed shot is attached to the camera. Specialized lenses can be obtained for virtually any requirement, such as taking photographs under water, or through a microscope.

c A **light meter** is used to determine the length of time that the film will be exposed and the aperture to which the lens should be set.

d The camera is focused, that is, it is adjusted so that the lens and film are the correct distance apart for the subject being taken. The camera is steadied, either by hand or on a **tripod,** and the shutter is released to expose the image onto the film for the required time.

a

b

c
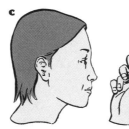

d

Film is processed by placing it in a developer, a stop bath and a fixer.
a The film is removed from the camera and rolled onto the **spiral** of the developing tank. This must be done in total darkness, otherwise the film will be spoiled.

b The spiral is placed in the **developing tank** (containing developer) and agitated so that all parts receive equal amounts of the chemical. This process is repeated with a chemical that stops the action of the developer, and finally with a fixer.

c The film is thoroughly washed in clean running water to rid it of all traces of the fixer.

d The strips of film are attached to **clips** so that they can be handled easily, and are hung up to dry, ideally in a purpose-built **drying cabinet.**

a

b

c
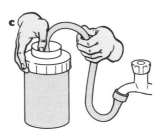

d

The image is printed by exposing it onto light-sensitive paper.
a Light is shone through the negative and onto the paper. A **safelight** provides working illumination that will not affect the printing paper.

b The paper is placed first in a developer **tray,** then when fully developed, rinsed in clean water.

c The image is made permanent by using a fixing chemical.

d The print is then washed thoroughly in running water to clear the surface of all trace of fixer. When the washing is complete the prints are dried; if a special **print dryer** is used it will ensure that the prints emerge flat.

a
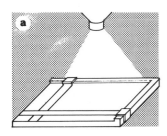

b
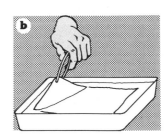

c

d
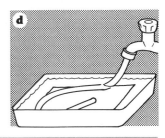

© DIAGRAM

3 Making books

The first books made from individual leaves were those developed by the Romans, consisting of wax tablets joined together at the spine. The advent of parchment in the third century BC led to the development of more portable leaved books, although many works were still written in scroll form on papyrus. Since those times, books with individual leaves have been made from strips of bamboo, palm leaves, wood, ivory and metal, and bound together with thongs of leather or plant sinew, or pierced and fitted with metal hinges.

The modern book is made of sheets of paper folded into leaves and fixed together at the spine, where the folds meet. Tools for making such books, by hand, from the manufacture of the paper itself to the decoration of the binding, are described and illustrated in this chapter. Although all these processes have been automated over the last two centuries, nothing can compare with a book that has been made from high-quality paper and bound and decorated by a craftsman-bookbinder.

This print of a bookbinding workshop comes from Diderot's "Encyclopedia of Industries." In France in the 18th century, the binding was not included in the price of a book, and so the purchaser had to enlist the services of a binder.

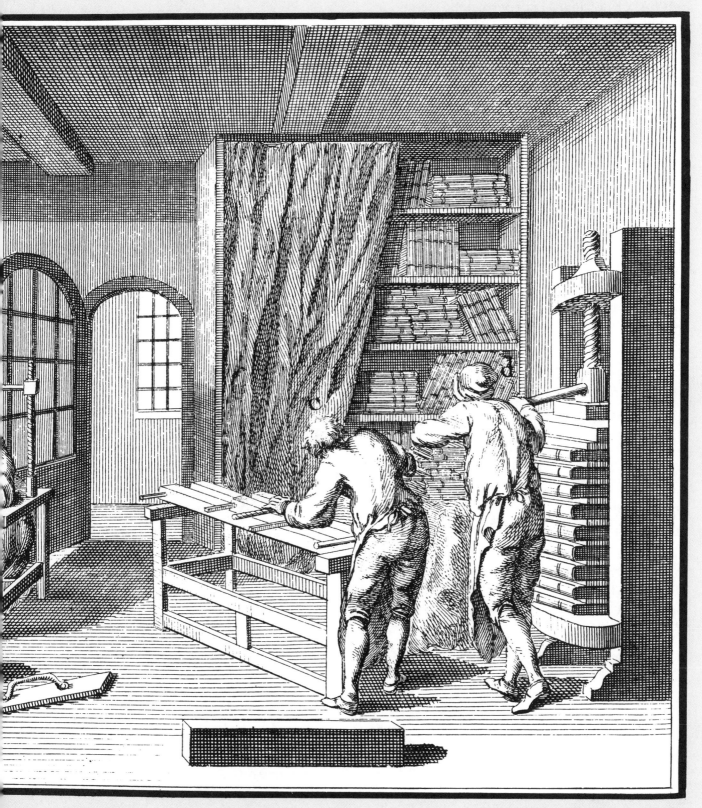

Papermaking

Paper is reputed to have been invented in China in 105AD. Knowledge of papermaking techniques gradually spread westward, reaching Europe only in the 12th century. Today, most paper is machine-made in factories, but traditional methods of breaking down materials into pulp and then reconstituting them into paper can be easily adapted for use at home.

This Japanese woodcut shows various stages in traditional Oriental papermaking— materials are being soaked in a basket in the river, beaten to a pulp with sticks, and dried in molds to form paper.

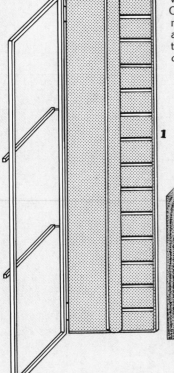
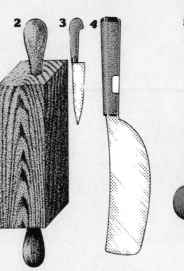
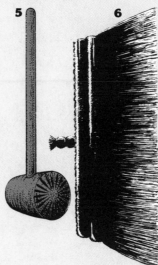

The craft of paper making reached Japan from China early in the seventh century. Today, the Japanese still use traditional processes to produce a great variety of high-quality papers. Examples of Japanese **papermaking** tools are shown left.

1 **Mold** for making fine tissue paper, usually from mulberry bark. This modern mold has a soft wood frame, copper hinges, and woven silk over a bamboo cover.

2,3 **Wood block** and **small knife** used to split inner bark from coarse outer bark.

4 **Paper-cutting knife.**

5 **Mallet** for beating bark.

6 **Brush** used for smoothing moist pulp in the molds.

The basic procedures for making hand-made paper are quite simple to master. A paper's character depends on the materials used and on the smoothness of the pulp.

a A **knife** is used to cut plant stalks into short lengths. Paper or fabric should be torn into squares.

b Stalks or fabric are put into a **galvanized bucket** and covered with water. Wearing **rubber gloves,** the paper-maker carefully adds caustic soda. When the soda has dissolved, he heats the bucket on a **stove,** stirring until the liquid boils, and lets it simmer 2-3 hours.

c After allowing the bucket's contents to cool slightly, the papermaker, again wearing rubber gloves, carefully strains the liquid from the fibers. The pulp is then thoroughly washed under a tap, first in a **sieve** and then in a square of closely woven **fabric.**

d The pulp is now pounded, either with a **pestle and mortar,** as shown below, or with a **meat tenderizer.** Alternatively, an **electric blender** may be used with extra water. If he wishes, the papermaker can next change the paper's color by adding various dyes.

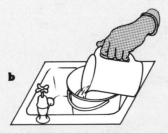

The papermaker's most vital tool is his **mold.** A simple home-made mold is shown below. The wood frame is fixed with waterproof adhesive and brass screws. A closely woven, man-made fabric is stretched over the frame and held with staples.

Other tools for home paper-making are shown here.
1,2 Knife and **scissors** to cut the old paper, cloth, or vegetable matter from which the paper is to be made.
3 Wooden spoon for stirring the fibers while they are being softened in a solution of caustic soda.
4 Sieve for straining liquid from the fibers.
5,6 Meat tenderizer and **pestle and mortar** for pounding. The smoothness of the pulp determines the character of the paper.
7 Iron may be used to smooth paper before sizing.
8 Electric blender, an alternative modern tool for obtaining a smooth pulp.

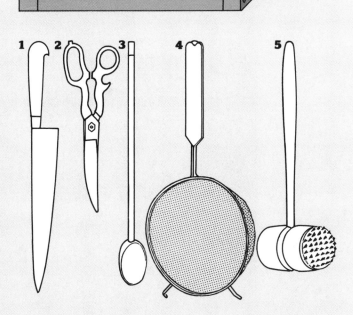

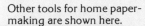

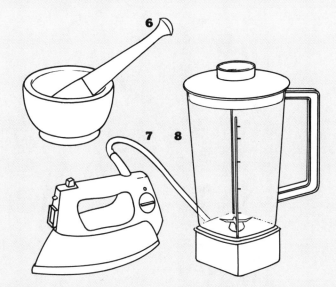

e The pulp is next added to water in a **vat**—perhaps a plastic tray. The **mold** is then lowered into the mixture and a layer of pulp collected on the fabric mesh. As the mold is lifted out, it is gently moved from side to side to obtain an even fiber distribution.

f If the papermaker is satisfied with the texture, thickness and evenness of the pulp in the mold, he then tips the mold slightly so that surplus water drains off at one corner, as shown below. If he is not satisfied, he tries another dip from the vat.

g The mold is placed on one end to allow the paper to dry, either in the sun on a warm, breezy day, or near a **radiator** or **stove.** When the paper is dry it is removed from the mold, placed between **blotting paper,** and pressed between two **boards** for 24 hours.

h For a smoother surface the paper can be pressed with an **electric iron.** To make the paper suitable for use with water-based inks or paints, size (culinary gelatin) can be applied with a **brush.** The paper is then placed between **blotting paper** and hung to dry.

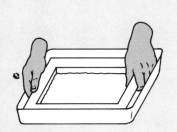

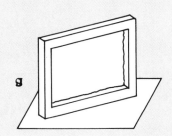

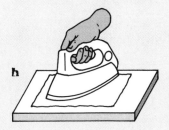

© DIAGRAM

Bookbinding 1

The binding of folded sheets of vellum into book form dates from the 4th century. Wood boards were used to keep the vellum flat and so the early volumes were heavy and cumbersome, but the introduction of printing on paper meant that books became lighter and more convenient in format, allowing the binder to develop the more delicate side of his craft.

The craft of bookbinding is illustrated in the woodcut on the right, made in 1568 by Jost Amman for Hans Sachs' "Ständebuch," or "Book of Trades." Sachs saw bookbinding as one of the noblest of the manual trades, ranking it with goldsmithing.

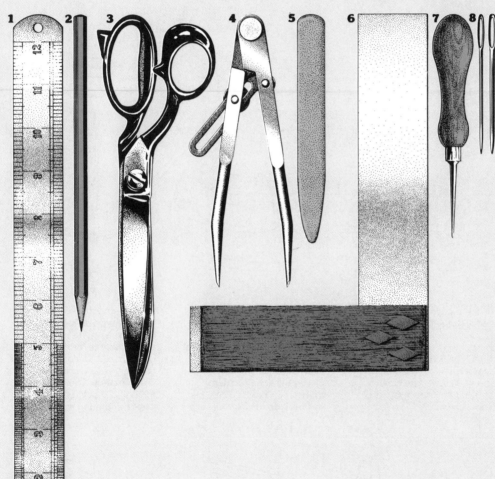

1 Steel rule.
2 Pencil for marking the boards and leather.
3 Shears or **scissors.**
4 Calipers or **dividers** used to equalize measurements on the book and the cover.
5 Bone folder; this produces a smoother fold than folders made of other materials, and will not mark the paper or the leather.
6 T-square used to ensure that the lines of the book are accurate.
7 Awl, needed for punching holes in the cover boards.
8 Needles used for stitching the sections to the cords or tapes.

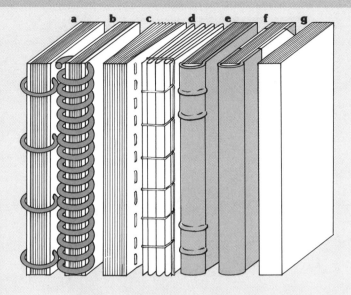

Many styles of bookbinding have evolved to cater for specific binding needs; some of the main types of binding are shown here (left).

a Ring binding, generally used to bind single sheets that cannot easily be sewn. Single metal or plastic rings are inserted through punched holes.

b Spiral binding is similar to ring binding, but the metal is in a spiral.

c Stab-sewing, also used mainly for binding single sheets; a row of stitches is made through the sheets from front to back.

d Stitched Japanese waterfall; these books are printed on one side of a long sheet of paper. This is then formed into concertina folds and sewn at the spine, leaving the outer edges of the "pages" still in folds.

e Stitched full binding with raised bands; the folded sections of the book are stitched to cords, which then form the raised bands on the spine.

f Half-binding; the spine and corners are covered with a second material, either leather or cloth. (Quarter-bound books have only the spine reinforced.)

g Perfect binding, often used for paperbacks. The pages are held together at the spine by glue only; there is no stitching.

1 Tenon saw used for cutting the stitch marks into the folded sections.

2 Backing hammer; the spine of the book is beaten with the hammer to make it assume its characteristic curved shape.

3,4 Cutting knives for use on leather and paper.

5,6 Paring knives used to thin the edges of the leather before it is folded over the cover. The knife with the bound handle was made from a sharpened saw blade.

7,8 Brushes for damping and pasting the leather, and for applying glue to the spine.

Bookbinding 2

Bookbinding by hand has developed into a highly skilled craft. Various machines have been devised to aid the craftsman, but the actual handiwork on the book, such as stitching, backing and gilding, is still done entirely by hand in order to maintain the high quality of the work.

The illustration reproduced on the right is of a craftsman-bookbinder in his workshop. The nipping press in which he is flattening a book is exactly the same in principle as those in use today.

The stages shown here are the basic steps in producing a full leather binding.

a The folded sections of the book are placed in the correct order and "knocked up" against a flat surface so that their backs are level. The sections are put into a **nipping press** to flatten them, and then into a **laying press;** cuts are then made across the folds with a **tenon saw** to produce stitching holes.

b The sections are placed against vertical cords strung from a **sewing frame,** and stitched firmly through the saw marks onto the cords. When the sewing is completed the cords are cut from the frame, and the book is pressed again to make it compact.

c The spine is lightly glued to hold the sections in place, then the raw edges of the pages are trimmed either with a **plow** or with a **guillotine.**

d The book's spine is rounded by hammering it on a flat surface, and then placed in the laying press; the spine is "backed" with a **backing hammer.**

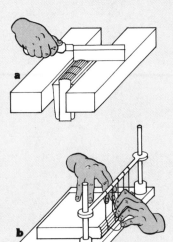

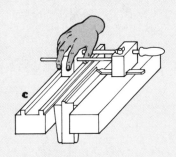

e The boards for the covers are cut to size, and the loose cords from the spine are laced through the boards and hammered flat. A hollow spine is attached to the backs of the sections.

f The leather is cut to the right size, and the edges are pared or thinned with a sharp, flat **paring knife;** this ensures that they will fold over neatly and easily.

g The leather is damped to soften it and then pasted all over to make it adhere to the book. The corners are trimmed and the leather is folded over the spine and boards.

h The endpapers of the first and last sections are stuck down to the insides of the boards to neaten the appearance of the binding. The leather is washed with damp cotton to remove any excess paste; it is then polished with a **polishing iron** if a smooth finish is required.

i The binding can then be decorated in various ways, such as tooling, embossing etc.

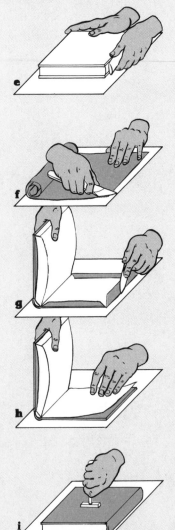

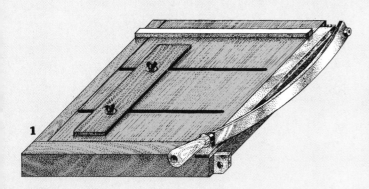

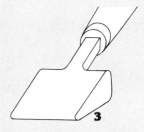

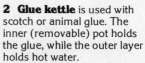

1 Card cutter is used to trim the book's cover boards to the correct size. The blade handle is raised, the card is placed so that the line to be cut coincides with the edge of the block, and the blade is brought down so that it slices away the unwanted card.

2 Glue kettle is used with scotch or animal glue. The inner (removable) pot holds the glue, while the outer layer holds hot water.

3 Polishing iron is heated and rubbed over the binding to smooth the leather.

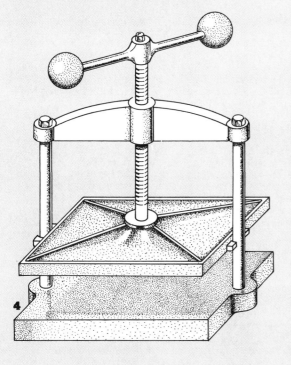

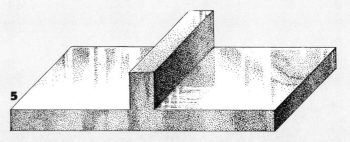

4 Nipping press is a small, powerful press used to keep the book flat and compact during binding. The book is screwed tightly into the press for short periods in order to expel any air that might be trapped between the pages.

5 Knocking-down iron is a heavy metal block used for ensuring that all parts of the book align correctly. The grip of the iron can be clamped into a press so that the edges of the book can be knocked firmly against the flat surface.

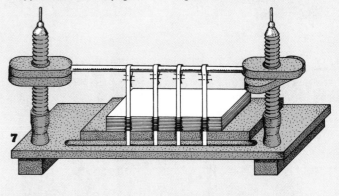

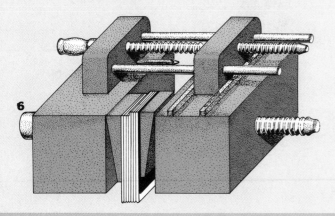

6 Plow is a tool for trimming the pages of books. The book is clamped into the vise, and a very sharp blade is run along the length of several pages at a time. The blade is then screwed in slightly further, and the process is repeated until all the pages are cut.

7 Sewing frame used for stitching the book sections together. Tapes or cords are strung vertically across the frame; the backs of the sections are laid against the cords and sewn firmly to them and to each other. The tapes can then be cut away from the frame.

©DIAGRAM

Gilding

Gilding has been used to great effect in the decoration of leather bookbindings, manuscripts of vellum or parchment, and a variety of other objects such as clocks and picture frames. Gold leaf is made to adhere to a surface by stamping with heated tools, or by burnishing. Each of these basic processes is briefly described here along with its tools.

Gold tooling on the jackets and spines of books has for hundreds of years been a popular way of decorating and enriching leather bindings. The book shown (left) was made for King Henry VIII of England, and was blind tooled.

Gold leaf for gilding is obtained in small books, as shown (left). Books usually contain 25 very thin, square sheets of beaten 23¼ karat gold.
Common leaf, made from various alloys, and **silver leaf** are also available.

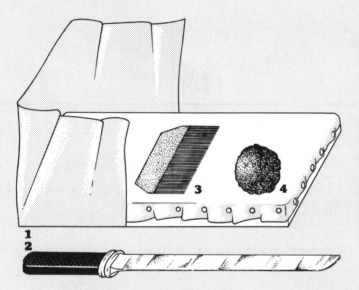

Several items are common to each gilding process.
1 Gilder's cushion with wood base and suede-covered pad. The gilder lays gold leaf on the cushion ready for used. This example has a **parchment shield** to protect the gold from drafts.
2 Gilder's knife used for cutting gold leaf.
3 Gilder's tip is a thin, flat brush used to pick up the gold. The gilder draws the tip through his hair to make the gold adhere to it.
4 Latex eraser, very soft for removing excess gold.

Heat is used to apply gold leaf in the following way.
a With a **brush** or piece of cotton, a special adhesive called glair is applied over the entire area to be gold tooled.
b Appropriate **finishing tools** are heated (see below).
c Petroleum jelly is applied thinly over the glair.
d A **gilder's tip** is used to position the gold leaf, which is then pressed flat.
e **Finishing tools** are cooled to the correct temperature by pressing them onto damp **cotton.** They are then used to stamp out the required design, since heat makes the gold leaf adhere to the glair.
f Excess gold is removed.

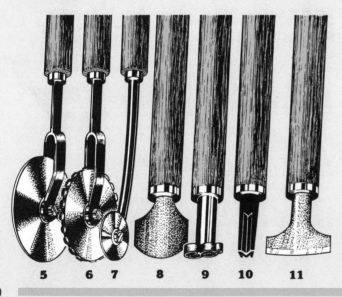

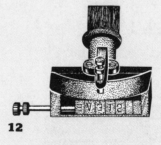

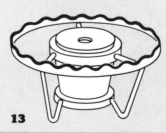

Finishing tools used when applying gold leaf by heat include those shown (left).
5 Fillet for plain lines.
6 Roll for patterned lines.
7 Farthing wheel for curves.
8 Gouge for curved lines.
9 Center tool for a motif.
10 Letter tool, also called a **handle tool** or **hand tool.**
11 Pallet for adding rules.
12 Spring typeholder to take letters for words.
13 Gilder's stove, heated electrically, with notches to hold the tool handles.

Gold was frequently used to decorate the inside of books as well as the outside, particularly in manuscript illumination. The detail (left) is an illuminated and gilded capital L from a decorated manuscript.

The applications of gilding can be extended for use on carvings and statues such as the one shown (right). The statue is of a seated Indra, and dates from the 13th century; the gilding gives the whole statue an air of opulence.

Examples of tools used for burnishing gold leaf are illustrated (left and below).
1 Quill pen with long slit for applying glair.
2 Breathing tube.
3 Agate burnisher, also known simply as an **agate.** Different styles of head are available.
4 Erasing knife.
5 Feather.
6 Bone folder, useful for preliminary burnishing.
7 Awl with fine point.

Stages in the application of gold leaf by burnishing are illustrated (right).
a Working on a hard, flat **burnishing slab,** the gilder first dusts the surface to be gilded with pounce, a fine powder for removing grease or moisture. A **feather** may be used to dust off the pounce. The gilder then uses a **quill pen** to mark out the required design in glair, a substance to which the gold will adhere. Any bubbles in the glair are pricked out at once with a fine-pointed **awl.**
b When the glair is dry, the gilder picks up a piece of gold leaf with a **gilder's tip.** He then makes the glair tacky by breathing on it through a **breathing tube.**
c The gold leaf is laid onto the tacky glair, and then covered with two sheets of paper. The gilder then uses an **agate burnisher** to rub over the area to be gilded.
d The covering sheets are removed, and the work examined. An **erasing knife** is used to correct mistakes.

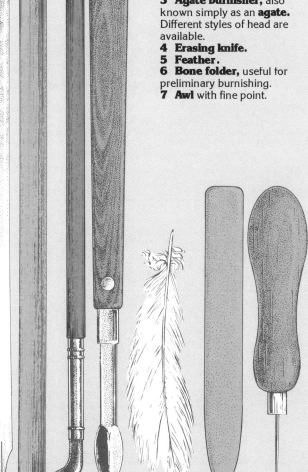

1 2 3 4 5 6 7

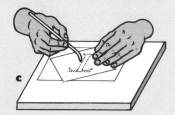

©DIAGRAM

4 Painting

Paint is a combination of dry pigment, a binder and a liquid medium. The resultant mixture determines, to some extent, the nature of the tools of the painter. The most common type of tool used by the painter is the brush, which is sufficiently absorbent to hold the liquid paint. The brush also has the capability, because of the flexible nature of the bristles, of being used in a variety of strokes so that the appearance on the receiving surface can be varied and regulated.

The precise qualities of the brushes chosen depend on the characteristics of the paint itself. Oil paints are sometimes used thickly, requiring strong bristle brushes for their application. At other times thin, translucent layers are applied, requiring soft, absorbent hair brushes, similar to those used in watercolor painting where the medium is water and the paint is applied in thin washes.

The nature of some paints, or of the ground to which they are applied, requires more specialized tools for their application. Fresco calls for large quantities of paint to be applied rapidly to the wet plaster ground, and so some fresco "brushes" consist of pieces of sponge tied onto handles. Encaustic, a technique popular in Roman times, involved painting melted colored waxes onto a panel and then "burning in" with a heated metal rod. In this century a technique has been developed for spraying pressurized paint through a nozzle, known as an airbrush, to produce very thin coatings of paint and even gradations of color. As further new paints and new painting methods are evolved, they will inevitably be followed by new tools for the painter.

The painting reproduced here is a self-portrait by Rembrandt van Rijn; the painter's brushes and palette can be clearly seen. One of Rembrandt's favorite subjects was himself with his painting tools, and he painted many variations on the theme.

Watercolor

Water-based paints include the opaque gouache and polymer paints, but the term watercolor is used primarily for the technique of painting in pure, transparent washes. Watercolor paper is prepared by soaking it in water and then drying it taped onto a board; the paper itself creates the white ground, and diluted pigments are painted onto it.

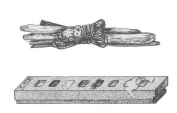

The detail (right) is from "The Ghost of Samuel Appearing to Saul," a watercolor by William Blake (1757-1827). The head is that of the Witch of Endor, who has called up Samuel's spirit; Blake's sensitive use of the watercolor captures her horror. Illustrated (left) are Egyptian brushes and a palette.

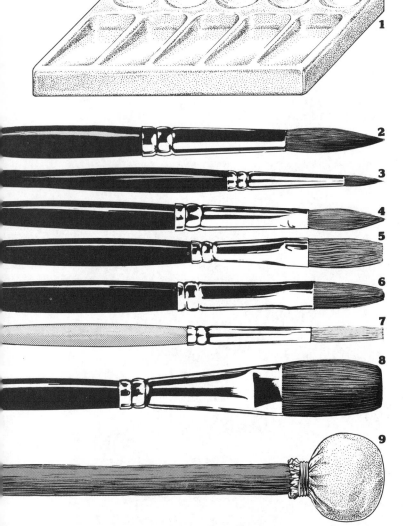

Watercolor brushes and **accessories** have been developing and refining since the 18th century, when watercolors first became popular in their own right rather than as preliminary sketches for oil paintings. Brushes now come in a wide variety of lengths, textures and thicknesses; each type of brush serves a different purpose.

1 Palette is a porcelain, glass or plastic surface, made either flat or with reservoirs, used for diluting the watercolors to the required strengths. The pigment, in block or paste form, is mixed with water by the artist.

2,3,4 Sable brushes are of a very high quality, and the hairs are very fine. Those with long hairs or heads hold a lot of paint and can be used for large areas; short-headed brushes can be used for small areas and fine detail.

5,6 Ox hair brushes have long heads to increase their paint carrying capacity.

7 Hog hair brush has a long flat head and a square tip.

8 Large flat is a brush used for color washing large areas.

9 Mahlstick is used to hold the painter's hand steady. It is a light wooden rod, often with a leather covered ball at one end.

Illustrated below is the method of using a **mahlstick** or **rest stick** (see left). The stick is held in the palette hand of the artist, and he uses it to steady his painting arm as he works.

Fresco painting

Fresco painting on plaster began over three thousand years ago; it reached its peak of popularity in the Italian renaissance, but is still used by some artists today. A cartoon, or sketch, is drawn first and its lines perforated; the plaster ground can then be marked through the holes. Wet plaster is laid on the area to be painted, so that the paints will combine with the plaster.

On the right is a fresco of the head of a saint by Domenico Veneziano; frescoes were frequently of religious subjects. The slightly luminous quality of the face is produced as much by the plaster ground as by the fresco paint itself. Shown (left) are an Egyptian pestle and mortar.

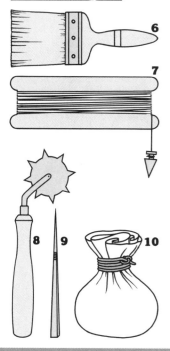

1 **Hawk,** a hand held palette.
2 **Scratch comb,** drawn over the first rough surface.
3,4 **Trowels** used for mortar and plaster.
5 **Float** for smoothing the various wall coatings.
6 **Wetting brush** for damping the coatings.
7 **Snapline and plumb** used to transfer straight lines to the plaster.
8,9 **Pouncing wheel** and **perforating point** for piercing the cartoon.
10 **Pouncing bag** full of charcoal powder. The bag is rubbed against the holes in the cartoon and marks the plaster underneath.
11 **Mortar and pestle** used for grinding colors.
12 **Muller and slab,** also used for color grinding.
13,14 **Spatula** and **palette knife** for mixing pigments.
15 **Broad, flat sable brush.**
16 **Italian-style fresco brush.**
17 **Swedish-style fresco brush.**
18 **Fitch brush,** with deeply chiseled tip.
19 **Square tipped brush.**
20 **Square pointed rigger brush.**
21 **Liner brush** for painting fine contours.
22 **Split tipped brush.**
23 **Sponge tipped brush.**

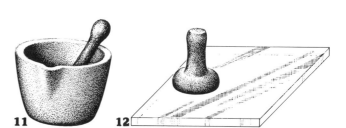

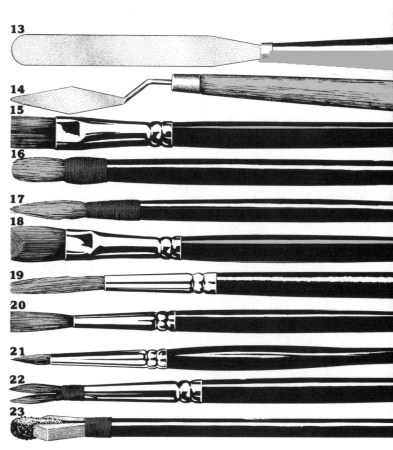

Oil painting

Oil painting was first used extensively by the van Eyck brothers in the 15th century. The translucence of egg tempera had proved unsatisfactory for rendering the soft, deep shadows of the newly popular realism in art, and painters experimented first with oil glazes over tempera and then with mixing the pigments themselves into the oil.

This self-portrait in oils (right) was painted by Velazquez in 1656. The artist has used the versatility of the oil paint to the full, laying it on thickly in the highlights and blending it delicately in the shadows.

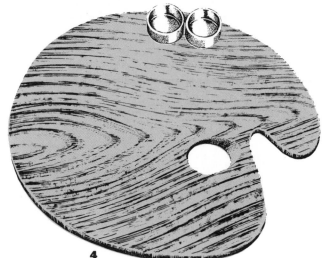

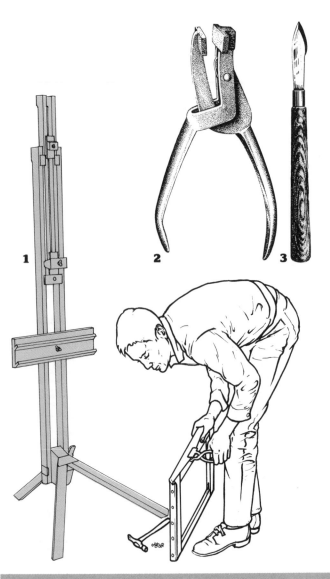

1 **Easel** for holding the canvas while it is painted.
2 **Canvas pliers** for stretching the canvas.
3 **Canvas scraper** for scraping impurities from the surface of the canvas.
4 **Palette** on which the paints are mixed, with **dippers,** small paint pots.

The method of using canvas pliers is illustrated on the left. The canvas is gripped firmly by the jaws of the pliers so that it can be pulled very tightly across the frame, and it is then secured with thumbtacks or nails.

Illustrated on the left are some of the many styles of **palette knife** available for use with oils. The artist uses a palette knife for blending two or more colors on his palette, and for applying the paint to his canvas if he wants a particularly thick block of color. If he wishes to alter the consistency of his paint, he can use a palette knife to mix it with oil; the most common oils in use are poppy, walnut and linseed.

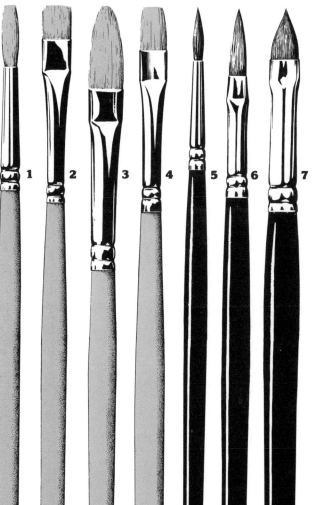

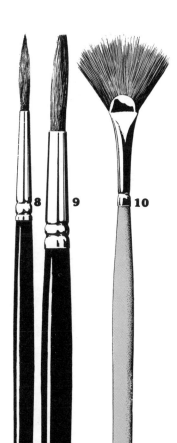

Brushes for oil painting must keep their shapes well so that they produce consistent strokes, and they invariably have very long handles in order to allow the maximum freedom of manipulation. For thicker paints, hog hair brushes are used because of their firmness, while sable brushes are more absorbent and are better for thinner paint. Fan brushes are used to blend one area of paint into another on the canvas.

  1 Round hog hair brush.
  2 Flat hog hair brush.
  3 Hog hair filbert.
  4 Hog hair brush with the bristles turning inward.
  5 Round sable brush.
  6 Flat sable brush.
  7 Sable filbert.
  8 Pointed sable rigger.
  9 Square pointed sable rigger.
10 Fan brush.

Signwriting

Signwriting originated in the distinguishing symbols displayed by shopkeepers over their premises; such symbols are known to have existed in ancient Egyptian, Greek and Roman civilizations. Gradually, wording that identified the proprietor or the trade began to be incorporated into the pictorial signs, and signwriting as we know it was developed.

The painting reproduced (right) shows the painting of an inn sign to celebrate the Duke of Wellington's birthday. The sign is being painted in public as part of the birthday festivities.

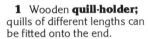

1 Wooden **quill-holder;** quills of different lengths can be fitted onto the end.
2 Quill filled with sable hair.
3 Hog hair brush with square end.
4 Sable pencil, a brush with a long, thin head of sable hair. The brush can be used for outlines and detailed work.
5 Hog hair brush, fanning out to a square end.
6 Square-pointed rigger.
7 Square-ended brush with nylon bristles.
8 Varnishing brush with hog hair bristles, used for varnishing the finished sign.
9 Dippers, small wide pots that hold paint or thinning medium.
10 Bridge used to keep the artist's hand away from the work.
11 Snap lines wound onto a reel. These lines can be used to produce temporary straight guidelines.

A **bridge** is used to keep the working hand at a distance from the wet, newly painted surface. The bridge is usually made of wood, and the feet are cushioned to protect the sign from damage; the artist rests his hand and arm on the flat top of the bridge (below).

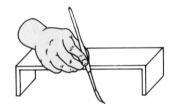

A **snap line** or **chalk line** consists of a length of twine rubbed with colored chalk. The line is secured tautly across the work and then lifted away in the center; when it is released it snaps smartly onto the work and deposits the chalk in a straight line (below).

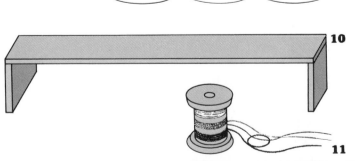

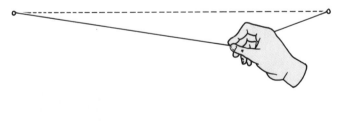

Airbrushing

Airbrushing is a technique that can be used to achieve great delicacy and accuracy in detailed tonal work. Color is propelled onto the paper in a fine spray by compressed air; a skilled airbrush artist can control the flow with great precision, blending and graduating tone very smoothly or applying a flat tone.

The example of the airbrushing technique shown (right) illustrates the gradual shading that can be obtained with this method of painting. Strong shadows and bright highlights can be produced by careful use of the brush.

The **airbrush** is held at the angle shown below, so that the ink will flow easily; this position also allows the wrist to move freely. The air hose is wound around the wrist to keep it clear of the paper and the brush.

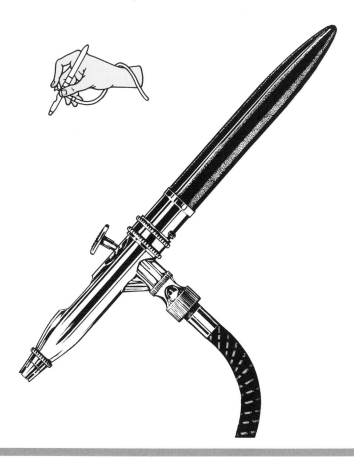

Before the **airbrush** is used, the color is diluted to the required strength, and the reservoir of the airbrush is filled with the solution. The strength of color used may be changed as work progresses if a wide variety of tone is required, or several different colors may be used.

a The drawing to be air-brushed is covered with a self-adhesive clear film (or ordinary clear film attached with transparent glue or gum).

b The areas to be colored first are cut out with a **scalpel** or **frisket knife.**

c The airbrush fills in the exposed areas, while the operator controls the density of the color with the trigger on the top of the brush.

d The colored areas are covered with film again, and further areas are removed.

e The procedure continues until all the detail is complete.

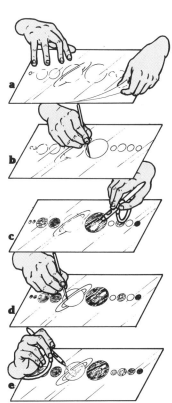

The **airbrush** is powered by compressed air, which is supplied either by an **electric compressor** (right) or by a **carbon dioxide cylinder.** The usual working pressure for the brush is around 25 lb (11 kg).

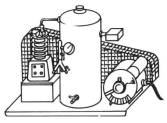

Miniatures

Miniatures are tiny paintings, often portraits designed to fit inside lockets. They are usually not more than 6 inches in diameter, and can be very much smaller, down to the size of a pin-head. The greatest Western miniaturists worked in England in the 16th and 17th centuries, and were headed by the master miniaturist Nicholas Hilliard.

The miniature reproduced (right) is a portrait of Sir Francis Drake, painted in 1581 by Nicholas Hilliard. The painting itself is only 1⅛ inches in diameter, which means that the brushstrokes on the ruff and the lace are minute.

1 Pencil used to make the original drawing.
2 Stylus for tracing the drawing onto the ground.
3 Sable brush size 000.
4 Thumbtacks for holding the paper over the ground.
5 Pins; when ivory is used as a ground, pins are used to hold the ivory leaf still.

6 Chamois used to clean grease from the grounds.
7 Pounce bag.
8 Paste brush; paste is used to secure parchment and vellum grounds.
9 Palette knife for mixing the pigments.
10 Feather used to dust off the pounce.

11 Oyster shell, a smooth shell used as a palette.
12 Glass slab and **grinder** used for blending the pigments into the liquid medium.
13 Miniature palette.
14 Hand-held magnifier, used when painting very fine detail.

15 Magnifying glass on a flexible stem to leave both hands free.

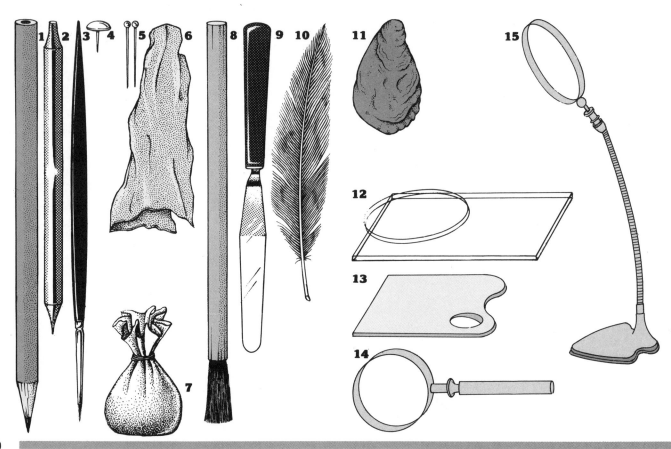

Tempera

Tempera is a water based paint that is mixed with a binder of egg yolk and then blended with distilled water. Tempera is generally painted on a surface of white gesso which, combined with the translucent appearance of the paint, gives the final painting an almost luminous quality; this was used to great effect in the many tempera paintings of Botticelli.

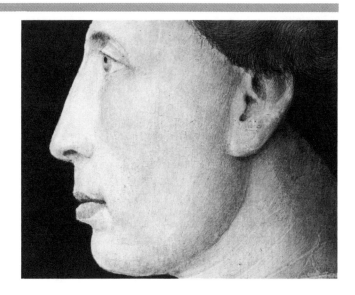

The tempera painting on the right is a portrait of Lionello d'Este, painted in 1447 by Giovanni da Oriolo. The translucent quality of the medium can be seen particularly in the delicate tones of the face.

1 Rasp used for preparing the wood grounds.
2 Sandpaper, also used to smooth the grounds.
3 Size brush; size is the preliminary adhesive and sealant.
4,5 Glass rod and **thermometer** used when preparing size.

6 Gesso brush.
7 Dropper, used to add water to the egg binder.
8 Palette knife used when mixing binder and pigments.
9 Egg separator; only the yolk is used in the binder.
10 Tea strainer used to strain the paints.
11 Sharp knife.

The ground for tempera is often a wood panel; this is smoothed with a **rasp** and with **sandpaper,** and then coated with gesso. Gesso is a mixture of size—a kind of gelatin glue—and whiting, and it gives a smooth surface ideal for receiving paint.

The binder is made by isolating the yolk of the egg, and then slitting it with a **sharp knife** so that its contents can be mixed with water and with the pigments. The paint is then strained, and is ready for use.

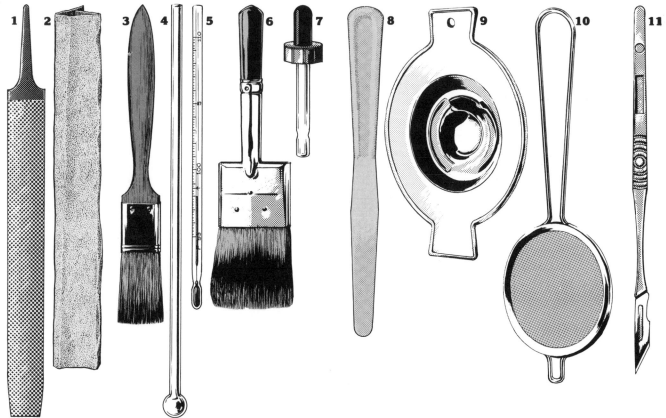

Stenciling

Stenciling is a method of transferring a design by painting through shapes cut in a thin sheet of metal, paper or a similar material. Stencils can be used for tiny designs, such as initials or small flower motifs, or for giant designs suitable for decorating an entire room.

The sprays of bamboo shown (right) were made by painting through a stencil cut from heavy paper. The repeat pattern was made by moving the stencil farther along the paper and repeating the process.

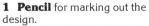

Stencils may be bought ready-cut in many shapes, sizes and designs.
7 Pattern stencils made in waxed paper.
8 Alphabet stencils made from thin metal.

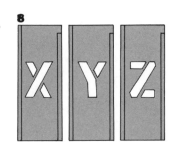

1 Pencil for marking out the design.
2 Sharp knife used for cutting out complicated parts of the design.
3 Scissors.
4 Bone folder used to crease the paper when cutting a repeat pattern.

5 Stencil brush for stippling the paint through the cut design.
6 Sponge; this can be used to dab paint through the stencil.

The technique for making and using a paper stencil is illustrated in the sequence (right).
a The chosen design is marked out onto the paper with clear lines.
b The design is then cut out of the paper, using **scissors** or a **sharp knife;** this leaves a paper stencil ready for use.
c The stencil is placed flat on the surface to be decorated, and the paint is applied over the top. The paint transfers onto the underneath surface only where there are holes in the stencil.

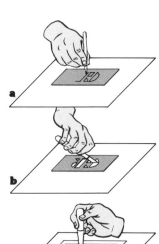

Rosemaling and tole painting

Tole painting and rosemaling are allied crafts which both involve painting bright, attractive designs, often floral in inspiration, onto a plain-colored background. The two crafts are products of a number of influences; they have a Scandinavian character, and also show an affinity to traditional English barge-painting.

Illustrated (right) are examples of rosemaling and tole painting The tin coffee jug has been decorated with rosemaling designs, and the wooden eggcup has tole flowers painted on the outside.

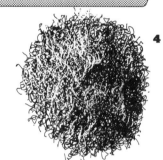

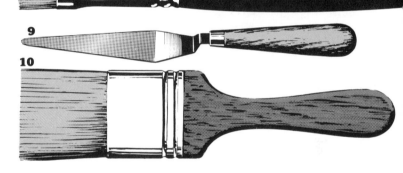

Rosemaling tools are illustrated above.
1 Fine sable brush.
2 Stylus for transferring the design.
3 Chalk stick.
4 Fine wire wool.

The three main stages in tole painting are illustrated (right).
a The wood to be decorated is rubbed with **wire wool** to smooth it. The background color is then painted over the entire surface.
b The tole designs are brushed on with **sable brushes;** ideally the artist should have a separate brush for each color, so that the clarity of the tones will not be dulled.
c When the paint is dry, the wood is varnished to give it a glossy appearance.

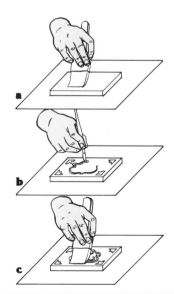

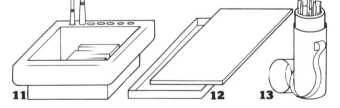

Tole painting tools are shown above.
5,6,7,8 Sable brushes in various sizes.
9 Palette knife for blending the paints.
10 Varnish brush; the wood used for tole painting is often varnished to protect the painting.

11 Brush basin used for cleaning brushes.
12 Covered palette; this prevents the paints from drying up during the work.
13 Brush quiver.

5 Pictures without paint

Pictures without paint can be made from paper, card, string, metal offcuts, natural objects—in fact, from any solid material. Many types of picture can be made from paper used in various ways. It can be cut into two-dimensional shapes, as in papercuts; this has for centuries been an honored craft in Oriental countries. Paper can also be shaped or folded into three dimensions, as with paper sculpture and origami, or it can be treated with a solid pigment as with brass rubbing and scratchboard.

Natural objects such as flowers and shells can be used to make pictures by arranging them decoratively on colored grounds. This was a traditional pastime at the turn of the century, and the survival of many examples proves the durability of such creations if they are carried out carefully.

Synthetic materials in bright colors, shiny finishes or unusual textures that are found in stores or as part of everyday objects can be the inspiration for modernistic collages. With a little planning and an element of artistic flair, the ordinary objects of today may become the art of tomorrow.

The print reproduced here shows a shadow artist at work producing a silhouette. The silhouette machine, as it is described, is a chair with one arm built up to form a screen. The paper is inserted into the screen, and the candle-light projects the model's profile.

Machine sûre & commode pour tirer des Silhouettes.

R. Schellenberg del. et sc.

Voici le caractère que j'assignerois à la Silhouette de cette jeune personne. J'y trouve de la bonté sans
beaucoup de finesse, de la clarté dans les idées, & le talent de les concevoir avec facilité, un esprit fort
industrieux, mais qui n'est point dominé par une imagination bien vive, & qui ne s'attache
guère à une exactitude scrupuleuse. On ne retrouve point dans la copie le caractère de gaieté qu'annonce
l'Original; mais le nez a gagné dans la silhouette — il y exprime plus de finesse.

Collage

Collage is the process of building a picture by securing solid materials onto a support. Paper, metal, wood, glass and plastic can all be used in collage. Natural objects such as seeds, pine cones, branches, leaves and grasses can be incorporated into attractive designs, and even substances such as sand, ash and powder paint can be used effectively.

The collage illustrated (right) was made of old tickets from a variety of sources. Stamped, printed or patterned papers and cards such as these make ideal materials for collage.

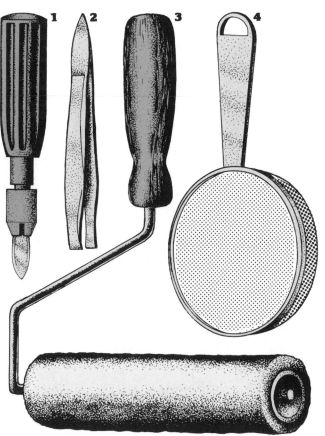

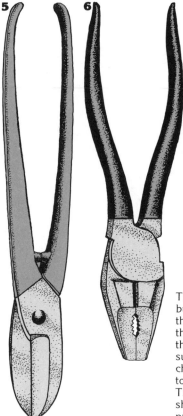

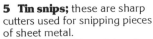

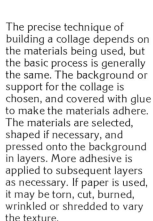

1 Craft knife used for cutting paper and plastic.
2 Tweezers for picking up small objects.
3 Roller used to apply adhesive.
4 Sieve; powder paint or sand can be shaken onto the collage through this.

5 Tin snips; these are sharp cutters used for snipping pieces of sheet metal.
6 Pliers, used to cut, bend and form lengths of wire and sheets of metal or plastic.
7 Sponge for spreading paint or adhesive.

The precise technique of building a collage depends on the materials being used, but the basic process is generally the same. The background or support for the collage is chosen, and covered with glue to make the materials adhere. The materials are selected, shaped if necessary, and pressed onto the background in layers. More adhesive is applied to subsequent layers as necessary. If paper is used, it may be torn, cut, burned, wrinkled or shredded to vary the texture.

Découpage

The name découpage comes from the French, meaning "applied cutouts." The craft began in the West in the 18th century, inspired by Oriental lacquer work, and was a very popular recreation in the following century. Cutouts are glued to a hard surface, usually wood, then varnished and polished to create a shiny, durable surface.

The box shown in this photograph has been decorated by the technique of découpage. The cutouts were applied to a prepared wood box, glued in place, and then varnished over to produce a smooth finish.

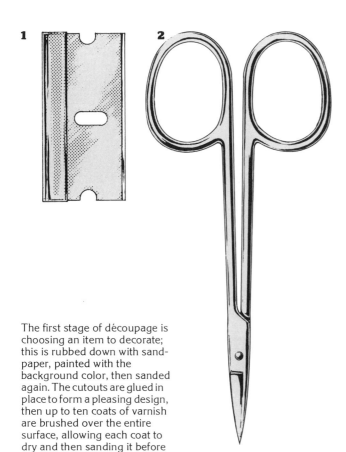

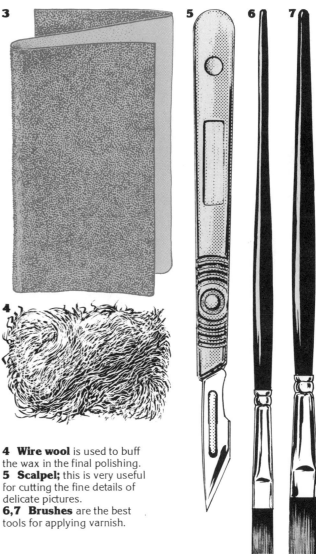

The first stage of découpage is choosing an item to decorate; this is rubbed down with sandpaper, painted with the background color, then sanded again. The cutouts are glued in place to form a pleasing design, then up to ten coats of varnish are brushed over the entire surface, allowing each coat to dry and then sanding it before the next is applied. The whole object can then be "antiqued" with a brown stain if desired to simulate aging; finally the surface is waxed and buffed with **wire wool** to complete the glossy finish.

1 Razor blade can be used to trim a picture when it overlaps an edge, or to produce an accurate match if part is to appear on a box lid.
2 Scissors are used for cutting out the pictures.
3 Sandpaper for smoothing the coats of varnish.

4 Wire wool is used to buff the wax in the final polishing.
5 Scalpel; this is very useful for cutting the fine details of delicate pictures.
6,7 Brushes are the best tools for applying varnish.

©DIAGRAM

Flower pressing

Flower pressing is a craft that became very popular in the 19th century, when the teaching of botany in schools stimulated an interest in collecting and preserving flora. Although some flowers fade when they are pressed, others keep their full colors. Leaves and ferns can also be pressed with great success.

The decorative effects that can be achieved by pressing and arranging flowers may be seen in the pressed flower picture shown (right). The flowers have been placed so that they form an attractive arrangement on the background.

A **flower press,** such as the one above, can be built by sandwiching sheets of firm card and blotting paper between two layers of ply. Pressure is applied by tightening the wing nuts. Alternatively, a heavy book, or a scrapbook under weights, may be used.

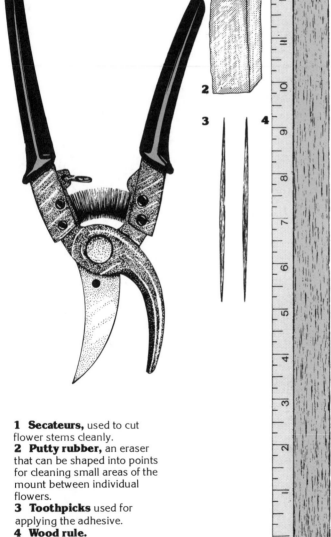

1 Secateurs, used to cut flower stems cleanly.
2 Putty rubber, an eraser that can be shaped into points for cleaning small areas of the mount between individual flowers.
3 Toothpicks used for applying the adhesive.
4 Wood rule.

Flowers and foliage must be dry and undamaged before they are pressed.
a The freshly cut flowers are smoothed out and put between sheets of blotting paper. The flowers should not overlap, otherwise they leave marks on each other.
b The sheets of blotting paper are placed between sheets of card and positioned in the **press.** The press is screwed down, or, if a book is used, the weights are placed on top of it. The flowers are pressed for at least six weeks; once they are dry and flat, they can be assembled into pictures and designs.

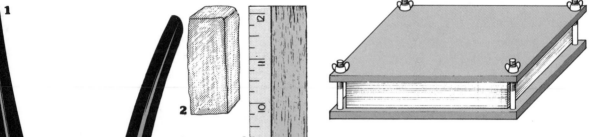

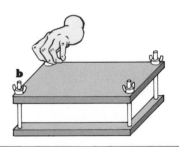

Shellwork

Eggshells, nut shells and sea-shells may all be used as materials for pictures and abstract designs. All the shells produce intriguing textures, and the surfaces may be painted or varnished for even more variety. Pasta shapes can be used in the same way.

Shown here are an eggshell mosaic (right) and a seashell mosaic (far right). The sea-shells have been selected and arranged according to their natural tones; the eggshells have been colored and crushed, and then arranged in a pattern on the paper.

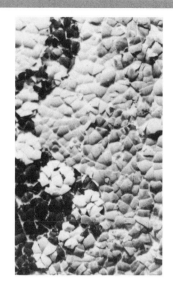

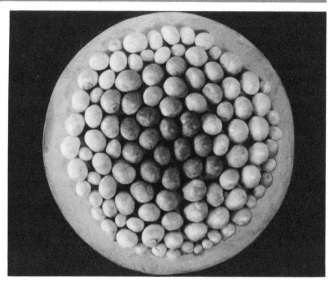

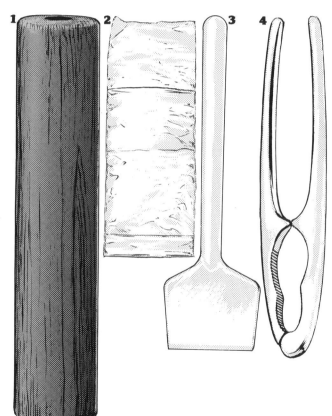

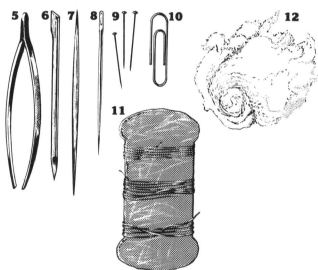

Egg shells are very fragile, and so require gentle handling to avoid spoiling them.

a The shells are placed in a **plastic bag** and gently crushed; a squeeze of the hand or a light touch with a **rolling pin** is generally sufficient pressure.

b Glue is spread over the chosen backing material. The pieces of shell are lifted one at a time and placed into position on the backing. The shells may have been colored or varnished beforehand, or the entire surface can be varnished when complete.

1 Rolling pin for crushing shells.
2 Plastic bag holds the crushed shells.
3 Gum spreader.
4 Nutcrackers.
5 Tweezers; these are used for picking up tiny shells.
6,7 Orange stick and **cocktail stick** for adhesive.

8 Darning needle used to pierce shells for threading.
9,10 Pins and **paperclip** for securing the work.
11 Fuse wire used in making seashell flowers.
12 Cotton; this is soaked in glue and used as a base for seashell flowers.

©DIAGRAM

Papercuts

Papercuts may take many forms, from the child's string of paper dolls to the intricate beauty of the traditional Oriental designs. The papercuts may be made from a single sheet of paper, or cut from several and joined or superimposed; whichever method is used, careful choice of paper and skilful cutting can make a pleasing work of art.

This traditional Chinese papercut is a fish shape called Fu Kuei Yu Yü, and is a charm meant to ensure that the recipient would have abundant wealth.

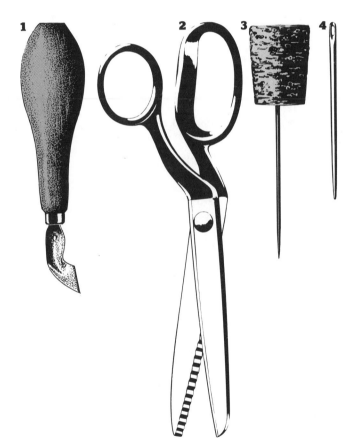

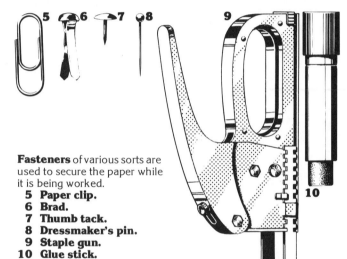

Fasteners of various sorts are used to secure the paper while it is being worked.

   5 Paper clip.
   6 Brad.
   7 Thumb tack.
   8 Dressmaker's pin.
   9 Staple gun.
10 Glue stick.

A simple papercut is made in the following way.
a The design is drawn out onto the chosen sheet or sheets of paper. The pieces to be cut away are clearly marked.
b Using a sharp **knife** or a pair of **scissors,** the unwanted portions are cut away from the sheet, leaving a design made from a continuous piece of paper.
Symmetrical patterns and doilies can be made by folding the paper several times before it is cut.

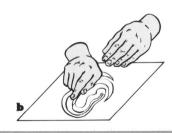

1 Lino knife with a very sharp blade.
2 Pinking shears for making jagged cuts.
3 Awl made from a darning needle held in a cork.
4 Bodkin used for piercing heavy papers.

Other tools that are illustrated elsewhere in the book are used for drafting and designing — for instance, pencils, pens, crayons, rulers, set squares, and compasses.

Silhouettes

A silhouette is a picture made by reproducing in one color, usually black, the outline of the model. The traditional subject for a silhouette is a profile likeness, although in the 19th century the clothing was often included so that the artist's skill could be shown in depicting the frills and flounces of contemporary fashion.

The silhouette shown (right) is a portrait of a young boy made in cut paper. The artist was one of the many seaside artists who plied their trade in the coastal resorts 20 or 30 years ago.

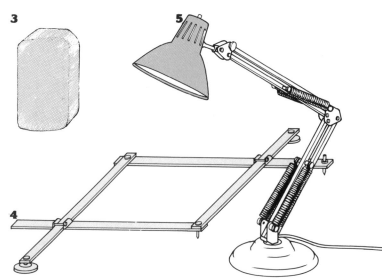

The tools required for silhouettes are very simple; it is the skill of the artist that makes the silhouette successful.

1 **Small scissors.**
2 **Pencil.**
3 **Plastic eraser.**
4 **Pantograph.**
5 **Adjustable lamp.**

The first method of producing a silhouette is shown (right).
a The model is placed so that the artist receives an exact profile. A strong light is shone behind the model so that the profile is thrown into relief.
b The artist then cuts the shape of the profile out of a sheet of paper, using sharp **scissors** so that every detail can be accurately reproduced.

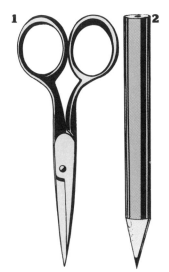

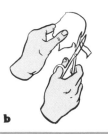

A second method of making a silhouette is shown in the sequence (right).
a The model is placed in front of a screen, and a lamp is shone so that the model's profile falls clearly on the screen. The artist then traces around the outline of the profile.
b This outline can then be reduced in scale with a **pantograph;** the tracing point is run along the outline, and causes the marking point to produce a smaller version on a piece of paper or card.

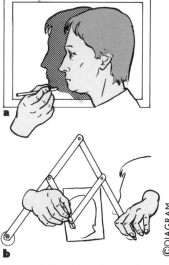

Scratchboard and sgraffito

Scratchboard (scraperboard) was a very popular medium for the artwork that accompanied 1950s advertising. Although now largely superseded as a commercial technique, especially since the advent of cheap color reproduction, it remains a popular craft for the individual artist. Using only very simple tools, it is possible to produce a wide range of effects.

Examples of scratchboard (right) and sgraffito (far right) are illustrated here. The scratchboard shows clearly the strong contrast achieved with this method, while the sgraffito uses several different papers of varying tones and intensities.

1 Pointed blade for cutting very fine lines.
2 Rounded blade gives a wider and deeper line.
3 Curved pointed blade set in a holder; this blade can lay bare broad areas.
4 Multiliner produces many parallel lines with each stroke.

To make scratchboard the artist coats specially surfaced board with ink, generally using black ink for the greatest contrast in tone. When the ink is dry it can be scraped away with **sharp tools** to give effects varying from fine lines to broad plain areas.

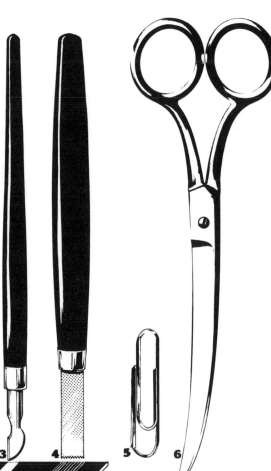

Sgraffito work takes two forms. One form uses the same method and materials as for scratchboard. However, when the ink is scraped away a multi-colored background is revealed rather than a white one.
The other type of sgraffito work, shown here, involves cutting through layers of paper. The tools for this method are as follows.
5 Clip used to hold the pieces of paper together.
6 Scissors with curved blades used for cutting.

Four or five sheets of exact size paper are clipped together. The pieces of paper should vary in color and texture. The **scissors** are then used to cut through the different layers in order to reveal the paper below through the cut shapes.

Paper sculpture and origami

Paper sculpture consists of cutting out paper shapes and scoring them to give a three-dimensional appearance. Origami is the ancient Oriental technique in which solid forms are built up simply by folding sheets of paper. White paper is often used for both these crafts, in order to give a strong light/shadow contrast to the finished form.

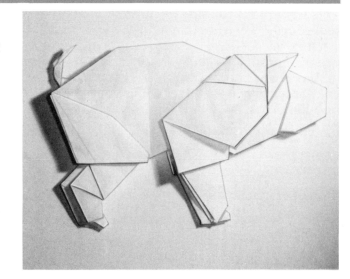

The pig shown right has been made in the ancient Japanese technique of origami. Two square sheets of paper were shaped into a three-dimensional form by a series of complex folds.

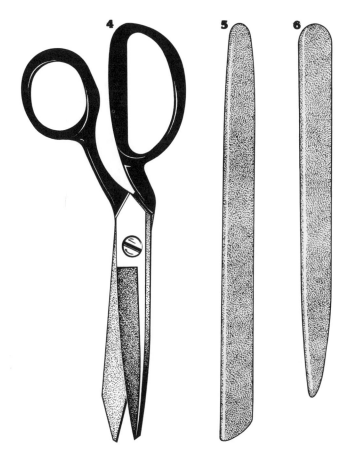

1 Blunt pen-knife, used for scoring lines on the paper shapes.
2 Paper punch, used to make holes for decoration or fastening.
3 Knitting needle can also be used for scoring.
4 Scissors for cutting out the shapes.

The underside of the flat paper shapes is scored by running the **blunt blade** or **knitting needle** along the chosen line. The scoring of the paper produces two facets that slope in opposite directions, and so catch the light.

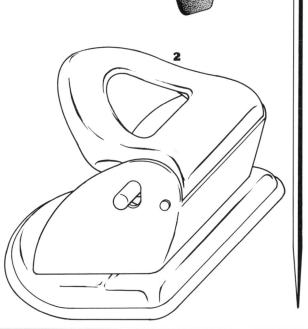

5,6 Bone folders are used to make the required creases in origami paper. The sheet of paper is repeatedly folded in a variety of directions, so that gradually a solid form is built up with the folded paper planes.

©DIAGRAM

Brass rubbing

The art of brass rubbing began as a method of reproducing ancient church memorial brasses, but any well-defined raised or engraved surface can also produce interesting results. Attractive rubbings can be obtained from gravestones, coal-hole covers, metal name plates, tooled bookbindings, and even coins and medals.

The brass rubbing shown on the right was made from a brass of Sir Thomas Walsch and his wife. The brass is in Wanlip, Leicestershire, England, and was made in 1393; the two figures are in the traditional pose of effigies, with their hands in the position of prayer.

1,2 Cobbler's wax or **heelball;** these sticks of waxy material produce the best rubbings. They can be obtained in several colors, and also in gold, silver and bronze finishes.
3 Weight to hold the paper in place while the wax is being rubbed on.
4 Soft wide brush used to clean the surface of the brass before the rubbing begins.

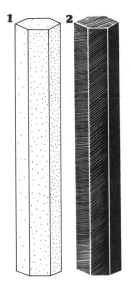

Permission must always be asked for a rubbing to be taken, in case the brass is old and valuable, and might be damaged.
a The brass is brushed clean, and the paper is secured over the surface with **weights.**
b The **heelball** is rubbed firmly over the surface of the paper, rubbing in one direction only for neatness.

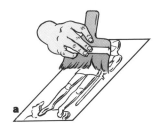

Nails and string pictures

Nails and string can be combined on a board to make interesting and delicate patterns. The shapes used as outlines are usually geometrical, so that the positions of the nails can be gauged accurately. String, colored thread, woolen yarn and metallic thread can be used to provide a variety of effects against different colored backboards.

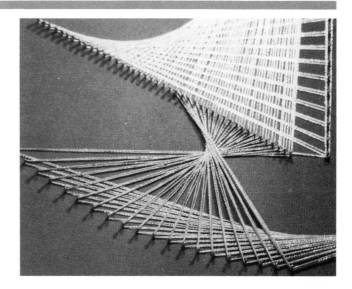

The nail and string picture reproduced here is a detail of a red and silver abstract based on the patterns made by sails in a harbor. The nail and string technique can be used to build up layered pictures or even three-dimensional sculptures.

1 Hammer used for knocking the nails into the board.
2 Compasses, useful for drawing accurate circles and circle sectors.
3 Needle tool, made from a darning needle stuck in dowel. This tool is used to prick out the preliminary nail holes.
4 Nail guide; the nail is slipped into the slot and hit home. When the guide is removed, it leaves the nail at a predetermined height.
5 Pusher; this tool also ensures that all the nails are pushed in to the same height.
6 Thimble.

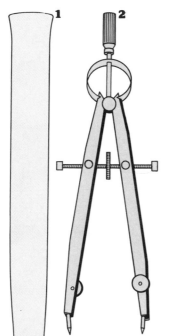

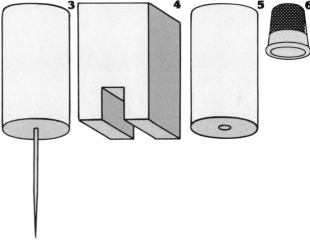

Accuracy is the key to making successful and evenly surfaced nail and string pictures.
a The design outlines are drawn onto the chosen backing board, and nails are driven in at regular intervals along these outlines.
b The chosen string or thread is secured invisibly to the starting nail. It is then wound to and fro across the design, taking a turn around each nail in sequence, before being secured neatly to the final nail.

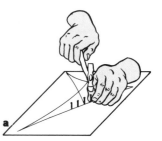

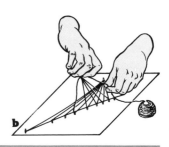

6 Clay and pottery

Clay requires three basic processes to turn it into permanent, waterproof objects. The first is that of shaping, performed when the clay is soft and malleable and has a high water content; its plasticity at this stage enables it to retain almost any shape and texture. The second process is that of firing—driving off the water chemically combined with the clay so that the object is made permanently hard. The third process, which waterproofs the clay, is glazing, which involves fusing a layer of glass onto the clay surface. All the tools of the potter relate to one or several of these processes.

Shaped and baked clay has a long and involved history, dating from 9000 years ago, yet in all cultures that have developed pottery the basic procedures are the same and so are the principles of the tools used. Primitive tribes use shaped sticks and textured tools to form and pattern the clay, just as the sophisticated commercial potter does. The nature of the kiln differs throughout the world, from the bonfire of African tribes to the modern gas or electric kiln, but the method of stacking and slowly firing the clay is universal. Despite the chemically controlled content of glaze used in modern times, the potter uses pouring, brushing and dipping tools to apply it just as his ancestors did. The basic nature of pottery tools for each of the various processes will not change because the basic nature of clay remains the same.

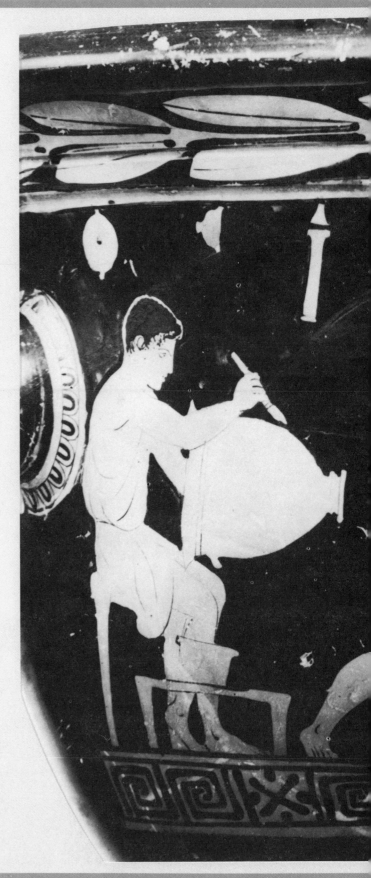

The pot shown here is an Attic red-figure vase in the bell-crater style, and was decorated by the Komaris painter c. 430-425 BC. The pot shows a potter's studio of the time; the figure on the left is painting a color decoration on a pot.

Clay preparation

Pottery is the art of shaping and molding pliable clays, and then firing them in a kiln to render the created shapes firm and stable. Clay in its original state is suspended in water; firing drives off the water that is chemically combined with the constituent materials, and fuses them together. Glazes are often added to make the ware waterproof.

This illustration is from Diderot's "Encyclopedia of Industries," published in the 18th century, and shows a man at work preparing clay for making crucibles. He is mixing the new constituents with broken biscuit-fired pots to give the new mixture added strength.

Pottery has been an instrinsic part of most civilizations for so long that archeologists have been able to learn a great deal about the lifestyles and technology of past cultures through pottery relics. Clay has been used in the past to fashion everything from water-pots to images of gods. Each civilization has had its own local clays, its own methods of shaping and firing the clay, and its own uses for the finished pots, and this variation has meant that the modern potter has a rich heritage of design and technique to inspire him.

Illustrated (below) are some traditional Chinese tools for shaping soft clay.
1,2 Clay-beating hammers used for building up large clay vessels without the use of a potter's wheel.
3,4,5 Hammer-stamps; the face of each stamp bears a relief carving, and the stamps are used for decorating the surfaces of clay pots.

Before clay can be used for successful pottery, it must be thoroughly prepared. Wedging is the term used to describe the process of expelling the air from the clay and ensuring that the clay body is thoroughly mixed.
a The ball of clay is cut in half with a **wire.**
b The hemispheres of clay are placed on top of one another with the cut sides of both pieces facing up; this ensures that the center of the original ball of clay is exposed to the kneading action.
c The two bits of clay are thoroughly kneaded into one another so that any hard lumps will be broken down, and all air bubbles will be expelled.
d The clay is reformed into a ball.
e The process is repeated, as many as twenty times, until the clay is thoroughly mixed and smooth.

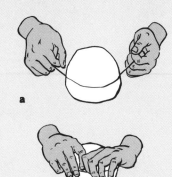

a

b

c

d

e

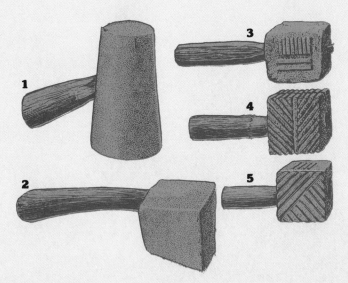

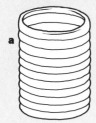

a Coiling is one of the simplest methods of producing clay pots. Cylindrical strips of clay are formed from the clay body, and then coiled on top of one another on a solid base; the final coiled texture can either be left as it is or smoothed off.

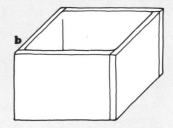

b Slab ware is made from slabs of clay that have been rolled out to an even thickness and cut into flat shapes. The slabs are formed into pots by sealing the joins with wet clay, or by pinching the slabs together at the corners where they join.

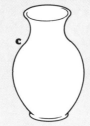

c Thrown pottery is a term describing ware that is formed on a flat, rotating **wheel.** The clay is placed on the center of the wheel, and as it revolves the clay is molded by hand pressure or with tools. The circular motion ensures that all sides of the pot are even.

d Molded ware is pottery that has been formed by pressing the clay against, or into, some kind of **mold.** Simple shapes can be formed by pressing the clay by hand against a shallow plate or basket; industrial molds shape the clay on both the inside and the outside.

Clays used by the potter are usually clay bodies—compounds of various clays and other constituents. Primary clays are decomposed volcanic rocks found on their original sites; they are therefore fairly pure. Secondary clays contain traces of other matter such as iron. Each clay has its own firing temperature and gives particular qualities to the finished article, so the potter mixes the clays in appropriate proportions in order to produce ware with specific qualities. To the basic clays he may add various constituents to alter or improve the thermal expansion, plasticity, fusion or color of the clay body so that he can determine the character of the finished product. Clay shrinks as it dries, but the shrinkage can be predicted and controlled by careful selection of the constituents.

1 Test sieve used to regulate the composition of clay slips.
2 Sieve.
3 Stiff brush for working the clay through the sieve.
4 Small brush.
5 Potter's knife.
6 Fettling knife.
7 Clay harp, used for cutting even slabs of clay.
8 Clay wire.
9 Twisted clay wire for thick or coarse clay.

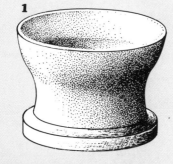

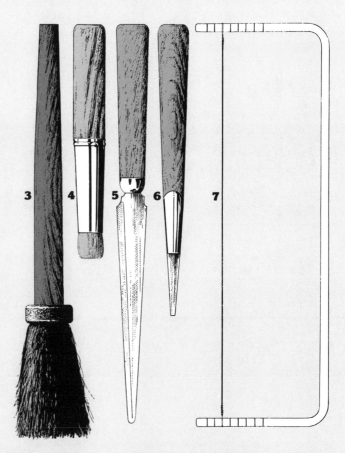

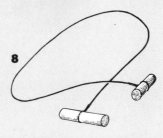

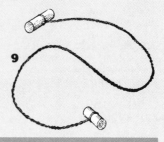

Working with soft clay 1

Soft clay is very pliable, and can readily be shaped and modeled by pressing, cutting, and carving. The clay can of course be modeled with the hands, but the many different tools that are available produce cleaner lines, smoother finishes, and more accurate marks on the clay than can generally be achieved with hand shaping.

The head shown (right) was formed from soft clay that was worked in a variety of ways to achieve the desired effects. The clay was kneaded, rolled, stretched, and also impressed with tools to form the features.

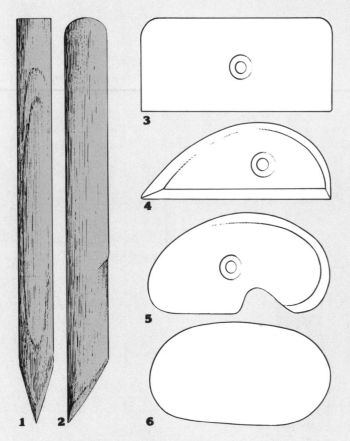

1,2 Bamboo tools, useful for cutting, trimming and decorating clay.
3,4 Boxwood ribs; these are used for forming thrown ware into accurate shapes and dimensions. The ribs are held against the clay shape as it rotates on the wheel.
5,6 Rubber kidneys.

7,8 Calipers used for checking the dimensions of clay articles. The arms of the calipers are on a pivot so that they can be extended and used for both internal and external measurements of hollow articles.
9 Template for shaping the sides of thrown pots to a given contour.

a A **shaping rib** is held against the inside of a thrown pot. As the wheel turns the pot, the rib molds the inside of the pot to a uniform curve.

b Calipers can be extended so that the points curve outward. In this way they can be used to take accurate measurements of the internal dimensions of the pot.

c A **template** is held against the outside of a thrown pot. As the wheel turns the pot, the template molds the outside surface of the article to a uniform shape.

d Turning tools are sharp-bladed tools that are used to shape a thrown pot as it is being turned on the wheel. As the tool is held against the pot, it incises the clay.

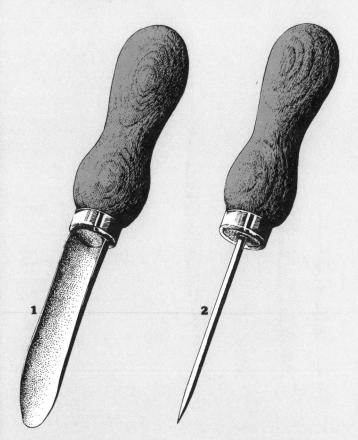

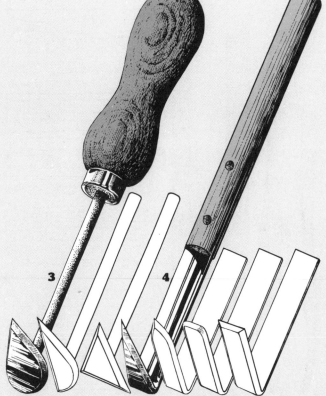

1 Piercer with a semicircular cutting blade. This tool can be used for pierced work, or for cutting accurate holes for spouts etc.

2 Needle tool; used mainly for trimming the rims of thrown ware, but can also be used as a stiletto for pierced work.

3 Stem tool with a variety of heads. The tool is held against pottery thrown on the wheel; each shape of head will make a distinctive line or curve in the clay.

4 Turning tool with a variety of heads. These tools are used mainly for shaping rims and bases on thrown ware.

©DIAGRAM

Working with soft clay 2

The plastic nature of soft unfired clay means that clay shapes need not be sculpted from a solid lump, but can be built up from many separate pieces of clay. When making a figure or a coiled pot, pieces of clay can be joined by smoothing and molding them together, or by smearing wet clay onto the join; either method produces a firm bond.

The terracotta figures illustrated (right) are from the sanctuary of Ayia Irini, Cyprus. The figures, which portray a wide variety of men, beasts and gods, were made in the 7th or 6th century BC.

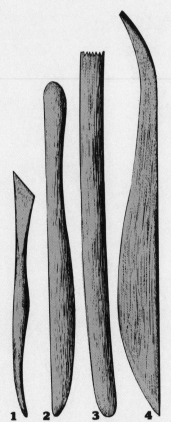
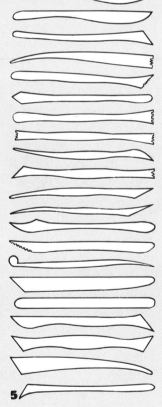
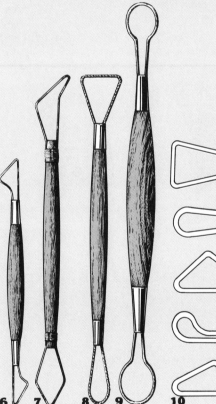
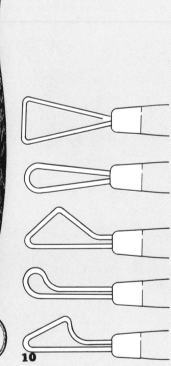

1,2,3,4,5 Boxwood tools in many shapes and sizes. These tools serve a variety of purposes; the larger tools can be used for forming large pieces of modeling, while the smaller tools are used for detailed work on sculpture and decorative ware. The tools with serrated or pointed edges can be used for producing textures and patterned finishes on a wide variety of clay work.

6,7,8,9,10 Wire ended tools used for carving clay and for hollowing out pieces of sculpture before firing. The tools can also be used on the surfaces of clay sculpture. The effect that each tool produces depends on the shape of its head.

The smooth-wire heads are suitable for soft clay, while the twisted-wire heads are useful for thicker or coarser-textured clay.

Coiled work is perhaps the simplest way of forming pots, although very attractive and decorative results can be achieved with variations of the basic method.
a Accurate cylinders of clay are cut from a block with a **coiler,** rolled by hand or extruded.

b A base is formed by coiling one of the lengths around itself on a flat surface. The clay is pressed together in each part of the spiral to ensure that the base is firm and solid.

c Other cylinders of clay are coiled on top of one another around the edge of the base. As the end of one length is reached, another length is molded onto it and the coiling continues.

d The pot is built into the desired shape, and the end of the final coil is smoothed into a rim. The ribbed sides of the pot can be smoothed out, or left in their attractive pattern.

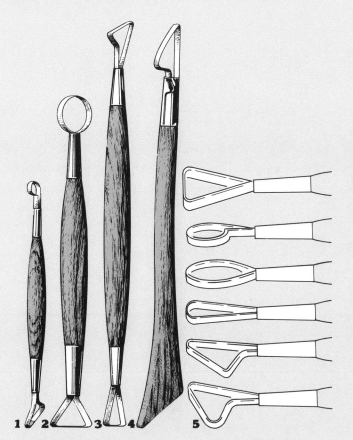 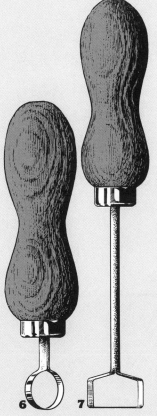 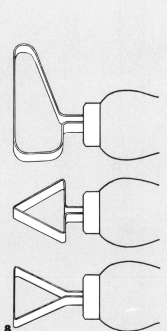

1,2,3,4,5 Ribbon tools in various shapes and sizes. The heads are formed from thin, flat strips of steel that make the tools both sharp and strong. They are used for all kinds of cutting, slicing and sculpting work.

6 Coiler, for making the accurate cylinders of clay needed for coiled work. As the coiler is drawn through a lump of clay, it cuts out a length of clay that is always of an even circumference.

7,8 Loop tools; these tools cut out different shapes of clay depending on the formation of the head of the tool. They can also be used for carving feet or decorative lines into thrown pots.

©DIAGRAM

Thrown pottery

Thrown pottery is the name used for pieces that have been shaped on a rotating wheel in order to give them an even, circular form. As the art of pottery has developed, the potter's wheel has become more sophisticated, but primitive tribes still form pieces on the same kinds of simple rotating surfaces that their ancestors used many centuries ago.

The illustration included (right) is from Jost Amman's "Ständebuch" or "Book of Trades," and depicts a potter throwing a pot. The potter is turning the wheel by moving its support with his feet.

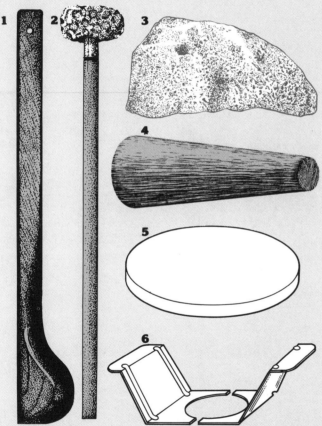

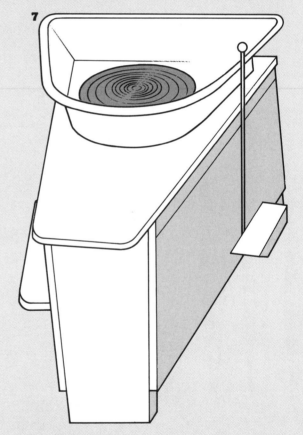

1 Throwing stick used for shaping narrow necks and curves on thrown pieces.
2 Sponge holder; the long handle enables the sponge to be used for mopping out the insides of tall or fragile pieces.
3 "Elephant ear" sponge for smoothing the surfaces of thrown pots.

4 Mandrel; this is used in the formation of hollow spouts for teapots etc.
5 Plaster batt, a porous surface on which the pot can be dried without adhering.
6 Pot lift for removing the pot from the wheel.

7 Electric wheel, controlled by either hand or foot pressure. The potter sits in front of the tray, and can control and vary the speed of the wheel by using the foot pedal or by moving the handle at the side of the wheel.

The advantage of the foot-operated control is that it leaves both the potter's hands entirely free for shaping the clay.

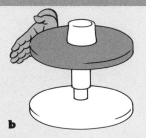

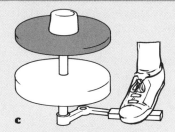

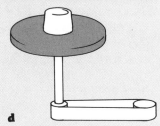

Rotating wheels have been used for many years as a method of producing accurate circular pots.

a The simplest method of rotating the pot involves placing it on a small flat surface that can be lifted and moved round as required.

b The addition of a **spindle** and **flywheel** makes the work of turning even easier. The potter can simply spin the wheel with his hand to rotate it, without having to lift the surface bodily.

c A **treadle** can be fixed to the spindle so that the potter can rotate the wheel with his foot, by a simple rocking motion. This leaves both his hands free to control and shape the clay.

d The incorporation of electric power in moving the spindle means that the potter has even finer control over his wheel. Subtle changes in foot pressure will produce the exact speed required for every stage of the work.

The basic principles of pot throwing apply to all kinds of pieces produced on the wheel, although of course the final size and shape of the pottery will depend on the potter's choice.

1 The clay is formed into a ball and held above the **wheel,** and then thrown onto the wheel as near the center as possible. The wheel is then turned while the clay is manipulated into the exact center and formed into a cone.

2 As the wheel is turned, the potter's thumbs are pressed into the middle of the clay; this begins to form a rudimentary hollow shape.

3 The potter uses his hands and various tools to press against the sides of the pot. He can increase the height of the pot, and shape the sides to the required contour.

4 The inside of the pot is smoothed in the same way as the outside—by the pressure and movement of the potter's hands and tools.

5 When the pot is the right shape and size, the potter cuts it free by drawing a wire between the pot and the wheel. The pot is then removed and allowed to dry before it is fired.

Articles such as teapots, cups, casseroles etc. can still be thrown on a wheel despite their irregular shapes. The basic body of the piece is thrown, and then handles, lips, lids and spouts are molded separately and attached to the body.

a Circular lids can be thrown on a wheel in the ordinary way; they can be made the right way up and then hollowed out, or they can be thrown upside down.

b Handles can be formed in several different ways. The traditional tapered shape is made by drawing out a large piece of clay into a curve, and cutting it at appropriate points. Other kinds of handles can be made from coiled or molded clay.

c,d Spouts can be formed on a **mandrel.** A clay slab is cut to the right size, and molded and sealed around the mandrel; the cone of clay is removed and cut to the required angle. Holes are cut in the clay body, and the spout is fixed to the perimeter.

e The separate pieces are molded onto the body, and sealed using wet clay.

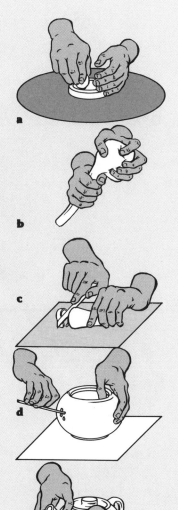

© DIAGRAM

Slab-formed pottery

Slab-molded pots are items that are formed from flat slabs of clay. The slabs are rolled out and cut into appropriate shapes, and then built into a structure by joining the pieces firmly at the edges. Curved forms can be made by bending the slabs, and the surfaces of slab work can be textured and decorated for added variety.

The picture (right) shows a clay structure made by the slab method of building up pottery. The rectangular shape of the house lends itself well to this technique, and even the tiles could be cut from clay slabs.

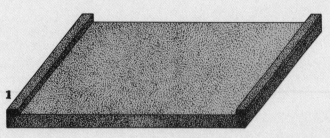

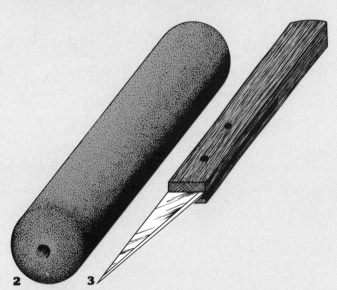

The principle of slab ware is very simple, and the slabs can be cut and formed into a wide variety of shapes.

a The clay is rolled out to an even thickness on a specially formed **board**. The runners at the sides of the board ensure that the pressure of the rolling pin is evenly distributed across the clay.

b The slabs are cut into the shapes required, using a sharp **knife** in order to obtain clean, accurate edges.

c When they are dry enough to be handled without damage, the slabs are joined at the corners or overlaps. Wet clay can be used to seal the joins, or the two pieces can be firmly pinched together. Cross-hatching with a **sharp tool** and the addition of water make the joints neat.

d The joining process is continued with all the slabs to produce the final shape.

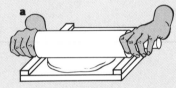

1 Modeling board with wood runners at the sides. As the clay is rolled, the runners govern the thickness of the slab.
2 Rolling pin used for rolling out the clay.
3 Knife for cutting the slabs into the required shapes.

Molded pottery

Complete clay shapes can be molded whole in several different ways. In slip-casting, the object may be shaped on all surfaces; with press molding, the mold shapes only one surface while the pressure applied shapes the other. Molds can be bought ready-made, or they can be made from existing objects or from a master shaped by the potter.

The photograph reproduced here shows the modeling room at a large Scottish pottery. The worker in the foreground is about to fill a plaster slip-casting mold with liquid clay in order to cast a pot.

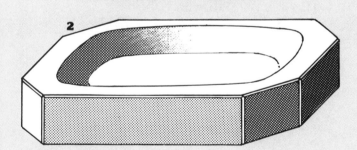

In press molding, slabs of clay are pressed against a pre-formed shape, usually of plaster or clay.
a If a **hollow mold** is used, the slab of clay is pressed firmly into the hollow of the mold. If a **hump mold** is used, the slab of clay is pressed firmly over the mold.
b When the clay has dried sufficiently it can be lifted away from the mold; it is then dried completely and decorated and fired as required.

Shown above are two types of press mold.
1 Hump mold; the clay is pressed over this mold to form a hollow vessel.
2 Hollow mold; the clay is pressed into this mold and the inside of the vessel is flattened by hand with a **sponge** or rubber **kidney.**

A plaster mold can be made in the following way.
a The shape is surrounded by a watertight barrier.
b The liquid plaster is poured around the shape.
c When the plaster has set, the completed mold is removed and dried.

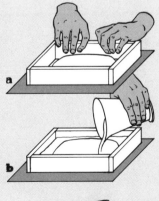

Slip casting involves pouring slip (liquid clay) into a porous hollow mold. The water in the slip drains away, leaving a firm clay shape inside the mold.
a Slip is poured into a two-piece **mold** through channels in the top; an escape hole for air allows the slip to reach all parts of the mold by preventing air locks.
b When the water has soaked away from the slip into the porous mold, both halves of the mold are removed. Any seam lines, or marks made by the slip channels, are smoothed off; the clay shape is lifted off the mold, dried, decorated, and fired.

©DIAGRAM

Raku pottery

Raku is a rapidly fired pottery that developed in Japan. The ware gains its characteristic appearance from the greatly sought-after accidental effects that result from the rapid firing and cooling. Raku bowls are often used in the Japanese tea ceremony, as these accidental effects provide excellent subjects for the contemplation that is central to the ceremony.

The raku bowl illustrated (right) was made in the early 17th century by the raku craftsman Donyu. The bowl is for use in the tea ceremony, and is called Tamamushi— translated as "a beetle with burnished wings."

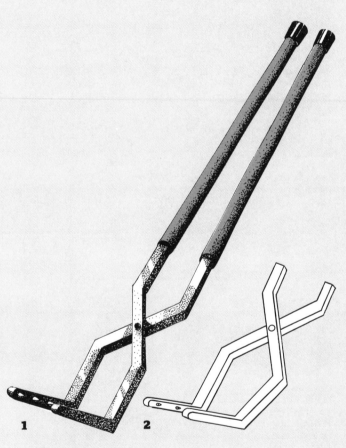

1,2 Raku tongs with jaws at different angles. The tongs are used for lifting the ware into and out of the kiln, and for holding the pots while they are placed in combustible materials and quenched in water.

The elementary steps toward producing raku pottery are described here, and pictured in the diagrams (right).

a The pottery is formed into the chosen shapes and given a preliminary firing; it is then covered with glaze.

b By means of the long-handled **raku tongs,** the pots are placed into a pre-heated kiln and become shiny; the pottery is then removed from the kiln.

c The hot pots are shut into an **airtight container** of combustible materials, in order to produce the characteristic raku finish.

d Using the tongs, the pots are then plunged into cold water so that they cool very quickly.

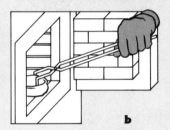

Additional equipment

General accessories useful to the potter include protective clothing, and equipment for storing and measuring the raw materials.
1 Storage bin.
2 Balance scales.
3,4 Storage canisters.
5 Asbestos gauntlet, used for protecting the hand against heat.
6 Rubber gloves for protecting the hands from contamination.
7 Protective **goggles** for use when dealing with chemicals or high temperatures.
8 Dust mask.

Additional tools for the potter include many items for handling and preparing the clays and glazes.
9 Ladle, for measuring out rough quantities of liquid.
10 Tub; this can be used for mixing slip or glaze.
11 Adjustable **modeling stand** with free-spinning turntable.
12 Tongs.
13 Funnel for transferring liquids from one container to another.
14 Bucket, used for storage or mixing glazes, plaster etc.
15 Electric mixer; the motor-driven blades are on a shaft that fits into the tub and hooks over the top.
16 Electric vibrator sieve used to refine large quantities of slip or glaze.
17 Blunger for the thorough mixing of slips or glazes. The blunger is filled with water, and then the dry materials are added to the water.
18 Pugmill, a machine used to recondition waste clay.

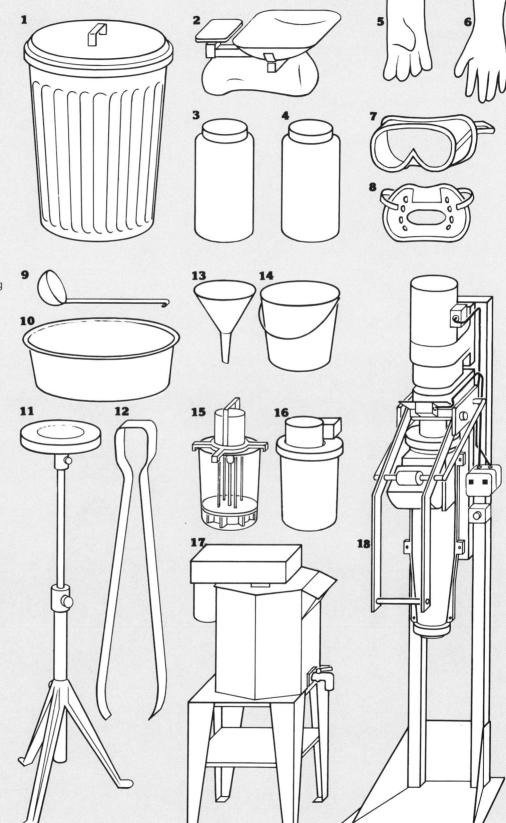

©DIAGRAM

Relief decoration

Much of the decorative quality of pottery can come from marks, patterns and textures made in the clay itself; that is, from some kind of relief decoration. Virtually anything can be used to mark clay, from fingernails to fabric, and every object or tool used will leave its own distinctive mark.

Shown (right) is a detail from an 18th century oviform earthenware jug. The jug was made by the firm of Wedgwood at the Etruria pottery works, and is ornamented with cameo leaves in a decoration known as amorini black.

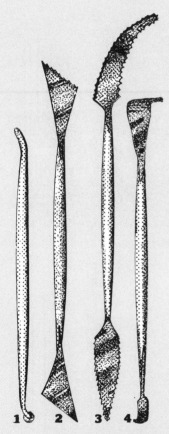

1,2,3,4,5 Steel **forming tools** with a variety of heads. Some of the heads have coarse or fine teeth, others have smooth edges, and some of the tools have heads that are at an angle to the body. The curved shapes of many of the tools make them particularly useful for reaching into crevices and curves of clay models and sculptures.

6 Steel **scraper** or **palette** with a serrated edge. Steel scrapers come in various shapes and sizes, and can be used to texture large areas of clay.

7,8 Roulette with various **heads.** Each head carries a different pattern; as the wheel is rolled across the work, the design is impressed into the clay.

9,10 Plaster stamps made in several different patterns. Plaster powder is mixed with water and then poured into a mold; when the plaster has set it is removed from the mold and carved into the required shape to make a relief stamp. The stamp is then used to mark the clay, and if a repeat pattern is wanted the same stamp can be used several times.

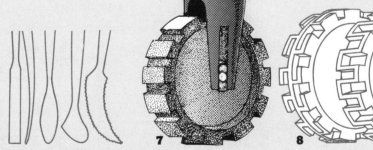

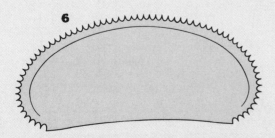

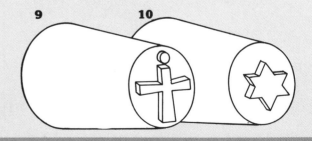

Relief decoration may also be achieved by applying separate pieces of clay to the pot or other article. Several tools can be useful for shaping clay to be used in applied decoration.

1 Extruding tool with several heads; the clay is forced through the head and emerges in a regular shape.

2 Cutter; these shaped blades are used in the same way as cookie cutters.

3 Tea strainer for producing clay strands.

4 Paddle used to beat clay additions into the surface of the article being decorated; this produces an interesting ripple effect.

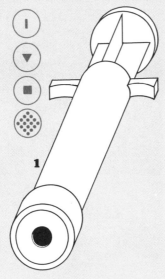

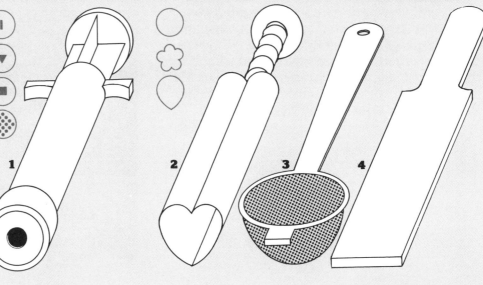

Some of the tools that can be used to produce relief decoration on pottery are shown at the right. The lines of pattern on the pot below illustrate the characteristic marks made by each of the tools.

5 Piercer.
6 Clay plane.
7 Bamboo tool.
8 Blunt **tool handle.**
9 Ruler, used for making straight marks on the clay.
10 Needle tool, used to produce stippled designs and to make fine lines.
11 Quill for producing a scratchy line.
12 Loop tool.
13 Sgraffito loop.
14 Sgraffito tool
15 Texture brush with stainless steel bristles.

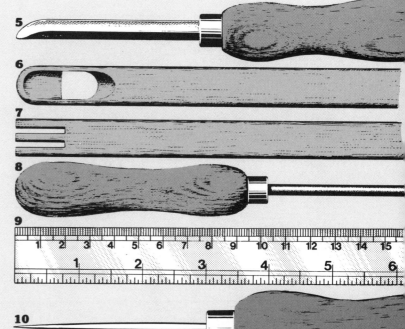

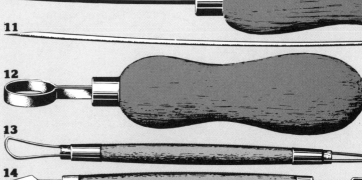

© DIAGRAM

Surface decoration

The surface of pottery can be decorated by means of colored or textured glazes. Powdered glaze is mixed with water and applied to the clay; when it is fired the glaze melts, producing a waterproof layer of glass on the surface of the pottery. Glazes can be applied to entire pots, or put onto the surface of the clay in patterns.

The photograph (right) was taken in a Danish porcelain factory and shows an artist hand-painting the porcelain with colored glaze. When the decoration is complete, the piece will be re-fired to make the decoration permanent.

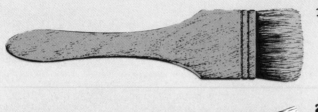

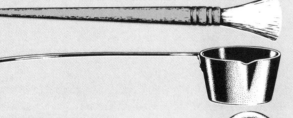

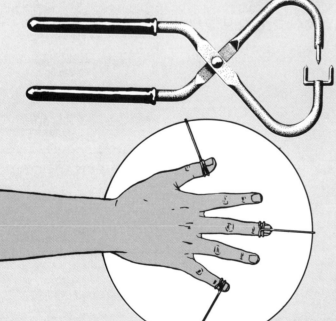

1 Flat glazer; this brush is soft and broad so that it leaves no brush marks in the glaze.
2 Glaze mop, a brush that holds a good deal of glaze so that it can be floated onto the pottery.
3 Ladle used for pouring glaze over articles.
4 Tongs for gripping ware while it is being dipped.
5 Plate dipper, a contraption that fits onto the fingertips and holds a plate lightly so that it can be glazed without finger-marks.
6 Spray gun used to apply an even coat of glaze.

Glaze can be applied to pottery in many ways. One of the most straightforward methods is that of dipping the vessel into a container full of glaze, and a similar technique involves pouring the glaze over the clay piece. Both these techniques can be used for glazing portions of pots, by regulating the parts that come in contact with the glaze. Glaze may also be sprayed onto the ware, for instance through a **blowpipe** or by means of a **spray gun,** and it can be brushed onto the ware with various types of **soft brush.** A **sliptrailer** can be used to apply thin lines of glaze, and of course once the glaze has been applied to the ware it can be patterned by swirling it, brushing on further colors, scratching through one layer of glaze to reach another, and many similar techniques.

Glazes are usually prepared from dry ingredients that are then mixed with water to form a suspension. Glaze is made up mainly of alumina, silica and flux; silica is the glass-forming ingredient, but on its own it will not melt below 1750°C; the other substances are added to melt the silica at lower temperatures. Thermal expansion and body fit have to be considered when glazing; if the thermal expansion of the clay is vastly different from that of the glaze, the body fit will be impaired and the glaze will become damaged on cooling.

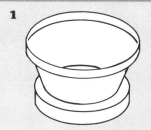

The wet glaze ingredients are ground, mixed and sieved.
1 **Test sieve.**
2 **Lawn brush** for use with the test sieve.
3 **Spatula.**
4 **Pestle and mortar.**
5 **Muller and glass slab.**

Various **brushes** and other pieces of equipment may be used to apply color to the pottery. Some of these brushes are shown on the right, and the pot below illustrates the characteristic mark made by each tool.

6   **Round sable brush.**
7   **Script brush.**
8   **Short one-stroke brush.**
9   **Flat duster.**
10,11 **Japanese brushes.**
12 **Sword liner.**
13 **Cut liner.**
14 **Fan brush.**
15 **Sliptraiier,** a rubber bottle with a narrow spout, used for trailing lines of slip or glaze in patterns.
16 **Feather,** used to draw one glaze into another in a decorative pattern.

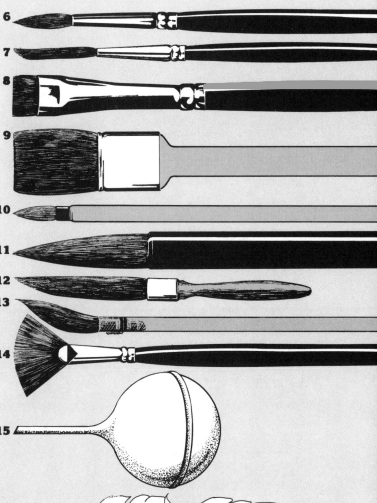

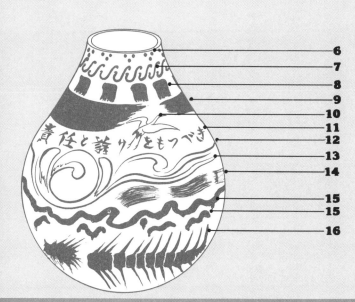

Firing clay

The first kilns were simply holes in the ground packed with unfired pots; bonfires were built over the top, and the heat hardened the pots. The modern kiln has been refined to such an extent that the heat can be regulated exactly, allowing the potter precise control over the character of the finished ware.

The illustration on the right shows workers loading a biscuit kiln. Biscuit firing is the first firing of unglazed pottery; this is the firing that drives off the water that is chemically combined with the clay.

Clay pots that are left to dry without artificial heat are weak and permeable. Although the clay appears to be quite dry, it still contains a considerable amount of water, and will become soft and plastic if moistened. In order to drive off the water that is chemically combined with the clay, it must be heated strongly. When this is done the clay's structure is irreversibly changed; it becomes hard, and will no longer mix with water. If a glaze is added, the pottery can be made totally waterproof.

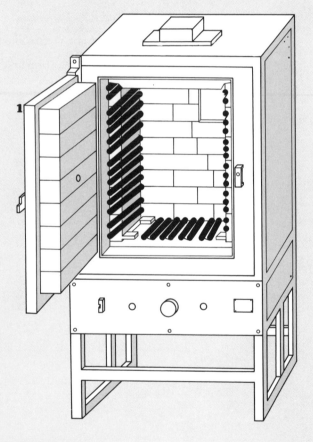

Pyrometric cones and **bars** **(a)** are a cheap method of monitoring the temperature of the kiln. The cones or bars are manufactured so that they will bend at a specific temperature, and are used in a group of three different grades.

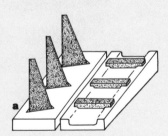

The first sags at a temperature below the optimum, and warns that the required heat is near; the second will be chosen to sag at the optimum heat, and the third will sag at a heat above the optimum. The kiln is turned off when the second cone's tip has bent down to the same level as its base **(b).**

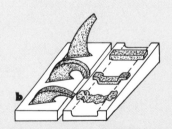

1 Electric kiln of a typical design. Because the heat comes from elements, and therefore no solid fuel is burned, the kiln does not need a chimney, although it has a vent hole for the escape of the fumes and water given off during firing, and to speed up the cooling. Specialized devices can be fitted to the kiln, such as an automatic pyrometer that will switch the kiln off when it has reached the required temperature.

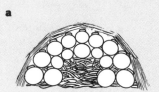

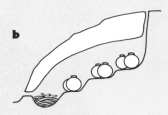

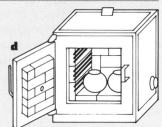

As man's understanding of the process of firing has increased, so kiln design has been modified to give him more control over the firing.
a African **bonfire kiln,** the simplest method of firing. The fire literally roasts the pots.

b Mexican **cross-kiln,** built into a bank. The fire is built at the foot of the bank and the unfired pottery is stacked into a central chamber. The heat is drawn up the channel to the ventilation hole, and fires the pottery as it passes through.

c Japanese **climbing kiln** consisting of several chambers. The heat from the fire passes through the first chamber and into the second, where it ignites extra wood to boost its heat level. This happens in each chamber until the last, which contains ware for biscuit firing.

d **Modern kiln;** this one is built of insulating brick. Modern kilns are usually fired by gas or electricity, but some people still prefer to use the traditional kilns that burn wood.

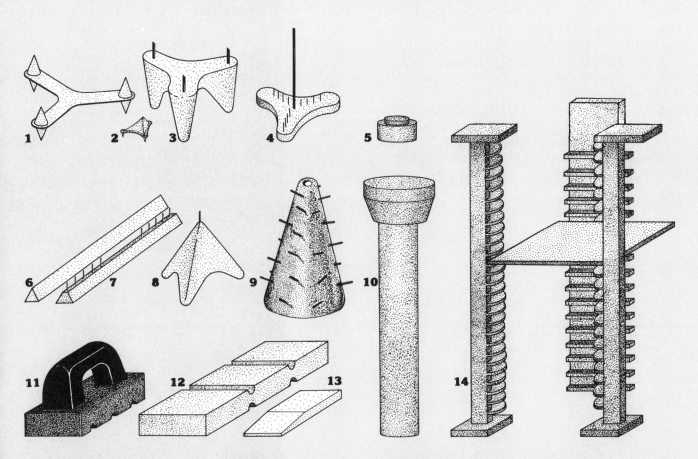

Kiln furniture is the term used to describe the accessories used in the kiln when stacking and firing the pottery.
1 **Stilt,** used for keeping pieces of ware separate from one another.
2 **Spur,** used in the same way as a stilt.

3 **High stilt** with nichrome wire points.
4 **Multiple stilt.**
5 **Shelf prop** with rim; the rim enables several props to be built up firmly to the required height.
6 **Saddle,** an elongated stilt.

7 **Bar stilt** with steel points.
8 **Pyramid stilt.**
9 **Bead tree;** the wires hold the beads and keep them separate.
10 **Shelf support.**
11 **Rubbing brick** with handle, used for cleaning kiln furniture.

12 **Rubbing blocks;** these are made of alumina, and are used to rub scars off fired pottery.
13 **Sorting chisel** for cleaning the plaster batts used as shelves.
14 **Tile crank,** a structure for holding tiles during firing.

7 Modeled and cast sculpture

The tools described in this chapter are those for modeling and casting sculpture. The principle of both modeling and casting is that the artist starts off with a soft material which is shaped and then allowed to harden in its new form. In the case of modeling, the material is malleable and plastic, and because it takes the impression of any tool brought into contact with its surface, the artist can work and shape the material into the form and texture that he wishes. The sculpture is then hardened by firing, or by allowing it to dry naturally in the air. Casting begins with a liquid, which is given shape by pouring it into a mold; it takes its shape and texture from the shape and texture of the inside of the mold. The hardening of most cast materials is a chemical process that takes place over several hours or several days. The tools for cast sculpture are mainly for mixing or melting the liquids, for making the molds, or for refining and polishing the surface of the finished cast. The evolution of casting spans many centuries— the Greeks, the Romans and the Ancient Egyptians all knew the skills for casting metal— and yet with the development of colored and transparent resins and other synthetic liquids, casting has become one of the most popular techniques for contemporary sculpture.

The medal shown in this photograph depicts Duval Janvier, a master medalist, at work striking a medal. This medal itself is the work of Alexandre Charpentier (1856-1909), a French craftsman who made many of these mementoes.

Building an armature

Sculpture on a large scale frequently involves building an armature, a kind of skeleton for the finished sculpture. An armature can be built from any firm material, such as wood, metal, wire or bricks; the main requirement is that it should support the weight of the sculpting medium that will be applied to it.

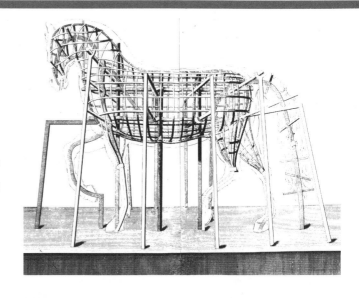

The armature illustrated (right) is a diagram from Diderot's industrial encyclopedia printed in the 18th century. This giant armature is showing the amount of support that is necessary for large sculptures.

An armature is necessary inside a sizeable sculpture because it prevents the large amount of sculpting medium from collapsing under its own weight. The most efficient armatures have the same basic shape as the projected form; for instance, an armature for a full figure would have extensions for the limbs and head as well as the structure for supporting the torso. The armature is built up by cutting, bending and joining the materials until a firm structure of the correct shape and size is reached.

1 **Hacksaw** for cutting wood and metal.
2 **Spirit level** used to check the accuracy of horizontal surfaces.
3 **Hammer** used for driving in clouts and nails.
4 **Screwdriver,** for use when the pieces are screwed together.
5 **Wirecutters** for trimming chicken wire etc.
6 **Vise;** when piping or strong wire needs to be bent it can be gripped at one end in the vise to provide good leverage.
7 **Gloves** should be worn to protect the hands from splinters and sharp wire.

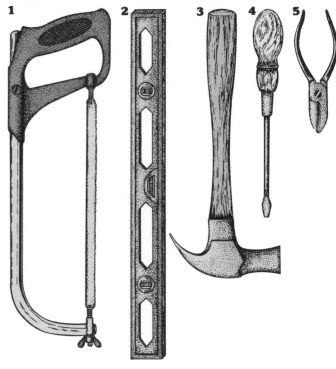

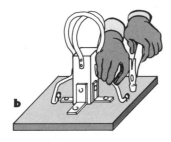

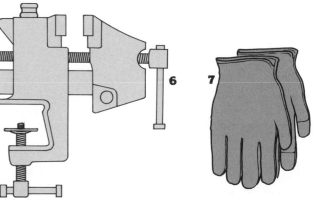

A simple armature for a head and shoulders sculpture can be built up in sections in this way.
a A strong piece of wood or metal is chosen for the main element of the armature and is attached firmly to a base.

b Wire, strips of metal, pieces of wood or any other appropriate materials are joined to the main column and molded or positioned to provide support for the skull part of the projected sculpture. Lateral pieces are joined on further down to support the shoulders.

Clay, terracotta, plaster

Soft clay and terracotta are very popular as media for sculpture, since they remain plastic and workable for a considerable time if they are handled carefully. All the tools mentioned in the section on working in soft clay can be used for soft clay sculpture, and the clay can be fired in the usual way.

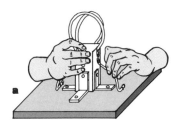

A clay (or terracotta) sculpture on an armature is modeled in the following stages.
a An armature suitable for the size, shape and material of the sculpture is made. Particular care must be taken that no dimension is too big.

b The clay is rolled into rough sausage-shapes, and these shapes are pressed onto the armature to build up the model in the correct proportions. As the work progresses the blobs of clay should be smaller, and more and more accurate in their shaping and placing.

c The planes and surfaces of the clay are worked and smoothed, with the hands or with tools, until the artist is satisfied with their appearance. The sculpture is finished by adding any detail or specific texture that is required.

Sculpting with plaster is a very specialized process because of the quick-drying nature of the medium. Also, plaster does not really pass through a plastic stage when it can be modeled in the same way as clay; instead it begins as a liquid that slowly thickens and hardens until it is solid. Thick plaster can be applied to an armature with a **spatula**, or strips of lint or coarse burlap may be dipped into liquid plaster and used to build up the form by binding them around the armature.

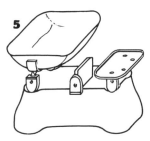

Dry, powdered plaster (dehydrated gypsum) is mixed carefully with water; this brings about a chemical reaction as the two elements combine and then harden.
a Powdered plaster is sprinkled into a container of water until small piles of plaster just break the surface of the water.
b The two constituents are left to stand.
c The sculptor puts one hand under the water and mixes the plaster thoroughly but gently, so that no air bubbles are trapped in the liquid.

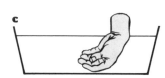

1 Spoon for measuring out dry plaster.
2 Ladle for handling the liquid plaster.
3 Scoop used for shoveling dry plaster.
4 Spatula, used for applying liquid plaster to the armature.
5 Scales; the dry plaster is weighed out on these.
6 Plastic storage bin for plaster powder.
7,8 Plastic mixing bowls.
9 Plastic bucket.
10 Armature support; this can be used to hold the armature in the correct position while it is being worked on.
11 Modeling stand.

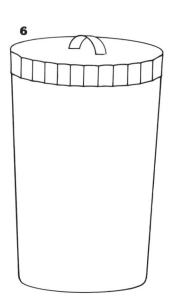

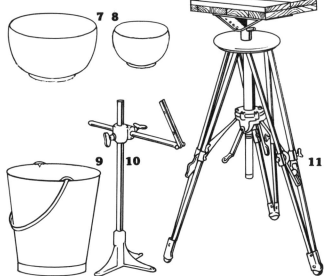

Shaping plaster 1

Once plaster has set, it can be cut, carved, filed, scraped and sanded in the same way as a soft stone, so very sharp steel tools can be used to great effect to refine the surface. Plaster can also be modeled directly by soaking strips of coarse cloth in plaster and then wrapping them round an armature.

1 Shears used for cutting cloth strips.
2 Hacksaw for cutting armature materials.
3,4 Gouges used for shaping the set plaster.

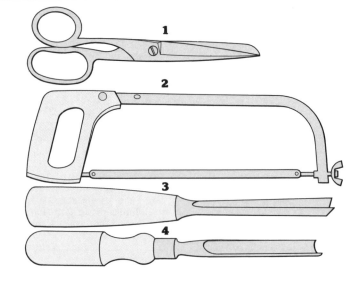

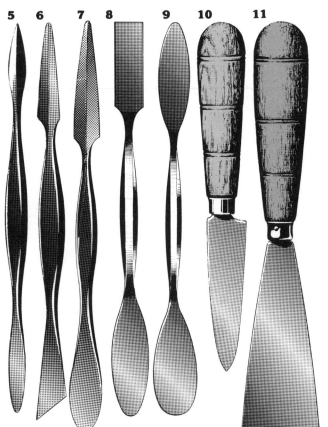

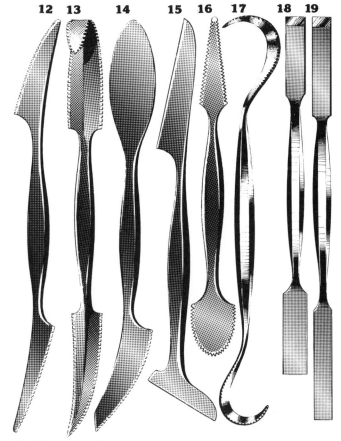

The following tools are used for shaping wet plaster.
5,6,7 Plaster-forming tools, made of steel to ensure that they leave a clean impression on the plaster.
8,9 Spatula-ended steel tools.
10 Plaster knife.
11 Broad-bladed scraper.

The following tools are used for shaping dry plaster.
12,13,14,15,16,17 Steel rifflers, tools with serrated edges.
18,19 Chisel-ended tools.

Plaster does not remain in a workable plastic state for more than a short time during the setting process, so it is necessary to build up the medium layer by layer.
a An armature is built of metal, wood, polystyrene or other suitable materials.

b Strips of burlap or scrim are dipped into liquid plaster and wrapped around the armature. These strips form the core of the sculpture and provide a textured surface that aids the adhesion of the subsequent plaster layers.

c Dollops of semi-solid plaster are applied to the core with a **spatula,** and smoothed into place to produce the approximate shape of the intended sculpture.

d When the plaster has set, the surface is filed, sculpted and shaped to the required form and finish.

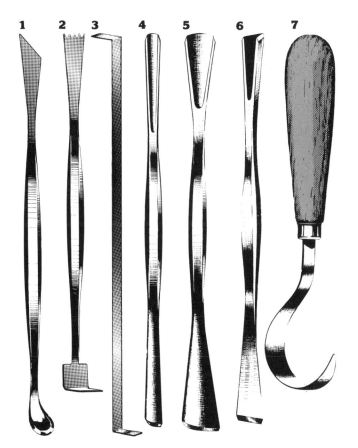

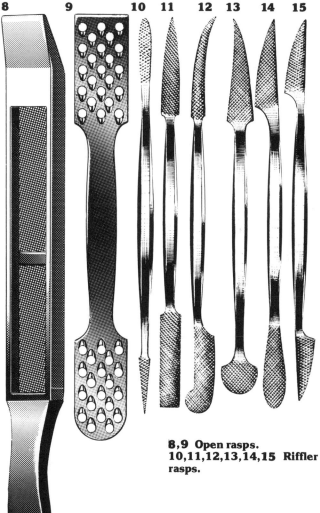

1,2,3 Assorted tools for shaping plaster.
4,5,6 Gouge-ended tools.
7 Steel hook.

8,9 Open rasps.
10,11,12,13,14,15 Riffler rasps.

Shaping plaster 2

Plaster is a popular material for taking casts, since it is easy to prepare, dries quickly, and accurately reproduces fine detail from the molds in which it is cast. Because plaster is cast cold, many kinds of plastics and synthetics may be used as mold materials without the danger of melting that exists when hot liquids are used.

The shaped plaster shown (right) is a detail of a ceiling frieze from Brockhall, England. Decorative plaster work of this kind was molded into numerous shapes, the most popular subjects being flower and plant motifs and geometrical designs.

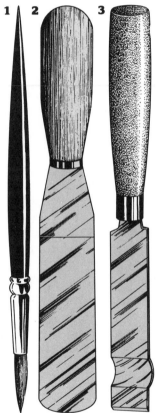

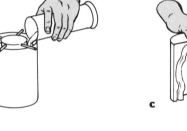

Synthetic molds for casting plaster can be made around almost any small, solid object.
a The original is placed in a suitable container, such as a can or a cup.

b The synthetic mold material is poured carefully around the original until the container is full.

c When the mold material has set, the container is removed and the mold is cut around with a **key knife** to release the original. This leaves a two-part mold that can be accurately reassembled and used for several plaster castings.

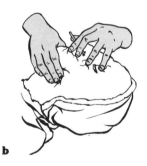

1 Soft brush for applying gelatin layers.
2 Spatula used to apply plaster over a gelatin mold.
3 Key knife; when used to cut a mold in two, the tool cuts an interlocking key that is used to reassemble it precisely.

A **mold** for making a casting of a face can be taken from life in the following way.
a The subject's face is painted with a gelatinous mold material; care should be taken that the subject can breathe properly, by inserting straws or pipes into the nostrils.

b When the gelatin layer has set, it is covered with a plaster layer to strengthen the mold.

c When fully dry, the mold is removed from the subject's face, and can be used for casting in the usual way.

Casting plaster from clay

Casting from a clay original is one method of producing a detailed and accurate plaster cast. The clay model is coated with a plaster **mold,** then the clay is removed and the mold is filled with plaster. The disadvantage of the process is that the mold can only be used once, since it is destroyed when releasing the final model. If reasonable care is taken when building the mold, however, this is a very reliable method of producing a well-finished plaster model.

1,2,3 T-square, spirit level and **pencil** may be used to measure and mark the shim line in the mold.

4 Shears for cutting shim.

5 Calipers, used to take measurements before and after the mold is applied, to ensure that it is even.

6 Rubber mallet; tapping the mold releases the cast.

7 Cross pein hammer, used like the mallet.

8,9 Rubber scrapers for removing excess plaster.

10 Rubber tubing; the mold is tightly bound with this.

11 Pliers for tightening wire binding on the mold.

12 Sponge for applying water and liquid soap.

13 Dusting brush.

14,15 Chisel and **mallet** for chipping away the mold.

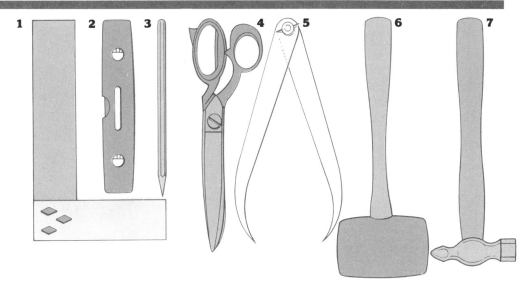

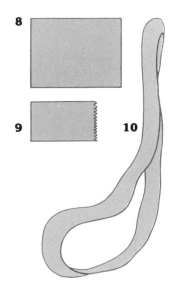

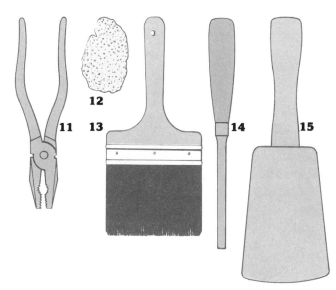

  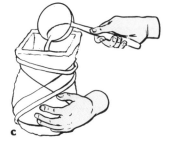 

Casting from a clay original involves first of all making a plaster **mold** around the clay.
a A wall of brass shim is built into the clay model; this will serve to divide the mold into two parts. Plaster is applied to cover the model.

b When the plaster has set, the two-part mold is broken open and the model discarded. The mold is dampened, and rinsed with liquid soap; the soap acts as a parting agent. The two halves of the mold are then sealed together.

c The mold is bound very tightly with wire and rubber tubing, to ensure that the two halves will not move. Liquid plaster is poured into the cavity; the parting agent prevents it from sticking to the plaster of the mold.

d When the cast plaster has set, the mold is tapped with a **hammer** or **mallet** to help release the casting. The plaster of the mold is then carefully chipped away, bit by bit, to reveal the cast model.

Papier-mâché

Papier-mâché literally means "chewed paper;" it is a fine paper pulp that can be cast and modeled into surprisingly strong structures. Newsprint or other unglazed papers are the best materials for papier-mâché, since they are very absorbent and can easily be pulped. The surface of dry papier-mâché objects can be painted and varnished.

The papier-mâché tray shown (right) was made in the 19th century by the firm of Jennings and Bettridge. The tray demonstrates the exotic shapes in which papier-mâché can be molded, which could not then be produced in any other suitable material.

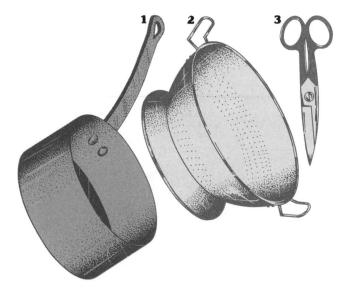

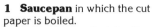

1 Saucepan in which the cut paper is boiled.
2 Colander for straining the pulp.
3 Scissors used to shred the paper so that it will pulp more easily.
4 Wooden stick or **spurtle** for stirring the pulp while it is boiling.
5,6 Paste brush and **paste bowl;** the pulp is mixed with paste to make it bond more strongly.
7,8 Paint brushes for decorating the finished papier-mâché.

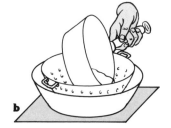

Papier-mâché is made from paper that has been boiled in order to break down the fibers.
a The paper is shredded, either with scissors or by tearing, and boiled in a saucepan of water until soft.

b The resultant pulp is strained through a colander, in order to remove any lumps and to ensure that the papier-mâché is of an even consistency.

c The strained pulp is mixed with a water-based paste. This acts as a binding agent to hold the paper fibers together.

d The pulp can now be cast in molds, or applied in layers to a base to build up a three-dimensional form. If the mixture is left to dry slightly, it can be modeled by hand or with tools.

Candlemaking

The craft of candlemaking began with the manufacture of ordinary domestic candles, and has developed into a decorative sculpture process in its own right. Liquid candle wax can be colored, perfumed, and whipped to make it frothy; when set it can be carved and sculpted like clay, or painted with colored or metallic waxes.

The engraving of a tallow-chandler or candlemaker right comes from "The Book of English Trades," published in 1839. The workman is dipping a rack of wicks repeatedly into a vat of wax to coat them thoroughly and build up finished candles.

1 **Scales** for weighing wax.
2 **Measuring spoons,** used when dye is added.
3 **Thermometer** for testing the wax temperature.
4 **Funnel** helps to avoid spills when filling molds.
5 **Pitcher** used to pour melted wax.
6 **Sieve** for straining dirty wax.
7 **Knitting needle** can be used to suspend the wick over a candle mold.
8 **Knife** for carving candles.
9 **Deep vat** for use when making dipped candles.
10 **Long shallow vat;** wicks are drawn through wax in the vat in order to make thin tapers.

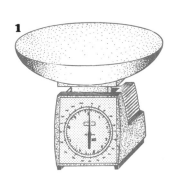

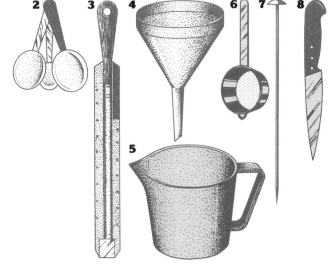

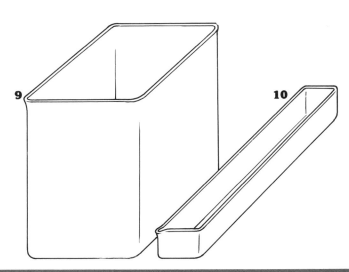

Candles can be molded in many different containers; cups, vases and tin cans may be used, or molds can be purchased in many shapes.
a The watertight **mold** is lined with a coating of silicone to prevent the candle wax from sticking. The wick is suspended from a **knitting** **needle** or **stick** across the top of the mold.
b The wax is melted to the correct temperature, perfume or color is added, and the wax is poured into the mold around the wick. When the wax has set, the newly formed candle is turned out and decorated.

©DIAGRAM

Modeling wax for casting metal

The lost wax process is a method used for making accurate and predictable metal casts. A positive form is modeled in wax, and a negative mold is made around the wax shape. The wax is then melted so that it runs out of the mold, and the cavity left is filled with molten metal; when cool, the metal is an exact replica of the wax model.

Auguste Rodin's sculpture "Despair" (right) was cast in bronze from a thin wax layer molded to reproduce the details of the original model. A bronze sculpture of this size has to be cast in a hollow shell, otherwise it would be both too heavy and too expensive.

Wax for modeling comes in different forms to suit the needs and preferences of the sculptor. Slabs or bricks of wax may be sculpted while firm, warmed and then modeled, or melted totally and cast into molds. Sheet wax may be cut and "soldered," or pressed into a mold to form a thin coating.

Tools for modeling wax are usually made of steel so that they can be warmed, and also so that they will make a firm impression on the wax.
1 Modeling tools, illustrating some of the shaped heads that are available on these implements.
2 Steel **dentist's probes;** these make excellent tools for modeling wax.

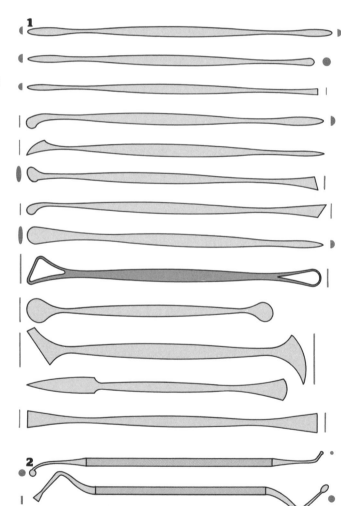

In order to melt wax for casting, the sculptor may use an electric **melting pot** (left). When the wax simply needs to be pliable, an **alcohol lamp** such as the one below is used to warm the **modeling tools;** in this way the heat is transferred to the wax.

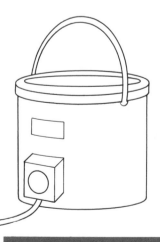

Foundry tools

To ensure that the metal for the cast will fill all the fine details of the mold, it has to be heated so that it will become molten. The melting and casting of the metal is done in a foundry. Because considerable heat is required to melt the metal, the foundry uses specialized equipment to cope with the handling and safety problems that arise. The metal is heated in a **crucible,** impurities are removed as they rise to the surface of the molten metal, and then the liquid is slowly and carefully poured into the mold and allowed to cool.

1 Two-man shank, used to carry a large crucible. The handle allows the crucible to be tipped in order to pour out the hot metal.
2 Pickout tongs for removing the top of the crucible and adding fresh ingots.
3 One-man shank for carrying a small crucible.
4 Lifting tongs used to lift the crucible from the fire.
5 Skimmer, a tool for removing impurities from the surface of the molten metal.
6 Crucible.
7 Ingot mold; spare metal can be poured into ingot molds and recycled.

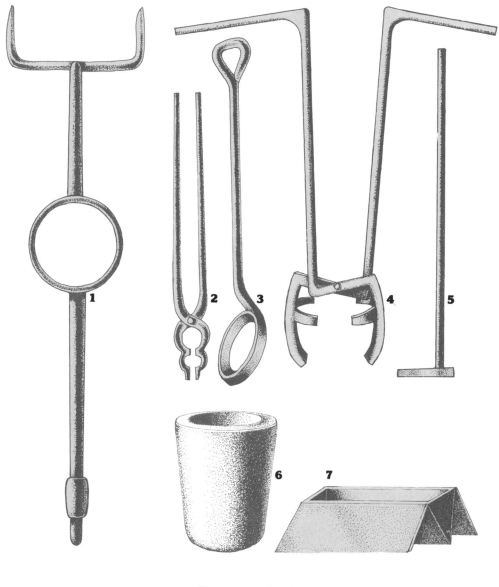

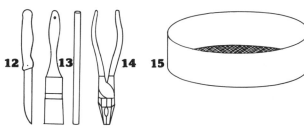

Protective clothing is necessary for foundry work, in case the molten metal spills or splashes over the workmen.
  8 Goggles.
  9 Asbestos mitts.
10 Leather apron.
11 Protective boots.

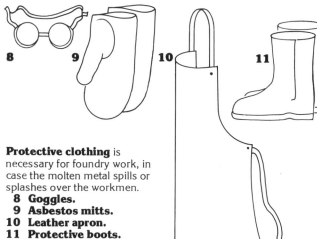

Sand casting involves pressing a model into a sand-packed **mold** and filling the impression with molten metal.
12 Knife.
13 Retouching tools.
14 Pliers.
15 Sieve.
16 Two-part mold.

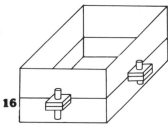

© DIAGRAM

Metal casting

 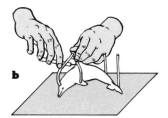 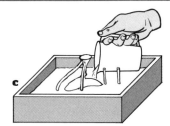 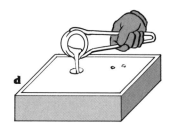

Casting from a solid wax model is perhaps the most straightforward way of using wax in metal casting.
a The wax is shaped (cast, sculpted, modeled etc.) into the form that the finished casting will take.

b Wax runners are attached to the model, and a wax funnel is applied to the top. The funnel is for the entry of the molten metal; the runners are for the release of the hot wax, and also they allow air to escape during casting.

c The model is placed in a container and surrounded with the mold medium. When the mold has set, the wax is melted so that it runs out and leaves a hollow in the mold.

d Molten metal is poured into the funnel and fills up all the cavities left by the wax. When the metal has set, the mold is broken open and the metal shape removed; unwanted metal is filed off, and the casting is chased and polished.

 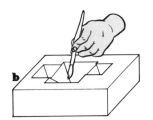  

A thin shell of metal can be cast over a core of another substance by using a thin layer of wax inside the mold.
a A model of the intended casting is made in clay, plaster etc, and a negative mold is made of this model.

b The inside of the mold is coated with a thin layer of wax. When the wax is cool, the central cavity is filled with a core of solid material, and the outside mold is removed.

c Runners are attached to the wax as described for solid wax casting. Long **nails** are driven through the wax and the core, and the mold medium is built up around this structure.

d The wax is melted out of the structure, leaving the core supported in the mold by means of the nails. The thin space left by the wax can now be filled with the molten metal; when the mold is broken off, the gaps in the casting formed by the nails are plugged with metal.

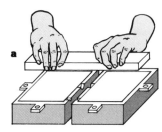 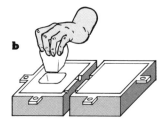  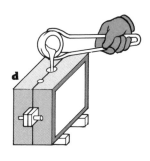

The basic principle of sand casting is shown above, very much simplified. Sand casting can be a very dangerous process, and should always be done under supervision and with the proper safety precautions.
a Both halves of a two-piece **mold** are packed with sand.

b A master model of the finished casting is pressed into the sand in one half of the mold. The model is removed, leaving a clear impression in the sand, and is pressed into the other half of the mold.

c Runners are cut into the sand surrounding the impressions, and the two halves of the mold are joined very precisely.

d The cavities in the sand are filled with molten metal. When the metal has cooled, the mold is removed and the casting is cleaned.

Metal finishing

When the casting emerges from the mold, it is covered with traces of the mold medium and is dull and lifeless in color; also, metal casts of the runners are still attached to it. The runners are removed, and the casting is cleaned with **wire wool** or a **wire brush.** Holes in the casting are enlarged with a drill and then plugged with metal, and the surface is· retouched by filing or graving; the entire casting is then chased to refine the surface. Finally it is immersed in an acid bath to complete the cleaning process.

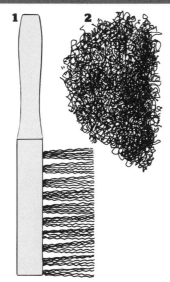

1 **Stiff wire brush.**
2 **Wire wool.**
3 **Graver.**
4 **Burin.**
5 **Gouge.**
6,7 **Files.**
8 **Hacksaw.**
9 **Drill.**

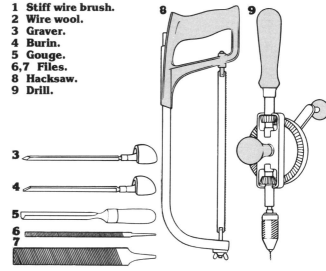

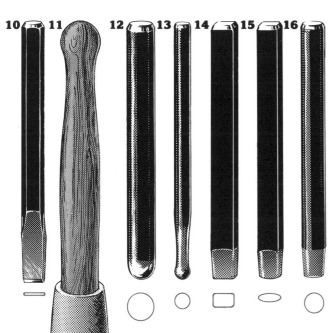

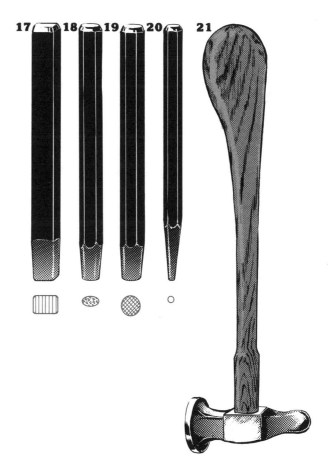

10 Cold chisel, used for removing the metal runners from the casting.
11 Mallet for driving the chisel.
12,13,14,15,16 Chasing tools with various shapes of head. These tools can be made by the sculptor to suit his own needs.

17,18,19 Matting tools; these give a light texture to the surface of the metal.
20 Punch with a small head, used to chase details that are inaccessible to the larger tools.
21 Chasing hammer used directly on the surface of the casting.

Polystyrene

Polystyrene is a versatile medium that can be molded, cut, carved, rasped, fused and colored. Expanded polystyrene blocks or sheets are excellent for ephemeral sculpture. Exact forms can be molded by expanding polystyrene granules in a shaped container; the granules expand when they are heated.

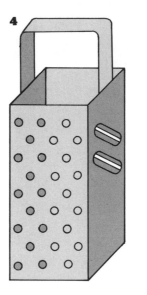

The photograph (right) shows a polystyrene mold being prepared for a concrete sculpture. The mold has been shaped from polystyrene blocks and assembled in a wooden frame; the concrete will be poured into the mold, and the polystyrene destroyed when the concrete has set.

Because polystyrene is so light, it is very useful as a core for large-scale sculpture in heavier materials such as plaster, concrete and resin. The form is roughed out in polystyrene blocks, and then the final material is applied to the surface.

Polystyrene can also be used as an original for metal casting. The form is sculpted in polystyrene foam, and then coated to provide a firm surface; it is then surrounded with mold material, and burned out when the mold is dry.

A **face mask** such as the one on the left should be worn when working with polystyrene, to avoid inhaling the toxic fumes given off when the material melts.

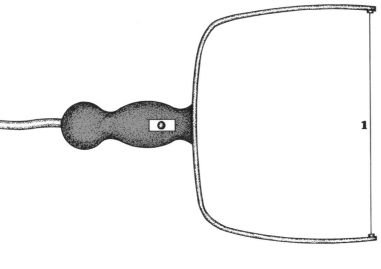

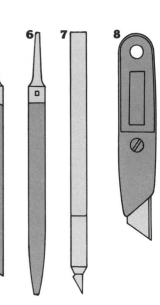

1 Hot-wire cutter; this is the most efficient tool for making clean cuts in the polystyrene foam.
2 Soldering iron for cutting channels in the polystyrene.
3 Heated metal spatula.
4 Cheese grater used for filing the foam.

5,6 Rasps.
7 Pencil knife; knives used for cutting polystyrene must be extremely sharp, otherwise they simply crush the foam rather than cutting it.
8 Craft knife.

Fiberglass

Fiberglass sculpture is generally a mixture of polyester resin and shredded glass fibers. The resin is the translucent material that picks up the mold details and gives the sculpture its smooth surface; this is then backed up with fiberglass and more resin, and produces a thin, hollow shell that has a great deal of tensile strength.

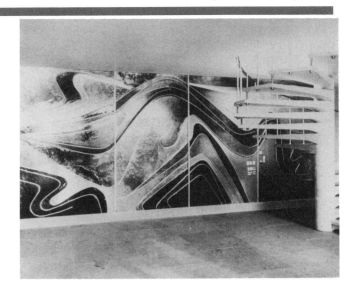

Shown in the photograph (right) is a fiberglass and resin mural. The resin was cast onto sheets of glass to ensure a flat surface, and then fiberglass matting and aluminum section dividers were laid into the resin.

Molds made of plaster are often used for fiberglass sculpture, since they can be chipped off when the forming is complete.
A layer of resin mixed with a catalyst and an accelerator is painted onto the inside of the mold; this is known as the gel coat.

Since toxic fumes are given off by the resin mixture, a **fume mask** should be worn throughout the mixing and application. Fiberglass is then stippled onto the gel coat, using a **brush** or a **finned roller** in order to produce a firm bond.

Further resin mixture is stippled onto the fiberglass, and this completes the hollow sculpture. This technique is used for large sculptures because of the high strength to weight ratio of the materials; large, strong hollow shells can be formed.

When the resin has cured fully, the mold is removed and the sculpture is trimmed with **snips** or **shears** and then filed and polished. Proper safety clothing, consisting of **protective overalls** and a **dust mask,** is worn to protect the sculptor from the fine glass particles produced.

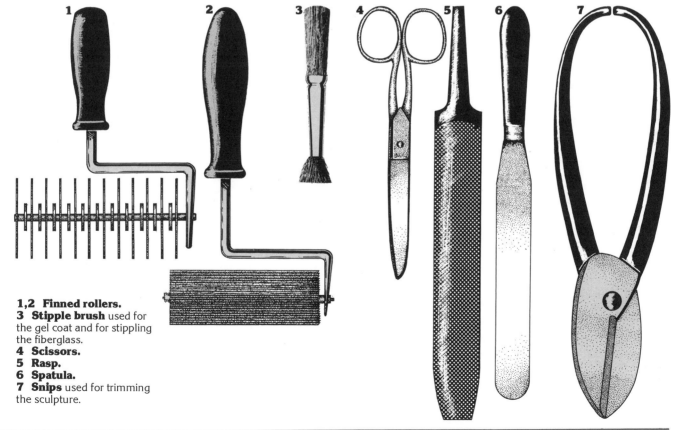

1,2 Finned rollers.
3 Stipple brush used for the gel coat and for stippling the fiberglass.
4 Scissors.
5 Rasp.
6 Spatula.
7 Snips used for trimming the sculpture.

©DIAGRAM

Resin and acrylic

Acrylics and other synthetic materials are becoming increasingly popular as sculpture media. The transparency or translucency of some of the synthetics enables sculptors to experiment with new visual effects in a way that was previously possible only with glass. Acrylic resins can also be cast, and will reproduce minute detail very accurately.

The photograph (right) shows acrylic furniture and wall panels by Michael Haynes. All the items shown are made from clear and colored acrylic sheet, and show the variety of forms that the material can be made to assume.

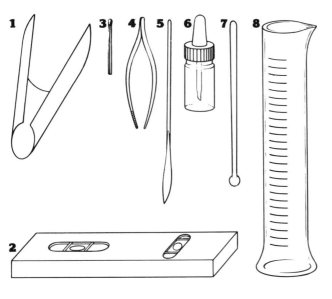

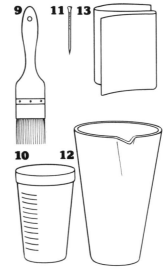

1 **Cardboard chute** used for transferring materials.
2 **Spirit level.**
3 **Matchstick** for applying small amounts of resin.
4 **Tweezers** are useful for positioning tiny objects to be cast in resin.
5 **Spatula.**
6 **Dropper bottle.**
7 **Glass mixing rod;** the shape prevents the formation of air bubbles in the resin.
8 **Measuring cylinder.**
9 **Paintbrush** for coating molds.
10 **Calibrated measuring cup.**
11 **Panel pin.**
12 **Mixing container.**
13 **Silicon carbide paper** used for polishing.

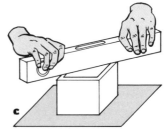
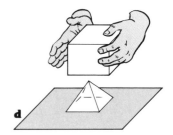

Resins are prepared and cast in the following way.
a The required amounts of resin and hardener are measured out and mixed in a **tall container** to help prevent the formation of air bubbles that would spoil the appearance of the cast.

b When the two materials are thoroughly mixed, the liquid is poured into a **mold** that has been coated with a release agent to prevent the resin from sticking. The mixture must be poured slowly and evenly to avoid trapping air.

c The level of the mold is checked with a **spirit level** to ensure that the casting will be even. The liquid is left to "cure" and harden; any air bubbles that form in this time are pricked with a **panel pin.**

d When the resin is thoroughly cured, the cast is released from the mold and polished with various grades of **silicon carbide paper** and **abrasive creams** until it achieves a glossy, transparent sheen.

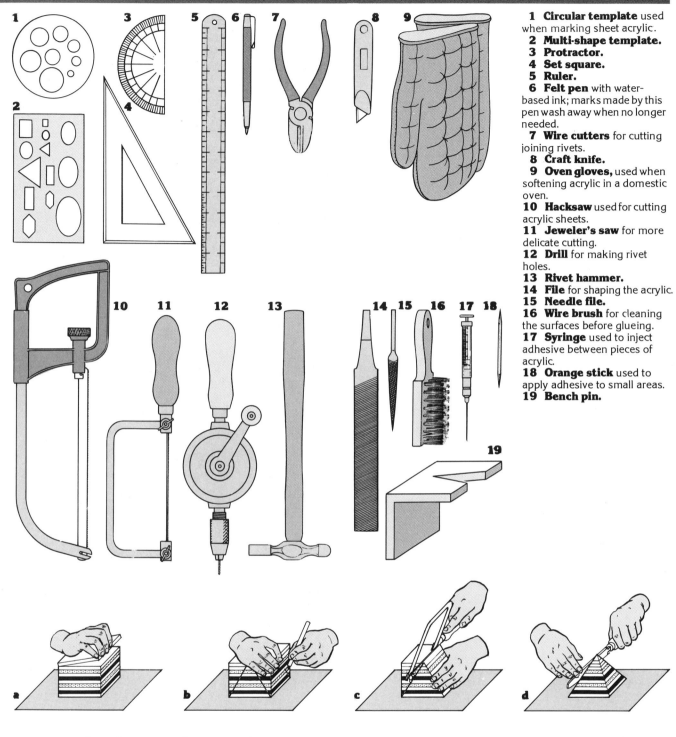

1 **Circular template** used when marking sheet acrylic.
2 **Multi-shape template.**
3 **Protractor.**
4 **Set square.**
5 **Ruler.**
6 **Felt pen** with water-based ink; marks made by this pen wash away when no longer needed.
7 **Wire cutters** for cutting joining rivets.
8 **Craft knife.**
9 **Oven gloves,** used when softening acrylic in a domestic oven.
10 **Hacksaw** used for cutting acrylic sheets.
11 **Jeweler's saw** for more delicate cutting.
12 **Drill** for making rivet holes.
13 **Rivet hammer.**
14 **File** for shaping the acrylic.
15 **Needle file.**
16 **Wire brush** for cleaning the surfaces before glueing.
17 **Syringe** used to inject adhesive between pieces of acrylic.
18 **Orange stick** used to apply adhesive to small areas.
19 **Bench pin.**

The technique for making sculpture from laminated acrylic sheets is shown above.
a The chosen pieces of acrylic are bonded by spreading each piece with adhesive and sandwiching the layers together.

b When the laminated layers are firmly bonded, the shape required is marked with a **felt pen,** using a **template** if necessary for an accurate outline.

c The shape is cut from the layers with a **saw;** all excess acrylic is cut away, and the felt pen marks are washed off the acrylic shape.

d The final object is filed to the exact form required, and then polished with a variety of **abrasive cloths.** Abrasive creams such as metal polishes can be used to achieve a high luster.

©DIAGRAM

8 Carved sculpture

Virtually the only principle that can be applied to all sculpture is that it is essentially three-dimensional, either in the round or in high or low relief. With carved sculpture, the artist begins with a solid block of the carving medium, and carves away the unwanted portions in order to leave a pleasing or beautiful form. With all carved sculpture, the reasoning behind the tools and their uses is the same whatever the material: strong, large tools are used to remove the large portions of unwanted material, and then progressively finer tools are used as the surface is refined. All the tools are either sharp themselves, such as the chisels used on stone and the knives used for chip carving, or are abrasive in some way, such as the woodcarving files and the abrasive-smeared wheels of the jade-carver. Until the 20th century, it was generally accepted in the Western world that sculpture should be representational, but the recent movements in sculpture have taken the art form to previously inconceivable limits. Sculpture can now be vigorously stylized, totally abstract, or even kinetic. The sculptor Henry Moore has described the feeling of freedom that came over him when he first made a hole entirely through one of his sculptures, and this new sense of freedom of expression in sculpture is one of this century's most significant contributions to the arts.

This stone relief comes from the bell tower of Santa Maria del Fiore, Florence, and depicts a stonecarver at work. His tools—hammers, chisels and pliers—can be seen lying beside his work.

Stonecarving 1

Stonecarving is the process of removing unwanted pieces from a block of stone until a sculpted form or finished design remains. Michelangelo considered that his task was to release the latent form trapped in each block of stone that he worked on, and any stonecarver's success depends on an ability to visualize the ultimate result of his work.

The print (right) of a stone-carver illustrates work in a statuary's shop. The sculptor is carving ornamental statues and busts of ancient and famous figures.

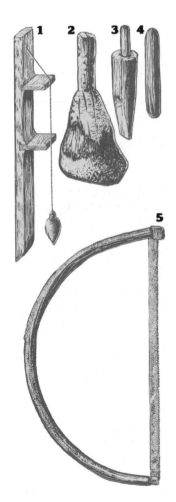

Stone is divided into three categories, depending on the way in which each type of rock was formed in the earth's crust. Igneous rocks include such types as granite and basalt; limestone and sandstone are sedimentary rocks, and meta-morphic rocks are those such as marble and alabaster. Stone varies from extremely soft to extremely hard, and the appropriate tools for a carving depend on the nature of the chosen stone. Many stones will take a high polish when the carving is complete, but others remain permanently matt and porous.

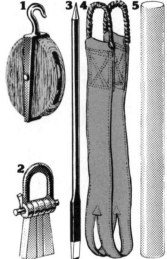

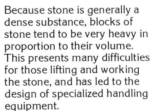

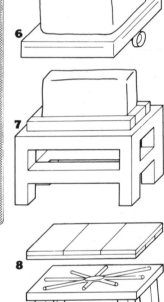

Some of the basic tools used for shaping and cutting stone have changed very little from those used in antiquity. The illustrations (left) show some ancient Egyptin stone-working tools.
1 Plumb line.
2 Wood mallet.
3 Wedge used for maneuvering stone blocks.
4 Wood roller.
5 Mason's bow saw.
6 Cradle for moving large blocks of stone.

Because stone is generally a dense substance, blocks of stone tend to be very heavy in proportion to their volume. This presents many difficulties for those lifting and working the stone, and has led to the design of specialized handling equipment.
1 Block, a pulley used when lifting heavy stones.
2 Lewis, a device that is locked into a hole in the stone and provides a loop for lifting.
3 Crowbar used to apply leverage to a block.
4 Sling for carrying the block.
5 Steel rollers aid the movement of the stone.

6 Samson, a small wheeled trolley.
7 Banker, a low, strong table that supports the block being carved.
8 Spider and turntable, a heavy-duty rotating surface resting on steel bearings.

 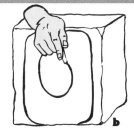  

These stages are the main steps that are followed by the sculptor when producing a stonecarving.
a A boulder is split, usually with **wedges,** to provide a stone of the right shape and size for the sculpture.

b Rough outlines of the sculpture are drawn on all faces of the block.
c The large unwanted areas of stone are stunned off the block, using a **point** driven with a **mallet** or a **club hammer.** Pieces can be struck away with an **adz** or a **bush hammer.**

d The surfaces of the sculpture are defined with **chisels;** these chip away flakes of the stone. The chisels are also usually struck with **mallets** to drive the tips through the stone with the correct force and direction.

e **Rasps** and **files** are used to smooth away the marks left by the chisels, and to give a preliminary shine to the stone. The final polishing can be done with abrasive papers or pastes, and soft cloth is used for the buffing.

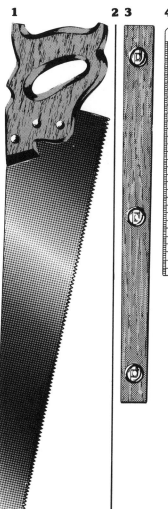

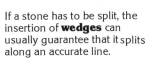

1 **Rip saw** can be used for cutting through soft blocks.
2 **Plumb line** for testing vertical surfaces.
3 **Spirit level** for gauging horizontal surfaces.
4 **Straight-edge,** used to ensure even cutting lines.
5 **Blocks of wood;** these can be slipped under the block of stone to provide gaps for inserting rollers.
6 **Wedge and feather inserts,** driven into the block to split off a specific section. The steel feathers protect the stone's edges.
7 **Wedges;** these stronger wedges are used on their own for splitting.
8 **Power drill,** useful for making exact indentations.

The bottom of the stone should be leveled so that it will stand firmly.
a An accurate horizontal is marked at the bottom of one edge of the block, and the stone is chipped into along this line. A **straight-edge** is placed in the groove, and the process is repeated on the opposite side until the two straight-edges are level.
b The stone on the other two sides is chipped away level with the corners.
c The island of stone in the center is gradually worked off in strips, the level being checked constantly.

If a stone has to be split, the insertion of **wedges** can usually guarantee that it splits along an accurate line.
a The sculptor marks out on all sides of the block a groove where the boulder needs to be split.
b **Wedges,** or **wedges and feathers,** are driven lightly into the stone at intervals around the line, ideally on all sides of the block.
c The wedges are carefully and systematically tapped with a **mallet,** one by one, until the two areas of stone are forced apart.

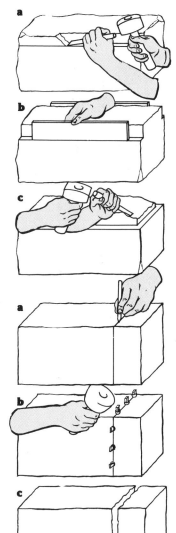

©DIAGRAM

Stonecarving 2

Picks are used to clear quickly large areas of unwanted stone from a block. The pick is driven against the surface of the stone and its force is conveyed laterally, causing flaking of the outside layers of the stone. The pick must not be used too forcefully or at too severe an angle, otherwise it may damage the crystalline structure of the stone further inside the rock; for this reason, the angle of the pick against the block is modified as the clearing of the surface nears completion.

1 Bush hammer, a flat-ended tool used like a pick. The many facets on the ends diffuse the force of the blow horizontally.
2 Double four-pointed pick.
3 Double-ended pick; each point has four facets.

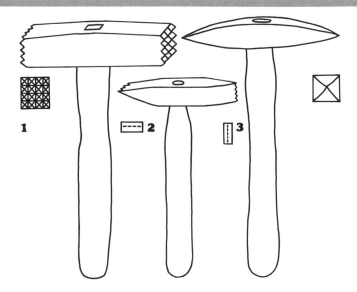

Chisels come in all shapes and sizes, to suit every need of the stonecarver. The length and thickness of the handle, the shape and width of the tip, and the angle and sharpness of the bevel, all depend on the job for which the particular chisel is intended.

1 Pitcher, with blunt square end.
2 Punch used for making indentations.
3 Point for finer indentations.
4 Claw; the edge of the chisel is marked with blunt serrations.
5 Claw bit and **holder;** the claw bit can be interchanged with others of different patterns.

6 Gouge, a chisel with a curved blade.
7 Fishtail chisel.
8 Bolster; this is a sharp version of the pitcher, and can be used for splitting small areas of stone.
9 Bullnose chisel.
10 Bullnose claw chisel.

11,12,13 Miniature chisels for use on small pieces or for working very fine detail.

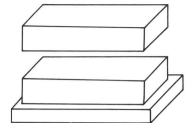

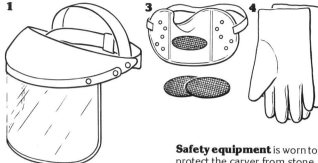

Illustrated (above) are **sharpening stones** suitable for use with stonecarving tools. The lower stone is in a **holder** so that it can be steadied while the tools are being sharpened. Oil is often used as a lubricant while sharpening.

The drawing (above) shows the technique for sharpening tools on the stones. The tool is held at an angle that corresponds exactly to the angle of the bevel required on the blade, and the tool is moved to and fro across the surface at this angle.

Safety equipment is worn to protect the carver from stone dust and from sharp flakes of stone.
1 Face mask in the form of an elongated visor.
2 Goggles.
3 Dust mask with spare filters.
4 Protective gloves.

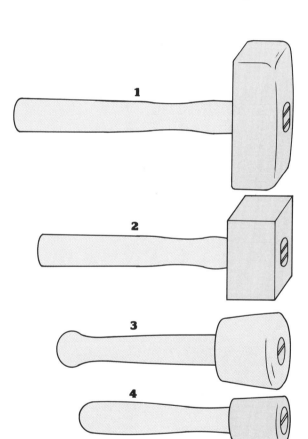

The **chisel** must be held firmly so that the carver can strike it squarely with the **mallet,** and also so that he can predict its mark upon the stone. Three firm ways of gripping the chisel are shown (right).
a With all fingers curled round one side of the chisel body and the thumb round the other.
b With the thumb wedged behind the head of the chisel.
c With the little finger wedged behind the chisel body.

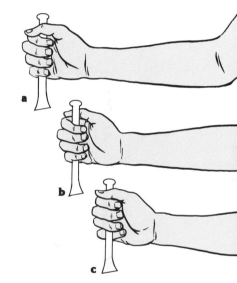

The angle at which the **chisel** is held against the stone changes as the work progresses.
a When large pieces of stone are being removed from the block the chisel is held virtually at right angles to the stone; the blow chips out a sizeable portion of stone and leaves a very uneven surface.
b The mason's stroke is used to define the planes of the sculpture more specifically; the chisel is held at a less pronounced angle to the stone.
c When fine finishing is needed, the chisel is held near the horizontal, in the carver's stroke.

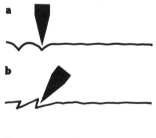

Hammers and **mallets** are used to drive the **chisels** into the stone. If the head of the chisel is flat, then a hammer is used; if it is rounded, a mallet is used. Both hammers and mallets can be made in various different woods and metals.

1 Steel hammer.
2 Iron lump hammer; this gives a duller blow than the steel hammer.
3 Wood mallet made of beech or lignum vitae for durability.
4 Dummy, a small mallet with a head of malleable iron.

© DIAGRAM

Stonecarving 3

Power tools of many kinds are available to the stonecarver. The tool heads usually have the same shapes and functions as their manual equivalents—the main difference is that they are driven by air or electricity rather than by the muscle-power of the carver. Power tools are expensive and noisy, and they produce fast-flying chips and a great deal of stone dust, but they save time and energy and enable the carving to progress rapidly. Extra safety precautions should be taken when using power tools.

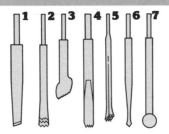

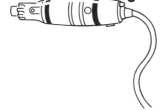

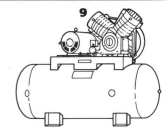

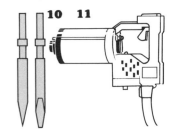

Heads available for a **pneumatic tool** include the following.
1 **Chisel.**
2 **Bush chisel.**
3 **Claw.**
4 **Ripper.**
5 **Frosting head.**
6 **Drill.**
7 **Rotary rasp.**

8 Pneumatic tool with air hose and socket for the heads.
9 Pump for pneumatic tool.
10 Heads for electric tools.
11 Electrically-powered tool body.

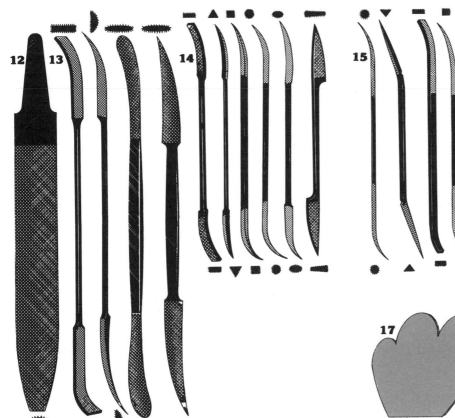

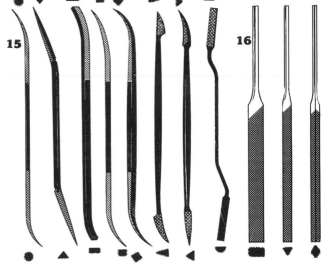

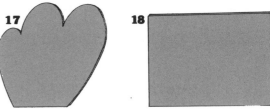

Filing can be used on both soft and hard stone to produce smooth curves and planes on the sculpture, either as a finish in themselves or as a final smoothing preparatory to polishing.

12 **Stone rasp.**
13 **Rasp rifflers.**
14 **File rifflers.**
15 **Needle rifflers.**
16 **Needle files.**
17 **Cock's comb.**
18 **Drag.**

Finishing stone

The finish left on a stone sculpture depends partly on the stone used: a soft stone, for instance, can be smoothed but not polished. Other factors are the tools used and the artist's preference. Sometimes a sculptor chooses to leave his tool marks evident, as in many of Rodin's works, whereas those of Michelangelo were often highly polished.

The photograph reproduced (right) shows a statue of Queen Hortense, by an Italian sculptor of the early 19th century. The statue illustrates very well the high polish that can be achieved on stone sculpture.

The basic steps needed to finish stone to a high polish are illustrated (right).

a The surfaces of the stone are smoothed with a **chisel** or **bullnosed claw** in order to remove the deepest marks made by the **carving tools.**

b The surface is made still more even by working it with a **file** or **riffler;** the finer the grade of file that is used, the smoother the surface will be.

c The stone is then buffed and rubbed with **abrasive blocks** and **compounds** so that even the faint marks left by the files are smoothed out. As polishing progresses, finer and finer grades of abrasive are used until the surface of the stone is glassy smooth.

d An extra gloss can be given to the stone by rubbing it with a **soft cloth** smeared with transparent oil.

a

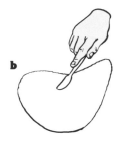

b

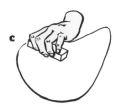

c

d

1 **Chisel** used for the final smoothing cuts.
2 **Bullnose claw** used for smoothing hollows.
3 **File;** this performs the preliminary refining.
4 **Riffler** refines the surface further.
5,6 **Carborundum** and **pumice blocks** for polishing.

7 **Garnet paper,** an abrasive paper made of crushed precious stones.
8 **Wet-or-dry sanding paper.**
9 **Emery cloth.**
10 **Polishing oil.**
11 **Soft cloth** for applying the oil.

©DIAGRAM

Wood sculpture 1

Wood has been used as a medium for sculpture by people of virtually every culture for over 5000 years. Wood is readily obtainable and easily worked with sharp tools, and its fibrous nature means that raised parts can be deeply undercut without any danger that they will break off, as often happens with stone, clay and plaster.

The wood relief reproduced (right) shows a monk at work carving a choir stall, and itself was originally part of a choir stall. The monk's tools can be seen hanging on the wall of his workshop.

Wood is classified into two types: hardwood and softwood. Hardwood comes from trees with broad, flat leaves, such as chestnut and oak; softwood comes from trees with narrow resinous leaves, such as pine. Hardwood is usually close-grained and more difficult to work, but it is more durable than softwood and takes a higher polish. Wood used for sculpture must be seasoned by consistent exposure to air before use—seasoning makes the moisture in the wood evaporate, and so reduces the risk of the final sculpture cracking, warping or shrinking.

A tree grows a new ring of wood every year, and each ring consists of many fibers that run vertically up and down the trunk. This fiber structure forms the grain, and the appearance of a piece of wood varies depending whether it is cut along or across the grain.

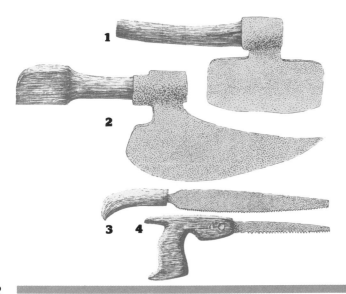

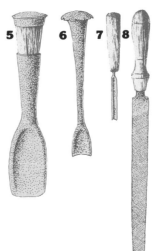

Illustrated (left) is a selection of old woodworking tools.
1,2 North American broad axes.
3 Egyptian handsaw.
4 Keyhole saw.
5,6 Hand-forged gouges.
7 Small gouge.
8 Rasp.

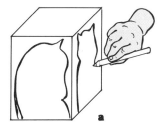
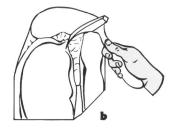
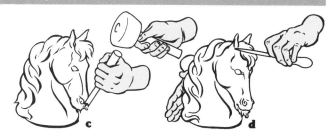

Sculpting in wood consists of carving out the planes of the final shape with more and more precision until they have the required shape and finish.

a The uncarved block of wood is marked on all sides with rough outlines of the finished shape.

b The main unwanted portions of the wood are removed in large chunks with a **saw** or an **adz;** the block takes on the rough proportions of the final sculpture.

c The form of the sculpture is more clearly defined by chipping or shaving portions of wood away with **chisels. Gouges** are used for cutting holes and indentations in the block where necessary.

d If a well-smoothed surface is required, the sculpture is refined still further by rubbing **files** of different grades over the wood. The surface can then be polished to produce a sheen.

While the wood is sculpted, the block must be kept stable so that the tools can be guided against its surface. This is done with various kinds of gripping mechanisms which are locked round the block.

1 Vise with two jaws for clamping the wood.
2 Clamp for holding small pieces against a bench.
3 Carver's bench screw; a block is screwed to the carving, then the block can be held firm in a vise.
4 Chops with cork-lined jaws for fragile pieces.
5 Workbench with **bench stops** and built-in **vises.**
6 Sandbag used to stabilize awkward shapes.

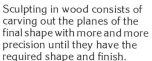
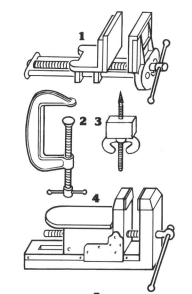
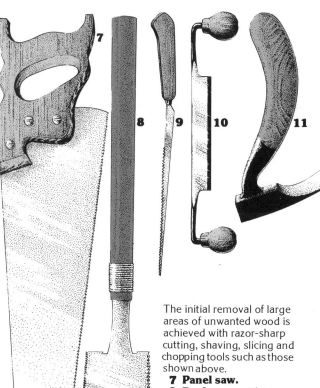
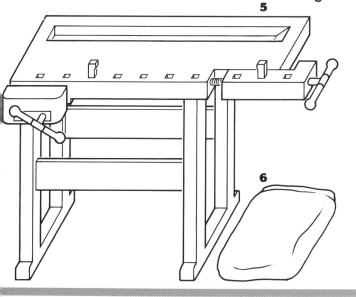

The initial removal of large areas of unwanted wood is achieved with razor-sharp cutting, shaving, slicing and chopping tools such as those shown above.

7 Panel saw.
8 Ryoba saw with two working edges.
9 Hikimawashi saw, similar to a **keyhole saw** and useful for cutting holes through the wood.
10 Drawknife; the knife is held with both hands and the length of the blade is pushed or pulled across the work.
11 Adz, an extremely sharp tool used with a chopping motion.

© DIAGRAM

Wood sculpture 2

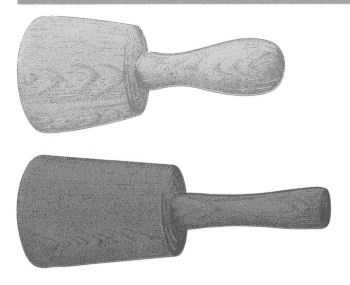

Mallets are wooden hammers used for driving chisels through the wood when carving. As they are made of wood, mallets are unlikely to splinter or split the chisel handles as a metal hammer might do. Mallet weights vary from very light (such as those of beechwood) to very heavy (such as lignum vitae). As the work progresses, and more delicate chisels are chosen for the carving, a lighter mallet is used for striking the chisels so that they will not cut into the wood too deeply.

The mallet is held in the carver's stronger hand so that he controls the blow accurately; the chisel is held in the other hand and is struck with the mallet (above). Both hands should be behind the point of the chisel at all times.

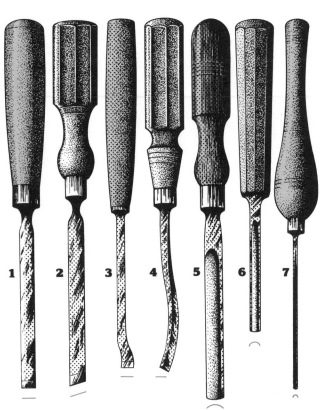

Chisels and gouges are used for the majority of the carving work in wood sculpture; they can be guided by hand, or struck with a hammer or a mallet. The shape and size of the blade determine the character of the mark made on the wood.

1 **Straight chisel.**
2 **Skew chisel** or **corner chisel;** the end of the blade is cut across at an angle.
3 **Short bent chisel.**
4 **Spade.**
5 **Gouge,** a chisel with a blade that is curved in section.

6 **Fluter,** a gouge with a deep channel.
7 **Veiner,** a very narrow gouge.
8,9 **Long bent gouges.**
10 **Macaroni tool,** a chisel with three straight edges.
11 **Parting tool,** a chisel with a V-shaped section.

12 **Short bent parting tool.**
13 **Long bent parting tool.**
14 **Fishtail tool;** the large blade spreads from the neck into a flat triangular shape.

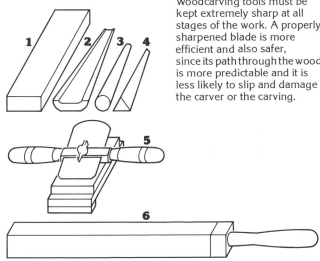

Woodcarving tools must be kept extremely sharp at all stages of the work. A properly sharpened blade is more efficient and also safer, since its path through the wood is more predictable and it is less likely to slip and damage the carver or the carving.

1 Rectangular **washita stone** for sharpening chisels and any other tools with straight blades.
2 Gouge slip, a curved stone used for sharpening both gouges with the bevel on the inside (in-cannel) and those with the bevel on the outside (out-cannel).
3,4 Sharpening point and triangle; these shaped and tapered stones are useful for sharpening tools with complex cutting surfaces.
5 Tool honer used to sharpen a variety of carving tools.
6 Strop, a wooden block covered in leather, for producing a really sharp finish on blades.

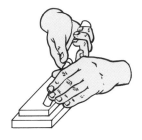

The surface of the slip stone is oiled, and then the tool to be sharpened is moved over its surface, held at the exact angle of the desired bevel. A curved gouge (above) is moved in a figure of eight, to ensure that all parts of the bevel are sharpened equally.

Files, rasps and **scrapers** are all used to abrade and refine the surface of the wood once it has been carved or sculpted to the required shape. All the tools come in grades varying from coarse to fine; the coarse grades are used on the surface first, and then the finer grades produce an even smoother finish.
1 Coarse flat file; the blade is made of steel and shaped into many small gouge-like cutters that pare off the unwanted material as the file moves over the surface.
2 Coarse round file.
3 Cabinet rasp.
4 Round rasp.
5,6,7,8 Riffler rasps in a variety of shapes. These slim rifflers are useful for reaching into awkward corners and curves.
9,10,11,12 Riffler files.
13 Rasp brush for cleaning the teeth of rasps and files when they become clogged with sawdust.
14 Curved rasp; this can be fitted round the hand and used for smoothing curves that are difficult to reach with a straight rasp.
15 Cabinet scraper for paring down large flat surfaces.

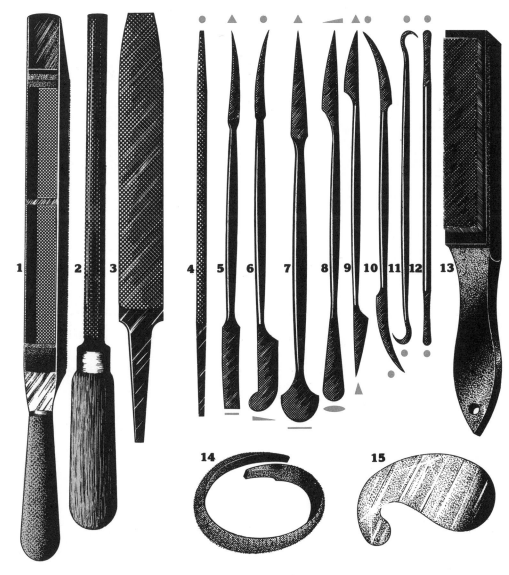

©DIAGRAM

Chip carving and finishing wood

Chip carving is a wood-carving method that involves shaving the wood away in layers to produce an incised pattern. The tools used for chip carving are small, very sharp knives with specially shaped blades.

The technique of chip carving is illustrated in the photograph (right). The sharp contrast between the two sides of each incision is typical of this kind of carving.

Chip carving designs are usually based on geometric patterns which have to be drafted and carved with extreme precision. The design is traced onto the wood and then each facet is carefully chiseled out of the wood piece by piece. Because the work is so precise, the **knives** for carving need to be kept very sharp so that there is no danger of them slipping and spoiling the symmetry of the design.

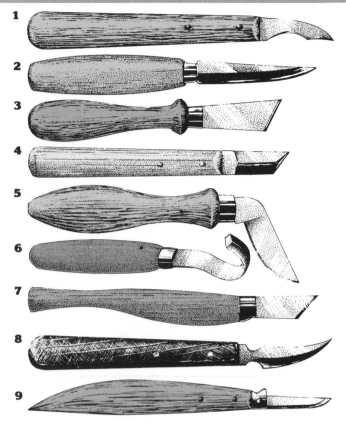

1 **Detail knife.**
2 **Swedish knife.**
3 **Broad-bladed knife.**
4 **Whittling knife.**
5 **Hooked knife.**
6 **Carver's hook.**
7 **Flat-bladed knife.**
8,9 **Detail knives.**

When doing chip carving, the **knife** must always be held so that both hands are behind the blade (right). The thumb of the working hand may be rested on the wood for support, but it too should be out of the cutting line.

If wood is left untreated it is very susceptible to heat, cold and damp. These adverse conditions can cause the wood to crack, flake, lose its color, and in extreme cases even to rot, so wood is usually protected by staining, sealing or polishing the surface in some way. Sanding smooths the surface, shellac and some oils and varnishes seal it, and waxes and polishes buff the surface to a shiny finish.

10,11 Soft brushes used for applying stains.
12 Spirit lamp; this is used to warm polishing oils. Warming them helps the oil to spread evenly over the wood, and also enables it to penetrate the wood surface more efficiently.
13 Sandpaper for smoothing the surface of the wood.
14 Linen rags used to apply and buff the wax finishes.
15 Tacky cloth; this cloth has a slightly sticky finish, and is used to remove dust and particles of sawdust from the wood.

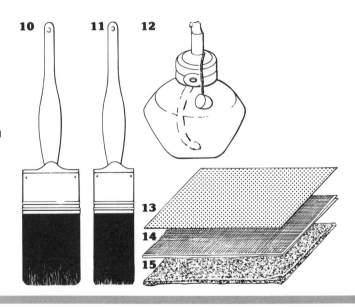

Ivory carving

Ivory is the base of one of the oldest drawings in existence—a prehistoric picture of a mammoth, scratched onto a tusk. True ivory comes from the elephant, but the teeth and tusks of seals, whales and hippopotami have all been used as substitutes.

The ivory carving on the right comes from an eleventh-century casket, and is a self-portrait by the ivory craftsman Engelramnus. He has depicted himself preparing an ivory tablet held by his son Redolfus.

These tools are ordinary Western tools that can be used for ivory carving.
1 Needle files; small, delicate files in assorted shapes for filing the ivory.
2 Coping saw used to cut fine pieces of ivory.
3 Bow saw, for slightly more robust cuts.

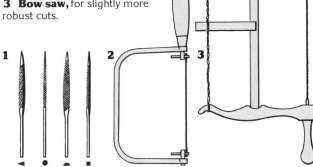

Hindus have developed a whole range of delicate tools especially for carving ivory.
4 Ari, a saw.
5 Kenchi, a pliers-like tool for cutting ivory into strips.
6 Chhuri, a paring knife.
7 Birka, a chisel.

8 File.
9 Hathouri, a hammer.
10 Groover.
11 Flat rasp.
12 Chhuri, a finishing knife.
13 Randa, a stippler.
14 Barma, a drill.
15 Drill-bow.

© DIAGRAM

Jade carving

Jade is one of the hardest stones used as a carving medium. No metal blade or file will cut jade, and so carving is accomplished by driving abrasive sands through the stone with various tools. Abrasives can be made of emery and carborundum, or crushed precious stones such as quartz, garnet and ruby. An ornate carving may take decades to complete.

The illustration of a jade-worker shown on the right contains many of the traditional tools illustrated on this page. The treadle wheel, bamboo eyeshield and metal carving head can be clearly seen.

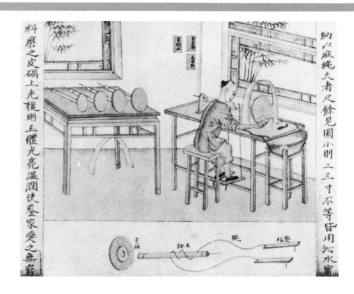

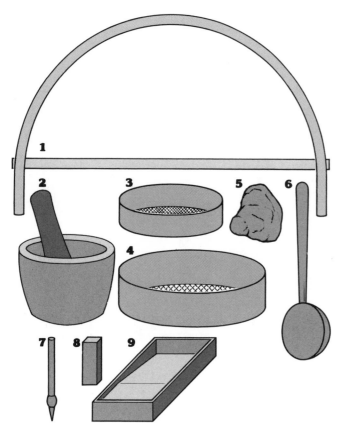

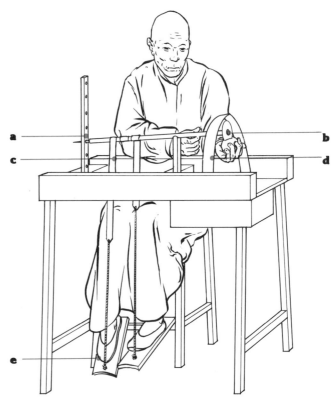

1 La ssǔ tzu, a saw made from a steel blade strung across a piece of bamboo.
2 Iron pestle and mortar used to crush the materials for the abrasives.
3,4 Sieves for grading the abrasive sands.
5 Oyster shell used to mix and sift the sands.

6 Ladle; the sands are mixed with water and poured continually onto the work.
7,8,9 Brush, stick ink and **inkstone;** ink is mixed on the stone and brushed onto the rough jade to outline the projected design.

Most of the tools used for grinding the abrasive through the jade are **steel heads** fixed to a **treadle-driven wheel.** The operator uses the treadles to spin the wheel as fast or as slowly as the work requires.

a Wood **bearing** used to support the wheel shafts.
b Carving head.
c Belt driving the shaft.
d Bamboo **eye-shield.**
e Treadles.

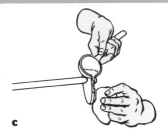
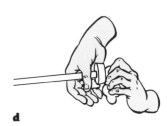

a **b** **c** **d**

A jade carving is designed by an experienced jade-worker, who studies the rough piece and decides upon the shape that will best enhance the jade's pattern and contours.
a The jade boulder is sawn into pieces of a manageable size.

b When the design has been chosen, its rough outlines are inked onto the piece of jade. As the work progresses, the master designer constantly studies the stone, and re-draws the outlines if the jade seems to require an alteration.

c The jade is carved with the abrasive sands, using the **steel heads** on the **treadle wheel. Bamboo drills** with diamond tips are also used to carve out portions of the pattern.

d When the form is complete, the jade is buffed and polished using **wood, leather** and **carborundum heads** on the wheel.

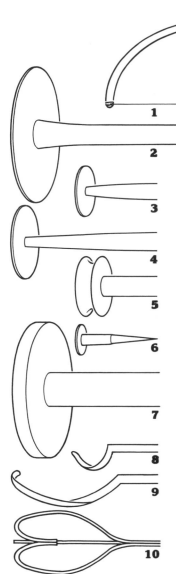

1 2 3 4 5 6 7 8 9 10

1 Wan kung chü; this saw has a single wire across the bamboo, and is used for cutting away unwanted jade from the design.
2 Cha t'o, large cutting disk.
3,4 Kuo t'o, small cutting disks.
5,6 Ya t'o, small grinding tools.
7 Mo t'o, large grinding wheel.
8,9,10 Wa-tzŭ, gouges used for hollowing out jade bottles and pots.

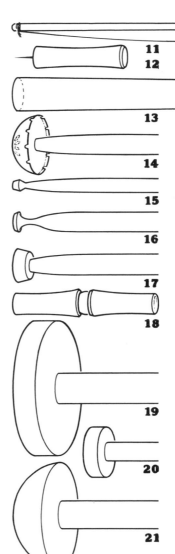

11 12 13 14 15 16 17 18 19 20 21

11 Drill bow, used to drive the drill heads.
12 Bamboo drill with a sliver of diamond set into the wire tip.
13 La tsuan, a large tubular drill.
14,15,16,17 Chuang ting, drill heads.
18 Bead polisher; two pieces of cut bamboo are rubbed around the sphere of jade.
19 Polishing wheel made of carborundum and shellac.
20 Wooden wheel covered with leather for polishing.
21 Wan-tzŭ, a curved polishing wheel.

9 Cabinetmaking

Cabinetmaking is the specialized craft that grew out of the trade of joinery. In the late 17th century, exotic and expensive woods began to supersede the commoner woods as materials for the furniture of the rich. Since the patrons were paying out a great deal of money for the materials, they insisted that the very finest items of furniture were produced for their outlay. Consequently, the craft of cabinetmaking, or the manufacture of fine furniture, was born. The woodworking skills used in cabinetmaking are of great precision, since a beautiful feature is made not only of the decoration but of the joints themselves, the grain of the wood, and the design of the entire piece of furniture. Accuracy in the execution of the design is of paramount importance, and so the tools for cabinetmaking are of the highest quality and made to the most stringent specifications. Most of the tools are developments of those used in the carpentry and joinery trades, adapted to cabinetmaking by making them more sophisticated and often smaller; all blades are sharpened to a razor-like finish. When a piece of furniture has been made by a cabinetmaker, whether it is a 17th century walnut bookcase or a modern Scandinavian pine table, a functional form has been made into a work of art.

The picture reproduced here is Sir John Millais' painting of Christ in the carpenter's shop. Although it was painted in the 19th century, all the tools illustrated are known to have existed in Christ's time.

Preliminary cutting

Felled wood must first be cut into manageable pieces so that it can be seasoned, sold, and easily measured for the cabinetmaker's requirements. Since green wood in particular tends to make tools stick as they cut, tools for preliminary cutting need to be both sharp and sturdy and so are usually made out of heavy-duty iron or steel.

The Japanese print illustrated (right) depicts a craftsman trueing up a log from a felled tree. Two types of ax are shown in the print.

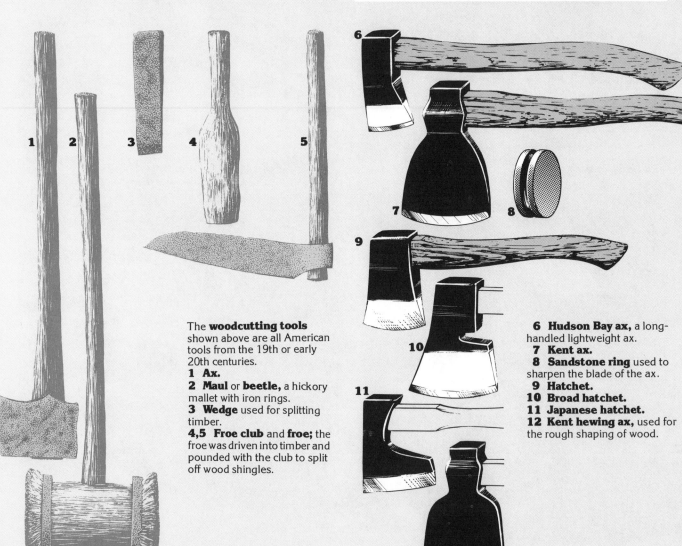

The **woodcutting tools** shown above are all American tools from the 19th or early 20th centuries.
1 Ax.
2 Maul or **beetle,** a hickory mallet with iron rings.
3 Wedge used for splitting timber.
4,5 Froe club and **froe;** the froe was driven into timber and pounded with the club to split off wood shingles.

6 Hudson Bay ax, a long-handled lightweight ax.
7 Kent ax.
8 Sandstone ring used to sharpen the blade of the ax.
9 Hatchet.
10 Broad hatchet.
11 Japanese hatchet.
12 Kent hewing ax, used for the rough shaping of wood.

A **one·man crosscut saw** is shown in use (above). The hand holding the main grip of the saw pushes it through the wood; the other hand, on the grip of the blade, pulls it back in a return stroke.

An **adz** is used to hollow out timber roughly (above). The adz is moved in a swinging motion through the wood, carving away more wood on each curving stroke.

The method of using a **froe** is illustrated (above). The left hand holds the froe so that the blade lies along the line to be split, and then the back of the blade is struck with a **froe club** to drive it into the wood.

Wood is split easily with a **splitting wedge** and **mallet,** as shown (above). The wedge is driven lightly into the line to be split, and then struck firmly with the mallet. As the wood begins to split, the wedge is moved farther along and the blow repeated.

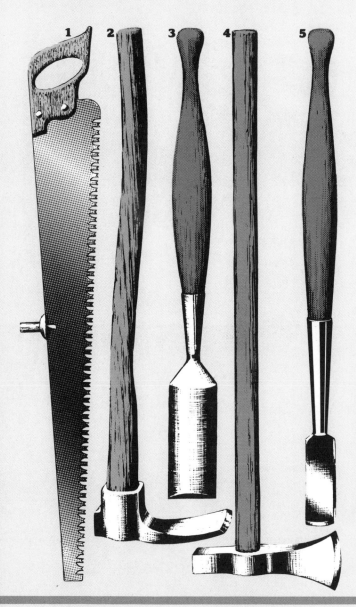

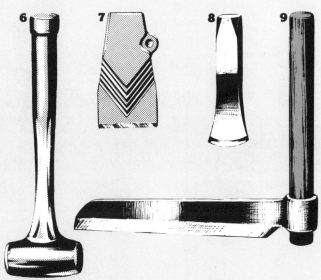

1 One-man crosscut saw.
2 Shipbuilder's adz with a lip on the blade.
3 Socket slick, a broad chisel for leveling hewn surfaces.
4 Woodchopper's maul used for splitting wood.
5 Bark spud, a tool for trimming away bark.
6 Dead-blow mallet; the hollow head is filled with lead shot so that there is no rebound to the blow.
7 Bucking wedge; the wedge is driven into the wood with a mallet.
8 Splitting wedge.
9 Froe used for slicing straight-grained woods.

©DIAGRAM

143

Cutting to shape

Saws are the tools most often used to cut the wood to the precise shape and size required for cabinetmaking. Saws are large blades with teeth on the cutting edges; these teeth are set (turned to the sides), and enable the blade to cut cleanly and efficiently through thick wood. Saws vary in size from the giant one-man crosscut saw (see p.143) to the tiny saw knives shown here.

The illustration (right) is a wood engraving by Thomas Bewick. It shows the inside of a cabinetmaker's workshop; the master craftsman and his assistants are working at a variety of tasks, with their tools strewn around them.

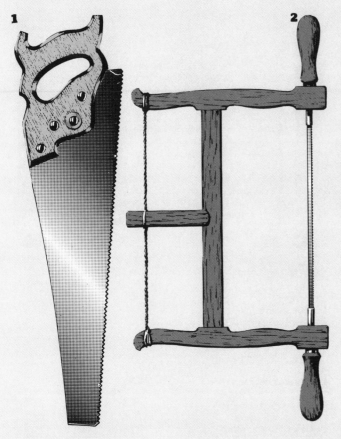

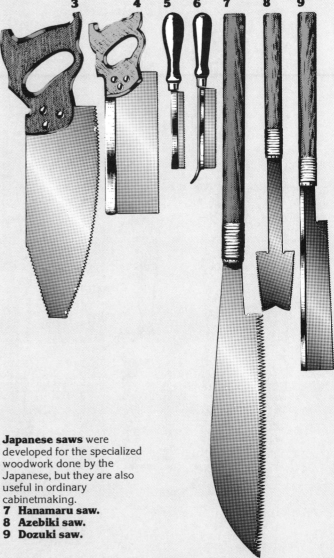

The **handsaw** was a prime tool of pre-mechanical cabinet-making, and various types were evolved, such as the **ripsaw, crosscut saw** and **panel saw,** to meet different needs of the cabinetmaker.

1 **Handsaw.**
2 **Bow saw;** the wire at the top is twisted to tighten the blade.
3 **Flooring saw.**
4 **Back saw.**
5 **Bead saw.**
6 **Blitz-back saw.**

Japanese saws were developed for the specialized woodwork done by the Japanese, but they are also useful in ordinary cabinetmaking.
7 **Hanamaru saw.**
8 **Azebiki saw.**
9 **Dozuki saw.**

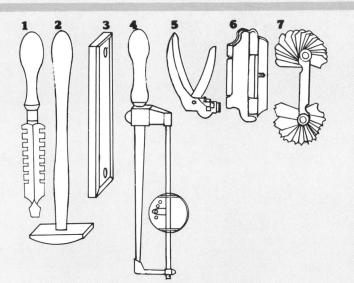

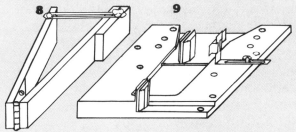

Saw accessories are used for sharpening and setting the saw teeth, and as aids to cutting.
1 Saw set for a handsaw.
2 Saw setting hammer used for bending the teeth.
3 Saw setting plate, used as an anvil for the setting hammer.

4 Saw sharpener.
5 Saw set.
6 Saw jointer.
7 Radius gauge, used to check the set of the teeth.
8 Taper jig, used as a guide when sawing diagonal lines.
9 Sawing jig.

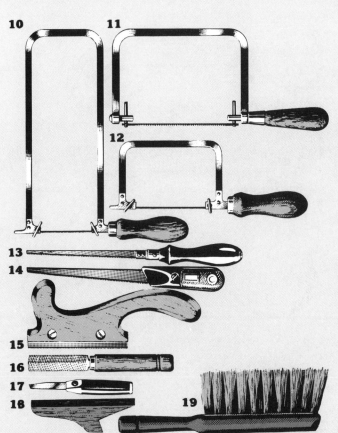

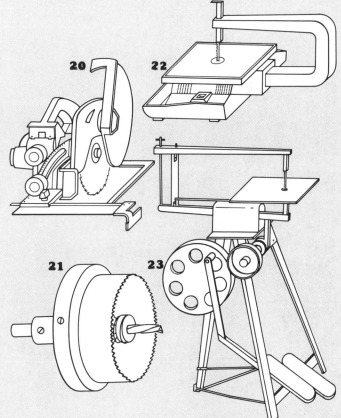

10 Deep-throated fretsaw.
11 Coping saw.
12 Piercing saw.
13 Keyhole saw.
14 Saw knife.
15 Dovetail saw.
16 Feather-edge saw file.
17 Adjustable knife with serrated edge.

18 Push stick; this is used for pushing small pieces of wood while they are sawn.
19 Bench brush.
20 Portable **circular saw.**
21 Hole saw.
22 Jigsaw.
23 Treadle fretsaw.

© DIAGRAM

Measuring and marking

Cabinetmaking is a very precise craft, and the cuts and joints made in the wood need to be extremely accurate to ensure that they marry correctly. Exactitude in the measuring and marking out of lines is therefore essential, and the cabinetmaker has at his disposal many instruments for measuring lines, angles, slopes, depths and rebates.

In the illustration (right) a Japanese craftsman is checking the level of a plank. In his right hand he holds a square, used to check right angles, and with his left hand he is holding the log so that he can see whether the surface is level.

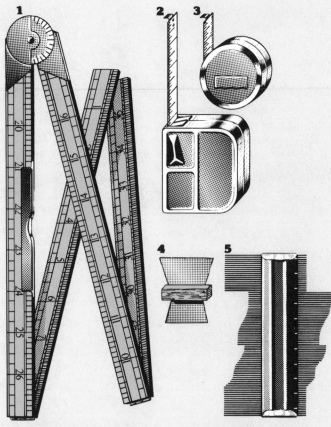

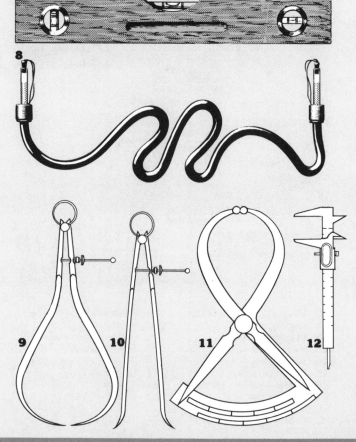

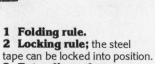

1 **Folding rule.**
2 **Locking rule;** the steel tape can be locked into position.
3 **Extending rule.**
4 **Dovetail template,** used to mark out joint angles.
5 **Template former,** used to duplicate complex contours.

6 **Musical instrument calipers** for measuring wood depths accurately.
7 **Spirit level.**
8 **Water level.**
9 **Outside caliper.**
10 **Inside caliper.**
11 **Double caliper.**
12 **Vernier caliper.**

The following **marking tools** are used in cabinetmaking.
1 Pencil.
2 Striking knife.
3 Marking knife.
4 Scratch awl.
5 Contour scriber; the plain point is run along the contour, and the scribing point reproduces the contour in a marked line.
6 Marking gauge.
7 Trammel heads.

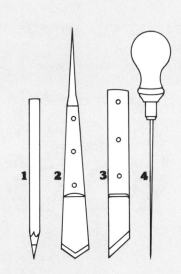

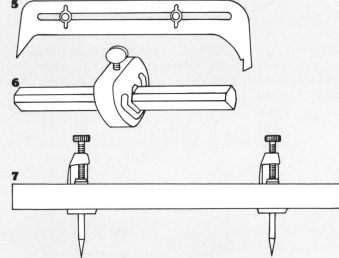

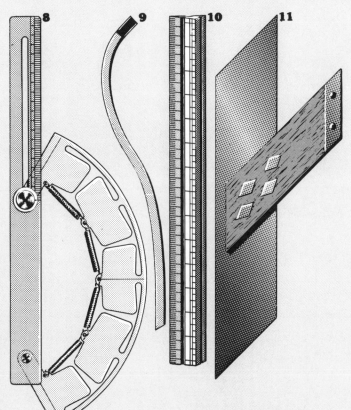

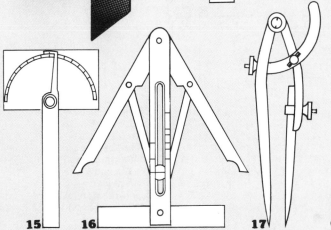

8 Adjustable ruler for drawing curves.
9 Flexible curve.
10 Architect's scale.
11 Miter square used in marking 45° angles.
12 Try square for checking right angles.
13 Sliding bevel.
14 Multipurpose square.

15 Stainless steel protractor.
16 Angle divider.
17 Loose-leg wing divider.

©DIAGRAM

Holding and clamping

Holding tools and implements are used in cabinetmaking for various puposes. Some tools are designed to hold the wood in place while it is being cut or marked, others to secure two pieces while they are being glued or jointed together. All of them work on the principle of applying pressure around the wood so that it cannot move out of position.

The rocking chair illustrated (right) is made in walnut wood, and the rods of wood have been bent by holding them in steam and then forcing them into shape on a pegboard. The steam softens the wood so that it does not split during the process.

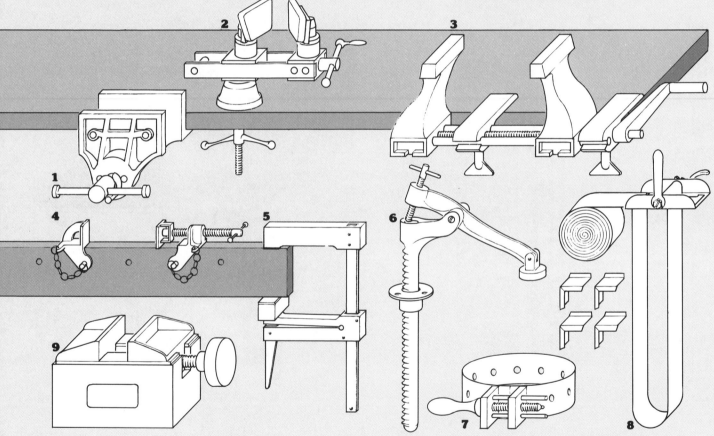

1 **Bench vise.**
2 **Universal vise** with a swivel.
3 **Multipurpose vise.**
4 **Clamp heads** that can be fixed up individually.
5 **Cam clamp.**
6 **Holdfast,** a lever-like clamp used to hold work to the bench top.

7 **Flexiclamp,** a belt clamp used particularly for circular assemblies of wood.
8 **Web clamp** and **corner pieces.** The joints of large items are glued and assembled, the protective corner pieces positioned, and the web tightened around the whole assembly.

9 **Auxiliary vise.**
10 **Clamp pad,** used over clamp jaws to protect delicate woods.
11 **Pinch dog,** used to hold flush joints during glueing. The harder the dog is driven into the joint, the firmer the bond will be.

A **pegboard,** such as the one illustrated below, is used to bend the pieces of wood used for curved chairbacks. The wood is softened in steam and then levered against the pegs; as it bends, more pegs are inserted to keep the wood in shape.

A **bending iron** (right) is an electric tool used for shaping curved pieces of wood. The gauge controls the amount of heat received by the wood, which can be held over the cylinder by the metal rings.

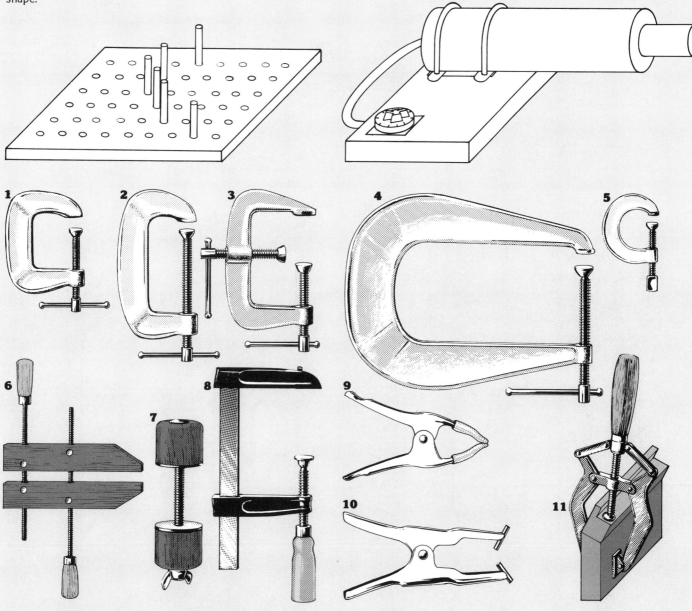

1,2 C-clamps.
3   Two-way edging clamp, used when pressure is required from the side as well as the top.
4   Deep-throated clamp.
5   Miniature clamp used for fine work.
6   Handscrew, also used for fine work.

7   Violin-maker's clamp.
8   Deep engagement clamp.
9   Spring clamp, a pincer-like tool.
10 Multispring clamp.
11 Universal clamp.

Specialized cutting

Cabinetmaking frequently calls for the cutting of complicated or difficult recesses, such as moldings, keyholes and joints, which can pose problems for the craftsman. The specialized cutting tools of the trade have been evolved to make these awkward cuts easier; many of the tools have shaped blades that cut out exactly the recess required.

This Genoese mandolin was made in about 1700, and has a wood body. The rose, which is the decorated centerpiece, was made by cutting out tiny sections of the wood to leave a pierced-work design.

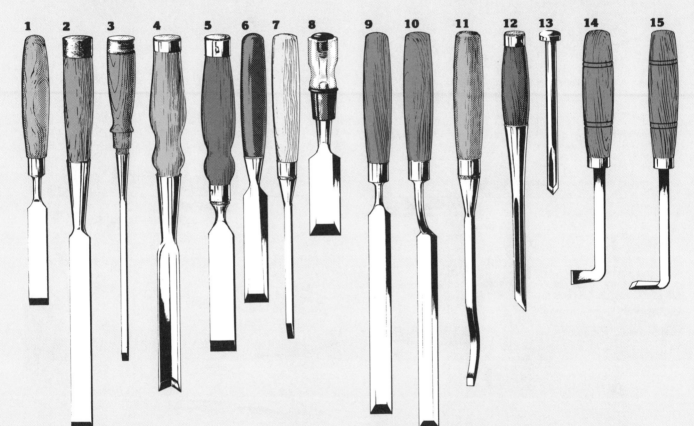

1 **Firmer chisel.**
2 **Socket chisel** with steel handle-end.
3 **Socket chisel** with leather handle-end.
4 **Socket corner chisel.**
5 **Heavy-duty chisel.**
6 **Bench chisel.**
7 **Deep-mortise chisel.**
8 **Butt chisel.**

9 **Paring chisel.**
10 **Bent paring chisel.**
11 **Swan-necked chisel.**
12,13 **Bruzzes,** chisels with angled blades.
14,15 **Drawer-lock chisels.**

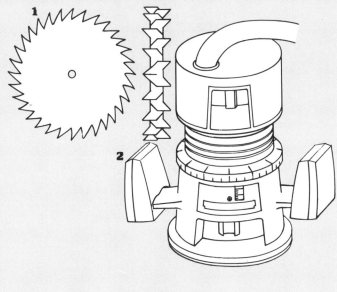

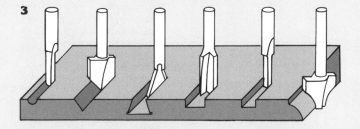

1 Dado blade for a drill, shown also in profile. The blade, when held sideways into the wood, cuts a slit.
2 Power router; this tool is fitted with a head and is moved across the surface that is to be routed.

3 Router heads in a selection of shapes. Some of the heads are for cutting recesses, while others are for shaping moldings.

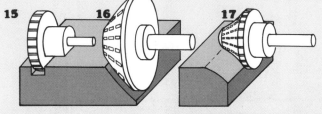

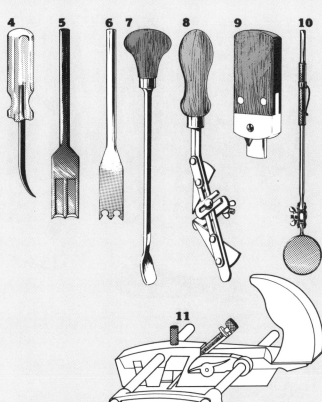

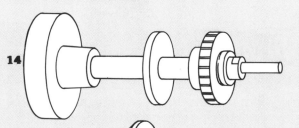

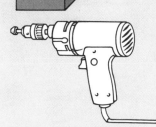

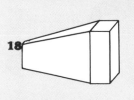

4 Nooker, a sharp tool for cleaning out incised corners.
5,6 Hinge chisels used to cut the channels for hinge fittings.
7 Violin-maker's gouge.
8 Groove cutter.

9 Purfling cutter.
10 Inspection mirror used for examining cuts that are outside the line of vision.
11 Plow plane; this tool is used to cut slits in the sides of wood.

12 Mortise chisel.
13 Tenon cutter.
14 Rotary cutter; this tool cuts grooves in wood.
15,16,17 Alternative **heads** for the rotary cutter.
18 Dovetail template, used to mark out dovetail joints.

The illustration (above) shows a **rotary cutter** attached to a **drill.** The shank is fixed into the chuck of the drill, and the cutter acts as the drill head.

Shaving and planing

Drawknives, spokeshaves and planes are used to pare down wood surfaces until they are even and regular. This process is not limited to flat surfaces; both concave and convex surfaces are catered for, and special blades have been produced to cut chamfers, cylinders and moldings. Miniature tools are manufactured for small or complex surfaces.

The chairs illustrated on the right come from the Harrod's catalog of 1895. The traditional shapes of the chair backs have all been formed from single pieces of wood by the use of drawknives and shaves.

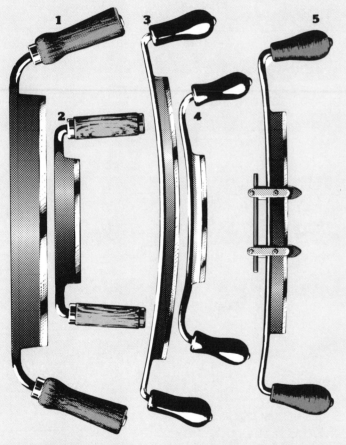

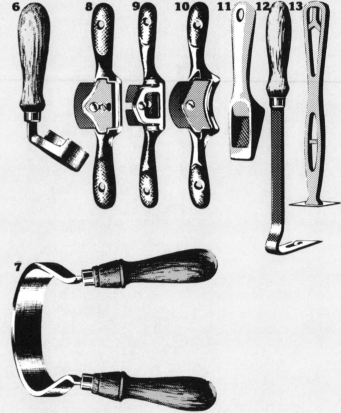

1 American-pattern drawknife.
2 English-pattern drawknife.
3 German-pattern drawknife.
4 French-pattern drawknife.

5 Chamfer guide; this drawknife has two blades that can be adjusted for cuts of various angles.

6 Scorp, a tool for roughing out hollow shapes.
7 Inshave, a blade used for concave surfaces.
8 Flat spokeshave.
9 Adjustable-throat spokeshave for fine paring.
10 Chamfer spokeshave.
11 Shaver, a paring tool.
12,13 Ship scrapers.

A **shaving horse,** such as the one shown (right), is often used by cabinetmakers and other woodworkers when paring or shaving. The work is held by the movable bar; the craftsman sits astride the bench, and can shave the work with long, unrestricted strokes.

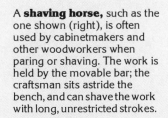

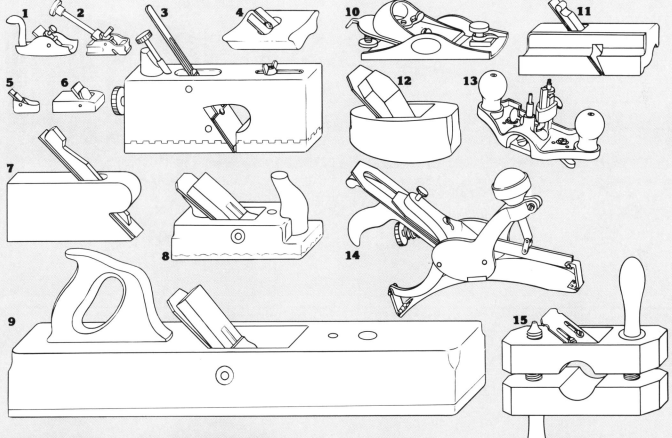

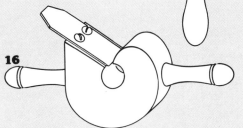

1 **Hollowing plane.**
2 **Palm plane.**
3 **Rebate plane.**
4 **Rail plane.**
5 **Finger plane.**
6 **Thumb plane.**
7 **Chisel plane.**
8 **Smoothing plane.**
9 **Jointer plane** for large areas and edge joints.

10 **Block plane.**
11 **Molding plane.**
12 **Curved plane.**
13 **Router plane.**
14 **Compass plane** with a flexible sole for either concave or convex cuts.
15 **Adjustable rounder plane** for cylinders.
16 **Rounder plane.**

Scraping and filing

Scraping and filing are methods of refining the surface of the wood in cabinetmaking so that it is both level and smooth. Files and rasps abrade the wood, leveling down uneven patches, while scrapers actually shave away minute slivers of the wood so that the surface is plane. Files and rasps are useful particularly in irregularly shaped areas.

The French commode table illustrated (right) was made by Thomas Chippendale, and shows the use of many precision tools. Drawers are very difficult items to make, as all the surfaces must be cut and then planed exactly so that they run smoothly and fit perfectly.

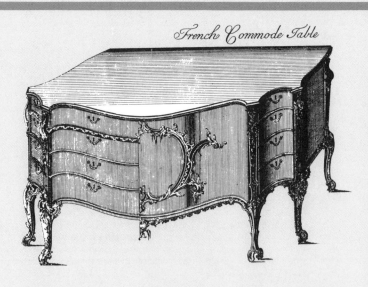

French Commode Table

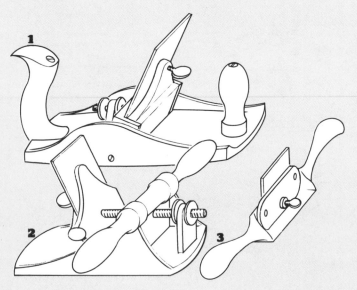

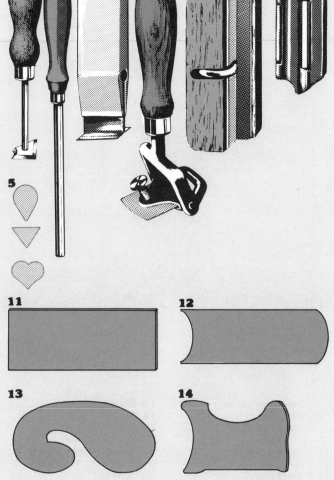

1 **Scraping plane.**
2 **Two-handed scraping plane.**
3 **Cabinet scraper** in spokeshave style.
4 **Shavehook.**
5 **Alternative heads** for the shavehook.
6 **Burnisher** for scrapers, used to produce the cutting hook on the blades.
7 **Four-bladed scraper.**
8 **Box scraper** used for the rough leveling of flat wood.
9 **Wheel burnisher** for scrapers.
10 **Scraper jointer.**
11,12,13,14 **Cabinet scrapers** in various shapes for smoothing flat and curved surfaces.

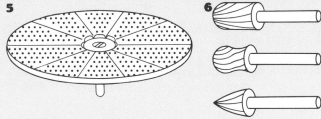

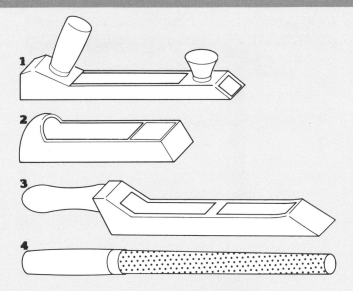

These **files** are the modern equivalent of dreadnought files; they have small cutting blades that vigorously abrade the surface of the wood.
1 **Plane-style file.**
2 **Box-style file.**
3 **Flat file.**
4 **Round file.**

5 **Flat rasp head** to fit onto a drill.
6 **Rotary rasp heads,** also used with a drill or motor tool.

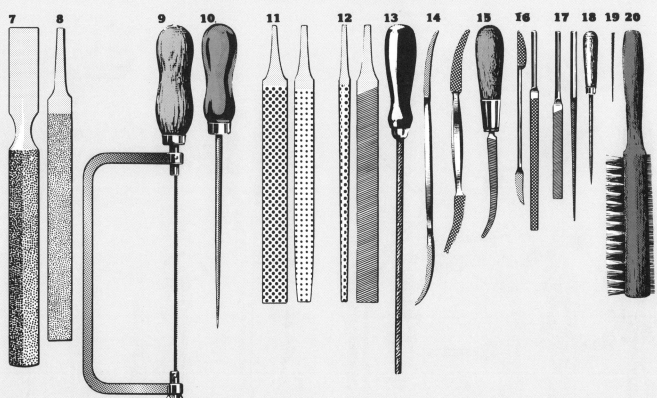

7 **Tungsten carbide rasp.**
8 **Tungsten carbide file.**
9 **Saw frame,** for an abrasive file blade.
10 **Tapered file.**
11 **Cabinet rasps.**
12 **Cabinet files.**
13 **Stickleback rasp,** a coarse rasp for smoothing keyholes and other crevices.

14 **Rifflers,** files with curved heads.
15 **Bent riffler.**
16 **Needle rasps.**
17 **Needle files.**
18 **Mousetail file.**
19 **Microfile.**
20 **File card and brush,** used for cleaning sawdust from the teeth of files.

Drilling and piercing

The term drilling can encompass many processes in cabinetmaking, from the making of tiny channels for minute screws to the cutting out of large holes to hold chair rungs or other cylindrical inserts. Drills work with a combination of circular motion and pressure to drive the tool through the wood.

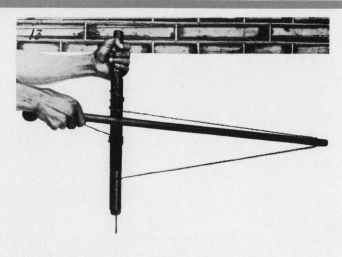

The Chinese bowdrill shown in the photograph (right) is a modern version of the traditional bowdrill that has been used in many countries for centuries. As the bow is moved from side to side, the drill bit turns rapidly.

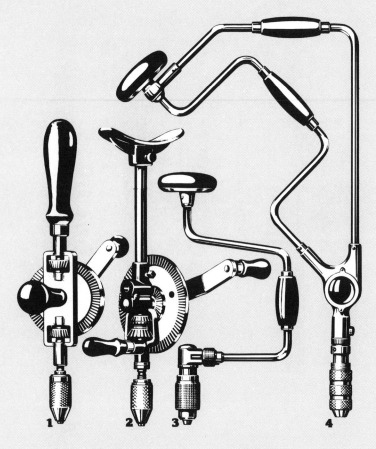

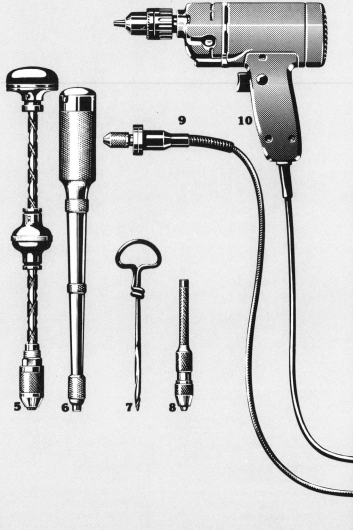

1   **Hand drill.**
2   **Breast drill;** the cup at the top of the drill is braced against the user's chest for extra pressure.
3   **Brace** or **hand brace.**
4   **Corner brace,** designed for use in awkward corners.
5   **Reciprocating drill.**
6   **Push drill.**

7   **Gimlet drill,** a small hand-driven drill bit.
8   **Pin vise,** used for gripping small drill bits and driven by a twirling action of the fingers.
9   **Flexible shaft** for an electric drill.
10 **Electric drill.**

1 Screw pitch gauge, used to check the pitch on screw threads.
2 Combination gauge for measuring thread width and pitch, and shaft dimensions.
3 Precision drill guide, used for drilling to a precise depth.

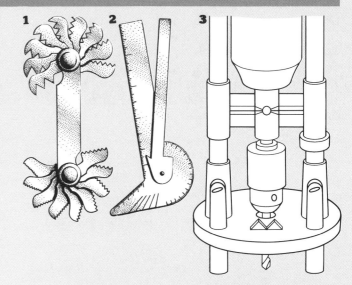

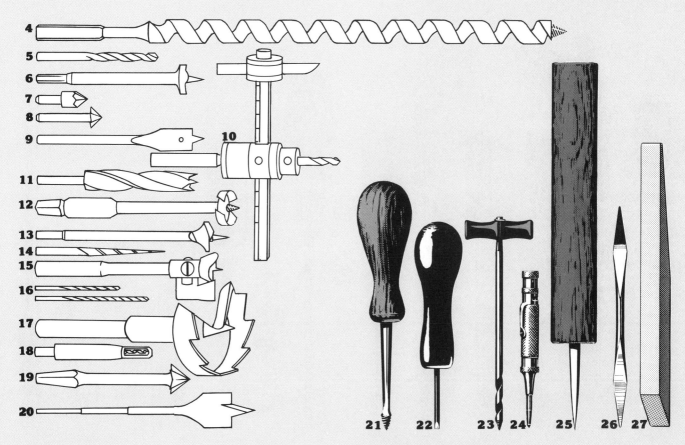

4 Ship auger, a heavy-duty drilling bit.
5 Twist drill bit.
6 Power-bore bit.
7,8 Countersinking bits, used for making the recesses to take screw heads.
9 Flat bit.
10 Circle cutter.

11 Brad point drill.
12,13 Power-bore bits.
14 Tapered bit.
15 Expansion bit.
16 Miniature drill bits.
17 Multispur bit.
18 Centering bit.
19 Countersink.
20 Spade bit.

21 Screw starter.
22 Bradawl.
23 Gimlet.
24 Automatic center punch.
25 Japanese gimlet.
26 Auger bit file.
27 Auger bit stone.
28 Drill-sharpening jig.

Securing

Joints in cabinetmaking are secured in four basic ways: by glueing, by screwing, by nailing, or by cutting interlocking joints. Frequently two (or more) of these techniques are used together for extra strength. Nails and screws, if used, are hidden by using them inside the article or by sinking the heads and plugging the holes with matching wood.

The armchair shown (right) was made in 1917 in the Cubist style. It appears as though all the pieces of wood are simply rested together, but in fact they are joined with hidden dowel joints. Chairs have to be secured very firmly, as they take strain in all directions.

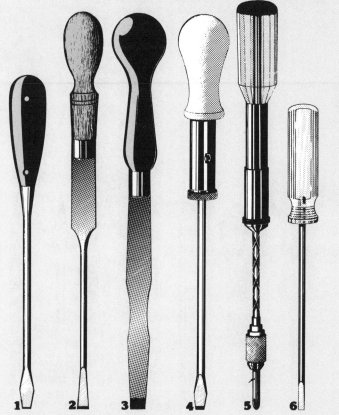

1 **Heavy-duty screwdriver.**
2 **Cabinetmaker's screwdriver.**
3 **London-pattern screwdriver.**
4 **Ratchet screwdriver.**
5 **Spiral ratchet screwdriver.**
6 **Parallel-tipped screwdriver.**

7 **Recessed-head screwdriver.**
8 **Midget screwdriver.**
9 **Wedge screwdriver.**
10 **Brad pusher.**
11 **Nail sets,** a series of tools for recessing the heads of nails.
12 **Glue injector.**
13 **Glue brush.**

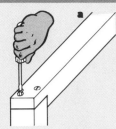
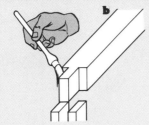
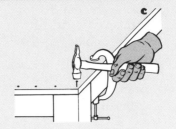
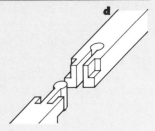

Four methods of securing joints are shown in the illustrations (above).

a A **screwdriver** is used to drive a screw into a pre-drilled hole. Screws can be obtained in all sizes for different tasks.

b Joints may be glued together. The glue is generally warmed to make it penetrate into the wood efficiently, and then brushed on with a **glue brush.** When the glue is tacky the pieces of wood are clamped together to dry.

c Joints may also be secured with nails or panel pins. The nail is struck into the joint with a **hammer; clamps** are often employed to hold the two pieces of wood together so that they will not move out of alignment when the nail is struck.

d Fancy joints are the most attractive and perhaps the most secure way of joining pieces of wood. Male and female parts of the join are cut so that they marry exactly when the pieces are assembled.

1 Steel claw hammer.
2 Pincers for removing old or crooked nails.
3 Warrington-pattern hammer.
4 Pin hammer for striking small nails or brads.
5 Cross pein hammer.

©DIAGRAM

Sanding, finishing, polishing

Wood is given its final smoothness by sanding and polishing the surface. Sanding consists of rubbing the wood with abrasives such as sand and emery; these abrasives are usually incorporated into a paper or pad so that they can be applied easily. The surfaces are finished by applying polish, wax, shellac or other varnishes.

This art nouveau table was made in 1902, and possesses the sinuous curves that were so popular with this genre. The mahogany pieces have been sanded and polished to such a high gloss that they shine as much as the gilt bronze fittings.

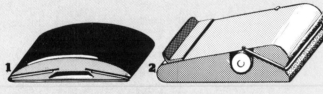

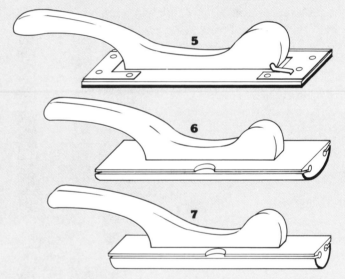

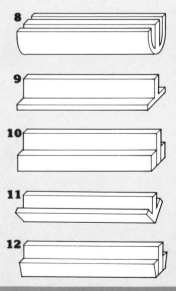

1 Sanding block in a convex shape.
2 Grit sander; this tool takes a belt of abrasive material.
3 Electric file or **belt sander,** used when large areas need to be smoothed.
4 Finishing sander.

5 Flat sanding plane.
6 Convex sanding plane.
7 Half-round sanding plane.
8,9,10,11,12 Contour sanders or **sanding slips,** shaped so that they can be used to smooth complex moldings.

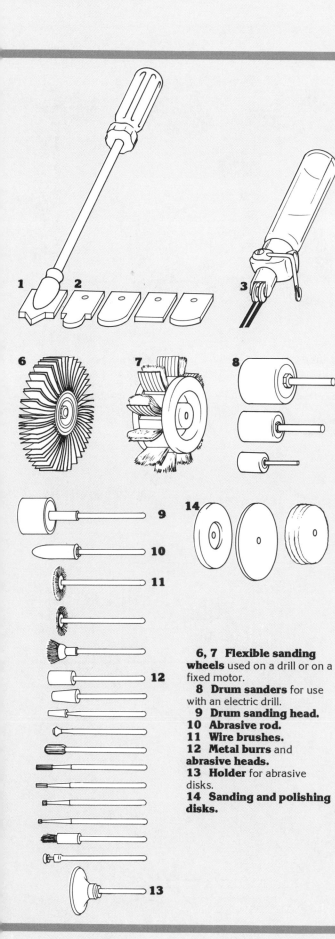

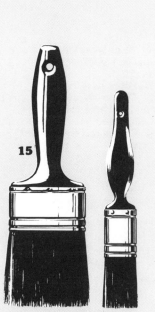

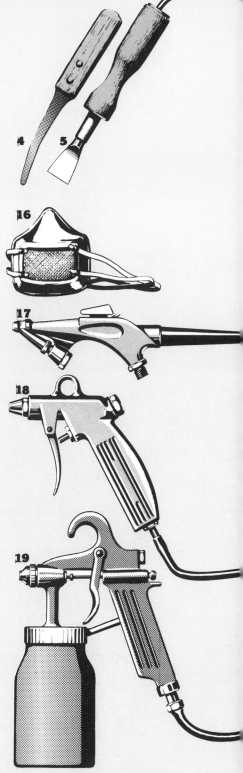

1 **Shaped sander,** used for sanding in awkward corners and joints.
2 Alternative **heads** for the shaped sander.
3 **Line stripper;** this wheel can be used to paint lines of color onto the wood before it is varnished.
4 **Burn-in knife** for applying shellac to blemishes or as a decoration.
5 **Electric burn-in knife.**

6, 7 Flexible sanding wheels used on a drill or on a fixed motor.
8 Drum sanders for use with an electric drill.
9 Drum sanding head.
10 Abrasive rod.
11 Wire brushes.
12 Metal burrs and **abrasive heads.**
13 Holder for abrasive disks.
14 Sanding and polishing disks.

15 Varnish brushes.
16 Respirator, worn for protection against dust particles.
17 Airbrush used for applying stains.
18 Air gun for spraying varnish.
19 Spray gun.

Picture framing

Frames for pictures can be made from many materials, including plastic, metal, papier-mâché and fabric, but the traditional material for classic-style frames is wood. The frame is generally made in four straight pieces, with the corners mitered (cut at a 45° angle) so that they join exactly.

The picture frame illustrated (right) is one designed by Chippendale, and is typical of the elaborate designs of his time. Around the frame, presumably intended for a seascape, are details representing various nautical subjects.

1 Miter template used when marking exact angles in the wood.
2 Miter vise.
3 Corner clamp used to hold the corner while it is being glued.
4 Combined square and miter.

5 Auxiliary vise, a tool for clamping frames as they are secured.
6 Miter guillotine; the slicing action of this tool cuts exact miters.
7 Mat cutter.

8 Framing band and **clamps;** a clamp is placed on each corner, and the band is tightened around the frame until the glue has set.

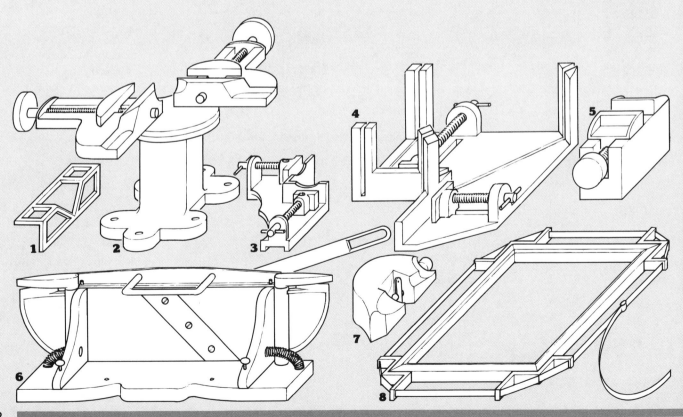

The method of making a simple picture frame is illustrated (below).

a A mat is made for the picture by cutting a piece of mounting card to the correct size for the proposed frame, and then cutting out an opening for the picture.

b The chosen frame molding is cut into the correct lengths for the four sides of the frame, and then an exact 45° miter is cut on each end of the molding pieces.

c The frame corners are joined with glue and with small nails, and clamped while they are drying so that they do not slip out of alignment.

d The picture is assembled in the frame. Glass, if used, is positioned first, followed by the mat, the picture, a protective piece of paper, and then a piece of thin board. The board is held in place by panel pins struck into the frame parallel with the board.

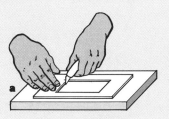
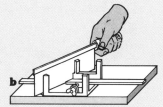

1 Molding scraper; this tool has a contoured blade so that it can reach into molding crevices.
2 Tack hammer.
3 Square-headed hammer, useful for striking in the panel pins that secure the backboard.

4 Screwdriver.
5 Nail set, a punch used to drive nail heads into the wood so that they can be concealed with a plug of wood or plastic wood.
6 Brad driver.
7 Brad squeezer, used to ease brads into the wood.

8 Pincers for positioning spring clamps.
9 Spring miter clamps; the clamps are squeezed into the mitered corners with the pincers, and take the place of glue and nails.

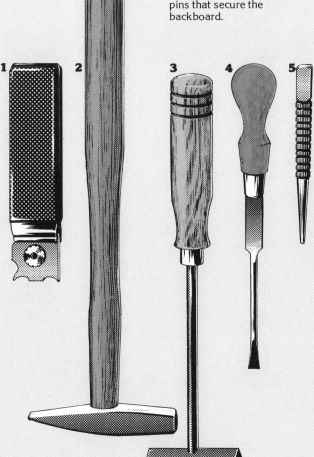
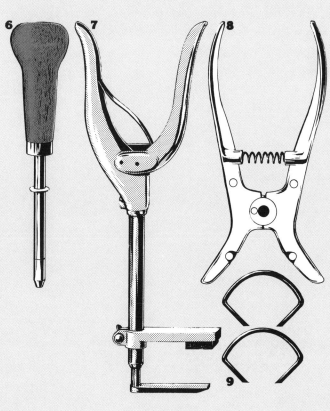

©DIAGRAM

Gesso

Gesso is a medium made basically from a mixture of whiting and animal glue. It produces a very smooth finish that is used as a base coat under oil paintings. Gesso can also be supplemented and thickened with shredded cotton to form a paste that can be modeled and shaped; thick gesso has been used extensively in the past for ornamental frames.

The elaborate mirror frames illustrated on the right were designed by Thomas Chippendale, and come from his "Gentleman and Cabinetmaker's Director." The frames have been built up with layers of thickened gesso.

1 Saucepan for melting the mixture.
2 Glass **stirring rod.**
3 Sharp knife used for shredding cotton.
4 Straining bowl, with a cover of fine muslin.
5 Pestle and mortar.

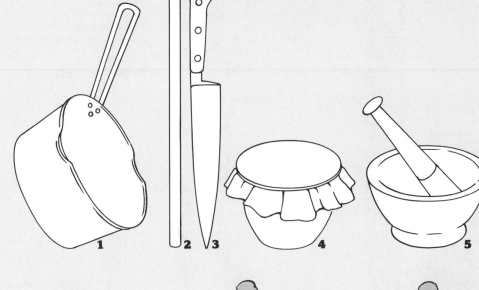

  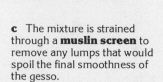

The procedure for making and using gesso is illustrated in the sequence (above).
a Water is added to the glue, and the mixture is boiled in a **saucepan** until the glue has dissolved and become clear and tacky.

b The lumps of whiting are ground to a fine powder with a **pestle and mortar,** and then mixed with the animal glue.

c The mixture is strained through a **muslin screen** to remove any lumps that would spoil the final smoothness of the gesso.

d For a thick gesso, cotton is shredded with a **sharp knife** and added to the mixture.

1 **Sandpaper** used to smooth the wood bases.
2 **Carbon paper.**
3 **Soft rag** for removing sawdust and dirt from the wood before the gesso is applied.
4 **Bristle brush** used for applying a base ground of gesso.
5 Smooth-ended **stylus.**
6 **Palette knife;** this can be used to apply large quantities of gesso.
7 **Soft brushes.**
8 **Clay-modeling tools.**
9 **Bamboo tool.**
10 **Dental probes** used to model the gesso.

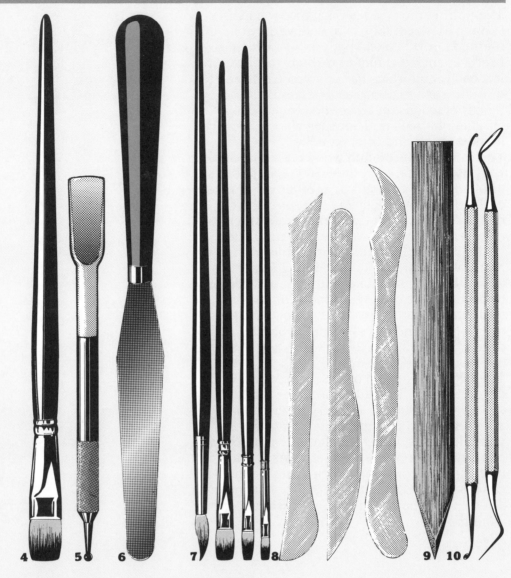

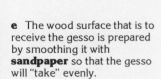

e The wood surface that is to receive the gesso is prepared by smoothing it with **sandpaper** so that the gesso will "take" evenly.

f The design to be interpreted in gesso is transferred to the wood by tracing over **carbon paper** with a smooth-ended **stylus.**

g The gesso is warmed slightly to soften it, and then applied to the wood with **soft brushes** in the pattern areas. It can then be modeled and shaped with a variety of tools, and built up in layers to form a raised design.

h When fully dry, the gesso can be sanded to make it smoother, and can also be painted with water-based paints and then varnished.

10 Wood decoration

The nature of wood makes it a very suitable surface for decorating in a wide variety of methods. It will take a high polish, which is useful in such techniques as high-relief carving; it is easily cut, which has enabled craftsmen to develop such methods as marquetry and inlay. Pieces of wood can be bonded together by laminating them, and because wood is porous it takes stains and colors readily.

The tools for decorating wood are many and various, but a large number of them are cutting implements of one sort or another, since most of the decorative techniques require some cutting of the wood. Carving and gunstock checkering are done with very sharp blades in shapes suitable to the work, while marquetry requires precision cutting of the pieces that are to be fitted together like a jigsaw puzzle. Wood-turning uses strong, sharp tools for shaving away the unwanted wood as the piece is turned on the lathe, and even Philippino bamboo decoration requires special knives to cut the bamboo to size.

The particular appeal of a piece of wood, well decorated and finished, cannot be imitated by any other substance, and very few materials are so satisfying for the craftsman to work upon. It seems, therefore, that no matter how convenient the mass-produced plastic and metal finishes on some articles may be, they can never have the same charm or even opulence as wood that has been lovingly designed and crafted.

The marquetry picture reproduced here depicts a marquetry worker at his trade. He is using a long-handled knife for cutting out the veneers; the knife rests against his shoulder for extra leverage.

Carving

Woodcarving is a craft that has been developed by virtually every nation, as a simple means of decorating this very common material. Woodcarving can be done on all scales; the carving may be as large as a totem pole or as small as the tiniest piece of doll house furniture, and each size of carving has its appropriate tools.

Shown in the photograph (right) are two carved figures that have been shaped out of wood and then stained with color. The particular carving technique used has made a design feature of the parallel cuts made by the chisels.

Illustrated (below) are some traditional Sumatran woodcarving tools.
1,2 Chisels.
3 Mallet, worn almost hollow from constant blows to the ends of the chisels.

Many of the tools for woodcarving are variations on basic **chisels** and **gouges;** a fuller range of these tools is illustrated in the wood sculpture section.

4 Chisel.
5 Gouge.
6,7 Sloyd knives.
8 Carver's hook.
9 Hobby knife.
10 Carving knife with a laminated steel blade.

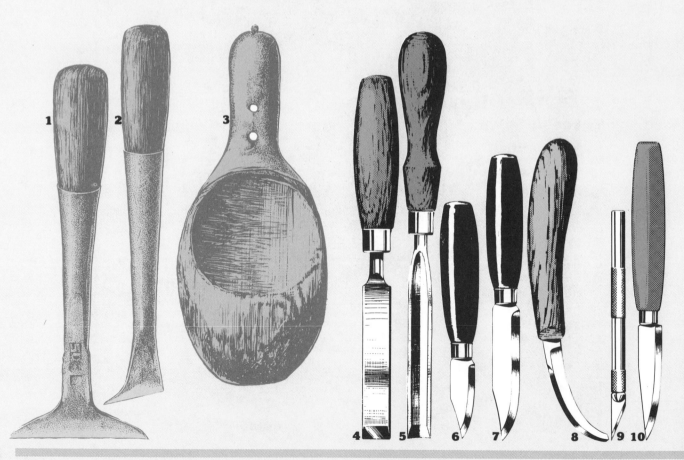

1 Woodcarver's punch; the punch is struck into the wood with a mallet, and stamps a pattern.
2 Alternative designs in which the punches can be obtained.

3 Rotary tool driven by electricity, fitted with a flexible shaft.
4 Heads for the rotary tool; these take the form of rasps and burrs.

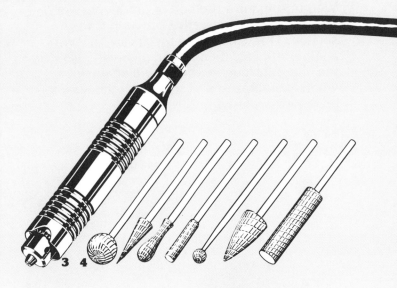

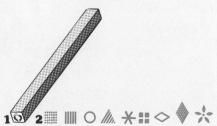

5 Detail knife.
6 Alternative blades for the detail knife.
7 Whittling knife.
8 Alternative blades for the whittling knife.
9 Miniature carving tool.
10 Alternative blades for the miniature tool.
11 Carving knife with its own protective cap.
12 Carving plane.
13,14 Heavy-duty scrapers.
15 Incising head.
16 Sharpening tool embedded with slivers of diamond.
17 Straight rasp.
18 File.
19 Bent riffler.
20 Riffler.
21 Needle file.

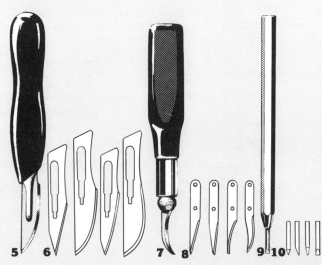

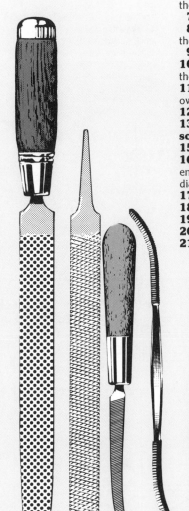

Woodturning 1

Woodturning is a method of producing wood shapes that are perfectly circular in cross section. This is achieved by placing the wood in a lathe, which is then turned at a high speed; the sharp turning tools are held against the wood as it rotates, and so cut an even incision all the way around.

The wood engraving reproduced here was made by the English artist Thomas Bewick, and depicts a wood turner at his lathe. His tools are behind him, on the window ledge, and in the rack on the wall.

1 Bow-driven lathe; the bow is moved up and down (or back and forth if held horizontal) and spins the lathe.
2 Treadle-driven lathe; this works on the same principle as the bow lathe, but the cord is driven by a foot treadle so that both hands are free for the work.

Centers of various designs are used to hold the wood securely in the lathe.
3 Dead center.
4 Revolving center.
5 Cup or **ring center.**
6 Two-pronged center.
7 Four-pronged center.
8 Modern lathe powered by electricity.

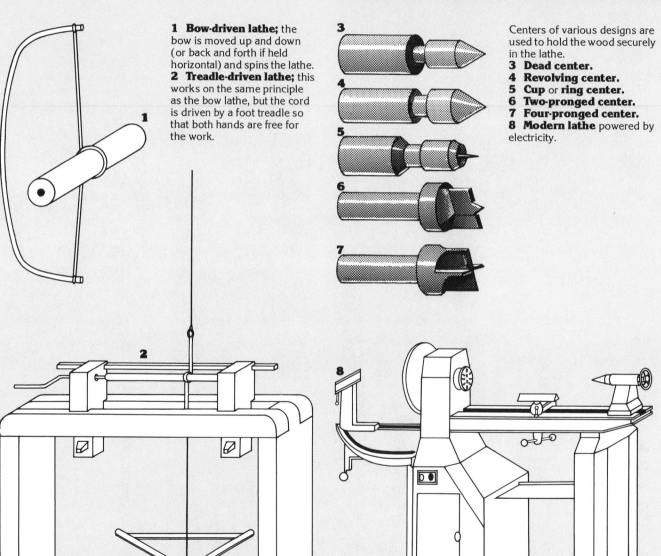

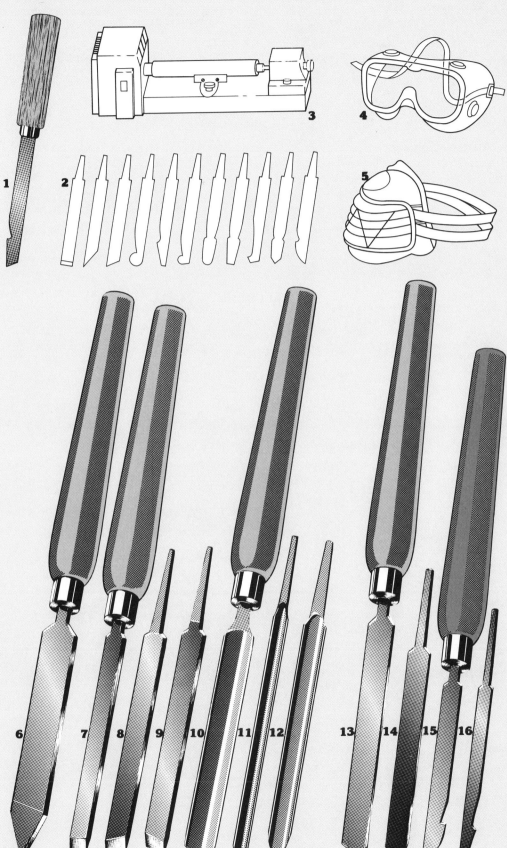

1,2 Miniature turning tools, only 7 inches in length. These tools are available in all the customary tool shapes, scaled down for miniature work.
3 Miniature lathe.
4 Safety goggles give protection from flying slivers of wood.
5 Dust mask should be worn when working with wood that gives off powdery sawdust.

Turning tools are strong-bladed chisels that carve into the wood as they are held against it.
 6 Parting tool, used for making the first incisions into the wood.
 7 Chisel tool.
 8 Skew right chisel.
 9 Skew left chisel.
 10 Roughing gouge.
 11 Spindle gouge.
 12 Deep gouge.
 13 Scraper.
 14 Round scraper.
 15,16 Side-cutting tools.

Woodturning 2

Oilstones and **slipstones,** such as those illustrated below, are used to keep the turning tools razor-sharp so that they cut efficiently and safely when held against the wood. Some of the stones are shaped linto curves so that the gouges can be sharpened easily.

A **strop,** illustrated (left), is used for the final honing of the newly sharpened tools. The strop is used as shown below; the tool is run across the leather strip so that its bevel is at the same angle as the leather.

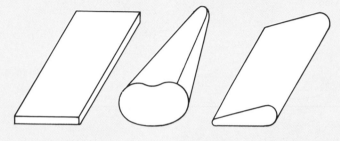

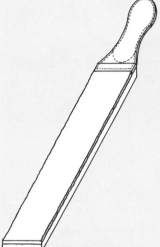

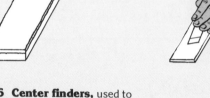

Other **woodturning accessories** are shown (below).
1 Sizing attachment used when forming columns of a specific diameter. When the correct dimension is reached, the attachment drops over the column and fits exactly.

2 Vernier caliper used when making exactly fitting lids and stoppers for turned articles.
3 Internal dial caliper.
4 Dividers.

5,6 Center finders, used to locate the exact center of wood cylinders.
7 Extendable steel rule.

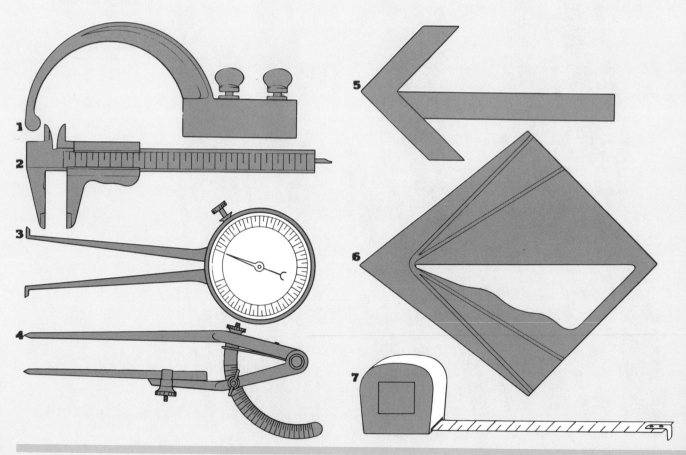

Laminating

Laminating is the technique of sandwiching layers of different woods together so that they produce a stratified effect on the sides intended to be seen. Laminated wood can be cut and shaped once the layers have bonded fully. It can also be fixed into a lathe and turned in the same way as any other wood.

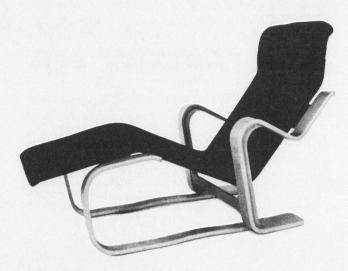

Shown in the photograph on the right is a chair made using laminated wood. The frame was formed by sandwiching together layers of wood of various colors, and then bending the frame to shape it to the required contours.

1 Steel ruler.
2 Set square.
3 360° protractor.
4 Miter block, used to cut exact angles in wood to be joined.
5 Marking gauge.

6 Bolt attachment, used for clamping pieces of wood while they are being glued.
7,8 Dowel cutters.
9 Plug cutter.
10 Dowel centers.
11 Doweling jig.
12 Jigsaw.
13 Smoothing plane.

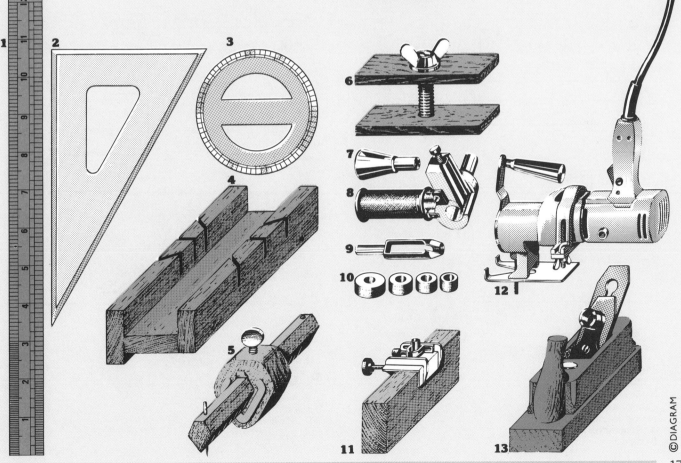

©DIAGRAM

Marquetry and veneering

Marquetry and veneering are related crafts that both use very thin slices of wood, known as veneers. Veneering involves applying or inlaying veneer of one color; in marquetry, veneers of different colors, shades and patterns are laid out to form a picture. The grain of a veneer reflects the tree that it was taken from and the way in which it was cut.

This example of marquetry (right) is a tabletop worked in a variety of woods of different tone and grain. The tabletop was made in the mid 18th century, and is attributed to the craftsman Oeben.

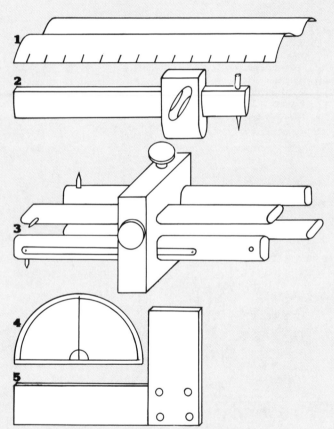

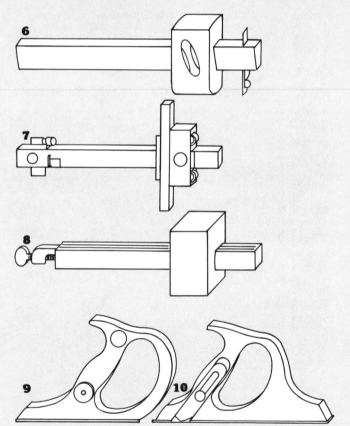

1 **M-section rule;** pressure can be applied to prevent the veneer from slipping during the cut.
2 **Marking gauge.**
3 **Compound marking gauge,** with four limbs that can be set individually.
4 **Protractor.**
5 **T-square.**

6 **Cutting gauge.**
7 **Inlay cutter;** this tool can be used to cut many shapes in the veneers.
8 **Mortise gauge.**
9 **Edge cutter** for trimming veneered edges.
10 **Strip cutter** used to make strips of veneer.

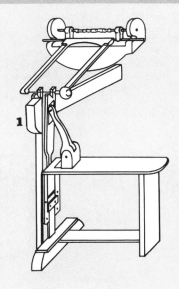

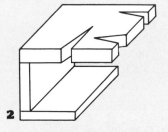

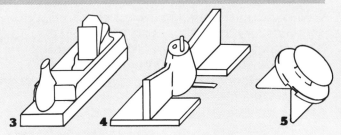

1 Marquetry cutter's donkey, a frame saw powered by foot so that both hands are free to move the veneer in relation to the blade.

2 Fretsaw cutting table, a multiple bench pin with slots of several sizes for use when sawing veneers.

3 Toothing plane, a plane with a serrated blade used to score marquetry grounds so that the glue will hold.

4 Router plane, used to cut out inlay recesses.

5 Corner trimmer used to even up perpendicular veneered surfaces.

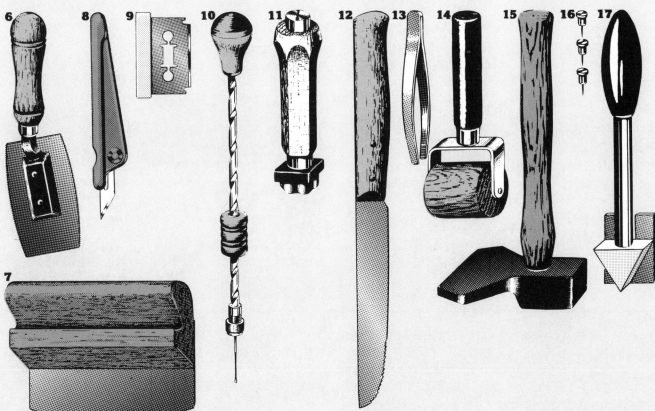

6,7 Veneer saws in two traditional patterns. The curved blades help to prevent the veneers from slipping or tearing as they are cut.

8 Marquetry knife.

9 Razor blade.

10 Fretwork drill used to make holes for the fretsaw.

11 Veneer punch, an irregularly shaped punch used when replacing damaged veneer. The wood surrounding the blemish is cut with the punch and removed, and then the punch is used to cut a replacement piece that will fit exactly.

12 Veneer knife.

13 Tweezers used for positioning tiny pieces.

14 Veneer roller used for smoothing veneered surfaces.

15 Veneer hammer, used not for striking but for applying pressure to the veneer after it has been glued into position.

16 Veneer pins used to hold the veneers in place while they are secured. The tiny points will not damage or mark the veneers.

17 Trimming chisel used to trim veneered edges.

Gunstock checkering

Gunstock checkering is a craft that grew out of a necessary task—that of providing a secure handgrip on gunstocks. In order to break the smooth surface of the stock, the wood is covered in the region of the grip with hundreds of tiny, even, crisscross lines, placed so that they form lozenges across the wood.

The shotgun illustrated (below) is an American example, and shows the traditional checkering on the stock. The diamond shapes of the checkering are arranged to fall along the stock, so that they do not cut across the grain unnecessarily.

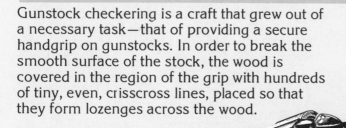

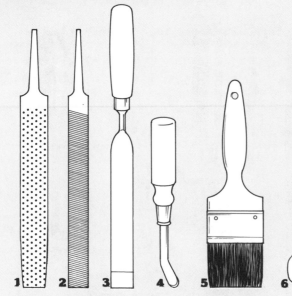

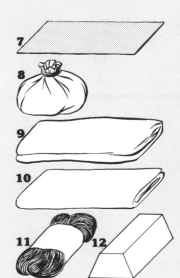

1 **Rasp** for preliminary preparation of the wood.
2 **File.**
3 **Chisel** used for shaping uneven parts of the stock.
4 **Heavy-duty scraper.**
5 **Soft brush** for staining and varnishing.
6 **Swab** for applying varnish.
7 **Sandpaper.**
8 **French polish rubber.**
9 **Wool pad** used for buffing.
10 **Soft cloth.**
11 **Wire wool** used for rubbing down coats of varnish.
12 **Tripoli wax** for polishing.

Checkering tools may be made at home by the craftsman; the following sequence shows the procedure for making a two-line **spacing tool.**
a The end of a steel rod is heated and then hammered so that it is square in section.

b The tool handle is cranked slightly to give it an angle, and then a square-bottomed groove is cut in the underside of the tool with a **hacksaw.**

c The sides of the tool are cut away at an angle so that each side of the tool is slanted to the same degree.

d Tiny teeth are cut into the sloping side of each blade, using a very small **triangular file.** The teeth should be evenly spaced so that they will cut through the wood cleanly.

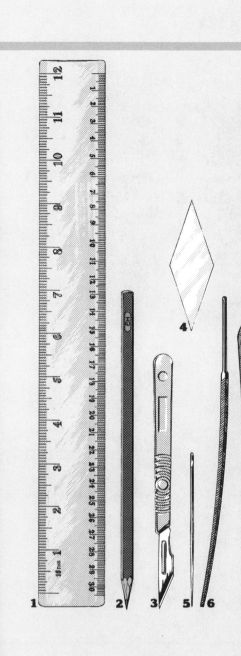

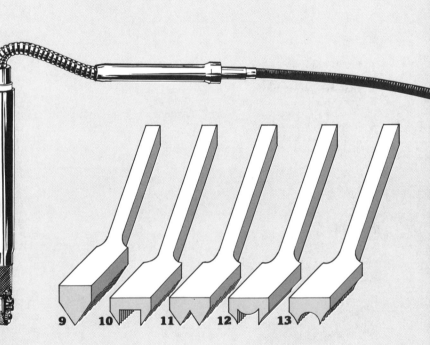

1 Plastic ruler; the flexibility of the plastic enables it to be bent slightly to conform to the shape of the stock.
2 Hard pencil.
3 Scalpel.
4 Diamond template, used to ensure that the two rows of lines are at the correct angle to one another.
5 Needle.
6 Bent needle file.
7 Narrow grooving tool.
8 Electric checkering head.

9 V-grooving tool.
10 Spacer for square-topped checkering.
11 Spacer for diamond-topped checkering.
12 Concave border tool used for making the final border around the checkered area.
13 Convex border tool.

The checkering patterns are made in the following way.
a The **diamond template** is laid along two sides of the area to be checkered, and two adjoining sides are marked with a **needle** or a sharp **pencil.**

b These lines are extended to the limit of the design, and then they are marked into the wood with the appropriate **spacing tool.** The spacing tool is then used to mark all the crisscross lines parallel with the first two guide lines.

c Each of the lines is deepened and regulated with a **grooving tool;** the shape of the final checkers will depend on the shape of the grooving tool used.

d The border of the pattern, where all the grooves have terminated, is neatened and shaped with a **border tool;** this may have either a concave or a convex section. The design is then polished and waxed.

Philippino bamboo decoration

Bamboo is a ubiquitous plant in many tropical countries, and is used for numerous ethnic arts and crafts. The natives of the Philippine Islands have developed their own attractive method of decorating bamboo wood; the technique involves attaching colored paper to the wood, and then boiling the bamboo to transfer the color to the wood.

The containers illustrated (right) have been decorated with the traditional Philippino technique. Each line of pattern has been produced on the bamboo wood by dyed paper cutouts or colored twine.

1 Small knife for cutting manila paper for the stencils.
2 Bark-trimming knife.
3 Curved knife used to slice the bamboo into sections.
4 Loguitip, a sandpaper-like leaf that is used for smoothing the bamboo.

5 Small basin for dissolving the dyes.
6 Betel nuts; these are used for polishing the wood.
7 Large basin carved out of wood.

The bamboo decoration is carried out as follows.
a A length of bamboo is trimmed of protruding bark, and then cut into long sections.
b The section is sanded with the abrasive **loguitip leaf.**
c Geometric shapes are cut out of dyed paper, and these are pasted onto the bamboo. Dyed twine is also wrapped around the cylinder.
d The tube is wrapped tightly in banana leaves and secured with twine, and then the entire object is boiled for several minutes; the heat causes the dye to transfer from the paper to the wood.
e The twine, leaves and paper are removed from the bamboo, and when the wood is dry it is polished with the meat from **betel nuts.**

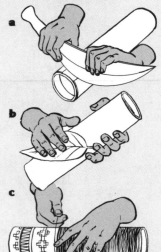

Pyrography

Pyrography, or pokerwork, is the art of decorative wood-burning. The name pokerwork comes from the first tool used for burning designs into wood—that is, an ordinary domestic hearth poker, which was heated in the open fire. Pyrographers today can use home-made patterned tools, or special electric pokers.

The panel illustrated (right) is a picture executed in pyrography by Ralph Marshall. The panel is dated 1834, and was copied from a painting by Henry Morland; the rich effects of light and shade are typical of pyrography at the height of its popularity.

1 Clamp used to hold the work while it is being decorated.
2 Bunsen burner for heating home-made tools.
3 Home-made poker; the head has been patterned with a file, and inserted into a wood handle.

4 Alternative heads for the home-made poker.
5 Electric poker and **stand;** the tip is heated by an electric current.
6 Alternative heads for the electric poker.

The principle of pyrography is the same whether a **poker, home-made** or **electric tools** are used.
a The tool is allowed to heat until its tip glows red hot.
b It is then held against the wood, and the pattern on the end of the head will burn itself into the wood's surface. The heads with plain ends can be drawn across the wood to scribe various lines.

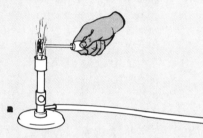

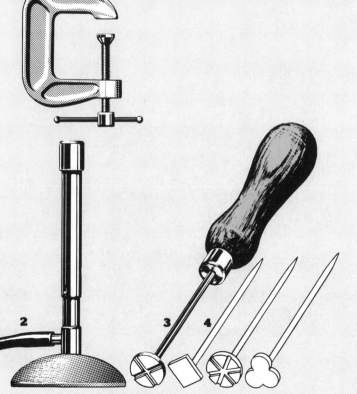

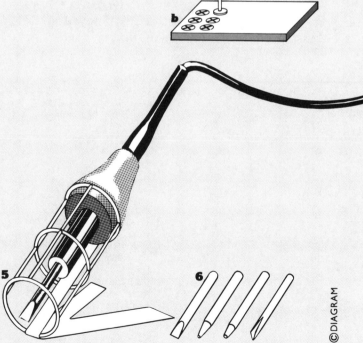

©DIAGRAM

11 Working with glass

Glass is a unique material, quite unlike any other medium used in the arts and crafts. When it is heated it becomes molten, but rather than being a liquid like molten metal, it is then viscous and malleable rather like plastic. When cool, glass solidifies into an extremely brittle solid which can not readily be carved or filed. It is one of the few craft materials that is generally transparent or translucent, and perhaps this characteristic above all has resulted in its widespread use for objects that combine beauty and utility.

The tools for working with glass can be divided into two kinds: those for shaping hot, molten glass, and those for working with cool, solid glass. Molten glass can be bent, stretched, molded, stamped, colored and blown, and tools have evolved to aid in all these actions. Solid glass can be cut, chipped, faceted, engraved and etched, and once again glassworking has its own tools for each process.

Apart from the advent of mechanization, the tools for glassworking have differed very little since the invention of each technique; depictions of 15th century glassblowers show them using blowpipes and pontils identical to those in use today. The main areas where glassworking is changing is in the development of new techniques. Modern materials can be used with glass, such as the concrete in which dalle-de-verre is set and the epoxy putty or resin used for mock stained glass and appliqué glass. The art nouveau and art deco movements in particular did much to develop new and beautiful methods of decorating glass.

The print reproduced here illustrates glassblowers from Diderot's "Encyclopedia of Industries." The pictures show the progress of a blown goblet from the attaching of the foot to its annealing in a slowly cooling oven.

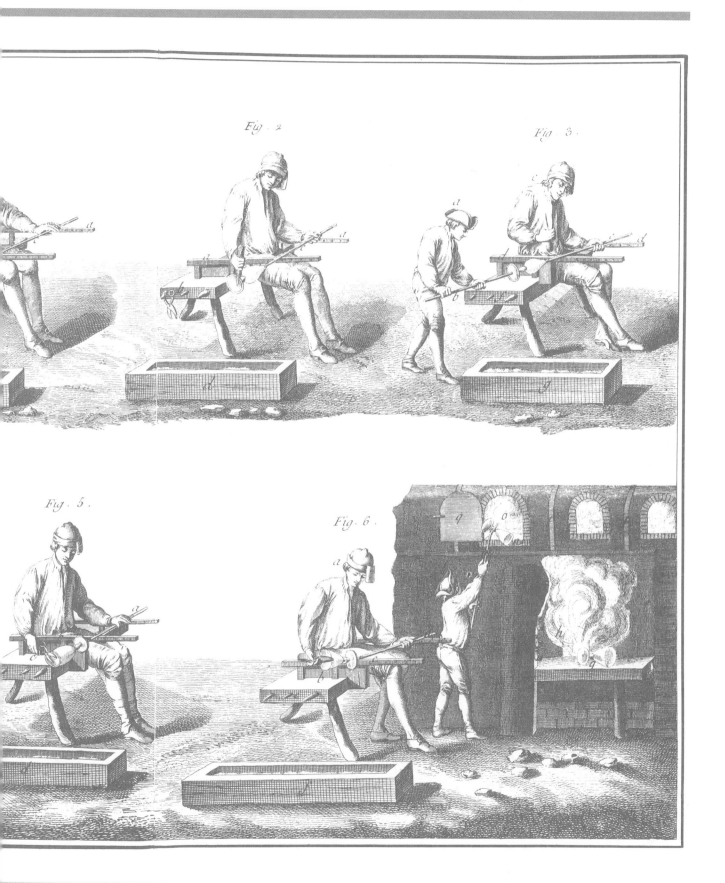

Fig. 2.

Fig. 3.

Fig. 5.

Fig. 6.

Glassblowing

Glassblowing was invented by the Syrians in the first century BC; they discovered that if molten glass was gathered on the end of a hollow rod, air could be blown down the rod to create a hollow vessel from the glass. The first blown glass was formed by blowing it into molds, but craftsmen later developed the technique of glassblowing without molds.

The photograph (right) illustrates one stage in the process of blowing a glass bowl. The vessel has been shaped and the bubble cut open at the mouth, and the rim of the bowl is being opened out with tongs.

Glass is formed mainly of silica, and the source of silica that is generally used is sand. The properties of the glass formed depend on the type of sand used, the additional materials used as fluxes, colorants and catalysts, and the method and speed of fusing the ingredients. The various materials are shoveled into a **crucible,** which is then placed in a **furnace** and fired; the heat causes the materials to melt and fuse into a viscous liquid, which when cooled forms brittle glass.

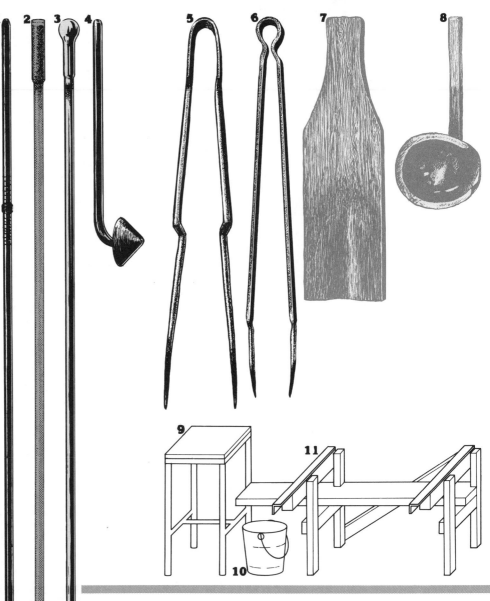

  1 Blowing iron.
  2 Pontil or **punty.**
  3 Gathering iron.
  4 Angled blowing iron.
  5 Jacks, used for shaping the necks and feet of blown vessels.
  6 Tweezers are used for nipping in the molten glass.
  7,8 Paddle and **wooden block,** used to regulate the shapes of blown items.
  9 Marver, a steel table for rolling the "gather" of molten glass.
10 Bucket used for cooling tools.
11 Glassblower's bench; the blowpipes can be laid across the flat arms.

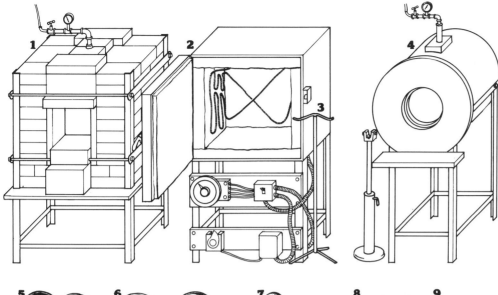

Glass for glassblowing is melted in a **furnace;** in large establishments the furnace runs continuously so that molten glass is always available.

1 Glassmelting furnace.
2 Annealing oven; the temperature of the oven is reduced slowly so that the glass does not develop flaws.
3 Pipe stand, used when heating the pipes at the furnace mouth.
4 Glory hole; if the glass loses any of its malleability during blowing, it is softened by holding it in this small furnace.

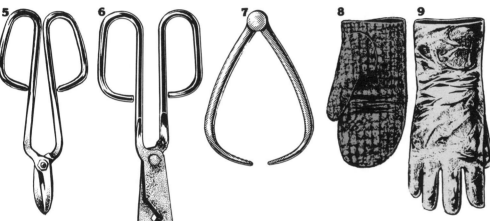

5,6 Glass shears; glass can be easily cut with these thick, strong blades.
7 Calipers used for checking measurements.
8 Asbestos mitt, used for protection from the heat.
9 Protective glove.

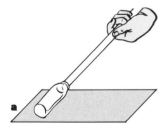

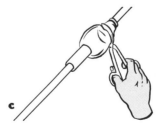

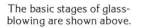

The basic stages of glass-blowing are shown above.
a A "gather" of molten glass is taken up on the **blowing iron** and rolled on the **marver** to ensure that it is even. This also slightly cools the outside layer so that the blowing will not burst it.

b A bubble of air is blown down the iron into the molten glass. This bubble is then increased by blowing until the glass is the desired shape, size and thickness.

c The **pontil** is attached to the tip of the glass, and the bubble is severed from the blowing iron by cutting it with **shears** or **snips,** or by dribbling a little water around the neck to cool the glass and then striking it firmly.

d The hollow vessel is then shaped as required. Extra molten glass for handles or feet is applied with the **gathering iron.** If at any stage the glass begins to lose its malleability it is returned briefly to the **furnace** to soften it slightly.

Patterned glass

a

b

c

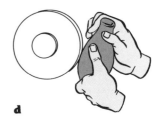

d

Cameo glass, such as the famous Portland Vase, is made from two different colors of molten glass.
a A vessel is formed (in this case, blown) from glass of one color; this will be the inner surface of the final vessel.

b When this vessel is slightly cooler, it is dipped into a container of molten glass of a different color so that it receives a coating of the second color. The vessel is now formed of two layers of glass.

c The chosen design is drawn onto the glass with a **wax pencil** or a **diamond-point engraver.**

d The glass around the design is cut away until the underneath layer of glass is reached. This leaves a relief design in one color of glass on a background of a different color.

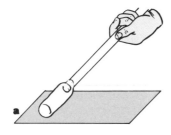

a

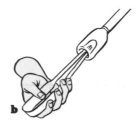

b

c

d

Air twists, which are often seen in the stems of wine glasses, are formed in the following way.
a A short, thick cylinder of glass is formed by taking a "gather" of glass and rolling it evenly on a **marver.**

b Several indentations are made in the end of the cylinder; the bigger the bubble that is required, the deeper the indentation must be.

c The ends of the indentations are sealed with molten glass. This traps air in the glass, forming bubbles in the cylinder.

d The cylinder is then heated to make it pliable. It can now be pulled out to a narrow rod suitable for a stem, and twisted so that the elongated air bubbles form spirals.

a

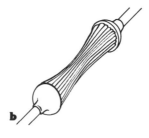

b

c

d

Millefiori means "thousand flowers," and is a method of glassworking that results in many tiny flower shapes packed together.
a Thin canes of colored glass are bundled together around a colored core, and are heated until they have fused.

b Each end of the bundle of canes is fitted into a special **cup.** The glass is then heated and the cups are drawn apart so that they stretch the bundle of canes until it is narrow and long.

c Rods made in this way are then sliced across, producing patterned disks. Several disks are packed together in a **mold,** and the spaces between the disks are filled with clear molten glass.

d If a paperweight or a similar object is being made, a thick dome of clear glass is dolloped onto the millefiori; this dome acts as a magnifier so that the minute detail of the colored "flowers" can be seen.

Flameworking

Flameworking is the manipulation of glass rods that have been heated to make them pliable. Flameworking was originally known as lampworking, and was used to form microscope lenses over a type of small oil lamp. The glass rods used for flameworking are traditionally clear, although colored rods can easily be obtained.

The small glass animal photographed here is typical of the kind of glass produced by flameworking. The animal has been formed from a solid lump of glass that has been softened by heating and then pulled into shape.

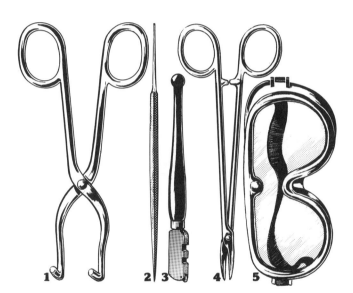

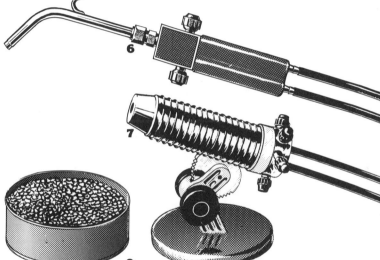

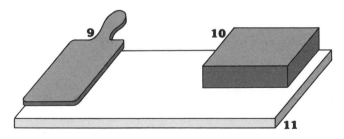

1 **Pincers** used to bend the glass.
2 **Triangular file** for scoring the glass along break lines.
3 **Glass cutter.**
4 **Forceps.**
5 **Protective goggles.**
6 **Hand torch.**
7 **Blow torch** on stand.

8 **Annealing tin** full of heat-retaining material.
9 **Carbon paddle** for shaping the glass.
10 **Carbon block.**
11 **Asbestos board** used to protect the working surface from heat.

The method for flameworking is illustrated above.
a The chosen rod is heated in the flame of a **torch** so that it can be manipulated. The glass is shaped into the required form by bending and pulling the molten rod.

b The finished form is then placed in an **annealing tin;** this allows the glass to cool very slowly, so preventing it from developing stress marks as it cools.

©DIAGRAM

Etching and engraving glass

Etching and engraving are two methods of decorating glass by removing minute amounts of glass from the surface of the object. In the etching process this is done by painting controlled amounts of weak acid onto the areas to be patterned; engraving consists of scraping or cutting away the surface so that a pattern appears.

Illustrated on the right is a wheel-engraved glass goblet. The bowl shown on the left is an example of glass etching, reproduced from the 1895 Harrod's catalog.

1 Brush used for painting on the acid.
2 Craft knife, used to cut away the pattern if a stencil is made of plastic film.
3 Razor blade.
4 Stylus.
5,6 Scrapers.

Hydrofluoric acid used on its own will produce a clear etch, which is a completely smooth indentation on the glass. If the acid is mixed with a bifluoride, such as ammonium bifluoride, the etch will have a frosted, slightly rough, appearance.

Most acids will not attack glass, so glass etching is a relatively modern technique made possible by the discovery of the properties of hydrofluoric acid. A 50% solution of this acid is sufficient to etch glass very quickly; 10% will yield a light etch.

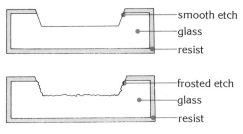

- smooth etch
- glass
- resist

- frosted etch
- glass
- resist

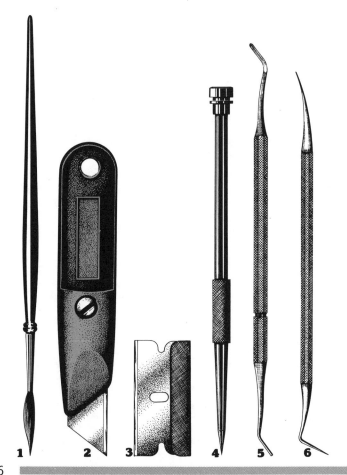

1 2 3 4 5 6

a   b

The principle of etching glass is shown in the two steps above.
a The parts of the glass that are not to be etched are painted with shellac, wax, or a similar acid-resistant substance. Alternatively, a resist stencil can be applied.

b When the resist has set, acid is painted over the glass and eats into the parts not covered with the resist. When the glass is etched to the required depth, the acid is rinsed off in water and the resist is removed with a solvent.

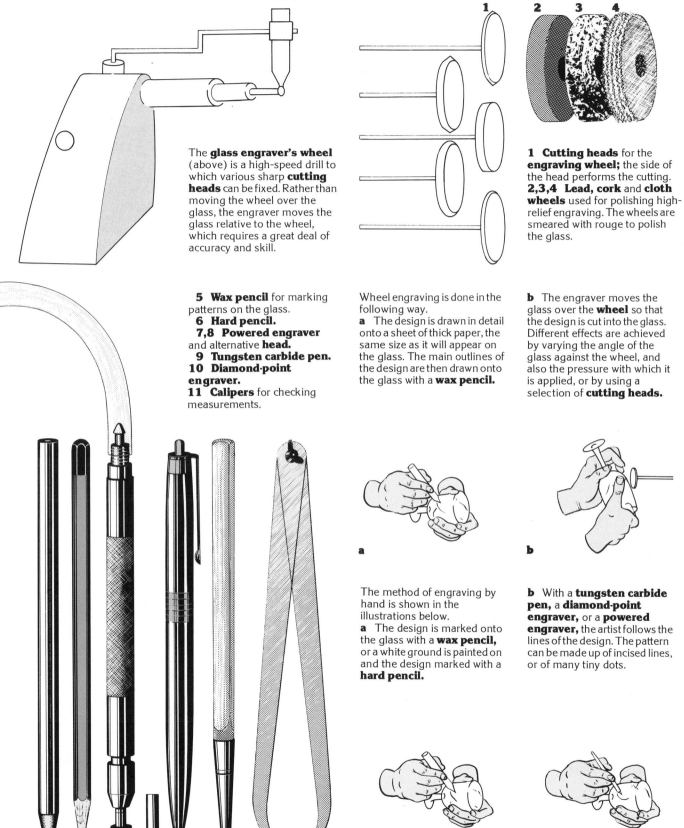

The **glass engraver's wheel** (above) is a high-speed drill to which various sharp **cutting heads** can be fixed. Rather than moving the wheel over the glass, the engraver moves the glass relative to the wheel, which requires a great deal of accuracy and skill.

1 Cutting heads for the **engraving wheel;** the side of the head performs the cutting. **2,3,4 Lead, cork** and **cloth wheels** used for polishing high-relief engraving. The wheels are smeared with rouge to polish the glass.

5 Wax pencil for marking patterns on the glass.
6 Hard pencil.
7,8 Powered engraver and alternative **head.**
9 Tungsten carbide pen.
10 Diamond-point engraver.
11 Calipers for checking measurements.

Wheel engraving is done in the following way.
a The design is drawn in detail onto a sheet of thick paper, the same size as it will appear on the glass. The main outlines of the design are then drawn onto the glass with a **wax pencil.**

b The engraver moves the glass over the **wheel** so that the design is cut into the glass. Different effects are achieved by varying the angle of the glass against the wheel, and also the pressure with which it is applied, or by using a selection of **cutting heads.**

a

b

The method of engraving by hand is shown in the illustrations below.
a The design is marked onto the glass with a **wax pencil,** or a white ground is painted on and the design marked with a **hard pencil.**

b With a **tungsten carbide pen,** a **diamond-point engraver,** or a **powered engraver,** the artist follows the lines of the design. The pattern can be made up of incised lines, or of many tiny dots.

a

b

5 6 7 8 9 10 11

©DIAGRAM

Stained glass 1

Leaded stained glass has for centuries been associated with grand architecture, especially with ecclesiastical buildings. Stained glass panels are now found in all manner of buildings, and, because of the influence of Louis Comfort Tiffany, as three-dimensional objects ranging from lampshades to room dividers.

The stained glass panel shown (right) depicts a medieval pedlar with his wares strapped to his back. The panel has been made from relatively few pieces of glass, and these have been painted to provide the extra detail required.

1 **Soft pencil** for designing and tracing the pattern to be cut.
2 **Soft wax pencil** used for writing on the glass.
3 **Steel rule** used for marking straight lines.
4 **Carbon paper** is useful for marking dark glass for cutting.
5 **Pounce bag;** white pounce is shaken over the carbon line to make it show up on the dark glass.
6 **Double-bladed cutter** for template cutting. The gap between the blades equals the width of the lead strips that will hold the glass.

7 **Glass cutter** with a steel wheel. The cutter is used to score the glass before breaking, and to nibble off surplus glass.
8 **Tapper** used to tap the underside of the scoreline so that the glass will break cleanly.
9 **Glass** or **plate pliers** can be used to break small pieces of glass along the scorelines.
10 **Grozing pliers** remove uneven pieces of glass from the cut shape.
11 **Circle cutter** scores perfect circles on the glass.
12 **Light box** used as an aid to accuracy during the assembly of the glass.

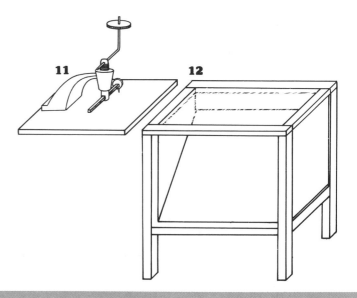

Glass for leaded panels may be prepared as follows.

a A full-size copy of the design is traced onto paper or cloth. This copy can then be used as a guide to mark the pattern lines onto a large sheet of plain glass that will act as a temporary base for the panel.

b The original design is cut into separate pieces, and each piece is used as a template. The template is laid over glass of the appropriate color, and scored round with a **cutter;** this scoreline is tapped and the excess glass is broken off.

c The pieces of colored glass are placed in position on the clear glass with wax, so that the entire panel can be held to the light for inspection. Paint, a type of vitreous enamel, is applied in the areas that require extra detail or special effects.

d The pieces of colored glass are placed on **racks** in a **kiln;** they are then fired at a moderate heat until the paint is bonded onto the glass permanently. When the glass pieces have cooled they are ready to be glazed.

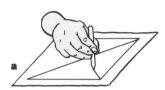

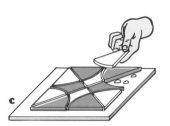

Brushes of many sorts are used to apply paint to the glass before the piece is fired to make the paint permanent.
1 Stippling brush used to dab color onto the glass to produce gradations of tone.
2 Large stippling brush.
3,4,5 Wooden stick, needle point and **quill** are all used to vary and refine the surface of the paint after it has been applied to the glass.
6 Broad hog brush for laying color washes and painting bold strokes.
7 Broad soft brush ideal for delicate strokes and for working with oil-based enamel paints.

8 Mottling brush used to apply matt color to large areas.
9 Badger brush, an excellent matting brush.
10 Firing kiln.
11 Kiln fork for placing the glass in the kiln.
12 Mixing tray for paints.
13 Glass bell preserves the moisture content of paints and stains.

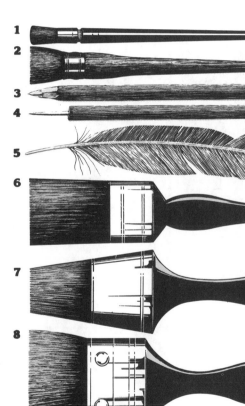

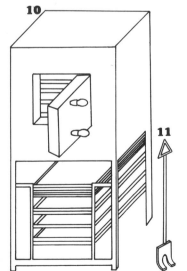

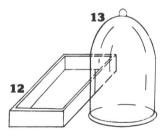

Stained glass 2

Glazing is the process of placing the glass pieces in their correct positions and fixing them with lead edgings. The strips of lead are known as cames or leads.
a In order to remove any kinks and to strengthen the lead the cames are gently pulled through a **lead vise.**

b Wood battens are nailed to the worksurface at right angles to each other; these will then serve as guides for two sides of the panel. Two edging cames are put in place and a **lathekin** is used to open up the leaves of the leads.

c The first piece of glass is fitted into the corner. It is knocked home with a stopping knife. A piece of lead came is placed around the glass, cut off at the correct angle, and pushed firmly against the glass with the knife.

d Once a glass shape and a came have been fitted together, **farrier's nails** are used to ensure that they are held firmly in place. All the glass pieces and the leads are assembled in this way, and when they are all in place the final outside cames are fitted.

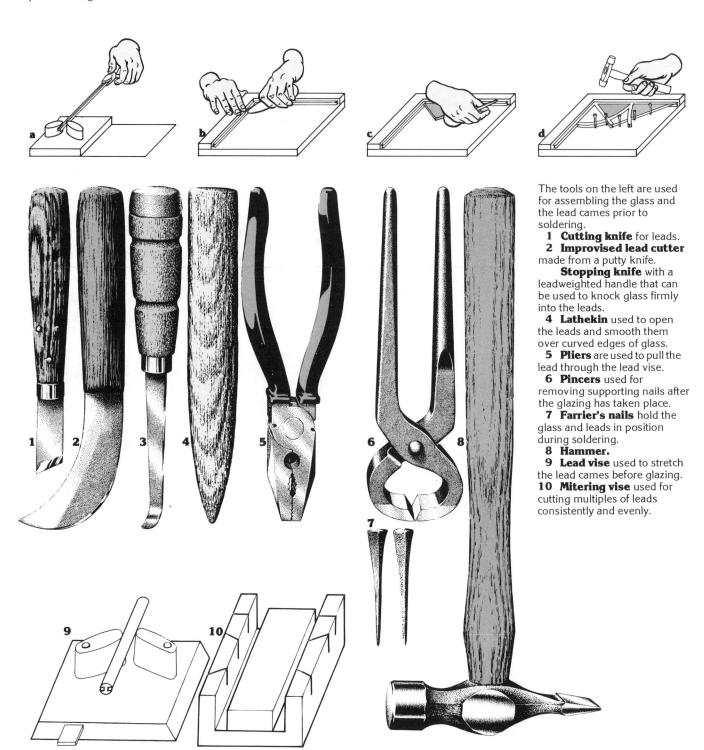

The tools on the left are used for assembling the glass and the lead cames prior to soldering.
1 Cutting knife for leads.
2 Improvised lead cutter made from a putty knife.
Stopping knife with a leadweighted handle that can be used to knock glass firmly into the leads.
4 Lathekin used to open the leads and smooth them over curved edges of glass.
5 Pliers are used to pull the lead through the lead vise.
6 Pincers used for removing supporting nails after the glazing has taken place.
7 Farrier's nails hold the glass and leads in position during soldering.
8 Hammer.
9 Lead vise used to stretch the lead cames before glazing.
10 Mitering vise used for cutting multiples of leads consistently and evenly.

Soldering joins the lead cames together so that the glass is held securely.

a The panel is scrubbed with a **wire brush** to clean it ready for soldering. Flux is then painted onto the lead joins to encourage the solder to "take" on the metal.

b Using a heated **soldering iron** each joint is soldered. The solder stick is held against the joint so that it will flow exactly where it is needed as soon as it becomes molten. When the solder has set, the two pieces of lead are permanently joined.

c The panel is turned over and all the joints are soldered on the reverse side to provide added strength. Any joints that need resoldering once the solder is dry are first cleaned with a **flat file.**

d The panel is weather-proofed if it is to be used in the outside wall of a building. This is done by painting the joints with cement putty and pressing the cames down to firm them. Excess putty is cleaned away with a **pointed stick.**

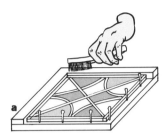

Shown on the right are tools used for soldering a stained glass panel.

1 Wire brush used to clean the panel before it is soldered.
2 Stiff-bristled brush for painting flux onto the joints to be soldered.
3 Flat file used to correct a poor solder. The surface of the lead is filed down so that a new solder can be made.
4 Pointed stick; any excess putty is removed with this.
5 Scrub brush used to distribute cement putty evenly over the panel.
6 Electric soldering iron with a **stand;** the hot iron can be placed on the stand for safety when it is not being held.

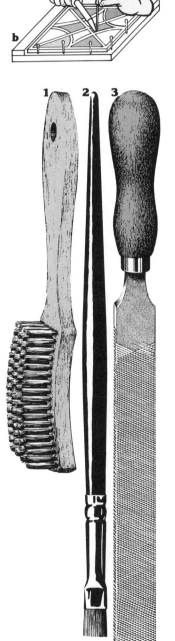

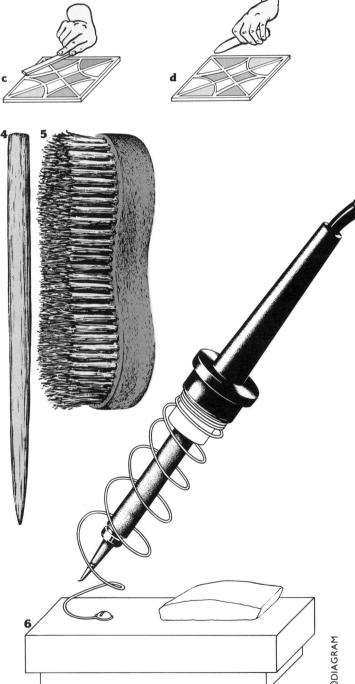

©DIAGRAM

Copper foil and glass

The use of copper foil in place of lead for stained glasswork has many advantages. Copper is a more versatile medium than lead as it can be wrapped around a wider variety of objects; it is also much lighter than lead and can be used for smaller, neater joins. Copper foil can be used to "lead" shell and stone slices.

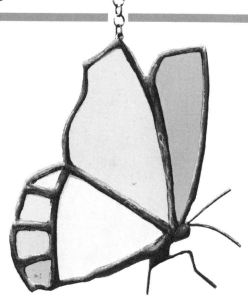

This decorative butterfly (right) was made in stained glass using the copper foil method of leading. Each piece of glass has been cut to shape and wrapped in copper foil strips, and the pieces have then been soldered together.

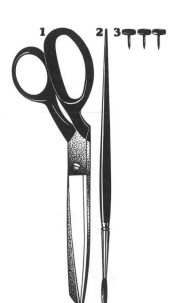

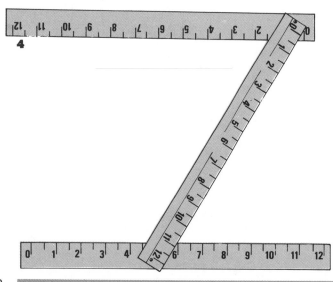

In addition to the usual tools for stained glass, the copper foil technique makes use of the following tools.

1 Scissors to cut the copper foil tape.

2 Small brush for applying flux to the panel.

3 Small nails are used during the assembly of the panel to hold the glass pieces firmly in place during soldering.

4 A **ruler jig** is used to produce consistent angles if geometric glass shapes are required.

A copper foil panel can be made as follows.

a A full size drawing of the proposed design is made on paper; there is no need to allow space for the leads, as the copper takes up very little room. The drawing is then cut up for use as templates.

b The pieces of glass are cut to fit the design by scoring around the templates with a **cutter** and then breaking off the excess glass.

c The edges of each piece of glass are wrapped in copper foil tape so that every section of glass is surrounded by a strip of copper. The glass sections are then fitted together in their respective places.

d The copper strips are soldered together wherever they touch. Unlike lead cames, which are soldered only at the vertices, the copper has to be soldered along every part of the "leadline." The panel is then turned over and soldered on the back.

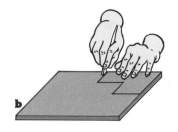

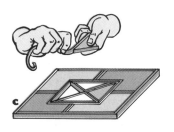

Epoxy putty and glass

Epoxy resin putty can be used to achieve an effect very similar to that of leaded stained glass. Black epoxy resin putty acts as the leads when placed on a base sheet of plain glass, and the areas between the "leads" can then be stained with transparent color. Epoxy resin can also be used to bind together freehand shapes cut from glass sheets.

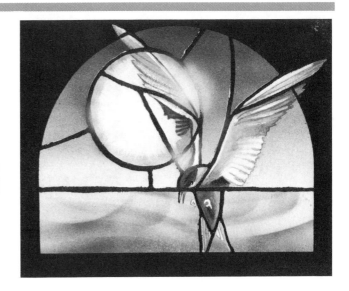

Shown on the right is a modern example of epoxy putty used to imitate the lead lines on stained glass. The spaces between the lines of epoxy putty have been painted to give the effect of different colors of glass.

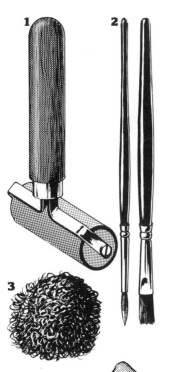

These tools are for making stained glass panels using epoxy resin.
1 Damp **rubber roller** used to press the putty onto the glass.
2 Selection of **fine brushes** for the application of paint or enamel to the glass.
3 **Wire wool** used to tidy up the edges of the dried lines of putty.
4 **Soft rag** moistened with methylated spirit or ether alcohol for cleaning the glass.
5 **Board** to act as a base for the glass panel during assembly.

Epoxy resin putty is used here in place of lead.
a An exact size sheet of glass is laid over the cartoon, and the shapes cut freehand from this sheet. The putty is rolled into lengths and sandwiched between the shapes to force it onto both surfaces.
b A **damp roller** is used to press the putty firmly to the assembled glass. When hard the putty is rubbed with wire wool to neaten the edges. The panel is then cleaned with a rag dampened with methylated spirit. Color—French enamels or acrylic paint—is applied. A variation of this method, glass appliqué, involves fixing the pieces to plate glass with epoxy resin.

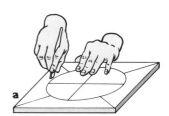

A stained glass panel involving no cutting can be made in the following way.
a An exact size glass sheet is laid over the cartoon. Strips of epoxy putty are rolled out and laid on the glass to follow the leadlines. The strips are then flattened with a damp **roller.**
b Once the putty is hard the panel is reversed and cleaned with a rag dampened with methylated spirit. The shapes are then painted so that the color overlaps the "lead" slightly. When the paint is dry, strips of putty are applied to the colored side to "lead" it.

Dalle-de-verre

Dalle-de-verre is a French name meaning "flagstone of glass;" it was the French who in the 1930s invented and perfected the methods used for working with dalle-de-verre, or slab glass as it is often called. Dalle-de-verre is usually set in concrete, although epoxy resins are becoming more popular as they are more weather-resistant.

Illustrated (right) is a dalle-de-verre panel made from slabs of glass set in concrete. The panel makes a design feature of the strong vertical lines produced by the supporting bars.

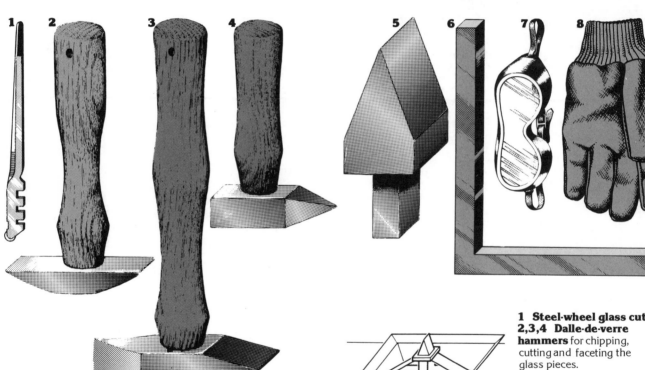

A basic slab glass cutting bench is set up in the manner shown on the right. The **anvil** is positioned over a **movable waste bin,** and **duckboards** are placed in front of the bin for the craftsman to stand on while working.

1 Steel-wheel glass cutter.
2,3,4 Dalle-de-verre hammers for chipping, cutting and faceting the glass pieces.
5 Steel anvil over which scribed dalles can be broken. The glass can also be faceted by chipping it against the anvil.
6 Iron L-angle is fastened to the front edge of the cutting table, and glass scored with a straight line can be broken over it.
7,8 Goggles and **gloves** should be worn for protection from flying splinters of glass.

A dalle-de-verre panel is made in the stages illustrated (below).

a A full-size drawing of the design is made, and the slabs of glass, or dalles, are cut to size to correspond to sections of the drawing.

b The faces and edges of the dalles are chipped and faceted by striking them with **hammers** on a **steel anvil.** This roughening causes them to reflect more light than if they were left flat.

c The dalles are positioned on a piece of greased paper marked with the design, and surrounded by **battens.** The spaces around the dalles are filled with concrete or epoxy resin until the level is flush with that of the glass.

d The surface of the concrete or resin is smoothed over with flat tools such as a **scraper** or a **plasterer's trowel.** When the panel is fully dry, the paper can be peeled off the back and the battens removed.

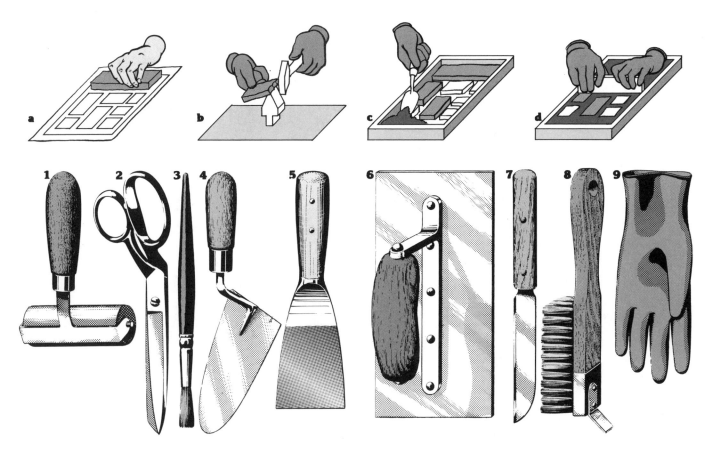

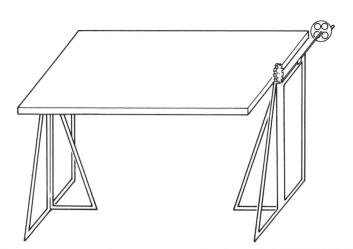

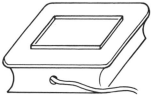

A **tip table** (left) provides support and ease of movement when casting a large panel, and a **vibrator table** (above) is useful to aid the dispersal of air bubbles from the casting mix.

1 Rubber roller used for applying grease to the slabs and the backing paper before casting.
2 Scissors for cutting the templates.
3 Brush for filling in narrow crevices before casting.
4 Brick trowel.
5 Scraper.
6 Plasterer's trowel.
7 Knife for patching up cavities in cast concrete.
8 Wire brush used to clean the glass before and after the casting.
9 Rubber gloves, used to protect the hands from concrete or resin.

©DIAGRAM

Vitreous and ceramic mosaic

Mosaics have been made through the ages from virtually every solid material, ranging from gold and precious stones through to eggshells and pasta. The famous mosaics of the Byzantine era, however, were made almost exclusively of glass, ceramic and stone. The fragments used may be arranged into a plane surface, or set at angles so that they deflect the light.

Reproduced (right) is a detail from a floor mosaic in a Sabian cave at Edessa, Greece. The full mosaic, which was made in AD 227-8, depicts the hero Orpheus charming the animals with his lute.

1 Mosaic hammer.
2 Glass cutter with a steel wheel.
3 Mosaic nippers.
4 Tile cutters, with a spring for extra power.
5 Tweezers used for picking up small pieces of mosaic.
6 Hardie, a small steel anvil used for breaking tesserae. The piece is held over the hardie, and struck with the **mosaic hammer.**

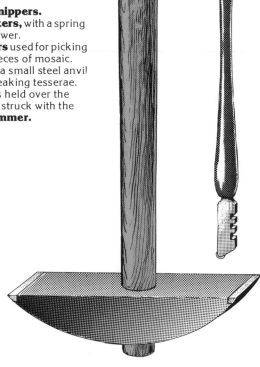

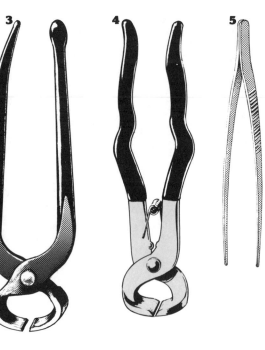

The illustration (right) shows some of the ways in which standard tesserae can be divided to produce mosaic pieces of various shapes and sizes. The cuts are made with the **nippers,** holding them at the edge of the tile and squeezing firmly.

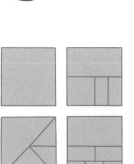

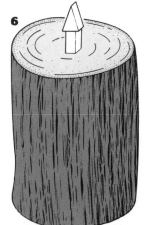

Much mosaic is set directly into its ground, or holding medium, but various methods have been developed so that the mosaic can be assembled in sections first. The indirect method, shown right, is one of these.
a An outline of part of the mosaic, reversed, is drawn onto craft paper and coated with gum arabic solution. The tesserae are arranged face down on the paper.
b When each section has been done in this way, the groups of tesserae are assembled on the prepared ground and the paper is peeled off.

The double reverse method, shown right, allows the artist to assemble the mosaic in sections but does not restrict the design to having a totally flat surface in the way that the indirect method does.
a The tesserae are grouped in clay, face up as they will appear in the final mosaic. They are then covered with muslin that has been soaked in glue.
b When the glue is dry, the tesserae are lifted out of the clay in one piece, held together by the muslin. They can then be assembled on the prepared ground.

1 Rolling pin for making flat clay tesserae.
2 Fettling knife for trimming the clay.
3 Tesserae cutter; the clay is cut and then fired as for pottery.
4 Tile cutter, illustrating some of the different shapes in which cutters can be obtained.
5 Serrated spreader used to prepare the ground in which the tesserae are set.
6 Clay board; the battens at the sides ensure that the clay is rolled evenly.
7 Automatic clay roller, with an adjustment for different thicknesses.

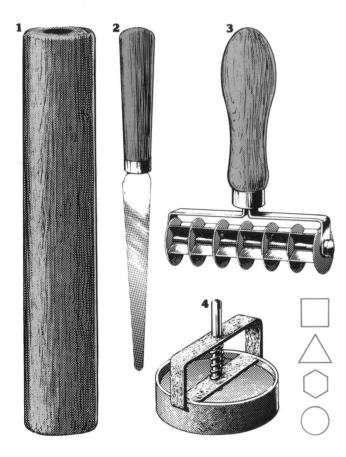

The pieces for mosaic need not be regular shapes; mosaics can be made from smooth pebbles of different colors, or from pieces of metal that have been cut to shape and arranged on a ground.

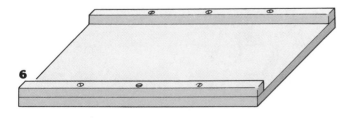

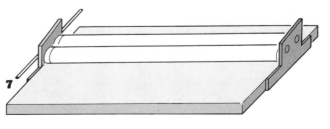

Enameling

Enamels are vitreous glazes that can be fused onto a metal surface to produce a durable decoration. The enamel is applied by placing it in position on the metal and then firing it in a small kiln to fuse the glass. Most enamel work uses colored glazes, although the technique known as grisaille uses monochrome enamels, usually gray with white highlights.

The example of enameling shown on the right is known as the Dunstable Swan, and is in the British Museum, London. The swan is just over an inch high, and dates from the 15th century; it was intended to be worn as a piece of jewelry.

1 **Porcelain pestle and mortar.**
2 **Sandbag.**
3 **Sieve.**
4 **Agate pestle and mortar.**
5 **Glass muller and slab.**
6 **Strainer.**
7 **Stiff brush.**
8 **Funnel.**
9 **Nailbrush.**
10 **Wire wool.**
11 **Paintbrush.**
12 **Wire tray** with foil **dishes** for drying enamels.
13,14 **Dropper bottle** and **spray bottle** for distilled water.
15 **Mixing palettes.**
16 **Wide-necked jar** for storage.

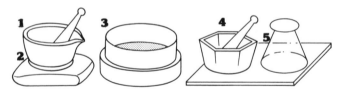

Enameling is a craft that requires careful preparation of the materials to guarantee good results.
a The enamel chunks are placed in a **porcelain mortar,** and broken up by striking the **pestle** with a **mallet.** A **sandbag** underneath cushions the blows.

b The enamel pieces are transferred to an **agate pestle and mortar,** and covered with distilled water. The grinding of the enamel continues under the water, which is changed at intervals so that the enamel is being ground and washed simultaneously.

c After the enamel has been dried, it is pushed with a **stiff brush** through progressively finer **sieve meshes,** so that it is separated into grades. Each grade is labeled and stored separately.

d The metal that is to be enameled is cleaned thoroughly, usually by pickling it in acid and then scrubbing it clean with a **nylon brush** or **wire wool.** This ensures that the enamel adheres evenly to the metal surface.

The following tools can be used when applying enamels.

1 Enameling stands in a variety of shapes.
2 Spray enamel gun.
3 Blowpipe spray.
4 Enameling brushes.
5 Needle tool.
6 Sgraffito tool.
7 Swirler.

8 Quill.
9 Tiny spatula.
10,11,12 Shaped tools for delicate enamel work.
13 Large swirler.
14 Metal chute used to scatter enamel.

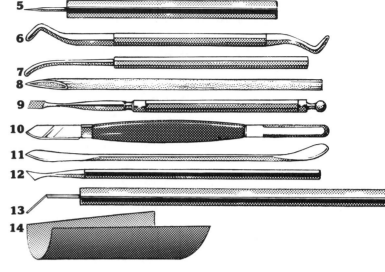

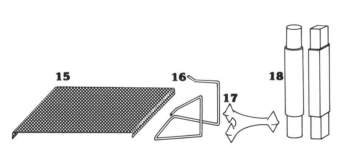

15 Kiln rack supports the work during firing.
16,17 Spurs in two designs. Pieces that are enameled on all sides can be rested on these during firing so that the enamel is touched at as few points as possible.
18 Carborundum stones.

19 Enameling tongs used to position pieces and racks inside the kiln.
20 Enameling fork for removing fired pieces.
21 Enameling kiln.

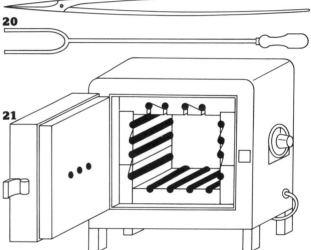

e Enamel is then applied to the surface that is to be decorated. The enamel powder may be dusted onto the surface, or it can be mixed with water or glue and applied with a **brush** or **spray.**

f The metal piece, with its coating of enamel, is placed in a **kiln** and fired for a period appropriate to the particular metal and enamel. The firing melts the glass in the enamel, and fuses it onto the metal.

g While the enamel is still molten in the kiln, patterns can be introduced by swirling—drawing a **pointed tool** through several colors of enamel in succession so that streaks of color are produced.

h When the enameled piece has cooled after firing, the stains produced on the metal by the heat are cleaned away by pickling or by rubbing with **carborundum stones.** This leaves the metal smooth and polished.

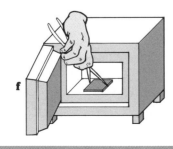

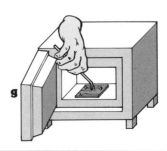

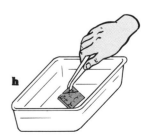

Foil and thread enamels

Specialized enameling techniques can add interest to the design of an enameled object and enhance its appearance. Gold or silver foil placed behind transparent enamel increases the brilliance of the color, and if the foil is also stamped the light is pleasingly diffracted. Enamel threads melt into attractive shapes when fired.

Illustrated (right) is an enameled medallion of the Holy Family, made by the Limoges school in the early 16th century. The enamel has been applied over foil to give the highlights a slightly luminous appearance.

1 Stamp made from pins stuck into a cork.
2,3,4 Stamps of various designs used to texture the foils.
5 Needle tool used to cut shapes from the foil.
6 Fiberglass brush for pressing the foil in place.
7 Agate burnisher.

8 Crucible holder for use when making enamel threads.
9 Steel rod used to draw the threads out.
10 Asbestos gloves needed for protection while handling the hot enamel.

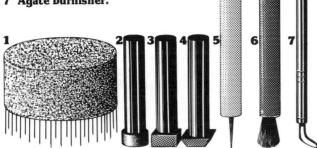

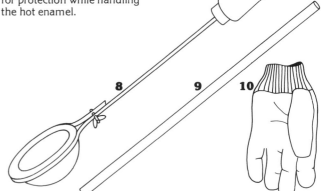

Enameling over foil creates a peculiarly luminescent effect.
a The chosen foil is cut to shape, and may be stamped with a pattern or an overall texture. It is positioned on the surface to be enameled, and burnished into place.

b The coating of enamel is painted or sprayed evenly over the foil, and then the entire piece is fired in the usual way. This method is effective only with transparent or translucent enamels, since opaque enamels do not allow any light to penetrate.

Enamel threads are made by drawing out hot enamel and allowing it to cool in thin lengths.
a The enamel is placed in a **crucible** and heated in a **kiln** until molten. The crucible is then removed from the kiln before the enamel cools.

b The crucible is gripped firmly in **tongs,** and a **steel rod** is dipped into the molten enamel. The rod is then pulled away to draw out a thread of enamel, which quickly cools in the air and can be broken into shorter lengths for storage.

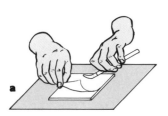

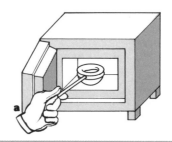

Cloisonné and champlevé

Cloisonné and champlevé are two ways of applying enamel in well defined areas. If two colors of enamel are placed side by side without a barrier they will mingle on firing; cloisonné overcomes this difficulty by creating barriers of metal between the areas of enamel, and champlevé places the enamels in depressions cut into the metal's surface.

The mask of Tutankhamen illustrated (right) shows examples of both cloisonné and champlevé work. The headdress is fused glass set in recesses in the manner of champlevé, and the bottom of the necklace is decorated with cloisonné blossoms.

Cloisonné tools are illustrated (right).
1 Needle-nosed pliers used for bending and shaping the cloisons.
2 Tweezers for positioning the metal cloisons on the background.
3 Paintbrush; this can be used to fill the cloisons with enamel.

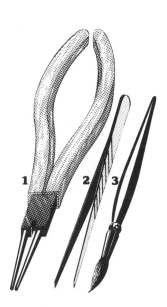

Champlevé tools are shown in the illustrations (right).
4 Gravers of various designs, used for cutting the recesses for the enamels.
5 Justifier, a tool with a flat head used for leveling the bottoms of the recesses.

Cloisonné consists of making fences (cloisons) to enclose the enamels.
a A strip of metal the correct length is bent to shape and the ends are soldered to form a cloison. Each cloison is then soldered onto the base.

b Each cloison is filled with an enamel, and when all the cloisons have been filled the object is fired. After cooling, the surface of the piece is smoothed and polished so that every cloison stands at the same height.

Champlevé is another way of ensuring that areas of enamel are kept separate.
a Depressions of the required shapes and sizes are cut with various sharp tools into the metal ground, leaving raised portions of metal to act as barriers.

b The enamel is then placed in the depressions, and fired and polished in the usual way. The effect can be similar to that of cloisonné, but champlevé can be used to apply small areas of enamel onto large pieces of metal that are to remain uncovered by enamel.

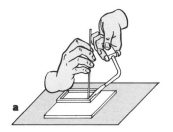

©DIAGRAM

12 Fine metalwork

Before the second century BC, all decorative metalwork was executed with hammers. The beating process spread the metal to the right thickness and area, and also shaped and contoured it if it was hammered on one side only. Large statues could be built up by riveting several of these hammered pieces together, or by securing them onto a wood core. Even when the lost wax process was evolved as a method of forming metal sections, the malleability of metal meant that hammering remained, and still remains, a very easy and effective way of shaping metal. Many of the metalworker's tools, therefore, are hammers, mallets and stakes of different types.

Hammering took on various refinements as the centuries passed; repoussé, chasing and stamping are all developments of the beating technique, and require their own versions of the hammering tools and punches. The invention of other processes made the metalworker's repertoire still greater; soldering, plating, inlaying and engraving all brought their appropriate tools.

The technological age has also made its contributions to metalwork. Mallets can be made of acrylic to reduce unwanted marks on the metal, electrically driven wheels speed up polishing processes, and tools can be machine-formed rather than laboriously hand-shaped. New processes, such as electroforming and the use of unusual alloys, are now earning their own places in the long tradition of craftsmanship in metal.

The print reproduced here depicts a goldsmith's workshop in the reign of Charles II, and comes from "A New Touchstone for Gold and Silver Wares," published in London in 1679. The craftsmen's tools can be seen hanging over the melting furnace.

Precious metals

The metals used in jewelry are generally chosen for their beauty, and so the precious metals— gold, silver and platinum—have always been in demand for the jeweler's work. Copper and also bronze (an alloy of copper and tin) have been used quite extensively, but both tend to oxidize and form an unsightly tarnish unless they are protected.

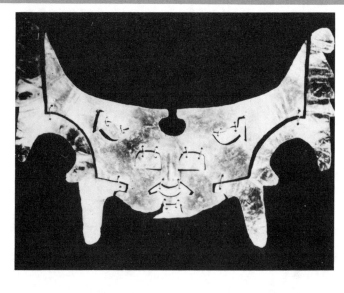

The nose ornament (right) is made from a cut and hammered sheet of pure gold, and is in the early Calima style of the Colombian goldsmiths. The ornament is in the Museum of Mankind, England, and formed part of the "Gold of El Dorado" exhibition.

Before the discovery of precious metals, shells, bones, ivory and pieces of bark and seeds were used as body decoration by primitive man. When gold, silver and precious stones were discovered, the ornaments became more elaborate and more intricate. Specialized tools were developed, and the basic form of these tools remains unchanged in their modern counterparts. All the tools below are from Ancient Egypt.
1 **Jeweler's anvil.**
2 **Goldsmith's hammer.**
3 **Jeweler's hammer.**
4 **Pincers.**

Gold is one of the most beautiful of all metals, and its rarity has made it highly sought after through the ages. Gold does not tarnish or corrode, and although it is soft, strength is added by alloying it with other metals, such as silver or copper.

Silver possesses a desirable combination of brilliance and malleability, and is a popular metal for jewelry work. Silver is more readily available than gold and is therefore not so expensive.

The **jeweler's bench** (below) is a piece of equipment that has remained virtually unchanged for decades. The bench has a semicircular section cut from it, and a sheepskin is strung under the gap to catch gold filings and dropped stones or tools. Most of the work is done over this skin, usually using the **bench pin**. The craftsman's stool is traditionally made from the semicircular section cut from the bench. Raised sides around the tray part prevent tools from rolling off the bench.

The jeweler's **V-clamp** (below) is a fork of wood that is fixed firmly to the bench. The work can be braced against the V-shape and hammered, cut, sawn and polished. The clamps come in a variety of sizes, and some have a small **anvil** fixed to the top.

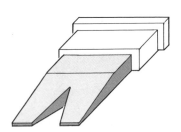

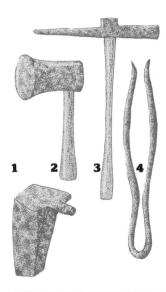

1   2   3   4

Platinum is a name meaning "little silver," and its properties of brilliance, malleability and ability to take a high polish strongly resemble those of silver. Platinum is usually alloyed with small amounts of iridium when used for jewelry.

Copper is a warm-colored ductile metal, and although it is not particularly hard its durability can be increased by cold-working the metal. As early as 3500BC copper was being intentionally alloyed with tin to produce bronze for tools and decorative work.

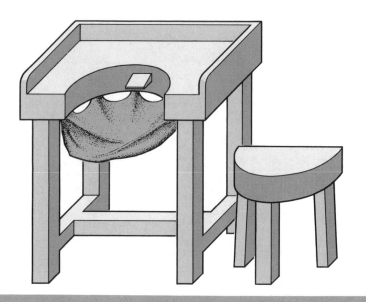

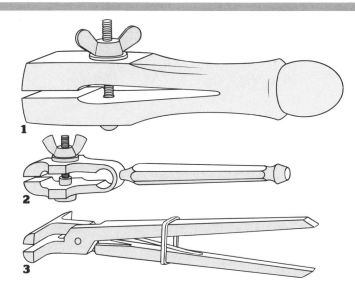

Clamps and vises are used to hold the metal in place as it is worked.
1 Screw clamp.
2 Pin vise, a smaller kind of screw clamp.
3 Slide pincers; a sliding band holds the jaws together when necessary.

The tools on the right are used to assess the length of metal needed when making rings.
4 Ring gauge; this is a series of ring blanks in regularly progressing sizes.
5 Ring stick or mandrel, a graduated stick for checking ring sizes.

Marking tools are used to trace out the cutting lines onto the metal.
6 Scriber, a needle-pointed marking tool.
7 Dividers; these are used to scribe circles and parallel lines.
8 Aluminum pencil, a sharpened rod of hard metal.

Snips are versatile cutting tools used for small pieces of thin metal where a saw is too cumbersome.
9 Compound action snips, a particularly strong cutting tool.
10 Plate snips, useful for cutting sheet metal.
11 Tinner's snips.

12 Shaping snips with curved jaws.
13 Jeweler's snips, sturdy sharp snips that will cut through a considerable thickness of metal.

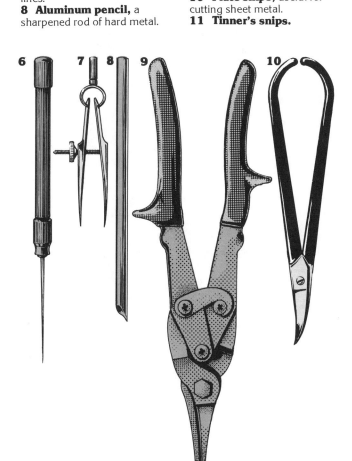

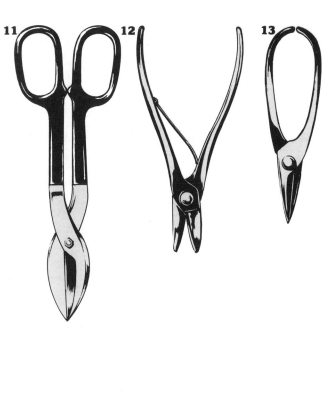

© DIAGRAM

Hammering and beating

The more ductile a metal is, the more easily it can be hammered and beaten to alter its shape, size or texture. Gold is the most ductile of all metals; one troy ounce can be beaten out to an area of 300 square feet. The tools used for hammering and beating vary according to the metal used, the object's shape, and the amount of pressure required.

The print reproduced (right) depicts the inside of an armorer's workshop, and illustrates many of the tools used in metalwork. The hammers and stakes being used in the print are very similar to those used by metalworkers today.

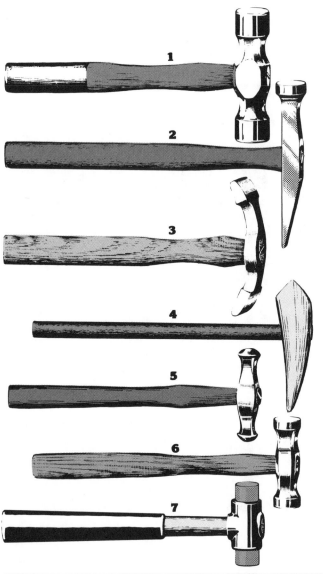

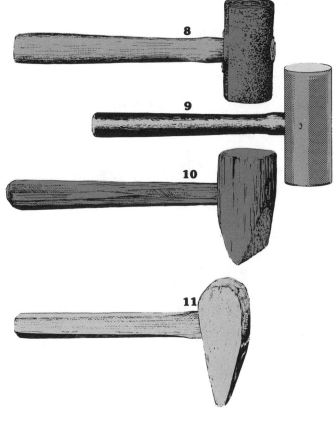

1 **Metal hammer.**
2 **Creasing hammer.**
3 **Border hammer.**
4 **Horn tip hammer,** made from the end of a bullock's horn weighted with lead.
5 **Blocking hammer.**
6 **Planishing hammer.**
7 **Acrylic hammer** that will not mark the metal.

8 **Rawhide mallet,** made from coiled treated cattle hide.
9 **Plastic mallet.**
10 **Round-faced boxwood mallet.**
11 **Raising mallet,** used particularly when forming hollow shapes.

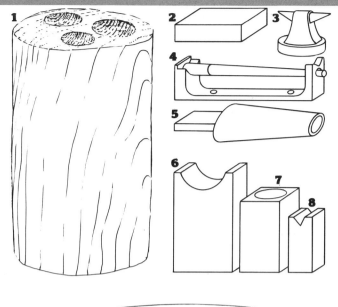

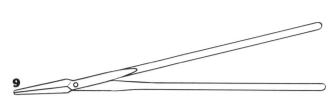

Hammering is done against smoothly shaped surfaces.
1 Tree trunk, an excellent natural anvil.
2 Metal bench block.
3 Bench anvil with shaped ends.
4 Ring mandrel, a tapered stick for shaping rings, in a **mandrel holder.**

5 Bracelet mandrel.
6,7,8 Wooden formers, carved blocks used as shaped anvils.
9 Annealing tongs; if the metal is too hard to beat, it is softened (annealed) by the controlled use of heat.

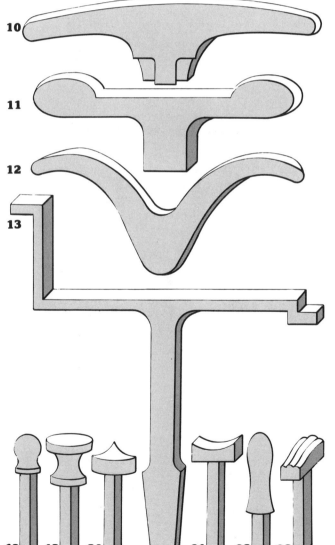

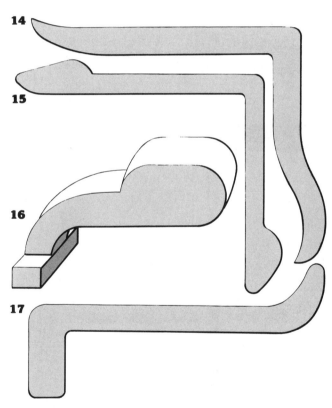

10,11,12,13,14,15,16 Large stakes in a variety of shapes. The stake is held firm is a **vise,** and the metal is beaten over the shaped ends.
17 Snarling iron for hollow shapes; one end is hooked over the rim and the other is struck sideways.

18,19,20,21,22,23 Small stakes for producing specific shapes in the metal. These also are held firmly in a vise while being used.

Sawing, piercing, filing

Sawing, drilling, punching and filing are all ways of rendering pieces of metal the correct shape for the work in hand. Pierced work is a method of decoration that involves cutting shaped holes out of flat metal in order to leave a latticework; this lattice can then be shaped, underlaid, enameled, or incorporated into a larger design.

The silver necklace shown in the photograph (below) is a daisy chain made the same size as real daisy blossoms. The silver was shaped by sawing and filing flat plates of silver until they achieved the correct shapes and contours.

Fine-bladed **saws** are used in jewelry work to make intricate perpendicular cuts in sheet metal.
1 Hacksaw.
2 Piercing saw, a jeweler's saw with a very fine, sharp blade.
3 Two **spare blades** for the piercing saw.

4 Center punch, a pointed punch used to make a preliminary mark for drilling.
5 Hand drill.
6 Spare bits for the hand drill.

7 End cutters, a pair of sharp clippers with straight jaws.
8 Metal punch for cutting out small holes in sheet metal.
9 Two-hole metal punch.

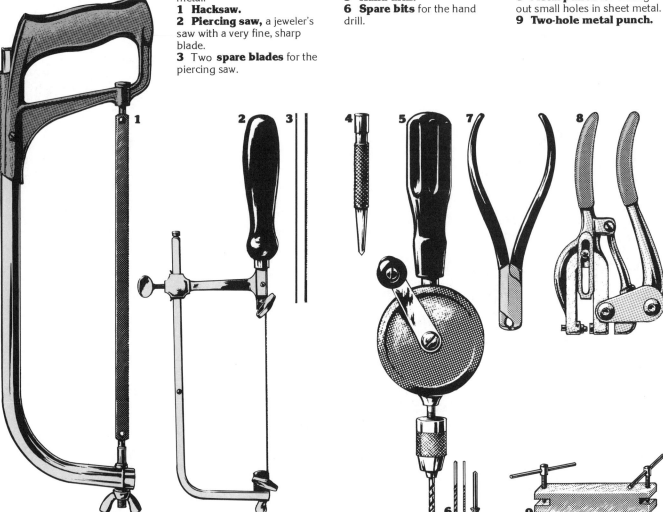

Pierced work involves drilling holes in the metal so that the saw blade can be threaded through.

a A **center punch** is used to mark a small impression on the metal so that the **drill bit** will not slip, and a drop of oil is added for lubrication.

b A hole big enough to take the blade of the **piercing saw** is drilled through the metal within the outline of the prospective hole.

c The **saw blade** is threaded through, teeth downward, and attached to the saw frame. The outline of the pierced work can now be traced with the saw cut; this process is repeated with every part of the metal to be pierced.

d When the pierced work is completed, the sawn edges are filed and polished to smooth and finish them.

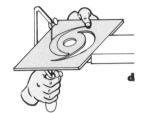

1 **Hand file.**
2 **Half-round file.**
3 **Knife-cut file.**
4 **Needle files** in various shapes.
5 **Handle** for needle files.
6 **File brush,** a wire brush used to clean debris from the files.

7 **Wire wool;** this is used to clean and polish the metal's surface.
8,9,10 Emery sticks, made by glueing emery paper onto wooden rods.
11 **Emery burnisher** for refining the surface of the metal.

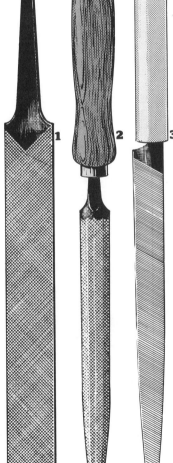
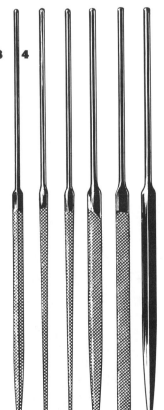
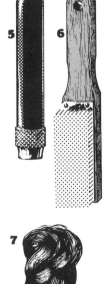

©DIAGRAM

Bending and stretching 1

Wiredrawing is the process of stretching a length of metal into a rod of a specific diameter and cross-section. The cross-section may be round, rectangular, triangular, half-round, or even more fancy depending on the shape of the hole through which the wire is drawn. Once the wires are formed they can be twisted, rolled, and bent into complex shapes.

This photograph of a Maltese silverworker shows the extremely delicate nature of filigree work. The tiny silver wires are laid out in shapes on the worktable, and the craftsman is carefully arranging them into a design.

1,2 Measuring gauges with graduated openings, marked with wire sizes. The wire is laid in the opening to determine its thickness.
3 Micrometer, another instrument for gauging the thickness of wire. The measurements are marked on the handle of the screw.

4,5 Drawplates with holes of various sizes and shapes. The wire is pulled through a selected hole to shape it to a particular size.
6 Draw swage; this tool makes use of complicated moldings in order to produce fancy wires.

7 Joint tool is especially useful for closing and smoothing the joints in chenier (metal tubing).
8 Drawtongs are the strong pliers used to grip the wire as it is pulled through the drawplate.

A **drawbench,** shown below, is used for drawing long or tough lengths of wire. The **drawplate** (see right) is held in a **vise** at one end of the bench; the wire is threaded through the plate and gripped in jaws attached to a belt, and the belt is winched by the craftsman.

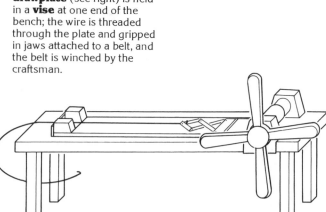

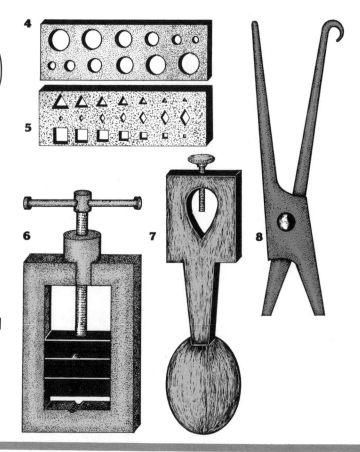

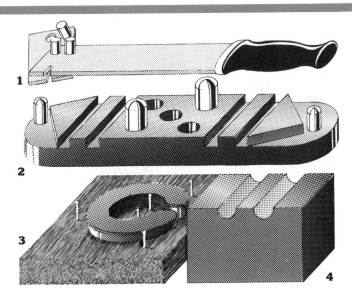

1 Wire-former, a hand-held tool for bending wire.
2,3 Wire-bending jigs; the wire is wrapped firmly round the posts on the jig in order to shape it.
4 Half-round former for making chenier (tubing). The semicircular channels are of different sizes.

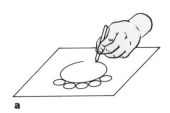

5 Jeweler's roll used to flatten wire and tubing.
6 Beating block for triangular wire. This block is made from part of an old railroad track; a V-shaped channel has been cut to hold the wire so that the third side of the triangle can be flattened.

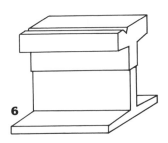

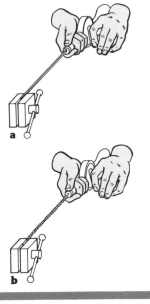

Chenier is the name given to decorative wire tubing; the process of making chenier is similar to that of wiredrawing, though slightly more complicated.
a A strip is cut out of metal plate, and one end is tapered slightly so that it will slip easily into the **drawplate.**
b The strip of metal is placed over a **half-round former,** and a metal or wood rod is hammered over the top to force the metal into the channel.
c The curved shape is put through an appropriate hole in a **drawplate,** and is pulled through the plate with **tongs.** This forms it virtually into a circle.
d The tube is then drawn through a **joint tool,** with the seam toward the top. The screw of the joint tool firms and smooths the join in the chenier, and the tube is now truly circular.

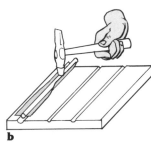

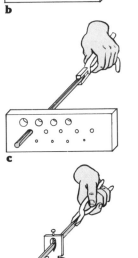

Filigree is a technique that involves forming patterns from bent and twisted wire, either on a background or as a latticework.
a The pattern to be interpreted in filigree work is drawn onto a piece of paper, and wires of the chosen type are twisted and coiled into flat shapes that correspond to the design.
b When all the parts of the design have been laid out in wire, the sections of wire are carefully soldered together at the points where they touch.

Wire can be evenly twisted, either in single or multiple strands, in the following way.
a One end of the wire is clamped firmly in a **bench vise.** The other end is fixed equally firmly into the chuck of a **hand drill.**
b The handle of the drill is slowly turned, so causing the wire to twist. The operator can control the action so that the wire is loosely or tightly twisted. Since this process produces extreme tension in the wire, the metal is kept well annealed.

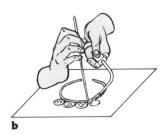

©DIAGRAM

Bending and stretching 2

Malleable metal can be not only hammered but also bent into decorative shapes. When wires are cut into even lengths and bent into loops they can be linked together in various combinations to form chains; pliers, fluting jigs and folding devices can be used to produce creases and undulations in the metals.

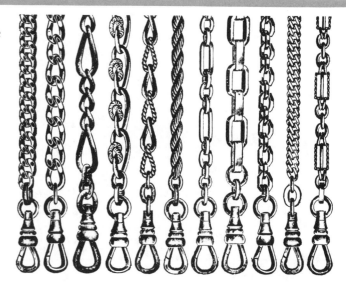

The chains shown in the reproduction (right) are watch chains that were advertised in a Sears Roebuck catalog at the turn of the century. Wrist watches were virtually unkown at this time, so every owner of a watch required a watch chain.

Chainmaking is a precise process, and care is needed to ensure that all the links are of even thickness and size.

a Wire of the required thickness is drawn through a **drawplate**, as described on the previous page.

b The wire is wound in a spiral around a **former;** the shape of the former will determine the shape of the links.

c The spiral of metal is sawn through on one side; this produces numerous pieces of curved wire that are all the same length and curved to the same shape.

d The pieces of wire can then be interlocked. The two ends of each link are aligned and pinched together firmly with **pliers** so that they will not come apart, and then soldered.

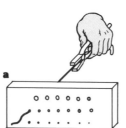

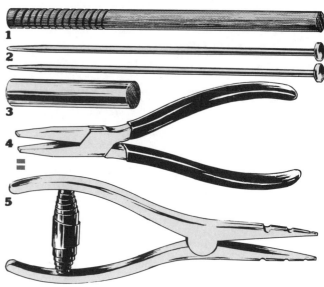

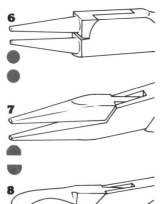

1 Link former made from a piece of spiral dowel.
2 Knitting needles placed together to make a former for oval links.
3 Link former made from a length of steel rod.
4 Flat-nosed pliers, useful for gripping wire.
5 Link-opening pliers; the action of the handles and jaws forces the links open.
6 Round-nosed pliers.
7 Chain-nosed pliers.
8 Loop-closing pliers with horizontal faces on the jaws.

A **fluting jig** consists of a pair of stakes over which the metal is hooked (right and below). When the metal is pulled downward, its rim assumes a ripple where it is bent by the jig.

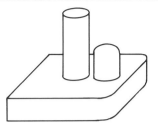

A **flatformer,** shown below, bends flat strips of metal into curved shapes. The metal strip is inserted into the device and the handle pulls the protruding part of the strip into a curve.

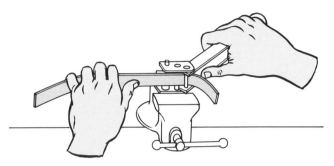

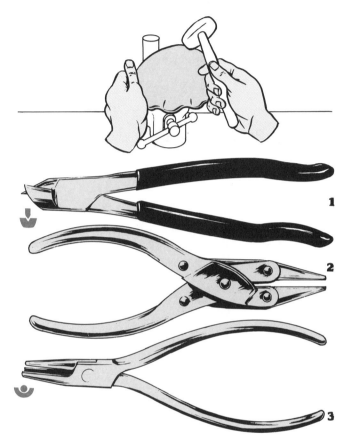

8

9

10

11

1 Bow-closing pliers.
2 Parallel-motion pliers; all parts of the jaw exert equal pressure.
3 Hollow-nosed pliers.
4 Ring-bending pliers.
5 Combination or **half-round pliers** — one jaw is flat and the other rounded.
6 Needle-nosed pliers.
7 Ring-holding pliers.
8 Tweezers for picking up tiny links.
9 Universal holder, a four-jawed gripper.
10 Folding iron; the sheet of metal is placed in the slit and can be bent over the tool.
11 Scorer for marking fold lines on sheet metal.

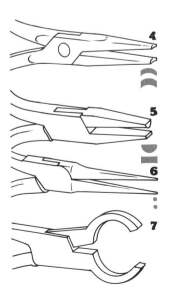

4

5

6

7

Magnifiers are useful when doing any delicate work such as chainmaking. On the right is a **jeweler's eyeglass,** and shown below is a **visor-style magnifier** that can be pulled into position when required.

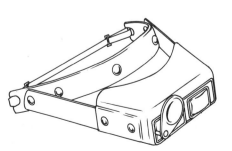

©DIAGRAM

Raised surfacework

Raised surfacework on precious metals covers a wide variety of techniques; repoussé, foil tooling, doming and graining are all methods of producing raised or embossed designs on the metal. Major cultures through history have used one or several of these methods for decorating their jewelry, armor and other metal artefacts.

The gold mask illustrated (right) was discovered in the 1870s by the archeologist Heinrich Schliemann, at the Mycenaean hilltop citadel in Greece. Schliemann thought that he had found the mask of Agamemnon, but in fact the mask is several centuries earlier, c. 1600-1450 BC.

1 Pitch bowl and **leather collar;** the pitch is used as a soft working surface for repoussé.
2 Fine-pointed punch for transferring the pattern to the metal.
3 Repoussé stylus, a tool for tracing round the preliminary outlines.

4 Repoussé punches; these are struck with **hammers** so that they mark the metal.
5 Chasing punches, also hammered into the metal.
6 Wooden creaser, a tool for producing striated textures.

Hammers are used to hit the punches so that they strike the metal cleanly and forcefully.
7 Chasing hammer.
8 Claw hammer.
9 Raising hammer.
10 Mallet.

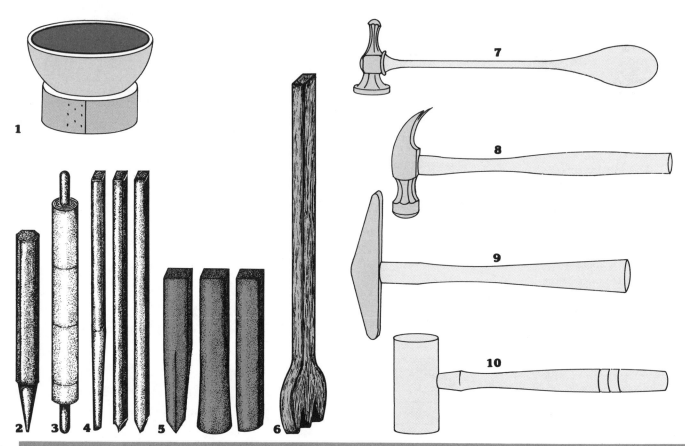

Graining is the process of making raised circular marks on the metal. Graining can be done by applying small beads of metal (see textured surface-work) or by using tools such as those shown on the right.

1 Counterpunch for making graining tools; the punch is struck over the counterpunch until the head is sufficiently hollowed.

2 Single graining tool, a punch with a hollow end. This punch is struck on the right side of the metal and forms small bead shapes.

3 Multiple graining tool.

4 Roulette graining tool.

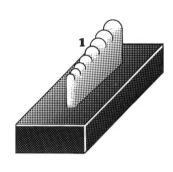

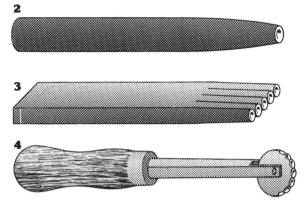

5 Wood **dapping block,** an anvil with hollows for depressing the metal.

6 Dapping punches; each punch fits a particular hollow in the block.

7 Steel **doming block.**

8 Doming punches.

9 Cutter; domes can be cut out to form hemispheres.

10 Textured block for tooling foil.

11 Pointed tools for use with the textured block.

12 Patterned tooling block.

13 Tools for use with the patterned block.

14 Fluting block.

15 Fluting punch.

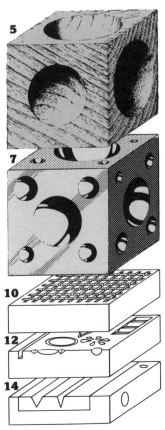

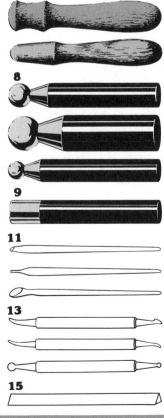

Repoussé is a French word meaning "pushed back," and the process involves pressing or striking the reverse surface of the metal so that a design appears on the front.

a The design is drawn out on a piece of thin paper the same size as the metal.

b The metal is placed on a **pitch bowl** and warmed slightly. The warming makes the metal adhere to the pitch so that it will not move during the work, and also it makes the metal a little more malleable.

c The paper carrying the design is placed on top of the metal, and the lines of the design are traced with a **stylus.**

d The paper is removed and the design is pressed into the metal, using **repoussé punches** and **chasing punches.** When the design has been made on the metal it is removed from the pitch bowl, and the front of the design is neatened by leveling the areas between the raised parts of the pattern. It is then returned to the pitch bowl face down, and the final touching up of the design is done with the punches.

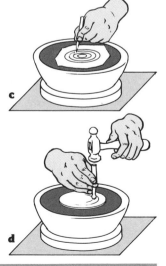

Textured surfacework

The surface of metal can be textured by cutting or scoring it with sharp tools, by stamping it with patterned punches, by etching it with acid, and by applying extra pieces of metal to vary its appearance. Variations in texture produce pleasing subtleties of light reflection and diffraction.

The example of textured surfacework (right) is a helmet from the Iraq Museum. The helmet has been decorated by chiseling and incising the surface in regular lines to give the appearance of a human head, complete with ears and hair.

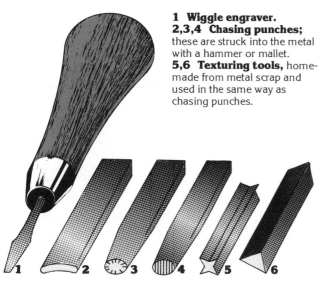

1 Wiggle engraver.
2,3,4 Chasing punches; these are struck into the metal with a hammer or mallet.
5,6 Texturing tools, home-made from metal scrap and used in the same way as chasing punches.

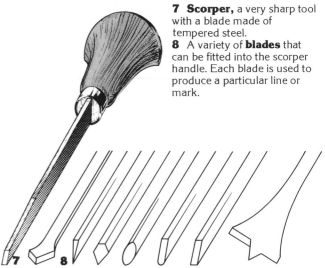

7 Scorper, a very sharp tool with a blade made of tempered steel.
8 A variety of **blades** that can be fitted into the scorper handle. Each blade is used to produce a particular line or mark.

A **wiggle engraver** is gripped firmly in the hand and moved from side to side through the metal (above left). This makes a wiggly line. **Chasing punches** (above) are struck into the metal with a hammer so that their pattern is transferred to the metal surface.

A **scorper** is gripped so that the thumb lies along the blade and can be used to guide the stroke (above). Variations in line can be achieved by altering the pressure on the tool, or by changing the angle of the tool against the metal.

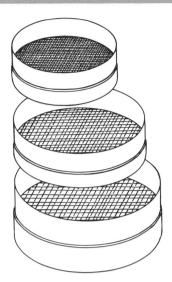

Graduated sieves (left) are used to grade the metal beads used in the graining process, stages of which are shown here (right).

a Tiny squares of metal are cut from a strip and laid on a **charcoal block;** they are then painted with flux.

b A **torch** is applied to the squares so that they melt into spheres.

c After grading, the metal beads are fluxed again and soldered onto the required ground.

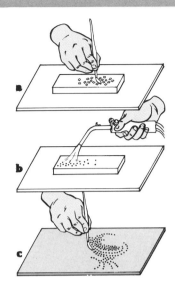

Etching with acid can be used to vary the texture of metal surfaces. The parts of the metal that are not to be textured are painted with stopping-out varnish, which is resistant to the acid, and the metal is immersed in an acid bath. The exposed parts will be eaten away slightly, leaving a mark in the metal. When the metal has been etched to the required depth, it is removed from the acid bath and rinsed. The varnish is then cleaned away from the untouched parts of the metal.

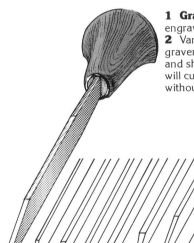

1 Graver used for metal engraving.

2 Various **blades** for use as gravers, all formed from steel and sharpened so that they will cut through the metal without difficulty.

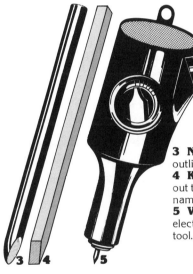

3 Namekuri tagane, an outline tool for Japanese inlay.

4 Kiri tagane, used to chisel out the recess cut by the namekuri tagane.

5 Vibro-engraver, an electrically powered engraving tool.

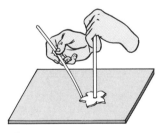

A **graver** can be used to cut long, flowing lines on the metal, or short marks for a rougher texture. As with the scorpers, the line can be varied by altering hand pressure or the angle of the tool.

A specialized Oriental method of inlay (above) involves cutting a shape from a thick sheet of metal and laying it into a thin chiseled recess. This results in a heavily textured final surface.

A **vibro-engraver** (above) can be used with various patterns of head to produce lines of varying quality. The head vibrates so that it cuts into the metal; the operator guides the tool so that it produces lines or areas of texture.

©DIAGRAM

Soldering

Soldering is the most efficient method of permanently joining two pieces of metal. The edges to be joined are butted up close to one another, and small pieces of solder (a slightly softer compound of the metal) are placed along the join. The metal is heated, and once the solder has melted and run into the join, the metals become one cohesive mass.

Brooches, scarf pins and similar objects, such as the examples illustrated (right), usually involve soldering when the pin is attached. Gold in particular is too soft to make successful pins, and so a pin of a harder metal has to be attached by soldering.

1 Jeweler's blowtorch with inlets for air and gas.
2 Acetylene torch.
3,4 Blowtorches.
5 French-pattern blowtorch.
6 Electric soldering iron.
7 Soldering iron to be heated in a gas flame.

8 Soldering bit, a device for guiding the molten solder into the join.
9 Mouth blowpipe made of brass, used to introduce an airflow to the work.

10 Spirit lamp can be used to evaporate water from borax flux.
11 Oil lamp, another torch device.
12 Rubber bulb for sucking up excess solder.

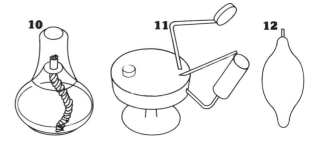

An **asbestos mat** is used as a stand for all the soldering implements, as shown below. **Safety goggles** should also be worn throughout the process, to protect the eyes both from heat and from glare.

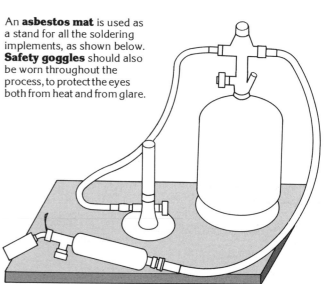

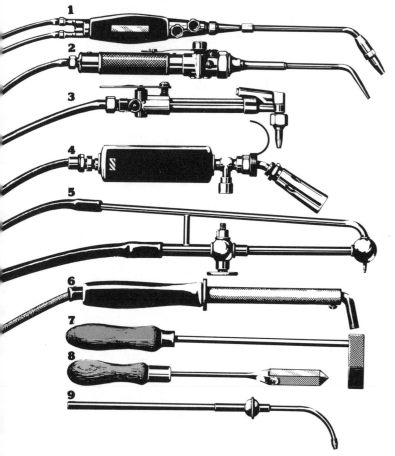

Solder is made by melting appropriate metals and then molding the mixture in a convenient shape.

1 Two-part solder mold.
2 Crucible for melting the metal.
3 Crucible tongs.

Flux, usually borax, is used to remove impurities from the solder so that it will flow readily into the join.

4 Slate mixing palette.
5 Borax cone and unglazed earthenware **mixing palette.**
6 Mixing brush.
7 Syringe full of solder and flux mixture.

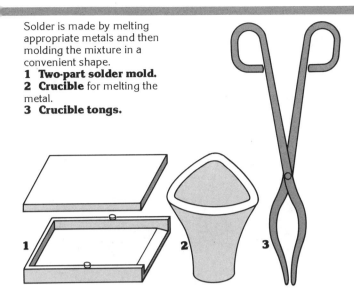
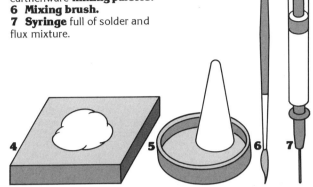

8 Solder snips.
9 Soldering tweezers.
10 Soldering clamp.
11 Soldering tongs.
12 Poker used to guide the solder into the join.
13 Bamboo tongs for removing pieces from the acid cleaning-bath.

14 Charcoal block; this can be used as a soldering base for small pieces.
15 Coiled asbestos base.
16 Carbon mandrel for soldering rings.
17,18 Third-hands, tools that grip work while it is being soldered.
19 Soldering stand.

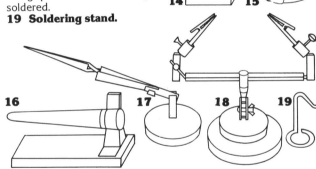

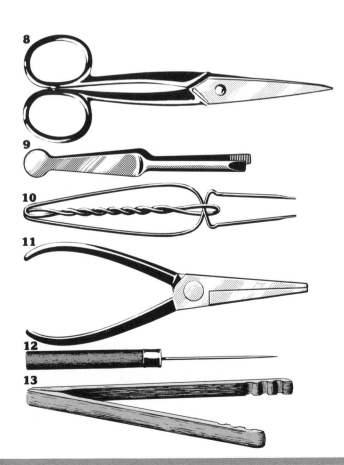

On the right is shown the basic technique of soldering.
a The two pieces of metal to be joined are placed in position, and painted with flux so that the solder will flow cleanly and freely.
b Tiny pieces of solder are applied to the join, and the whole piece is heated. The metal has to be heated most at the part of the join furthest from the solder until the solder runs and seals the join.

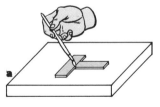
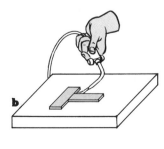

©DIAGRAM

Preparation for casting

The technique for casting precious metal has been known for centuries; the ancient Egyptians were skilled jewelry casters, and in South America it was a cast gold statuette that finally confirmed the legend of El Dorado. Casting from a model reproduces intricate detail or complex forms that could never be made by cutting or beating.

The salt cellar illustrated (right) was cast in gold by Benvenuto Cellini; he made it in the 16th century for Francis I, King of France. Salt was so precious a commodity that elaborate containers were made for it, and placed in front of the host at meals.

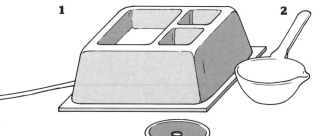

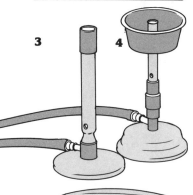

1 **Electric wax pot** used to melt the wax and keep it warm and molten.
2 **Porcelain ladle;** the porcelain retains the heat so that the wax does not solidify.
3 **Burner** for warming tools.
4 **Wax-melting burner.**
5 **Wax extruder,** a gun that forms pellets or wires of wax in various diameters.
6 **Wax press,** a syringe used with different nozzles to produce wax in wires or fancy shapes.

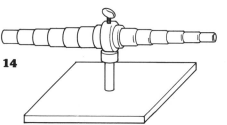

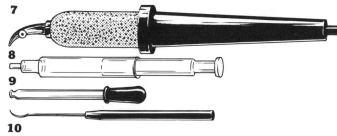

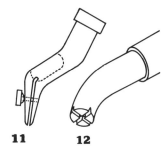

7 **Wax pen** with a well for the molten wax.
8 **Wax syringe.**
9 **Dropper** for molten wax.
10 **Needle tool.**
11,12 **Reservoir tools** of various designs. These tools have shaped heads that are used to mold or extrude the wax, and the reservoir in each head holds a supply of warm wax.
13 **Spirit lamp** for warming tools and softening wax.
14 **Stepped mandrel** used as a base for building wax ring forms.

The basic method of modeling a wax ring form is illustrated in the following sequence.
a A sufficient quantity of wax for the model is melted slowly so that it does not burn or boil. Boiling introduces unwanted bubbles into the wax.

b A **stepped mandrel** is used as a base on which to build the ring. The use of the mandrel ensures that the ring will be even in diameter and of a predictable size.

c The modeled ring form is removed from the mandrel when it has solidified. Any further modeling is done with warmed tools, and then the entire surface can be smoothed by dipping the form quickly into acetone.

d Sprues of wax wire are applied by "soldering" the two pieces of wax together with warm tools. The sprues will form channels in the mold material, and when the wax has been melted out these channels will be used to carry hot metal and to release trapped air.

a

b
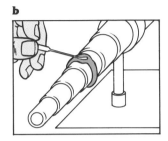

c
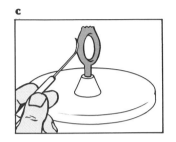

d
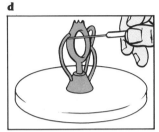

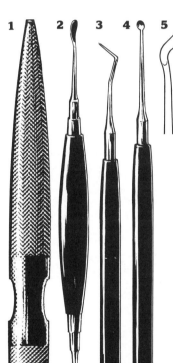

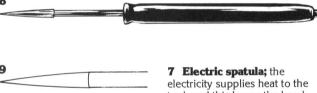

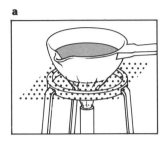

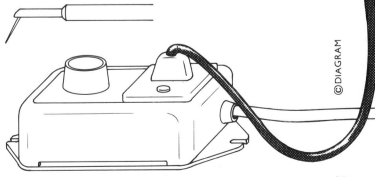

Modeling tools are usually made of steel so that they conduct heat. The tools are warmed so that they make the wax pliable as they touch it.
1 Wax file.
2,3,4 Wax-modeling tools.
5 Various **heads** that can be found on modeling tools.
6 Glass slab used as a building base for modeling larger forms.

7 Electric spatula; the electricity supplies heat to the tool, and this keeps the head permanently warm so that the wax can be modeled more easily.
8 Electric wax welder.
9 Heads for an electric spatula.

©DIAGRAM

Casting

The principle of casting is that a positive model is used to make a negative mold; a metal positive cast in this mold will reproduce the original model in every detail. As well as wax, most combustible natural materials such as pinecones, leaves and flowers, insects and some shells can be used as the original model.

The photograph (right) illustrates an Ashanti brass weight in the form of a lion. The weight was formed by the lost wax casting process, and was cast in a hollow shell.

1 Investment scoop; the investment is the material from which the mold is made.

2 Measuring cylinder used to determine the volume of metal needed to complete a casting. The cylinder is partly filled with water; the model is placed in it, and the exact rise in the water level is noted. The model is removed, and metal pieces are added to the cylinder until the water again reaches the higher level.

3 Investment proportioner gauges the proportion of powder to water for the investment mix.

4 Rubber bowl for mixing the investment.

5 Investment blender; this machine can be used to mix very smooth blends of investment.

6 Casting flask with a fitted **sprue base.**

7 Flask vibrator used to eliminate air bubbles from the mold.

8 Vacuum extractor; when the wax has been melted from the mold, an extractor is used to create a vacuum so that the metal will flow readily into the cavity.

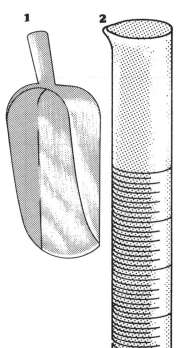
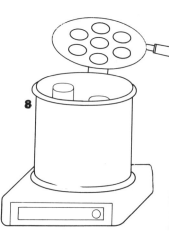

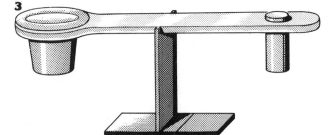
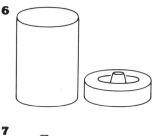
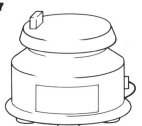

A simple casting can be done using a cuttlefish as the mold. The process requires only basic tools, such as a **small saw** and **sharp knives.**

a The cuttlefish is cut in half with a **small saw,** and the two faces are sanded smooth.

b The shape to be cast is cut into the two halves of the mold, ensuring that all the lines marry when the halves are joined. The two pieces are bound together strongly with wire, and can then be used as a mold and cast with molten metal.

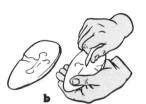

1 Crucible used for melting the metal for casting.
2 Long-handled crucible.
3 Sprue cutter, used for clipping off the excess sprues of metal after the mold has been removed.

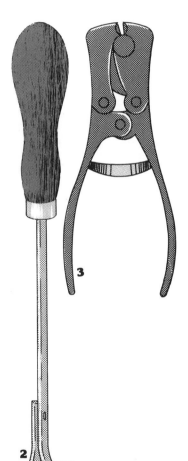

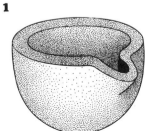

Investing is the process of creating a mold around the original model (right).

a The investment powder is mixed with water to the correct creamy consistency.

b The model to be invested is attached via a wax cone to a **sprue base;** a **flask** is fitted to the base and filled with investment mix.

Casting is the process of filling the cavity in the mold with molten metal to produce a finished piece.

c The metal that is to be cast is melted in a **crucible** until it is red hot. Any impurities are removed from the surface of the molten metal so that they will not marr the casting.

d The metal is poured into the cavity in the **mold,** and allowed to set.

e When the metal is cool, the mold is broken and chipped away from the casting. The sprues that carried the molten metal to the casting are snipped off with **sprue cutters.**

f The casting is placed in an acid bath and scrubbed with **wire brushes** to clean away all traces of the mold material. When the casting is properly clean it can be buffed and polished in the ways suitable to the metal.

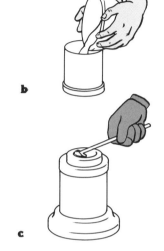

©DIAGRAM

Inlay

Inlay is the process of forming a depression in one metal and filling this with another metal or an alloy, usually of a different color. The depressions to be filled can be formed by casting them in the metal, by etching them away with acid, by cutting them away with sharp tools, or by compressing the metal with punches and dies.

The gunstock decoration shown in the photograph (below) is a superb example of metal inlay. The gun was decorated in gold by Ken Hunt, and the inlay has been carved in some parts and engraved in others.

Metal inlay is designed to produce a decorative contrast between the colors of the ground metal and the inlay metal. Consequently dark metals such as bronze and some copper can be effectively inlaid with gold, silver and brass, while paler metals such as gold and silver might be inlaid with niello or oxidized copper for contrast. The technique known as parquetry involves inlaying shapes of various metals in a close-fitting "patchwork" design.

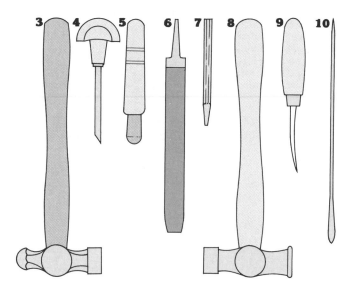

Damascene inlay is done by hammering the inlay metal into gouged recesses.
a The pattern to be damascened is drawn out onto the metal, and a sharp **graver** or **scorper** is used to cut away the metal in the pattern areas. At the edges of each incision the craftsman undercuts the ground metal slightly to provide purchase for the inlay metal.
b The inlay metal is placed in the recesses and hammered into the grooves so that it spreads into the undercuts and is secured. The entire surface is then smoothed and polished.

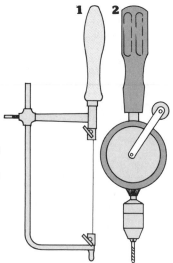

1 Piercing saw for cutting sheet metal.
2 Hand drill.
3 Hammer used to beat parquetry metal into place.
4 Graver or **scorper.**
5 Agate pestle for grinding niello alloy.
6 File used to reduce gold to powder. The powder is mixed with mercury for inlaying, after which the mercury is evaporated.
7 Narrow punch.
8 Hammer.
9 Burnisher used to smooth the inlaid surface.
10 Niello spatula.
11 Pestle and mortar for mixing gold and mercury.
12 Pair of clams can be used to hold the work.

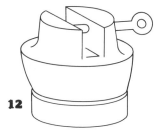

Japanese stratified alloys

Japanese stratified metalwork is made from many thin sheets of metal laminated together and then cut and beaten to expose the various layers. The metals used are generally gold, silver and copper, pure and in alloys, and the original sheets need to be very thin so that the maximum variation of color can be achieved in the laminated block.

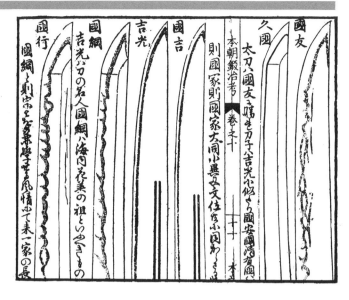

The blades shown (right) are from traditional Japanese swords, and illustrate the principle of stratification. The patterns along the cutting edges were produced by the skilful forging of different metals to give strength to the blade; each pattern identifies the sword's craftsman.

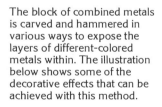

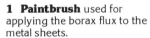

1 **Paintbrush** used for applying the borax flux to the metal sheets.
2 **Leather sandbag** on which the work is rested.
3 **Blowtorch** used for the soldering process.
4 Various **drill bits** for marking the laminated block.
5 **Punches** for distorting the metal surface.
6 **Files** used to flatten the distorted surfaces.
7 **Scorper;** holes and channels can be dug in the block to expose the layers.
8 **Rolling mill** used to flatten the original sheets of metal.

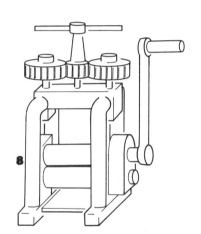

The block of combined metals is carved and hammered in various ways to expose the layers of different-colored metals within. The illustration below shows some of the decorative effects that can be achieved with this method.

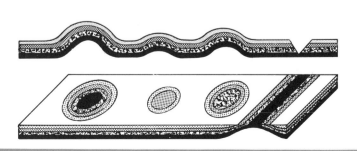

The principle of the stratified alloys is very simple but produces a rich and attractive effect.

a The chosen sheets of metal are rolled in a **mill** so that each sheet is of an even thickness throughout. The sheets are then soldered together in a random order so that there is as much variation as possible within the block.

b When the block is complete, the surface is drilled, gouged and channeled to reveal the strata. In some places the metal is punched or hammered into domes which are then filed down to show further metal layers.

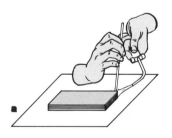

Amerindian jewelry

Jewelry made from silver and set with turquoise has been made by various North American Indian tribes, particularly the Navajo, for the last hundred years. Characteristic designs have evolved which the Indians have made peculiarly their own, and Indian craftsmen have developed esoteric methods and tools for working their designs on the silver.

The belt shown in the photograph (below) is made in a typical Amerindian pattern. Each section of the belt has been individually cut, stamped and patterned with embossing dies.

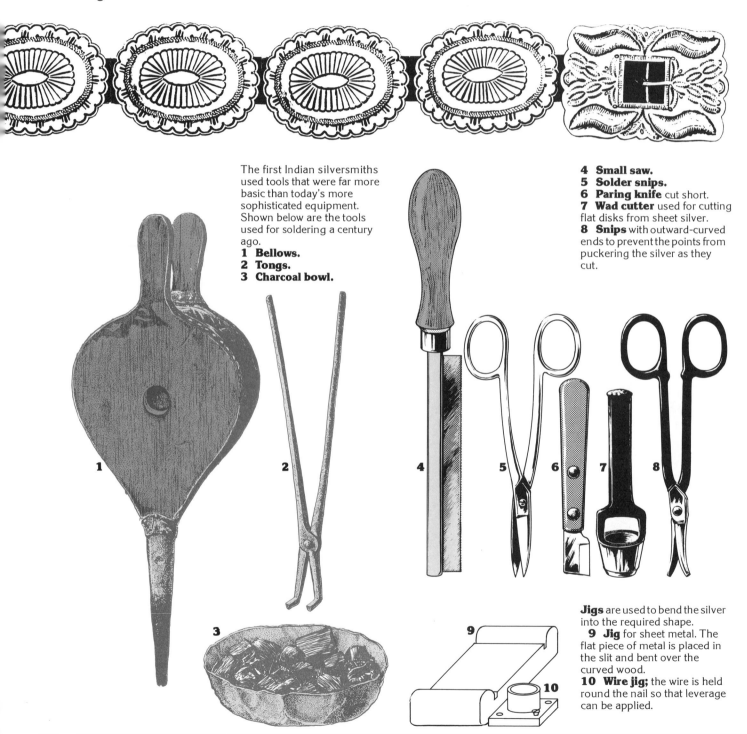

The first Indian silversmiths used tools that were far more basic than today's more sophisticated equipment. Shown below are the tools used for soldering a century ago.
1 Bellows.
2 Tongs.
3 Charcoal bowl.

4 Small saw.
5 Solder snips.
6 Paring knife cut short.
7 Wad cutter used for cutting flat disks from sheet silver.
8 Snips with outward-curved ends to prevent the points from puckering the silver as they cut.

Jigs are used to bend the silver into the required shape.
9 Jig for sheet metal. The flat piece of metal is placed in the slit and bent over the curved wood.
10 Wire jig; the wire is held round the nail so that leverage can be applied.

During the first half-century of North American Indian silversmithing, the only source of silver was coinage. This was melted down with a proportion of cartridge brass and cast in small bars, or ingots, in a mold.
1 Ingot mold.

Carved stone **molds** are used to cast pieces of ornate jewelry.
2 Two-part mold; the design is carved into one piece, then the halves are joined and the cavity filled with molten metal.
3,4,5 Knives used to carve the designs into the mold.

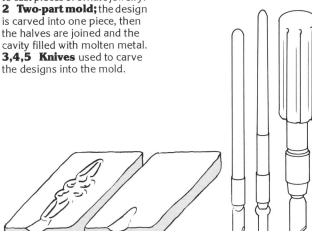

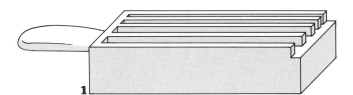

6 Round-faced mallet made of wood.
7 Lead block used as an anvil when hammering shallow disks.
8,9 Cone anvil and **cone punch** used primarily in button making. A flat disk is placed on the anvil and struck with the punch to shape it into a cone.
10,11 Fluting anvil and **fluting punch.**
12,13 Female and male embossing punches. The female punch is stamped onto the front of the silver to outline the shape to be embossed, and then the shape is raised by stamping it from the back with the male punch.
14 Flat anvil.
15 Flat-faced dies used to stamp relief designs.
16,17 Wooden anvil and **smooth punch** used for rounding disks.
18,19 Bead anvil and oval **bead punch.**
20,21 Round **bead anvils** and their appropriate **punches.**
22 Scalloping punches.
23 Detail punches.

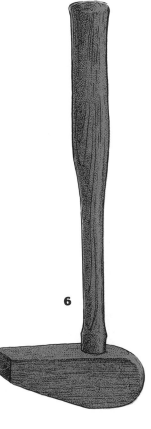

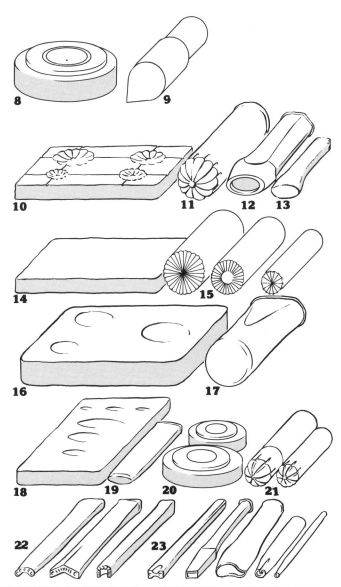

Finishing and polishing

Finishing and polishing are the final stages in working with precious metals, and are the stages that are most often skimped or deemed unnecessary. However, a flawless finish on a piece of metalwork can only be an asset to its appearance, as it sets off the beauty of the metal and demonstrates the skill of the craftsman.

The 17th century silver items shown here form a set of writing accessories. They comprise: tray, inkpot, sandbox, and a bell for summoning the servant to post the letter. The items are made in English silver, and are finished to a high polish.

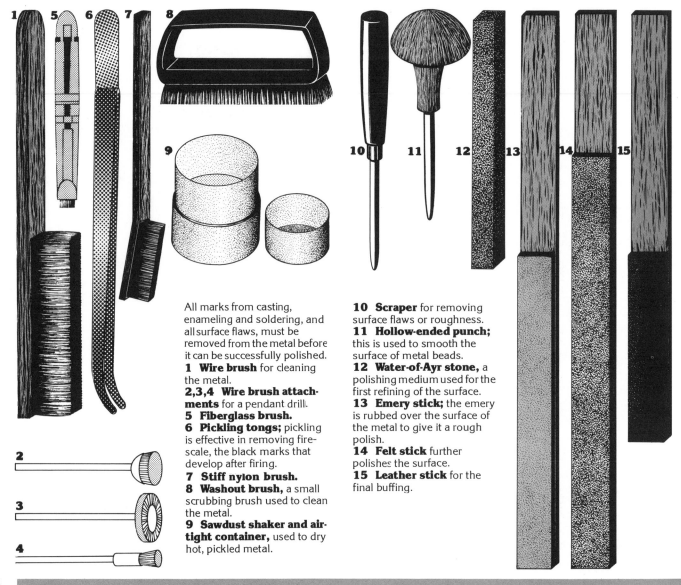

All marks from casting, enameling and soldering, and all surface flaws, must be removed from the metal before it can be successfully polished.

1 Wire brush for cleaning the metal.

2,3,4 Wire brush attachments for a pendant drill.

5 Fiberglass brush.

6 Pickling tongs; pickling is effective in removing firescale, the black marks that develop after firing.

7 Stiff nylon brush.

8 Washout brush, a small scrubbing brush used to clean the metal.

9 Sawdust shaker and airtight container, used to dry hot, pickled metal.

10 Scraper for removing surface flaws or roughness.

11 Hollow-ended punch; this is used to smooth the surface of metal beads.

12 Water-of-Ayr stone, a polishing medium used for the first refining of the surface.

13 Emery stick; the emery is rubbed over the surface of the metal to give it a rough polish.

14 Felt stick further polishes the surface.

15 Leather stick for the final buffing.

A **double-spindle polisher,** illustrated below, can be used with various cleaning and polishing attachments. Tripoli, a polishing compound, is used on some of the attachments, and jeweler's rouge (a finer grade polish) on others.

Very little polishing medium is required on the buffs; the work is done by the fast movement of the **buff** against the metal.

a The chosen buff is attached to the **spindle** and set in motion, and the block of **tripoli** or **rouge** is held gently against the buff so that only a very light coating is transferred.
b The piece to be polished is held against the buff, at such an angle that the moving wheel cannot "grab" the piece out of the operator's hands. It is advisable to wear **goggles** to protect the eyes from dust and fragments.

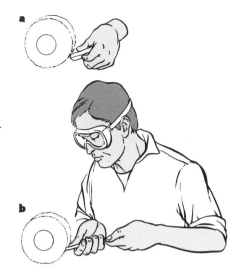

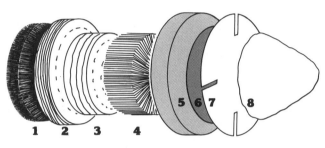

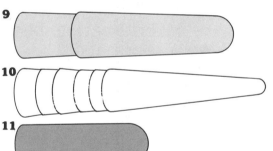

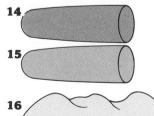

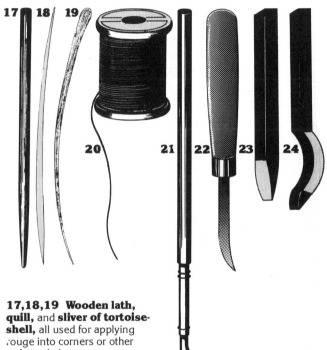

1 **Bristle brush.**
2 **Muslin buff** for tripoli.
3 **Cotton buff** for rouge.
4 **Poly-mop,** a soft polishing mop.
5 **Wooden lap,** a smooth wooden polishing wheel.
6 **Knife-edge lap,** also of wood, for polishing crevices.
7 **Split buff.**
8 **Taper buff.**
9 **Felt ring buffs.**
10 **Emery shells;** these are cones for polishing the insides of rings.
11 **Hard felt buff.**
12 **Tripoli block.**
13 **Abrasive tripoli block.**
14 **Jeweler's red rouge.**
15 **Golden rouge block.**
16 **Chamois polishing cloth.**

17,18,19 **Wooden lath, quill,** and **sliver of tortoise-shell,** all used for applying rouge into corners or other awkward places.
20 **Linen thread;** this can be charged with rouge and threaded through small openings in pierced work.
21 **Agate burnisher** for final smoothing.
22 **Steel burnisher.**
23 **Hallmark punch.**
24 **Curved hallmark punch** used to mark the insides of rings.
25,26 **Finger cots** used to protect polished jewelry from finger marks.

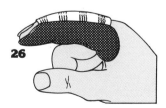

© DIAGRAM

13 Lapidary and beadmaking

Lapidary work is the cutting and shaping of precious and semiprecious stones for jewelry. Beads are also included here as they are similar to stones in their relationship to jewelry; both are used to provide pattern and decoration in transparent, translucent or opaque color as a contrast to the metals generally used as backgrounds.

The factor that determines the nature of many of the tools for lapidary work is the hardness of many of the most popular stones. Diamond, emerald, sapphire and ruby are all very hard stones, amethyst, malachite, tiger eye and agate rather softer, but all of them have to be ground against very hard or abrasive surfaces. Carborundum and emery are used for the softer stones; diamond itself, in the form of abrasive grits, is used for the harder stones. Consequently many lapidary tools are merely vehicles for the various abrasives.

The cutting of facets in stones, which is performed to make them reflect extra light, is an important but relatively recent aspect of lapidary work. Before the great popularity of faceted stones in the 15th and 16th centuries, stones were frequently shaped and polished into domed forms, called cabochons. Jewelry and lapidary work have always provided chances for designers and craftsmen to show their skill and originality, and today is no exception. After the ornate creations of the 19th century, which reached their climax in the works of Carl Fabergé, this century has seen a movement toward stark simplicity and beauty of design, characterized particularly by the modern design influence of the Scandinavian countries. Traditional skills are being transformed; such techniques as faceting are not outmoded, but are applied with originality and flair to such tasks as cutting reflective surfaces on metal or resin blocks, and to shaping asymmetrical stones.

This photograph shows the workshop of Carl Fabergé (1846-1920). Fabergé specialized in the creation of fantastic objets d'art from combinations of precious metals, gems, and semiprecious stones such as jade, malachite and lapis lazuli.

Rock hunting

Finding and recognizing the rough stones that will be attractive or valuable when cut and polished requires experience, and the use of a variety of tools for testing the stone's properties. Stones can be identified by color, hardness, specific gravity, facet angle and light diffraction; careful examination is necessary for these to be firmly established.

The illustration on the right comes from a book called "Familiar Lessons on Mineralogy and Geology etc." published in London in 1821. Rock collecting is described in the book as one of the most agreeable pastimes of those visiting coastal resorts.

Rock-hunting tools are used to dig out rough stones, and to help the collector make preliminary examinations so that he can decide whether their characteristics are promising.

1 Rock hammer for breaking up small boulders.
2 Chipping hammer.
3 Rock pick used to chip away at boulders.
4 Hoe pick.
5 Gad-pry bar used for loosening ore or rock.
6 Gem scoop used to scrape rubble out of crevices.

7 Splitting chisel, a tool used to break up rocks into manageable pieces.
8 Wedging chisel with a pointed tip.
9 Narrow chisel used for probing rock pockets.
10 Lightweight **ultraviolet lamp** used for gem identification.

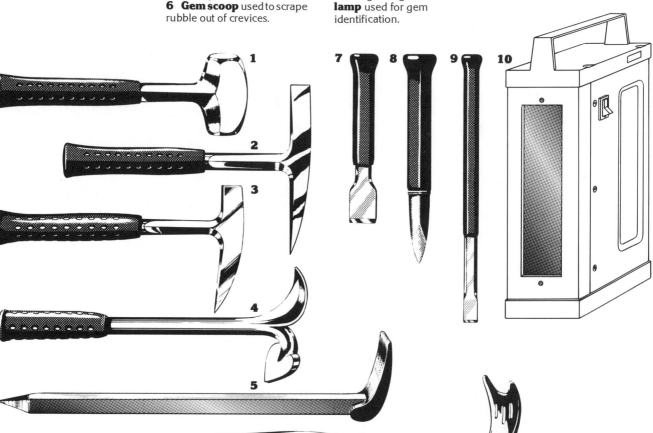

Classifying gemstones

1 Eye loupe.
2 Linen tester, a small magnifying glass.
3 Illuminated coddington; this magnifying lens has a small beam of light that passes through the lens and onto the stone.
4 Dichroscope, a device for carrying out detailed examinations of a stone's structure. The stone is held by the attachment in front of the lens.
5 Focusing magnifiers, worn on a headband as goggles.

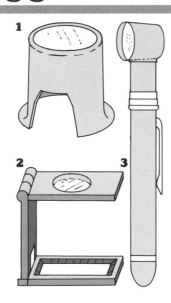

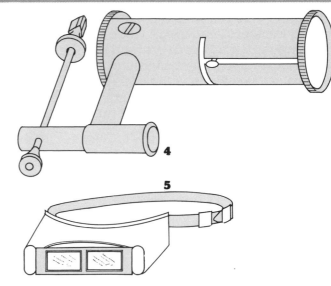

6 Tweezers with a locking device so that the stone will not slip while it is being examined.
7 Gem holder with claws that grip the stone firmly.
8 Contact goniometer, a tool that is used for measuring the facet angle of a crystalline stone.

9 Emerald filter; this glass distinguishes emeralds from the numerous other green stones.
10 Hardness tester used for grading stones.
11 Cleaving blade, a sharp steel bar used to split stones so that their facet angles can be measured.

Mohs' scale of hardness is used to grade gemstones, based on the principle that a harder stone will mark a softer one. Talc, the softest stone, is grade 1; diamond, the hardest, is grade 10. The grades of some other stones are listed (right).

Diamond	10
Sapphire	9
Ruby	9
Topaz	8-9
Chrysoberyl	8½
Emerald	8
Aquamarine	7½
Beryl	7½
Zircon	7½
Tourmaline	7-7½
Agate	7
Amethyst	7
Carnelian	7
Chalcedony	7
Onyx	7
Tiger eye	7
Garnet	6½-7½
Jade	6½-7
Haematite	6½
Opal	6
Moonstone	6
Lapis lazuli	6
Turquoise	6
Obsidian	5
Malachite	4-5
Coral	3½
Jet	3½
Pearl	3½
Amber	2-2½

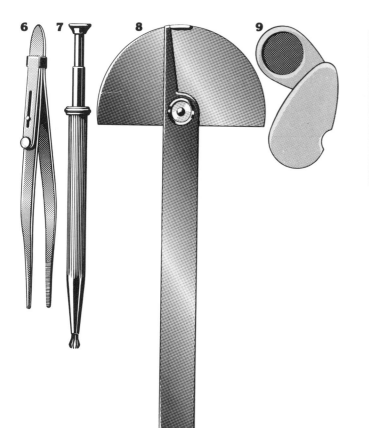

Cutting and shaping

Most precious and semiprecious stones are harder than steel, and so cannot be cut with steel tools no matter how sharp the blade may be. Abrasive grits have to be used to make the actual fissure in the stone, and the various blades are used only as a means of driving these grits through the stone; diamond chips can be incorporated into many blades.

The slab of semiprecious stone shown in the photograph on the right has been cut with a slab saw to give it a flat surface. The stone will be cut into further slices so that sections for cutting and shaping can easily be taken.

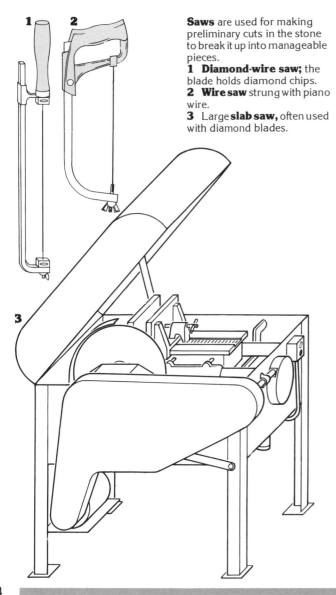

Saws are used for making preliminary cuts in the stone to break it up into manageable pieces.
1 Diamond-wire saw; the blade holds diamond chips.
2 Wire saw strung with piano wire.
3 Large **slab saw,** often used with diamond blades.

4 Adjustable rectangle template used as a pattern.
5,6,7 Templates in fancy shapes; these are traced onto the stone as cutting guides.
8 Tungsten carbide pencil for marking stones.
9 Aluminum pencil.

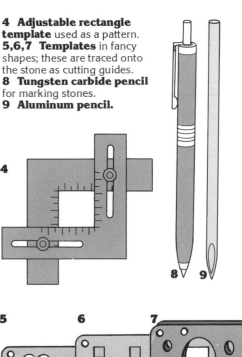

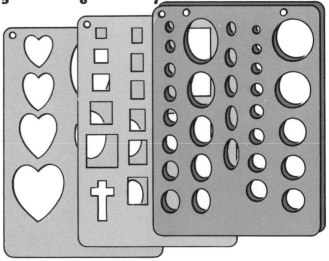

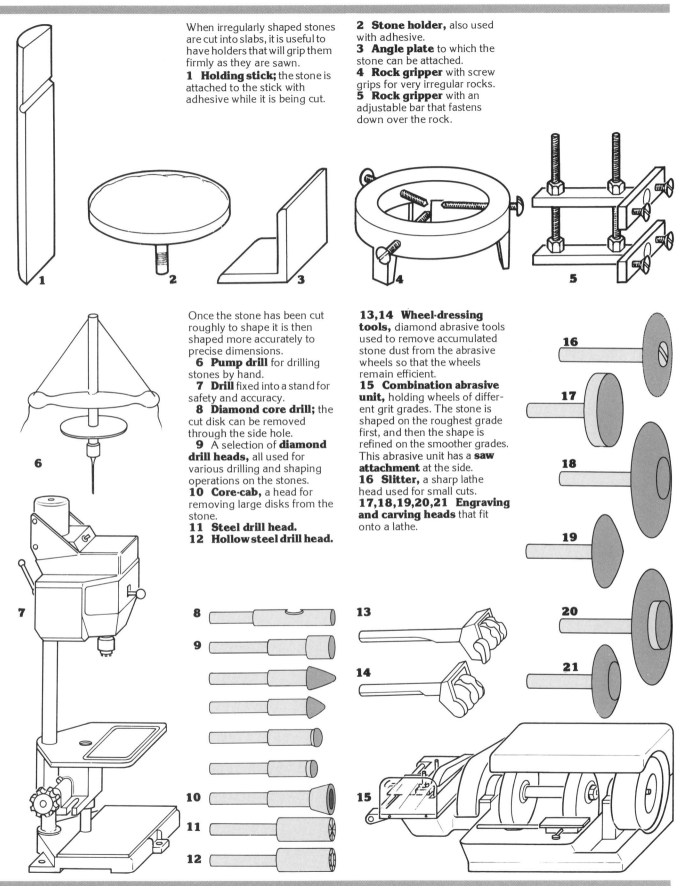

When irregularly shaped stones are cut into slabs, it is useful to have holders that will grip them firmly as they are sawn.

1 Holding stick; the stone is attached to the stick with adhesive while it is being cut.

2 Stone holder, also used with adhesive.

3 Angle plate to which the stone can be attached.

4 Rock gripper with screw grips for very irregular rocks.

5 Rock gripper with an adjustable bar that fastens down over the rock.

Once the stone has been cut roughly to shape it is then shaped more accurately to precise dimensions.

6 Pump drill for drilling stones by hand.

7 Drill fixed into a stand for safety and accuracy.

8 Diamond core drill; the cut disk can be removed through the side hole.

9 A selection of **diamond drill heads,** all used for various drilling and shaping operations on the stones.

10 Core-cab, a head for removing large disks from the stone.

11 Steel drill head.

12 Hollow steel drill head.

13,14 Wheel-dressing tools, diamond abrasive tools used to remove accumulated stone dust from the abrasive wheels so that the wheels remain efficient.

15 Combination abrasive unit, holding wheels of different grit grades. The stone is shaped on the roughest grade first, and then the shape is refined on the smoother grades. This abrasive unit has a **saw attachment** at the side.

16 Slitter, a sharp lathe head used for small cuts.

17,18,19,20,21 Engraving and carving heads that fit onto a lathe.

Faceting and polishing

The beauty of precious and semiprecious stones is enhanced when they are polished to a high gloss, and some of the transparent stones can be given more "fire," or reflected light, by faceting. Faceting is the process of cutting regular planes on the stone in a predetermined pattern that is related to the stone's crystalline structure.

Shown (right) is St Edward's crown, part of the Crown Jewels of the British monarchy. The crown contains approximately 440 precious and semiprecious stones, set in gold with silver decoration.

The first precious stones used for decorating jewelry were not faceted at all, but smoothed and rounded into the cabochon style; a cabochon is a stone with a flat back and a domed face. It was discovered, however, that some stones reflected more light if they were cut into facets, and so the face was cut into regular planes as in the rose cut. The backs of these early cut stones were still flat, but through experiment lapidaries learned to shape the bottom of the stone into a point (known as a pavilion) that further increased the gem's "fire."

The cuts illustrated (right) are shown from the top and from the side.

a Cabochon cut, with a flat back and a domed face.
b Baguette cut; this cut is particularly suitable for emeralds and sapphires. A true baguette cut has the same cuts on the back as on the face.
c Rose cut, a cut that was particularly popular for early faceted stones.
d Trap cut; the face is similar to a baguette, but the back is cut into a pointed pavilion.
e Antique cushion, a fancy cut for rectangular stones.
f Brilliant cut, often used for modern diamonds.
g Fancy cut used for a pear-shaped stone.

Gauges are used to take accurate measurements of stones and settings at all stages of the work.
1 Stone-size gauge.
2 Spring gauge.
3 Stone-size gauge; this version can be folded away.

4 Micrometer, an adjustable tool that is closed around the stone and allows the size to be read from a graduated scale.
5 Contact gauge used in diamond polishing.
6 Angle gauge for measuring the angle of the table (top) of a faceted stone.

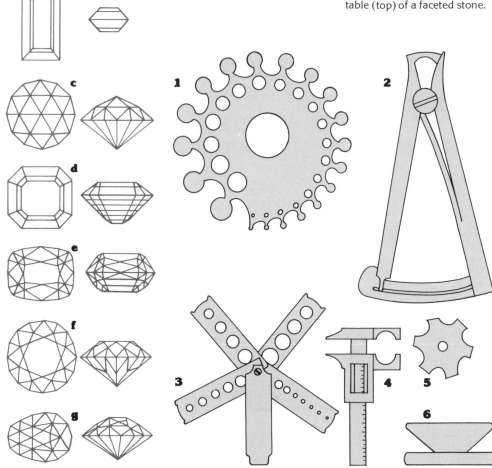

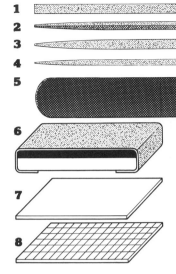

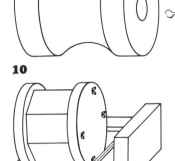

1,2,3,4 Diamond files used for shaping and polishing.
5 Silicon carbide abrasive board.
6 Silicon carbide sander.
7 Glass slab used for hand-polishing stones.
8 Scored perspex slab, used with grits for hand polishing.

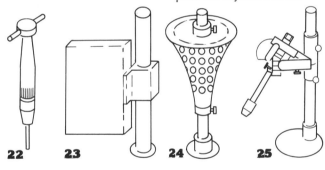

9 Wooden polishing wheel, made on a lathe so that the circumference is true.
10 Tumbler, often used to polish baroque (irregularly shaped) gemstones.
11 Vibrating lap; this polisher vibrates gently, abrading and polishing the stones on its surface.

During polishing, the stone is secured with wax to a **dopstick** to provide a grip.
12 Hardwood dopstick.
13 Steel dopstick.
14 Suction dopstick.
15 Cone-ended dopstick used for faceted stones.
16 Lap stick used in the faceting head.

17 Dopping wax.
18 Heated palette used to melt dopping wax.
19 Knocking-off block, against which the dopstick is struck to remove the stone.
20 Wood knocking-off stick.
21 Syringe full of diamond recharging compound for laps.

22 Hand-held faceting head; the stone is dopped to the end and the tool is adjusted to the correct angle against the lap.
23 Hand rest for use with hand-held faceting tools.

24 Jambpeg used as an elementary faceting head; each hole is at a set height and angle, and the **lap stick** is placed in the appropriate holes.
25 Mechanical faceting head.
26 Faceting unit with lap plate and adjustable head.

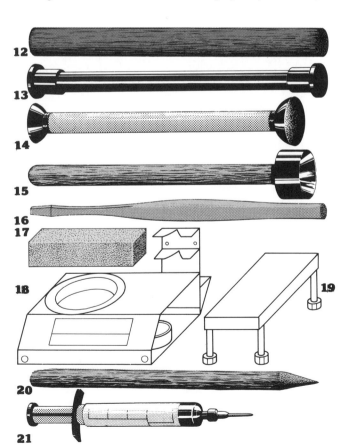

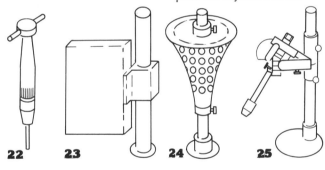

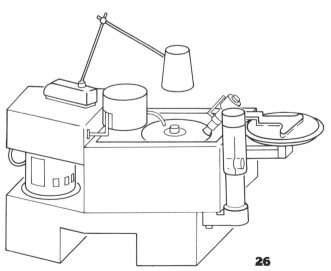

© DIAGRAM

Mounting and setting

The settings used for mounting gemstones perform the functional service of holding the stones in place and of protecting them against unexpected blows that might otherwise dislodge them. Some settings are designed to be as unobtrusive as possible, but others are developed so that they become design elements in their own right.

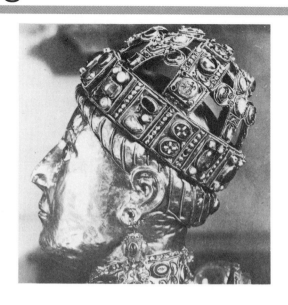

The head shown (right) is a detail of the statue of Saint Foy, in the treasury of the French cathedral of Conques. The statue was made in the 10th or 11th century, and the settings of the precious and semi-precious stones are typical of that period.

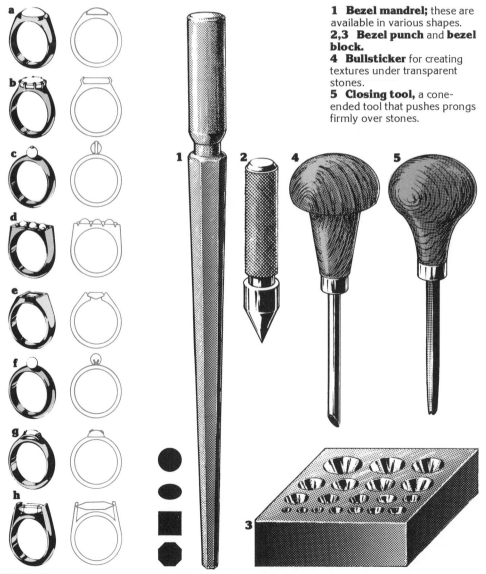

The styles in which gemstones have been mounted and set in the past have been determined by a number of factors. Fashion has played an important part; for instance, the widespread use of faceted stones in Elizabethan times led to the development of inconspicuous settings such as the claw setting, in which the minimum surface area of the stone is covered by the metal. The development of more complex techniques has also affected style; for example, pearls were generally set in the Middle Ages by driving a rivet right through the pearl, but as this spoiled the appearance of the stone a method was developed for fixing pearls invisibly. Shown (right) are some of the variations in setting and mounting styles.

a Bezel setting.
b Claw setting.
c Riveting.
d Graining.
e Flush setting.
f Invisible setting for pearls.
g,h Two modern settings for gemstones that have been cut into unusual shapes.

1 Bezel mandrel; these are available in various shapes.
2,3 Bezel punch and **bezel block.**
4 Bullsticker for creating textures under transparent stones.
5 Closing tool, a cone-ended tool that pushes prongs firmly over stones.

A bezel setting for a single stone brooch is formed in the following way.

a The shape of the stone is marked with a **scriber** on the metal that is to take the setting; the metal is cut along this line.

b The bezel is formed from a strip of metal that is soldered into a ring. The required tapered shape is imparted to it by hammering it on a **bezel mandrel** or by punching it in a **bezel block.**

c After being checked for size around the stone, the bezel is joined to the metal base by soldering it all around the circumference. A pin is soldered to the back at this stage.

d The stone is dropped into the middle of the bezel, and a **bezel pusher** is used to smooth the metal rim down over the stone, so holding it firmly in place.

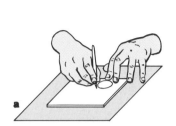
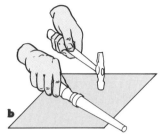
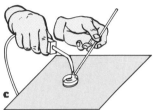
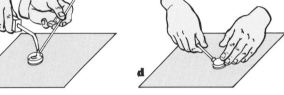

1 Ring clamp, used for holding a ring while it is being worked on.
2 Bezel pusher used for smoothing bezel edges.
3 Holding fixture; the work in progress can be jammed into the V-shape.
4 Bezel roller, for smoothing larger bezels.

5 Prong lifter, a tool for altering the positions of prongs without damaging them.
6 Prong-bending pliers for closing prong fixtures.
7 Prong pusher.
8 Burnisher, a steel or agate smoothing tool.

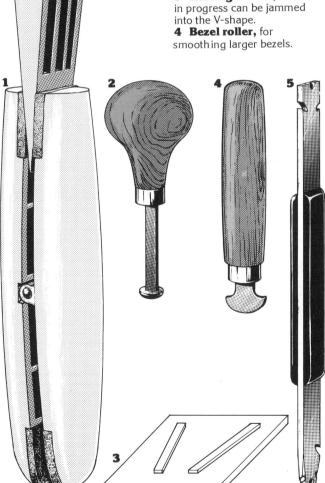

Beadmaking

Beads are small objects that have been pierced for stringing together. They are usually used for necklaces and other decorative purposes, although in ancient times particular beads were often endowed with mystical and magical properties, and so had to be designed and shaped to set formulae handed down through the ages.

The beaded basket shown (right) was made by threading glass beads onto fibers taken from pineapple leaves, and then weaving the threads together. The beads, in several different colors, have been arranged so that they form a regular pattern.

The earliest beads ever worn were probably plant seeds; shells and fossils were used later, and so were the teeth of animals and humans, with holes drilled through them for stringing. By the Neolithic period beads were being made from bone and pebbles. The Egyptians were the first to make beads from faience, the forerunner of glass, and they also made very beautiful beads from precious stones such as lapis lazuli, carnelian, turquoise and amethyst. Many civilizations learned to make beads from gold and silver, and eventually from glass and crystal also.

Illustrated (right) are some of the many kinds of beads that have been worn at different times through history.

a Plant seeds.
b Shells.
c Teeth; these examples are the eye teeth from several wildcats.
d Bone, in this case the vertebrae of a snake.
e Roots and tree bark.
f Carved wood.
g Unglazed clay.
h Pearls.
i Gold disks.
j Coral.
k Glass shapes.

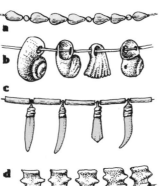

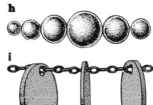

Beads made from rolled paper can be easily decorated and are surprisingly durable. Shown (right) are some of the paper strips that can be used, showing also the shape of the resulting bead. The strip of paper is coated with paste, and then rolled evenly over a **rod** or a **pencil** (right) until the end of the strip is reached. The bead is slipped off the rod, allowed to dry, and then decorated with paints and varnish.

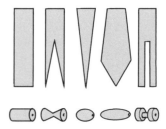
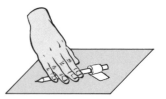

Wood beads can be made quite simply from small twigs, particularly those with interesting bark.
a The twigs are notched all round at regular intervals, using a sharp knife such as a **whittling knife.**
b The twig is sliced through at every notch, so that single bead shapes are formed. The center of each one is pierced with an **awl** or a **bodkin** so that the beads can be strung.

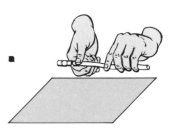
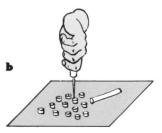

240

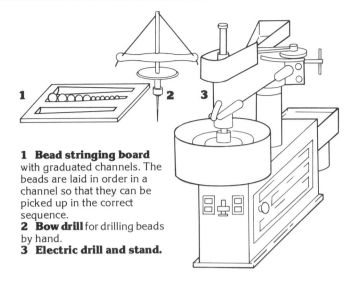

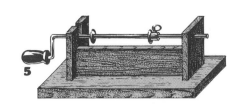

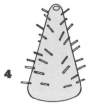

1 Bead stringing board with graduated channels. The beads are laid in order in a channel so that they can be picked up in the correct sequence.
2 Bow drill for drilling beads by hand.
3 Electric drill and stand.

4 Bead tree used when firing clay beads; each bead is placed on a separate piece of wire.
5 Bead wheel used for painting stripes on beads; the bead is placed on the shaft, which is then turned with the handle (right) while the stripe is painted.

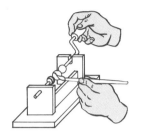

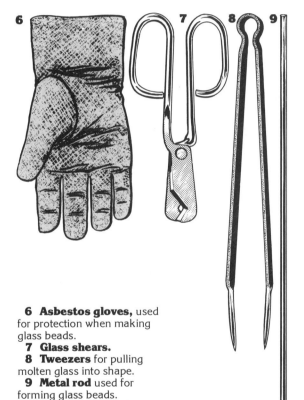

6 Asbestos gloves, used for protection when making glass beads.
7 Glass shears.
8 Tweezers for pulling molten glass into shape.
9 Metal rod used for forming glass beads.
10 Blowpipe for molten glass.

Glass beads may be made from an elongated section of blown glass.
a A "gather" of molten glass is taken from the furnace on the end of a **blowpipe,** and a bubble of air is blown into the gather.

b This section of hollow glass is then pulled out into a thin length, and cut into pieces with **glass shears** so that beads are formed with holes already in their centers.

Another way of forming glass beads is shown on the right.
a Long cames, or sticks, of glass are assembled around a **metal rod** and heated until they fuse.
b When the glass is cool, the metal rod is withdrawn and the tube of glass that remains is cut into sections with a **file** to form individual beads.

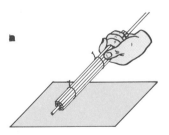

©DIAGRAM

14 Thread preparation

This chapter illustrates and describes the tools involved in preparing natural fibers for use in textiles, and also those tools used in coloring and dyeing fibers; dyeing can take place before or after the threads have been woven. Natural fibers of many kinds can be used in textiles; the fibers may come from animals, as with the various types of wool, or they may originate from plants, such as the fibers of hemp, cotton and mulberry.

The tools used for the preparation vary with the size and nature of the fibers. With wool, the material is prepared by combing the fleece across toothed cards to remove the tangles, and then spinning it into regular threads; cotton, by contrast, has to be beaten on a net in order to clean the dirt from the fibers and to make them even and fluffy before it is spun. Spinning is the means of converting a bundle of separate fibers into a continuous thread that can be used for weaving, knitting or knotting, and different ages and different regions of the world have evolved their own methods, varying from the simple hand-held spindle of many tribes to the electrically powered spinning wheel. The fibers can be dyed to any color of the rainbow once they have been prepared, and although many chemical dyes have recently been developed, none are quite as subtle or as beautiful as those produced by the various plantstuffs that have been known and used for centuries.

The print reproduced here illustrates the thread preparation stage in the 18th century Irish linen industry. The linen fibers are being spun into thread by the woman on the left, while the woman on the right makes ready the thread fcr weaving.

Preparing natural fibers

Natural fibers suitable for processing into textiles can be harvested from a surprising variety of flora and fauna. Wool can be obtained not only from sheep, but from goats, llamas and even angora rabbits. In the plant kingdom, fibers are derived from the cotton seed, hemp and flax stems, and the bark of the paper mulberry.

The illustration (right) shows a pastoral scene, with peasants in the foreground preparing flax. The flax has been retted (partially rotted) in water so that the softened fibers can be twisted into thread.

The bark of the paper mulberry tree is used for making fabrics in many Pacific islands. The bark is stripped, and then flattened and textured with patterned beaters.
1,2,3,4,5,6,7 Beetles or **beaters** used to flatten the bark fibers.

Hemp and flax fibers are processed in similar ways. The fibers are cleaned, stranded, beaten, and then prepared for spinning.
8 Rippler; the fibers are drawn through this to clean them of bark and dirt.

9 Nail bed used to separate the fibers into strands.
10 Scutcher for beating the fibers.
11 Bar with textured surface; hanks of fiber are drawn through the hole and around the bar to remove unwanted plant tissue.

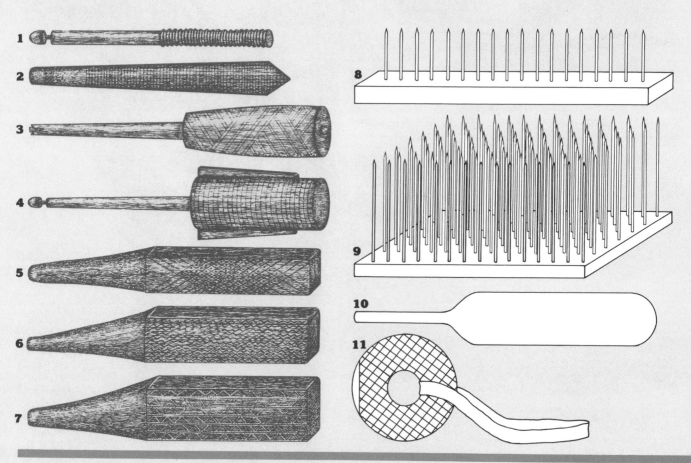

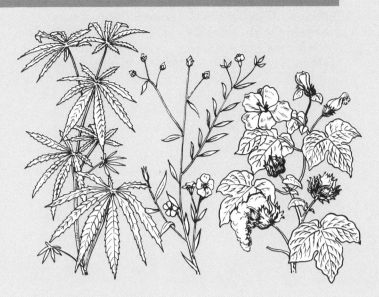

Illustrated (right) are three of
the plants that yield natural
fibers suitable for conversion
into textiles.
a Hemp.
b Flax.
c Cotton.

Wool needs to be carded before
it can be spun. The carding
regulates the strands of wool
and combs out the tangles
that have formed in the fleece.
1 Cards are made of wood
and covered with wire combing
teeth.

Cotton is prepared by placing
the balls of fiber in a string
hammock and beating them
with willow rods until they are
soft and even.
2 Willow beater.
3 Hammock suitable for
willowing cotton.

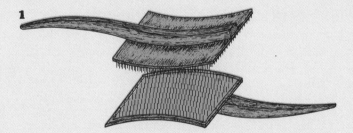

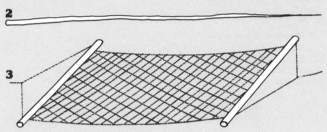

Carding is done with lumps of
wool from the sheared fleece.
a A rough hank of wool is
placed on one of the **cards**
and teased out to cover the
full area of the teeth.

b The second card is stroked
across the first until all the
wool has been transferred to
the second card. This procedure
is repeated five or six times
until the wool is well combed
and forms a roll, called a
rollag, on the card.

Natural fibers are felted and
scoured by immersing them in
very hot water and scrubbing
them vigorously. This cleans
and softens the fibers and
helps them to form into even
strands.
4 Rubber gloves.
5 Bowl.
6 Jug.

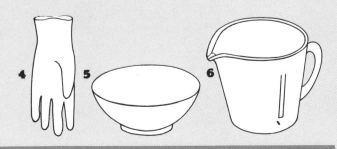

Dyeing

Dyeing natural fibers is a rewarding task, since they readily absorb all kinds of organic dyes that can be gathered and prepared from plantstuffs. The plantstuffs are chopped small, and then boiled to extract the pigment. The fibers to be dyed are added to the solution with a mordant that makes the dye "take," and the ingredients are boiled.

Illustrated (right) are examples of tie-dyeing and of batik. The tie-dyed fabric exhibits the characteristic radiating effect, and the batik shows the crackle effect that appears on the fabric as a result of the tiny cracks that appear in the wax.

1 Pestle and mortar for crushing dyestuffs.
2 Scales used to weigh ingredients.
3 Hatchet for chopping dyestuffs.
4 Thermometer.
5 Glass stirring rod.
6 Mixing spoon for the dyes.
7 Tongs used to lift the fibers in and out of the vats.
8 Wooden fork for stirring the fibers.
9 Measuring spoons for dyes and mordants.
10 Strainer for removing unwanted plant material.
11 Dyeing vat.
12,13 Bucket and **bowl** for mixing and dyeing.

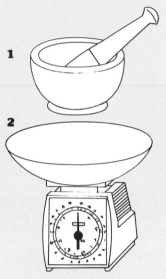
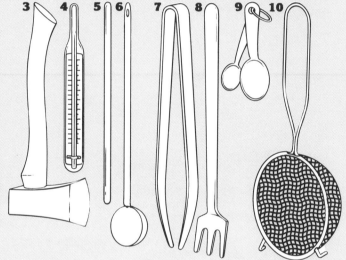
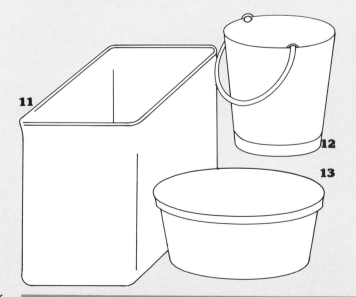

Substance	part used	color
Prickly pear	fruit	pink
Madder	root	red
Onion	skins	orange
Goldenrod	flower	yellow
Bracken	fern tips	pale green
Indigo	leaves	blue
Elder	berries	lilac
Logwood	wood	purple-gray
Birch	bark	light brown
Walnut	hulls	dark brown

Tie dyeing is a pattern-producing dyeing process that involves binding portions of the fabric tightly with string or by other means so that the dye cannot reach them.

1 Pin used to hold the fabric in place while it is being tied.

2 Needle and thread; the thread can either be stitched into the fabric or wound around it.

3 Clothes pin can be used instead of thread to hold the fabric.

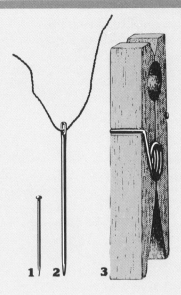

The pattern produced by tie dyeing will depend on whether the fabric is folded, gathered, crumpled or simply tied randomly.

a The fabric is tied tightly in the chosen design; the thread must be extremely tight so that no dye can creep under it.

b The fabric is dyed in the normal way. The dye will color all those parts of the fabric that are not protected by the string. When the dye is dry the strings are removed, and the fabric is pressed to remove all folds and creases.

a

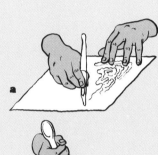

b

In batik dyeing, resistance to the dye is provided by a wax coat.

4 Funnel for applying hot wax to large areas.

5 Wax crayon; this can be used to produce a blurry pattern on the fabric.

6 Tjanting, a tool for applying hot wax in fine patterns. A metal reservoir holds the melted wax.

7,8,9 Skewer, needle tool and **nail;** these can be used to trail hot wax across the fabric.

10 Double boiler for melting wax safely.

11 Alcohol lamp; this can be used to keep the wax in the tjanting molten.

12 Electric wax palette.

Batik can be used to produce intricate patterns, provided that the wax is kept liquid so that it can be drawn onto the fabric accurately.

a The wax is melted, and applied to the areas of the fabric that are not intended to take the dye. The wax is left to harden, and then the fabric is dyed in a low-temperature solution.

b When the dye has taken, the fabric is washed in very hot water to remove the wax. The clean fabric is dried, and the process is repeated with any other colors required.

a

b

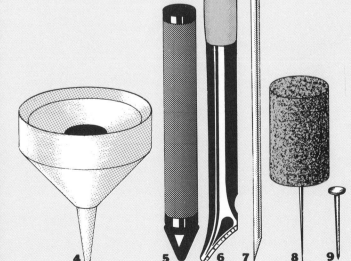

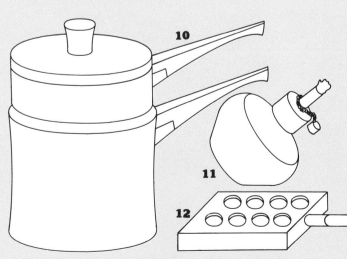

Spinning

Spinning is the technique of twisting fibers so that they cling together and form a continuous yarn. This can be done on a hand spindle, which is basically a weighted rod, or on a spinning wheel, which speeds up the process considerably. Flax is generally wound onto a distaff before it is spun, as this helps to prevent the long fibers from tangling.

The photograph on the right was taken in Ireland at the turn of the century, and shows a woman spinning thread on a type of spinning wheel known as a castle wheel.

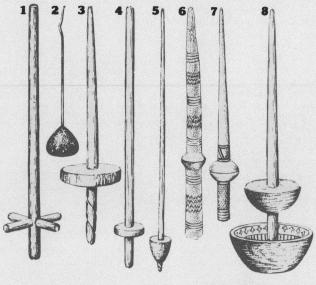

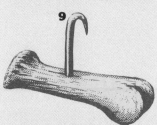

1 **Wood spindle** with a cross onto which the yarn is wound.
2 **Chinese wire spindle.**
3 **Navajo spindle.**
4 **Andean spindle.**
5 **Egyptian spindle,** c. 1500BC.

6 Bronze Age **pottery spindle.**
7 **Bone spindle** from the Bronze Age.
8 **New Mexican cup spindle.**
9 **Chinese spindle** made from metal in a section of bone.

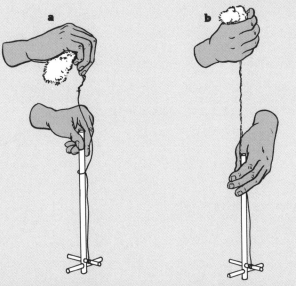

Shown (left) is the method of using a **spindle** with a dowel cross.
a A "leader" of ready-spun yarn is attached to the spindle and to the roll of unspun wool.
b The spindle is spun with one hand, while the other hand slowly feeds out wool.

c When the spindle reaches the floor, the yarn is wound onto one hand and then onto the spindle.
d When the spindle is full of yarn, the dowels that form the cross are pulled out and the ball of yarn is slipped over the end of the spindle.

1 Distaff used for holding prepared fibers. The fibers are carefully arranged on the distaff so that they require the minimum of manual regulation during spinning.
2 Andean distaff.
3 Hedgehog or **flyer,** with hooks used to feed the yarn onto the bobbin. As one part of the bobbin is filled, the yarn is looped over another hook to fill the next part of the bobbin.
4 Electric spinner.

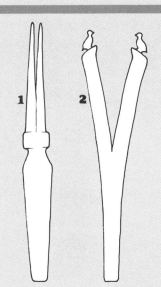
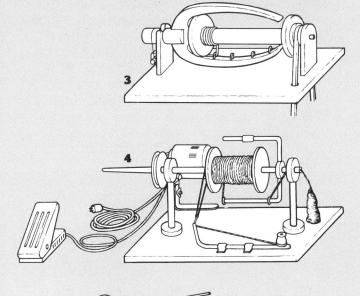

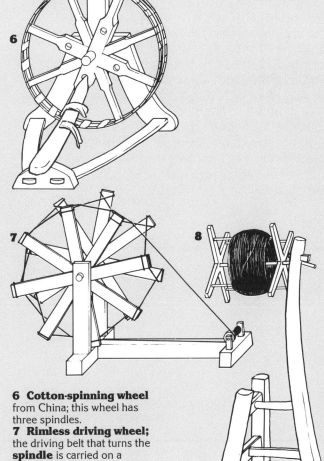

5 Spinning wheel with a **hedgehog** or **flyer** for feeding the yarn bobbin. The wheel is operated by a treadle at the bottom.

6 Cotton-spinning wheel from China; this wheel has three spindles.
7 Rimless driving wheel; the driving belt that turns the **spindle** is carried on a network of cords connecting the spokes.
8 Hemp-spinning wheel.

©DIAGRAM

15 Weaving

Weaving involves forming a web or a cloth by interworking two sets of fibers. The warp, which goes from top to bottom on a vertical loom or front to back on a table-top loom, is set up first, and then interwoven with the weft or woof, which goes from side to side. Some areas of weaving, such as basketwork, use adaptations of this basic principle, such as having a warp of radiating fibers that are woven with a weft in a circular fashion, beginning from the center and working outward.

The principle behind weaving in any fiber is surprisingly consistent; the basic over/under or tabby weave is found all over the world, in fabric, baskets, chair seats and matting in every fiber from cotton to coconut. Variation is brought into each craft by altering the basic weave, and by introducing extra colors or threads of a different thickness.

The tools of the weaver include those needed for making ready the fibers to be woven—knives and bark-strippers for basket canes and the implements used for warping thread come into this category. The weaving tools themselves range from the four-stick "loom" of the American Indians to the many shedded floor looms of the cloth weaver. The history of craft weaving has included such landmarks as the development of the heddle system, the setting up of the Gobelins tapestry works in the 15th century, and in our own century the development of new weaving techniques such as three-dimensional "soft sculpture" weaving and sprang.

This tapestry is the central panel from the "Life of Christ" tapestry in Rheims Cathedral, and depicts the Virgin Mary weaving a strip of braid decorated with floral designs.

PLANTATIO

Weaving 1

The successful weaving of fabric depends a good deal on the way in which the yarn and the loom are prepared. The warp yarn is made ready for the loom by winding it into skeins and attaching it carefully to the loom at even intervals; various tools exist to assist in this process, and also to help the weaver to produce an even weave on the loom.

The wood engraving reproduced here was made by the English artist Thomas Bewick, and depicts a weaver at his loom. His spare bobbins are in the basket on the floor.

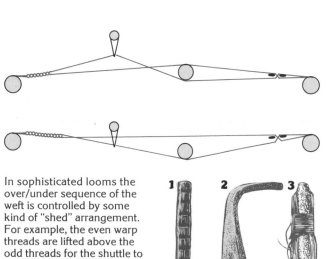

In sophisticated looms the over/under sequence of the weft is controlled by some kind of "shed" arrangement. For example, the even warp threads are lifted above the odd threads for the shuttle to pass in one direction, and then lowered for it to pass back, as shown in the diagrams (above).

Illustrated (right) are examples of ancient and ethnic **looms** and **weaving accessories.**
1 Egyptian **warp-spacing bar.**
2 Egyptian **weft beater.**
3 Egyptian **shuttle** with the thread still in place.
4 Horizontal ground loom.
5 Bow loom strung over a pliable branch.
6 Warp-weighted loom; the warp threads are kept taut by stone weights.
7 Quill loom; the weft used in this loom incorporates colored porcupine quills.
8 Backstrap loom, a kind of loom still used in many countries. The weaver leans back to tauten the warp threads.

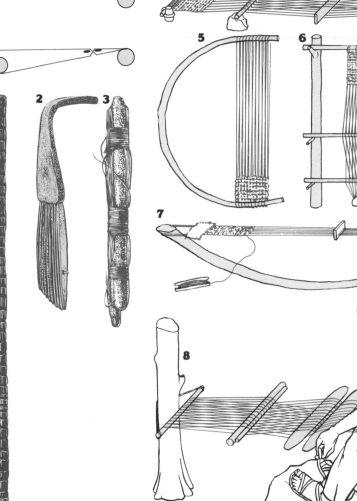

1 Weaving tablets, used for making a strip of decorative fabric. The tablets are pierced with five holes and strung with yarn; the different sheds are made by turning the cards forward and back, and the shuttle is inserted after each turn.

2 Chinese **ribbon loom** used for weaving narrow strips of silk ribbon.

3 Inkle loom; this loom can be used for weaving long strips of braid.

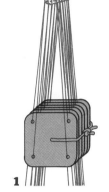

1

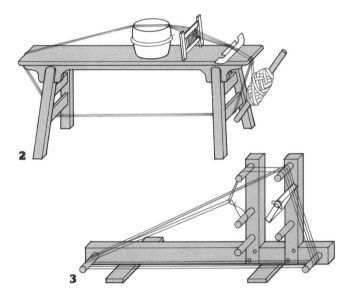

2

3

The technique of finger weaving, used for making braids with diagonal or chevron patterns, is illustrated (right). This particular sequence is for making a diagonal stripe.

a The chosen colors of yarn are cut into long threads, roughly twice the length of the band required.

b Each thread is doubled, and attached with a loop knot to a **pencil** or a **weaving stick.** All the threads of each color should be knotted side by side.

c The outside thread on the left is taken under the second thread, over the third, and so on alternately to the last thread.

d The thread that is now on the extreme left is woven in turn under and over the threads to its right.

e This sequence is continued, always using the thread on the extreme left, until the strip is as long as required.

f The end of the braid is neatened by sewing up the yarn ends with the final weft thread.

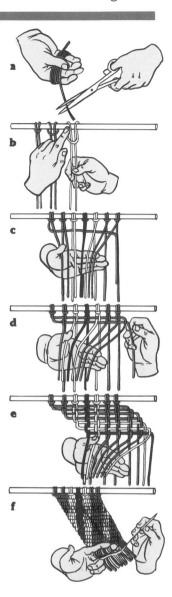

a

b

c

d

e

f

4 Warping frame used for preparing the warp threads for the loom. The way in which the threads are wound on the frame ensures that they can be transferred to the loom in the correct order and with the minimum of tangles.

5 Niddy-noddy used for preparing skeins of wool.

6 Swift; this implement expands to hold skeins of different lengths.

7 Spool rack used for feeding out the yarn.

8 Warping mill, a frame used for preparing very long warp threads.

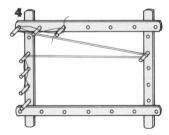

4

5

6

7

8

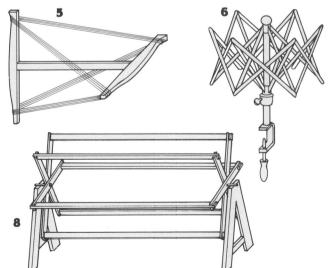

Weaving 2

1 Frame loom, a simple loom for weaving rectangles of fabric. The warp is made by winding the yarn to and fro across nails hammered into the frame, and **weaving sticks** are used to form sheds.
2 Table loom fitted with **rollers** so that considerable lengths of fabric may be woven.

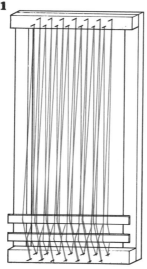

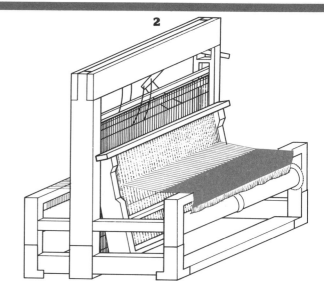

3 Rigid heddle; the heddle is the device used to separate the threads used for the different sheds.
4 Wire heddles; each thread has its own heddle wire in this arrangement.
5 Raddle used for spacing the warp threads correctly.

6 Shaft sticks; these are inserted into the warp threads as they are prepared for the loom, and keep the different sheds separate while the loom is being threaded.
7 Shed stick.

8,9 Reed hooks used for catching the yarn through the heddles.
10 Threading hook, also used for threading the heddles.

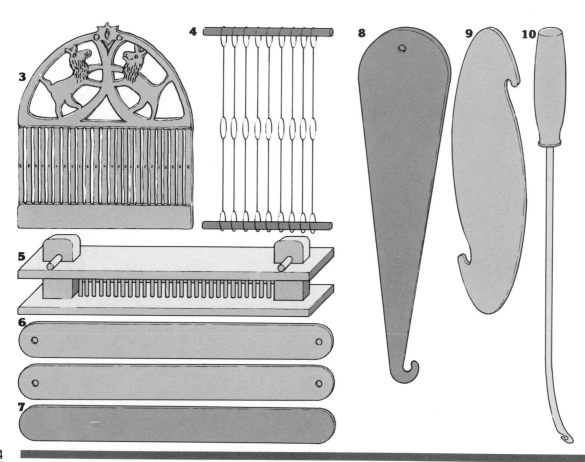

The tools shown on the right are used particularly for tapestry weaving.

1 "Butterfly" of yarn; when many colors are being used for the tapestry, small lengths can be formed into butterflies to keep them tangle-free.

2,3,4 Bobbins, designed to hang down the back of the tapestry during work.

5 Beater used to beat down the weft.

6 Tapestry needles used for sewing in the loose ends and joining pieces woven in different colors.

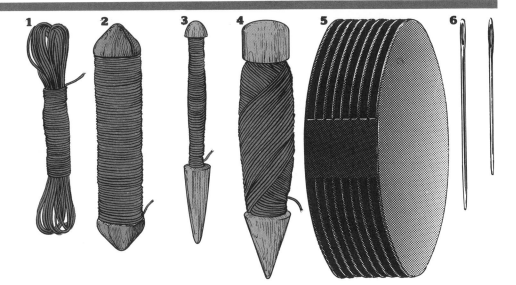

7 Shuttle; this is the simplest form of shuttle, with the yarn simply wound around the center.

8 Stick shuttle.

9 Boat shuttle; this shuttle carries a **bobbin** of yarn inside the frame.

10 Bobbin winder, used for producing bobbins that are evenly covered with yarn. A strip of brown paper, wound on first, secures the yarn end.

11 Beater in the shape of a comb.

12 Stick beater.

13 Brush for raising the nap on woven fabric.

14 Fulling shears used for trimming the nap.

15 Needles, one ordinary length and one extra long, for weaving in yarn ends.

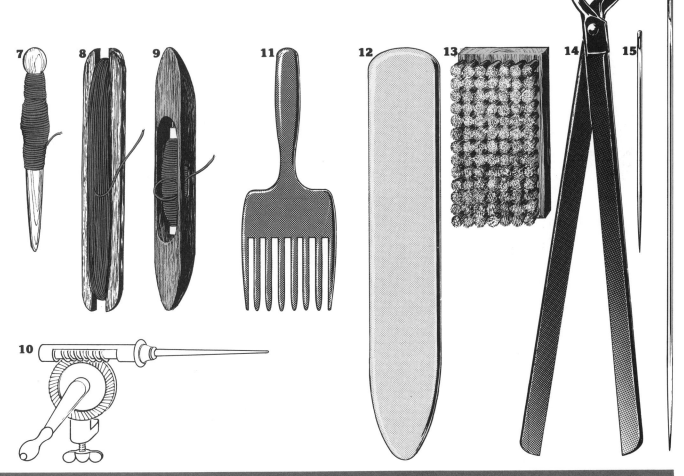

© DIAGRAM

Rugmaking

Rugs can be made using many common techniques, such as weaving, rushwork and knotting, but the particular method known as hooking is almost exclusive to rugmaking. A backing canvas with a very open weave is used as the rug base, and short pieces of yarn or strips of fabric are knotted into this canvas in such a way that the ends stick up in tufts to form the rug's pile.

Illustrated (right) is a traditional Persian carpet; the geometric and floral elements are typical of Persian rug design. The technique of rugmaking can also be adapted for designs that include large, bold or abstract elements.

1 Indelible marker used for drawing designs onto the backing fabric.
2 Fabric slitter, with circular blades driven by a handle.
3 Thumbtack used to hold paper secure when designing.
4 Carpet tack for mounting canvas onto a frame.

5 Large needle used for joining and finishing canvas.
6 Lacing sets used to hold the backing securely.
7 Craft knife used for cutting canvas to size.
8 Pile gauge; the strands are looped around the gauge so that they are all the same height.

9 Spiral holder for strips of fabric or for strands of yarn.
10 Rug hook for looped rugs.
11,12 Latch hooks for knotted rugs; these hooks take the yarn through the canvas and bring it back to the surface.

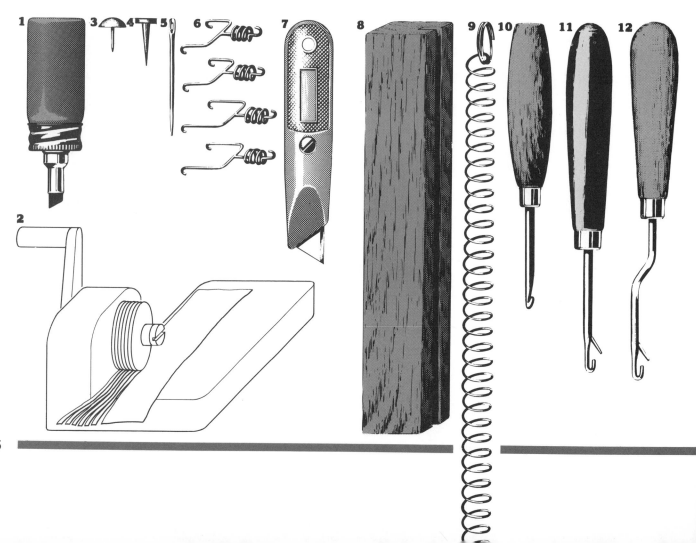

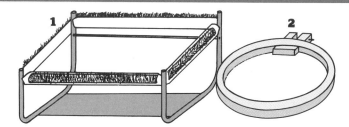
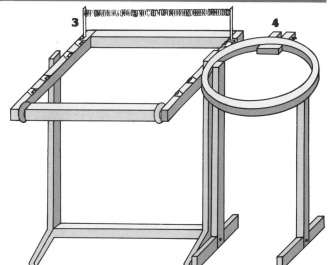

Rug frames are used to keep the canvas taut during hooking. The frames shown (above) are hand-held.
1 Spiked frame; the rug is pressed into position over the spikes, and can be tightened by turning a handle.
2 Circular frame.

The frames illustrated (right) are floor-standing models that leave both hands free for the work.
3 Square frame with a spiral **holder** for the working strands.
4 Circular frame.

5 Speed hook; this semi-automatic hook considerably speeds up work on looped rugs.
6,7 Punch needles.
8 Whisk broom; this is used for cleaning lint away from the work.
9 Rug shears for slitting and trimming the loops.

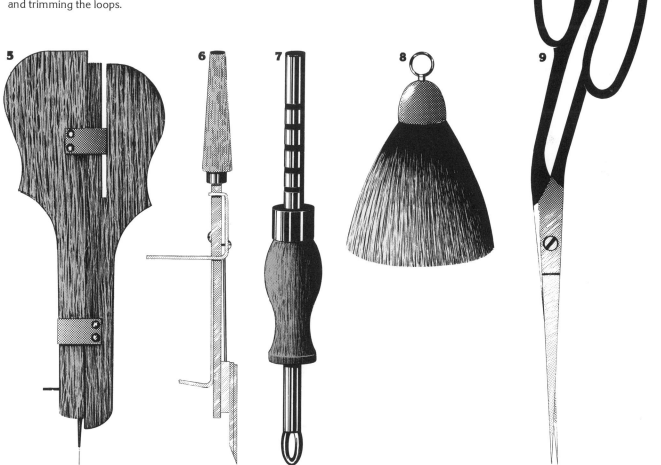

Rushwork

Rushwork articles are made with dried grasses that are interwoven in the same way as the rods for basketry. Rushwork tends to be softer than basketry, as the fibers are not so stiff, and it has a smoother finish. Also described here are corn dollies, the traditional fertility symbols made for many centuries in rural England.

Shown on the right is a table mat woven from rushes. Two different weaving methods have been used to produce two effects in the mat; the center has been woven with a simple tabby weave, and the outside border has been made with paired rushes twisted between the main stakes.

A rush is tested for strength before it is used; any weak rush is removed by pulling the thin end gently but firmly. The rushes are then wiped with a damp cloth to clean them and to remove the air and water from inside the stems.

1 Secateurs used for cutting the rushes.
2 Mallet used for beating and softening.
3 Measuring tape.
4 Craft knife used for trimming.
5 Wet cloth for damping the rushes.

6 Funnel; this is used as a gauge for making bundles of rushes of even thickness.
7 Packing stick.
8 Fid, a long tapering cone used for stretching holes in the rushwork.
9 Wrapped brick used to hold down partly woven sections of the work.

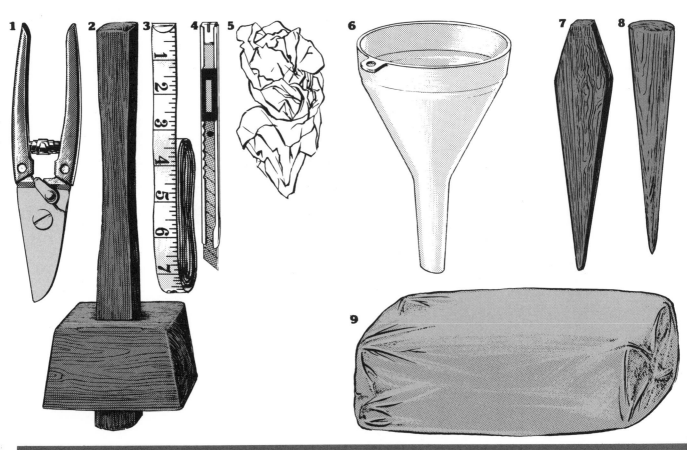

1 Rush threader.
2 Bent wire used for pulling rushes through narrow gaps in the work.
3 Packing needle used for fine finishing work.
4 Lacing awl.
5 Sailor's palm, a thimble palm used with the awl and needle.
6 Cork mat and **glass-headed pins** used to keep the work in place during weaving.

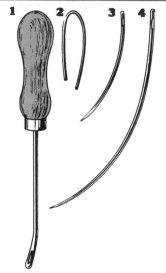

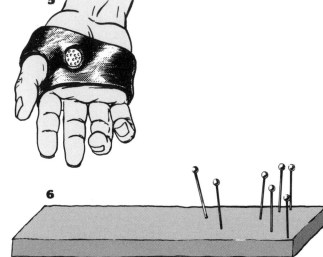

The procedure for making a round rush mat is shown in the illustrations (right).
a Long, straight rushes are chosen for the main stakes of the mat; they should be considerably longer than the width of the mat in order to allow for a border.
b The stakes are woven into a simple tabby (over/under) check to form the central motif of the mat.
c The weaving around the central motif is done with a paired rush. A rush is bent at a point slightly removed from the center, and then looped over one of the main stakes.
d The rush is woven around the central stakes, twisting it between the stakes to form a weave on both sides of the mat simultaneously.
e A new rush is joined as the first one comes to an end, and the process is repeated around the mat.
f To make a border, the **rush threader** is inserted into the weave and used to pull down the end of each stake around the edge of the mat.

The sequence (right) shows the method of forming a horseshoe-shaped corn dolly.
a A number of hollow straws, such as those from wheat, rye or maize, are prepared by cutting the ears off with sharp scissors.
b Several of these straws are made into a core by forming them into a bundle and binding the bundle with wire.
c Five long straws are attached to the end of the bundle; these are the straws that will form the traditional corn dolly weave.
d The straws are woven around the core by placing one straw over its neighbor; the second straw is bent over the first, and twisted round to lie over the third straw. This weave continues until the core has been covered.
e The ends of the straws are neatened off by tucking them under one another.
f The dolly is bent into the shape of a horseshoe, decorated with a spray of oats, and tied with a ribbon.

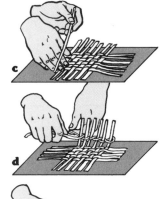

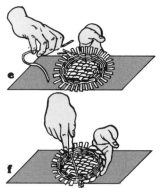

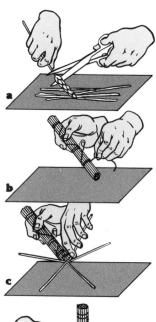

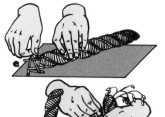

©DIAGRAM

Basketry

Basketry is a craft with a history spanning thousands of years, yet the basic methods of stripping, preparing and interweaving the willows have changed very little in that time. Several tools have evolved to speed up various processes, such as the cleaves for splitting willows into even strands, but most tools are still made according to traditional patterns.

Shown on the right is an example of basketry. The weaves used in basketry can be simple, as in this example, or they may be complex and executed with fibers of several colors, as in many of the articles produced by Oriental basketmakers.

1 Bagging hook, used for cutting down withies (willow rods).
2 Willow knife.
3 Billhook used for trimming and shaping the withies.

4 Willowbrake, a tool used for stripping and peeling the withies.
5 Three-way cleave used for slicing withies into three even parts.
6 Four-way cleave.

7 Shop knife used for pointing the withies so that they can be inserted easily into the work.
8 Picking knife used for trimming the finished basket.
9 Shears for cutting and trimming stout withies.

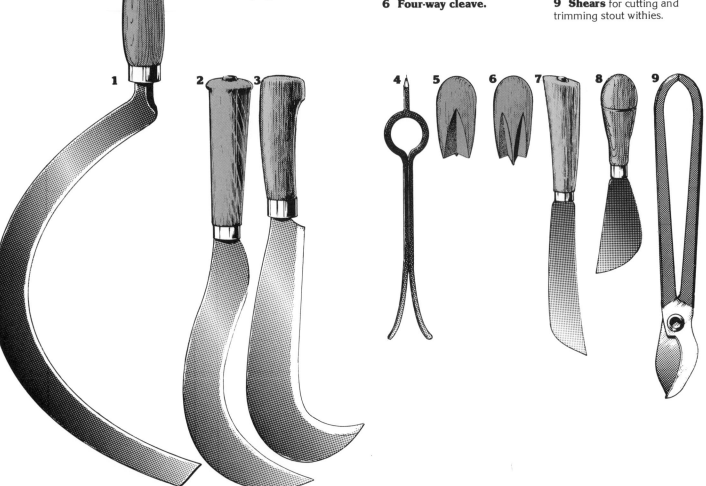

The illustration (left) shows the method of using a **willowbrake.** The withy is inserted into the brake and pulled through; this loosens the bark. It is then pulled through in the opposite direction to clear away the loosened bark.

Shown (below) are two types of **shave;** these work as small planes for cutting strips of willow. A small blade is inserted into a slot in the shave, and adjusted to the required position; the blade is then fixed in place with a small screw.

The method of using a **shave** is illustrated (below). The shave is clamped in a vise, and a willow strand is pulled through the stock and across the blade; this converts the strand into flat strips suitable for binding finished baskets.

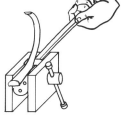

1 Kinking tongs, used for bending the ends of rods so that they can be finished off neatly.
2 Commander, an iron bar used for straightening canes and rods.
3 Grease horn, used when lubricating the bodkins.

4 Sponge for damping the withies to soften them.
5 Solid bodkin.
6 Hollow bodkin; this makes an opening in the weave, and the withy is inserted through it.
7,8 Rapping iron and **beater,** used for tapping down rows of weave.

9 Lacing awl used to carry withies through the weave.
10 Tapestry needle for use with split binding.
11 Boards clamped together so that they can be used to grip flat pieces of basketry.

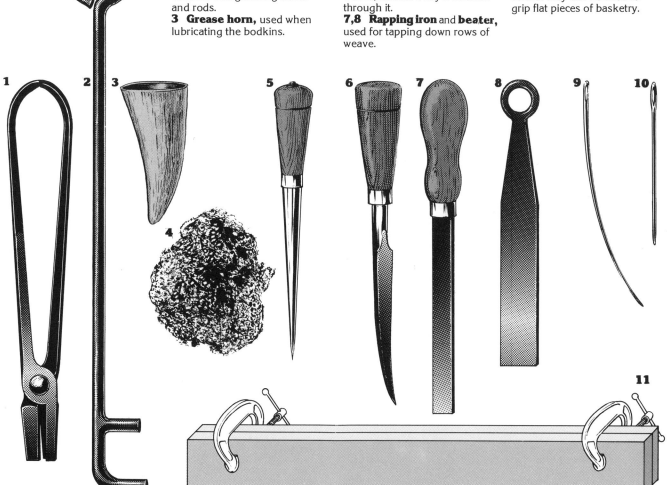

©DIAGRAM

Canework

Cane has for many years been a popular material for making furniture, usually by splitting the canes and then weaving them into patterns that are both decorative and strong. The cane most commonly used is rattan, a climbing palm that has very tough stems; even when the cane is split into thin slices the material has a great deal of strength.

Illustrated (right) are two examples of cane seating. The cane strips have been interwoven in various directions, and each cane is individually secured in the chair frame by taking it down through a small hole and wedging it tightly.

1 Scissors used for cutting the cane.
2 Craft knife for notching and splitting the cane.
3 Spline chisel used for removing old cane strips from furniture that is to be renovated.

4 Knitting needle used for clearing old cane from the holes around chair seats etc.

5 Caning pegs used for securing the cane during weaving.
6 Pin hammer.
7 Fine bodkin.
8 Basketmaker's bodkin.
9 Side cutters used for cleanly nipping off the ends of canes.

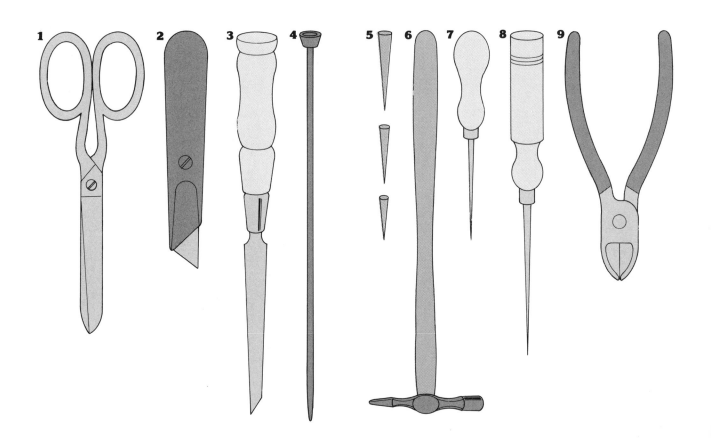

Spalework

Spalework and white oak basketry are similar techniques used for making simple and strong baskets from wide strips of straight-grained wood. Whereas the strips used for canework are often rounded on one side, because they are half-sections of small stems, the strips used in spalework are slices taken down large branches, and so are flat on both sides.

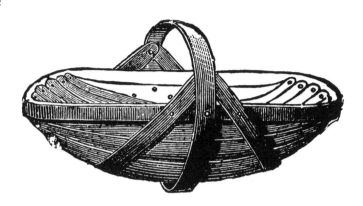

Illustrated (right) is a garden basket from a shopping catalog issued earlier this century. The basket, or trug, is made in a traditional style from strips of straight-grained wood.

1 Cleaving adz used for splitting the wood.
2 Froe, also used for splitting.
3 Small froe.
4 Shave horse used when shaving off the strips for spalework.

5 Mallet used for striking the froe.
6 Drawknife; this can be used for planing off strips over the shave horse.
7 Sharp knife for white oak basketry; this is used for splitting the wood.
8 Scaleboard plane used to make long, flat shavings.

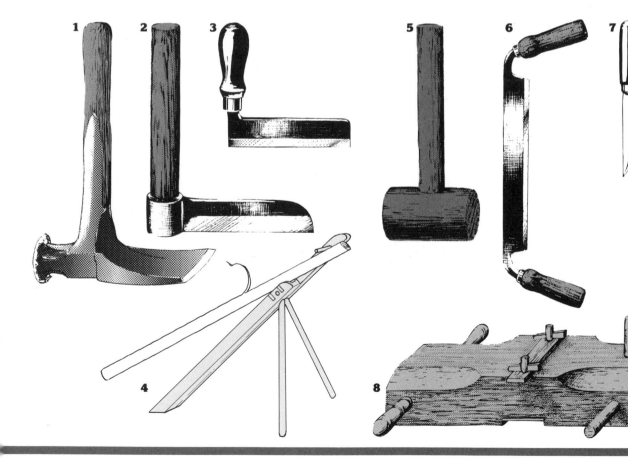

16 Knitting and knotting

The word knitting is derived from the Anglo-Saxon word cnyttan, which means "to weave threads by hand," and this is exactly what the knitter or knotter does. Each of the techniques described in this chapter consists of making knots or loops in the thread used until a firm fabric or decorative filament is produced.

The tools of the knitter and knotter are very straightforward. They generally consist either of tools for looping one thread through another, such as knitting needles and crochet hooks, or for holding the working thread, such as tatting shuttles, netting shuttles and lace bobbins. The threads for techniques such as macramé and bobbin lace are knotted and twisted by hand rather than with tools.

Perhaps because the knotting crafts are especially delicate, and also because they were often popular with the leisured classes, the tools designed for these crafts have always been delicate and beautiful. Crochet hooks have been fashioned from silver, ebony, mother of pearl; tatting shuttles have been made in filigree silver, enamel and ivory. Although the modern versions of the tools may not be so beautiful, they are nevertheless easily available and very durable, and the shapes themselves remain as elegant as ever. The knitting and knotting techniques, rather than dying out in the wake of machine-made lace, are being used as media for designs of great originality and abstract beauty by the textile artists of today.

Shown on the right is a painting called "The Visit of the Angels," painted c. 1390 by a painter known as the Master Bertram. The early date of the painting illustrates the early evolution of such complex techniques as knitting with several needles.

Knitting needles and accessories

Knitting is a thread-knotting process usually carried out on two straight needles, with the addition of extra needles for special purposes. The date and area of the origination of knitting are impossible to establish, but certainly the craft was well established in European countries in medieval times.

The example of knitting (right) shows various different stitch combinations. The patterns in this piece were all formed from the basic plain and purl stitches combined with slipped stitches.

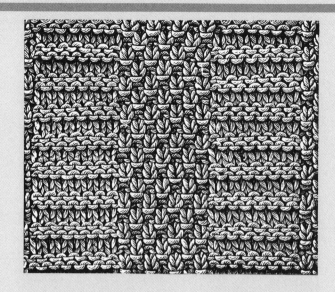

Knitting needles have been made of many substances through the years, such as bone, wood, tortoiseshell and amber, but most ordinary needles nowadays are made from metal or plastic.
1 Large needles for producing large stitches in fancy knitting; these examples are made of wood.
2 Metal knitting needles.
3 Circular needle, used for knitting a seamless tube such as a sweater.
4 Plastic needles.
5 Cable needles; these needles are pointed at both ends so that stitches can be slipped on and off each end.

6 Needle gauge, used to check the sizes of knitting needles. The American numbering system is shown in brown, and the English (metric) system in black.

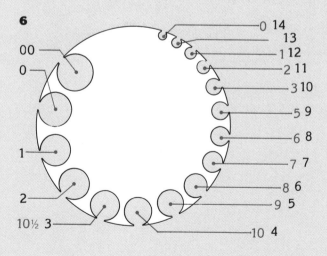

The basic plain knitting stitch, described here for right-handed knitters, is shown in the sequence (right).

a The right needle is slipped into the first stitch on the left needle.

b The working end of the yarn is wound around the tip of the right needle, which is then drawn back through the stitch, carrying the loop of yarn with it.

c The old stitch is slipped over the tip of the left needle, leaving a new stitch on the right needle.

Four **cable needles** are used to form seamless tubes of knitting, as shown (right). The stitches are divided into three groups, and each group threaded onto one cable needle; the spare needle is used to knit the new stitches onto each section.

A **circular needle** can also be used to knit up garment necks and other types of seamless knitting (right). All the stitches are threaded onto the needle, and the knitter moves the stitches around the circle as they are worked with the two needle ends.

1 Knitting needle holder made from carved wood.

2 Novelty **knitting needle case.**

3 Row counter; the small dial is turned at the end of every row of stitches, so that an accurate record can be kept of completed rows.

4 Needle tip used to protect the needle point.

5 Point protector made from a cork.

6 Measuring tape.

7 Yarn holder.

8 Stitch holder used to hold stitches while they are not being worked.

9,10 Special-purpose needles.

11 Ring markers used to mark off sections of the knitting.

12 Scissors.

13 Crochet hook used for making chain stitches when required.

14 Darning needle used for sewing up knitted garments.

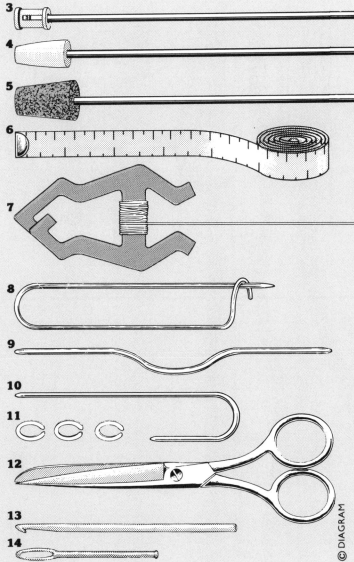

© DIAGRAM

Frame knitting

Frame knitting is used for making seamless, hollow tubes of knitting, either in the form of thin cording, or as shaped pieces for stockings and similar articles. The yarn is looped around a number of raised points, and then a new row of stitches is formed by hooking the previous stitches over the yarn.

The print on the right shows a Japanese woman making a cord by knotting it over a circular frame. The frame ensures that the spools of thread remain in the correct order as they are braided.

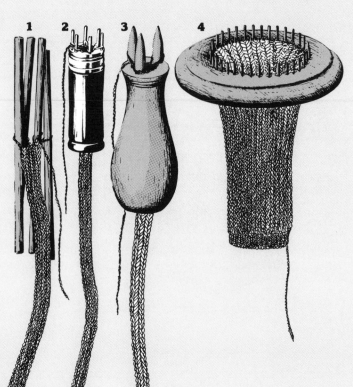

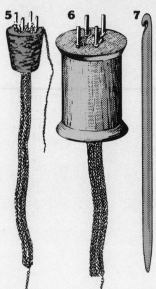

1 Amerindian knitting frame made from four sticks; the yarn is looped over each stick in turn.
2 Ebony and ivory frame.
3 Ivory frame.
4 Wood ring used for frame knitting.
5 Hollow cork with metal pegs.
6 Thread spool converted to a knitting frame.
7 Crochet hook used for looping the stitches over each other.

The principle of frame knitting is shown in the sequence (above).
a The preliminary stitches are formed on the pegs by taking a loop of yarn around each peg.

b The yarn is then taken round the outside of the first peg, and the loop already on the peg is hooked over the new yarn. This process is repeated with each peg in the circle, and then continued for as many rounds of the pegs as required.

268

Beadwork

Beadwork is thread work that incorporates beads into the stitching. This can be done by threading the beads onto yarn that is then knitted up in the usual manner or looped over shaped formers; alternatively, the beads may be strung on thread that is then used as the weft thread on a bead loom.

The example of beadwork shown (below) is a quirt, or horsewhip. The thong is made from braided animal hide, and the loop is made from fabric with beadwork incorporated into the decoration.

1 Pierced purse mold for a beaded purse. The band for the purse top is made by stitching it through the pierced holes, and the body of the purse is then looped around the mold.
2 Purse mold for a long beaded purse.
3 Purse mold for beadwork made using the frame knitting technique.
4 Cable needles for knitting up circular shapes.
5 Bead needles; these are long and fine so that several beads may be threaded on them.
6 Bead loom.

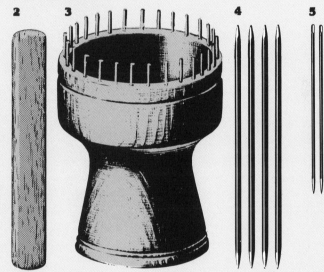

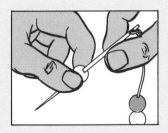

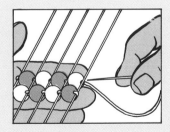

Bead weaving is done in the following way.
a The **bead loom** is threaded with warp threads to the desired width, and sufficient beads to decorate one width are threaded onto the weft. The end of the weft is attached to a **bead needle.**

b The weft is laid under the warp so that one bead appears in each gap in the warp. The weft needle is then returned over the top of the warp threads, and threaded through each bead in turn so that they are secured in place.

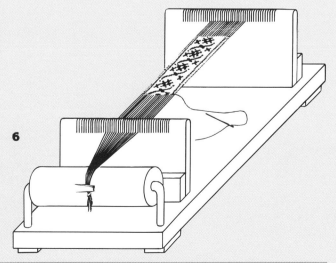

6

Knitting machines

Knitting machines have been developed to duplicate mechanically the stitches made when hand knitting, only to do so considerably faster. The handpiece of the machine is moved back and forth across the stitching area, and it performs the stitches dictated by punched cards that have been previously fed into the machine.

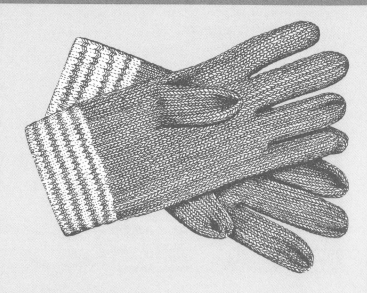

Illustrated (right) is a pair of gloves made on a knitting machine. The machine was programmed with one stitch for the basic knit of the gloves, and with another for the fancy border around the wrist bands.

The illustration (below) shows a typical modern **knitting machine.**
1 Yarn tensioner.
2 Punched card.
3 Handpiece.
4 Completed knitting emerging from the machine.
5 Spools of yarn.

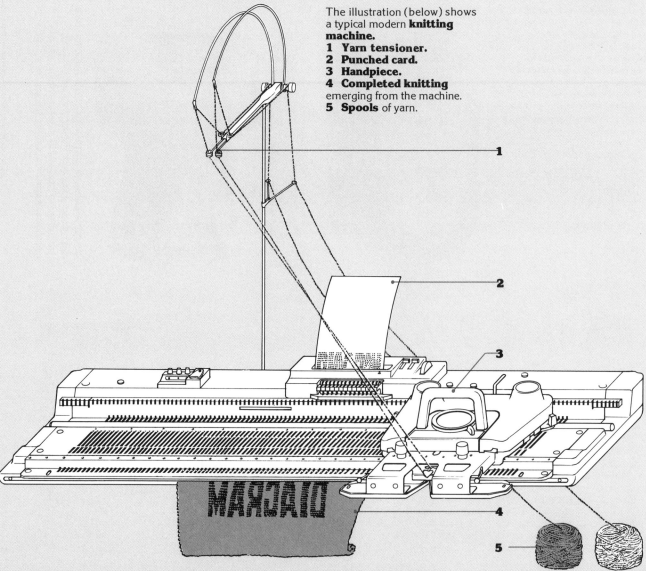

A **yarn winder,** illustrated (right), is used to prevent knots and tangles from impeding the machine's progress. The yarn is wound onto the winder from the purchased skein, and passes through an eye which halts the yarn at knots so that they can be untangled.

Illustrated (far right) are several styles of **needle pusher.** These are the parts of the machine that determine changes in the basic stitching scheme of the knitted fabric being worked.

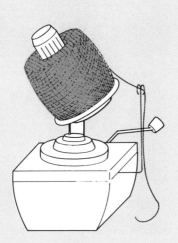

Various **accessories** are used with the knitting machine.
1 Work hook.
2 Latchet tool
3 Transfer tool.
4 Seven-needle transfer tool.
5 Spare needle.
6 Bar pusher.

7 Weights, used to ensure that stitch tension is equal throughout the piece.
8 Machine brush.
9 Card clamps.
10 Card guide pin.
11 Card punch.

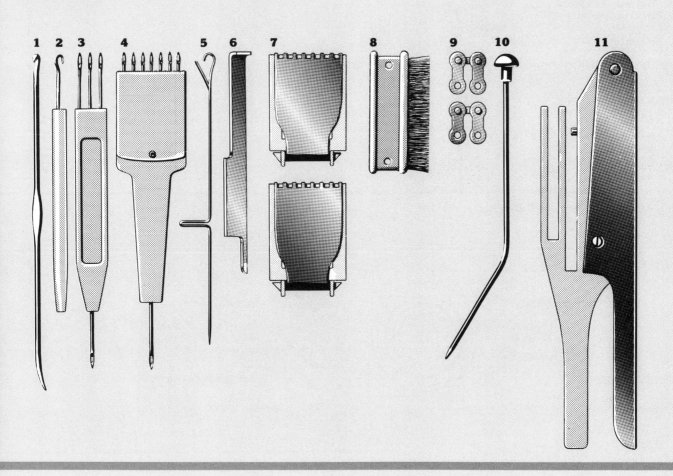

©DIAGRAM

Bobbin lace

Bobbin lace is formed by twisting many tiny threads in a predetermined pattern so that they form a piece of flat lace. The name comes from the numerous bobbins on which the threads are wound to keep them tidy and to provide tension on the work; complex patterns can require hundreds, or even thousands, of individual threads.

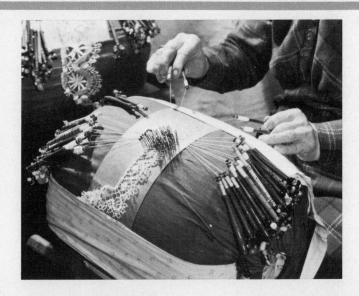

The photograph (right) shows a piece of traditional bobbin lace being made. The paper is pricked out and marked with pins, and the threads are being twisted and knotted in the required sequences.

1 Stiletto, in the shape of a fish, used for pricking out the lace pattern.

2 Pins with decorative beads; the pins are used as guides, and the thread is twisted around them.

3,4 Glass-headed pins from Venice.

5 Plain wood bobbins.

6 Pricking template used as a pattern.

7 Spring; this is attached to the front of the working pillow and keeps the bobbins in the right order.

8 Bobbin winder.

9 Lace board, a small board onto which the finished lace is wound.

10 Lace measure an ancient tool used by laceworkers to measure a day's work.

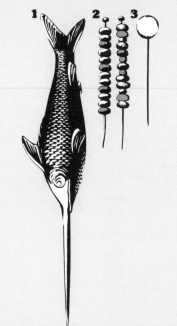

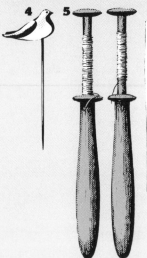

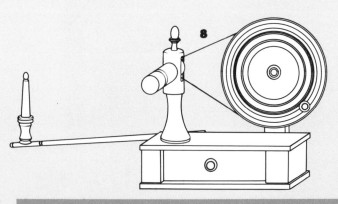

1 **Olivewood bobbin** from France.
2 **Boxwood window bobbin.**
3 **Boxwood bobbin.**
4 **English ivory bobbin.**
5 **Named ivory bobbin;** these were often given as love tokens.
6 **Painted bobbin** from Russia.
7 **Bamboo bobbin** from India.
8 **English bobbin** with pewter washers.
9 **Brass bobbin.**
10 **Barrel bobbin** from Austria; the barrel keeps the thread clean.

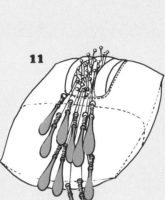
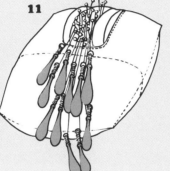
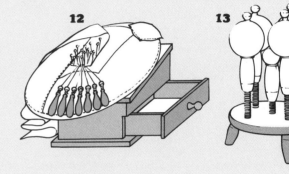

11 **Lace pillow** with a wheel at the back so that the finished lace can be wound into a bag to keep it clean.
12 **Circular lace pillow** that rotates to allow easy access to all parts of the work.
13 **Lacemaker's lamp;** the sphere in the center held a floating wick.
14 **Lace pillow** shaped like a muff.
15 **Lace pillow** and **adjustable stand.**
16 **Diffusers;** these globes diffused the light from a lamp so that all parts of the work were lit evenly.

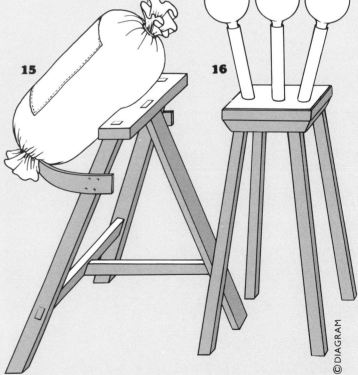
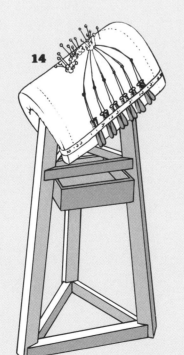

©DIAGRAM

Crochet

Crochet is a method of knotting a thread by drawing it into a chain by means of a hook. The basic stitches can be combined into sequences to produce many variations of pattern and texture; crochet can be as delicate as fine lace, or as chunky as macramé; the technique is adaptable to threads of any thickness.

The example of crochet work shown (right) illustrates the way in which large, flat areas can be built up by a spiral of crochet stitches. Each stitch is hooked into a loop made by a stitch in the preceding row of the spiral.

The size of the stitches made in crochet is determined by the diameter of the **crochet hook** that is used.
1 Crochet hooks in graduated sizes. Modern hooks are usually molded from metal.

2 Hardwood hook.
3 Rosewood hook.
4 Kelp hook.
5 Multiple crochet hook with heads of different sizes.
6 Sheath for the multiple tool. When in position, the sheath allows only the chosen hook to protrude.

All crochet stitches are variations on the basic chain stitch shown (right).
a A small slip-knot is made in the end of the thread to be crocheted, and a **hook** of suitable size is inserted into this loop.
b The loop is pulled tight over the hook, then the hook is brought down to pick up another portion of the working thread. The hook is turned slightly so that it grips the thread securely.
c The new loop is drawn through the original loop, which passes over the tip of the hook to form the first stitch of a chain. This is repeated as many times as required.
d The chain that has been formed now acts as the base for further rows of stitches; each new stitch is looped through one of the stitches in the previous row.

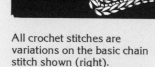

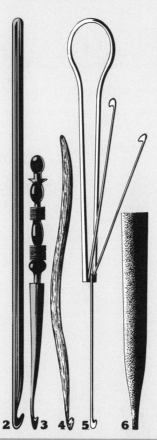

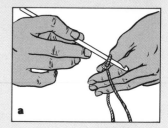

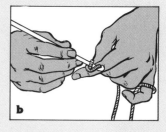

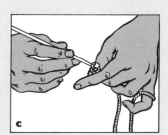

Hairpin crochet, lucet work

Hairpin crochet and lucet work are variations of the chainmaking principle of crochet. Hairpin crochet gains its name from the curved pin upon which it is produced; it is a technique that yields a long web of fine lace. Lucets are used to produce single chains of thread which can then be couched or crocheted in their turn.

The lace illustrated on the right was made by linking lengths of hairpin crochet with ordinary crochet stitches. The hairpin crochet exhibits the characteristic feathery appearance.

1 Steel pin used for wide hairpin crochet.
2 Pin with adjustable slider.
3 Wood pin with slots in various places so that different widths of lace can be crocheted.

Lucets are small harp-shaped tools used for making chains; the thread is looped around the two horns, and then hooked over subsequent loops to form a chain.
4 Ivory lucet.
5 Wood lucet.

Hairpin crochet consists of a series of loops secured in the center.
a The thread is wound around one bar of the **pin,** and a small **crochet hook** is used to take up a stitch and pull it through the stitch that is already on the hook.
b The thread is then wound around the other bar of the pin, and again a stitch is picked up when the thread returns to the center. Completed stitches can be gently slipped off the rounded end of the pin to make room for further work.

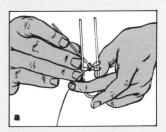

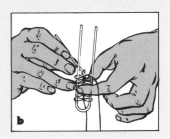

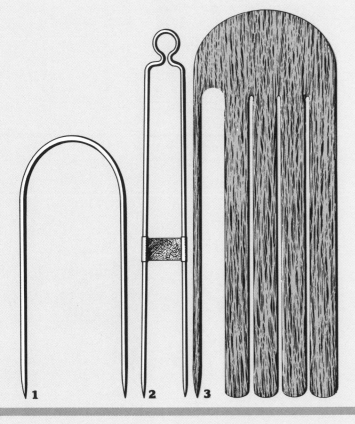

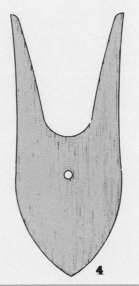

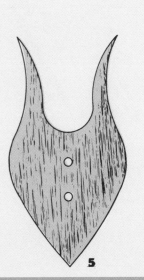

©DIAGRAM

Macramé, tatting, netting, knotting

Macramé, netting and tatting are three ways of forming decorative knots in thread in order to produce lacy patterns. All three types of knotting can be done with any thickness of thread, although traditionally tatting is very delicate while macramé is particularly associated with coarse jute and hemp threads.

The lacy panel illustrated (right) is made from embroidered netting. A regular mesh is netted first, and this can then be decorated with embroidery, needleweaving and other techniques.

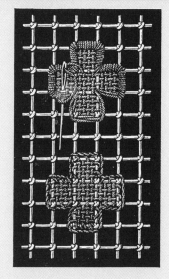

Illustrated (left) is an example of macramé. The technique was originally a Turkish craft used for making decorative fringes on shawls and veils, but it has now developed into a craft in its own right.

1,2 Bone bobbins for macramé threads.
3 Glass-headed pins for pinning out macramé.
4 T-pins.
5 Knotting shuttle made of ivory.
6 Scissors.
7 Crochet hook used for finishing macramé and knotting.
8 Needle with a large eye so that it can take coarse threads.
9,10 Two types of **macramé board.**

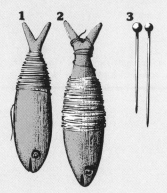

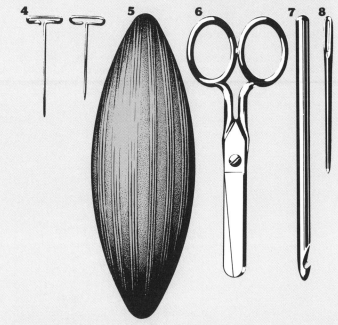

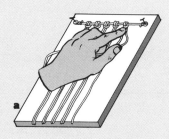

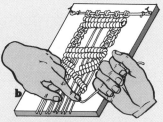

Macramé is generally worked from a series of parallel threads.
a The macramé threads are cut into even lengths, and these are knotted in a row along the top of a **macramé board.**

b The threads are then used in pairs and groups to form a wide variety of decorative knots; the threads may be braided or twisted, and wood beads are often threaded over the working threads so that they appear in the pattern.

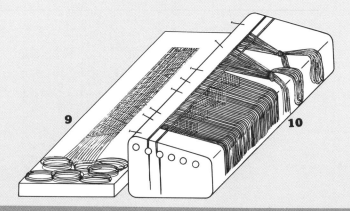

1 **Tatting shuttle,** showing the way that the thread is wound over the central core.
2 **Tatting shuttle.**
3 **Rubber band,** used to secure balls of wool so that they can be used as makeshift shuttles.
4 **Fancy shuttle** made of wood.
5 **Shuttle** for loosely spun wools such as mohair.
6 **Tatting hook** on a chain so that it could be hung from the waist.

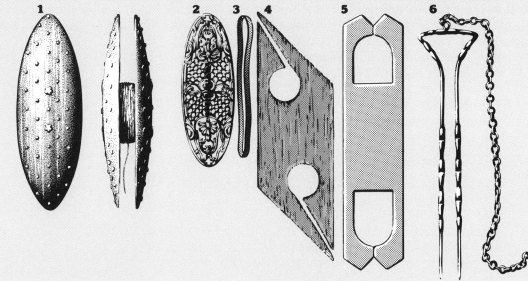

7 **Large netting needle** suitable for hammocks.
8 **Large netting gauge.**
9 **Netting shuttle.**
10 **Steel netting needle.**
11 **Case** for netting tools.
12 **Gauges** for fine netting.
13 **Netting needles** carved from tortoiseshell.
14 **Single-ended netting needle.**
15 **Netting needle** made of tortoiseshell.
16 **Netting box** containing **netting tools** and a **stand** for securing the work.

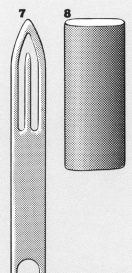

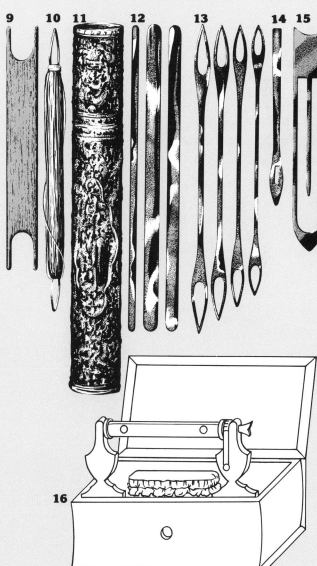

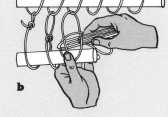

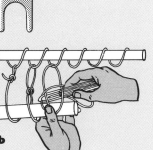

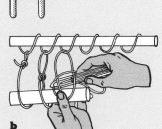

The technique of netting with a large thread is shown in the sequence (above).
a   The thread is wound onto a **netting needle,** and a series of loops is made by knotting the thread loosely round a **stick** or **dowel.**

b   A **gauge** is placed under the first row of knots, so that the next row will be even. The second row is made by threading the needle through a loop and over the gauge, and then knotting it at the top of the gauge.

16

©DIAGRAM

17 Needlework

In the late Stone Age, the people living in Northern Europe wore clothes made from several pieces of hide sewn together in a primitive manner by threading thongs through punched holes. In Southern Europe the discovery of contemporary bone needles suggests that woven fabrics were already being stitched together, since bone would have been too weak to pierce leather. The art of sewing fabric, therefore, dates back many thousands of years.

Needles and other sewing tools have changed remarkably little in appearance since ancient times. The iron needles used by the Egyptians and introduced to Europe in the Middle Ages were exactly the same in principle as their bone forerunners, and shears were used for cutting out fabric in the late 19th century just as they were in Roman times. The inventions of the sewing machine in 1830 and the band-knife cutting machine in 1860 were the first major changes in sewing tools since the Stone Age. The introduction of electrically powered tools for domestic use has been the major contribution this century to the history of sewing tools. Electric irons are now used instead of flat-irons for pressing tailored work; sewing machines and even scissors can be driven by electricity. Perhaps even more important, however, has been the revival of interest awakened by the various arts and crafts movements at the turn of the century in the rich heritage of needlework techniques and tools that exists throughout the world.

This photograph was taken at the turn of the century in a London school. The girls in the picture are being taught needlework, and the boards at the front of the class display stitching samples.

Measuring, marking, cutting

Dressmaking requires very accurate measuring and cutting of the pieces of fabric to ensure the success of the final garment. Seams must be even, hems level, curves smooth and cuts clean so that the pattern pieces will fit together correctly when they are stitched. Clearly marked cutting guides and sharp scissors help the dressmaker at every stage.

This photograph, taken at dressmaking class in 1915, shows a girl cutting out major pattern pieces from fabric laid on a large table.

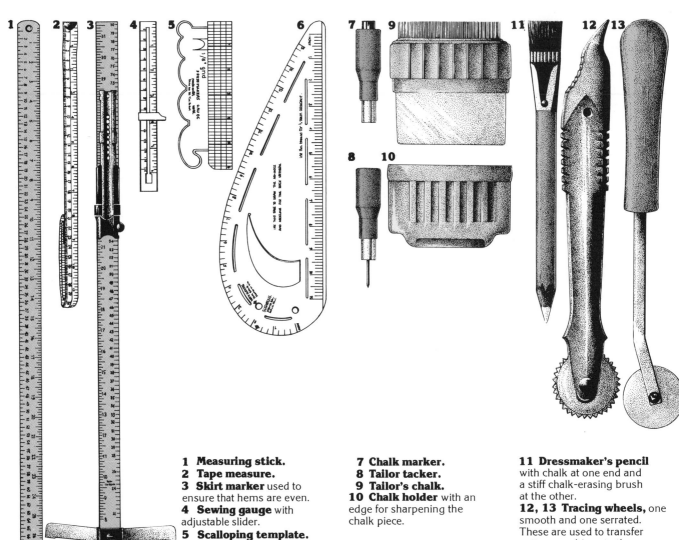

1 **Measuring stick.**
2 **Tape measure.**
3 **Skirt marker** used to ensure that hems are even.
4 **Sewing gauge** with adjustable slider.
5 **Scalloping template.**
6 **Curve square** used for measuring curves.

7 **Chalk marker.**
8 **Tailor tacker.**
9 **Tailor's chalk.**
10 **Chalk holder** with an edge for sharpening the chalk piece.

11 **Dressmaker's pencil** with chalk at one end and a stiff chalk-erasing brush at the other.
12, 13 **Tracing wheels,** one smooth and one serrated. These are used to transfer pattern markings to the fabric.

Scissors are sophisticated cutting implements formed by two cutting blades joined at a fulcrum. When the handles are brought together, the blades meet in a cutting action. The first implement used for cutting textiles was simply a shaped knife-blade. The advantage of two blades for accuracy was soon realized, and at first these were formed rather like sheep shears from a single piece of sprung metal. These developed into the two-bladed scissor design that is still used today.

1 Cutting-out knife from Ancient Egypt.
2 Iron shears.
3 Iron scissors from the 1st century AD.
4 Steel scissors inlaid with gold, from 18th century France.

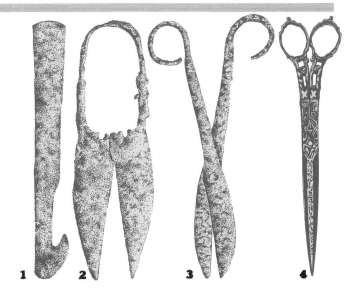

1 2 3 4

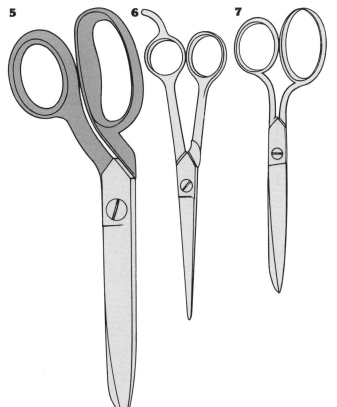

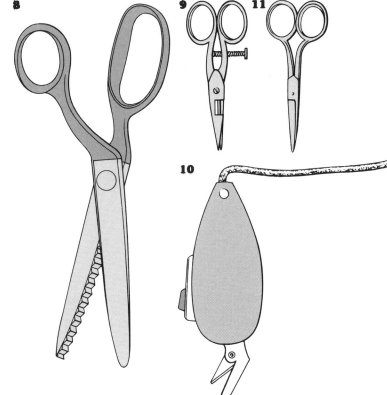

5 Dressmaker's shears; the handles are bent upward so that the blades can lie flat when cutting out fabric.
6 Hairdresser's or **lingerie scissors** used for cutting fine fabrics.
7 Trimming scissors.

8 Pinking shears with blades that cut a series of small zigzags to prevent fraying.
9 Buttonhole scissors; the special design of these scissors means that buttonhole slits can be cut without damaging the surrounding fabric.

10 Electric scissors.
11 Embroidery scissors with short, pointed blades.

Needles, pins, tailoring aids

Needles and pins have been used since the Stone Age. The first simple needles were carved from slivers of bone and used to carry thonging through holes punched in animal hides. As man's domestic skills evolved, needles were made finer and sharper so that they could themselves pierce holes for the thread.

Shown (right) is a pack of needles offered for sale in the 1895 Harrod's catalog. The needles are all sharps, one of the most popular all-purpose needles.

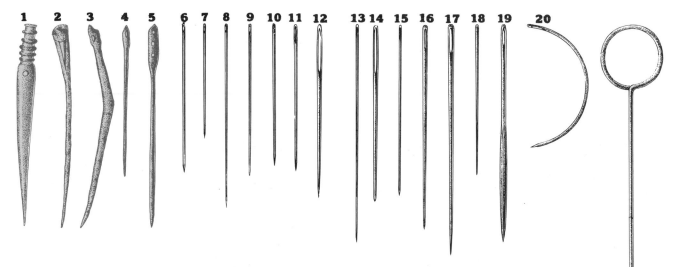

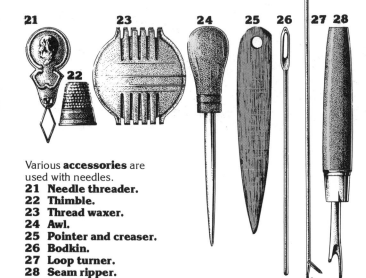

1 Bone needle with an eye and notches for carrying the thread. This needle is from Ancient Egypt and is about 5000 years old.
2 Bone needle from the Early Iron Age.
3 Bronze needle from Egypt.
4,5 Bronze needles from Ancient Rome. One needle has multiple eyes so that the thread can be secured against slipping.

6 Sharp, a needle used for hand-sewing.
7 Between or **quilting needle.**
8 Straw, a tacking needle.
9 Ball-point needle used with knits.
10 Self-threading needle; the thread is drawn into the eye through a slot.
11 Embroidery needle.
12 Chenille used for yarn embroidery.
13 Bead needle used to apply beads and spangles.
14 Tapestry needle.
15,16,17 Darners.
18 Glover, a small needle with a triangular point.
19 Sailmaker; this needle also has a triangular tip.
20 Curved needle.

Various **accessories** are used with needles.
21 Needle threader.
22 Thimble.
23 Thread waxer.
24 Awl.
25 Pointer and creaser.
26 Bodkin.
27 Loop turner.
28 Seam ripper.

Sewing aids are used by the dressmaker to help shape and form the garments.

1 Iron.

2 Press mitt for shaping small curved seams.

3 Tailor's ham for pressing shaped areas.

4 Seam roll, a cylindrical pad on which seams can be pressed open.

5 Tailor's board.

6 Sleeve board, a small ironing board used for pressing sleeves.

7 Needle board, a block with steel needles covering the surface. This is used for pressing fabrics with a thick pile.

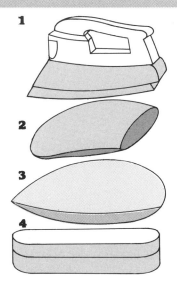
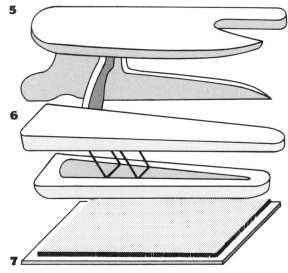
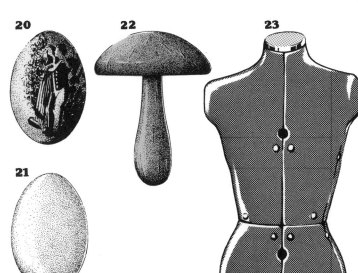
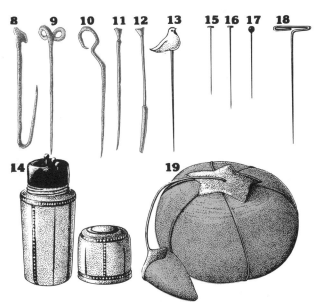

The first **pins** used in antiquity were those that could be found ready-made—fish bones and thorns. Through the ages, pins have been carved from bone and wood, and fashioned from gold, silver, ivory and bronze.

8 Roman bronze pin.

9 Egyptian bronze pin.

10 Iron pin, forerunner of the safety pin. The point could be bent back and secured behind the ring.

11 Bone pin.

12 Bronze pin with a point protector.

13 Glass-headed pin from Venice.

14 Pin-poppet, a type of pincushion with a lid.

Modern pins, like modern needles, are generally made of steel, although there are several designs of pin to choose from. Pins are no longer a luxury, since they can be made very cheaply with specialized machinery.

15 Flat pin, a steel pin with a flat head.

16 Dressmaker's pin, a long fine pin that will not mark delicate fabric.

17 Glass-headed pin.

18 T-pin.

19 Pincushion with a separate **emery bag** for cleaning rusty pins.

Sewing accessories are designed to make the seamstress's task easier and more pleasant.

20 Darning egg, a smooth shape over which fabric is stretched for repair.

21 Hand cooler, made of natural stone or of porcelain and used to cool the sewer's hands.

22 Darning mushroom, a wood shape used in the same way as the darning egg.

23 Tailor's dummy, a life-sized form on which garments can be fitted and tailored.

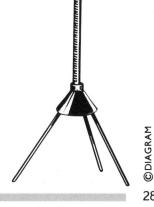

©DIAGRAM

Sewing accessories

The many small and delicate implements used in sewing have lent themselves over the years to dainty ornament, so that the tools have become objects of craftsmanship, beauty or elegance. Tools for the rich were often ornamented with gold, silver, ivory, ebony, pearl and carved wood, and sets of matching implements were often manufactured as gifts.

The sewing kit (right) was advertised in the 1895 Harrod's catalog. The kit contains spools of thread, silks, buttons, needles, pins, tapes and thimbles.

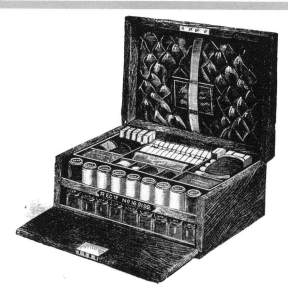

Shown here are some historical examples of **sewing accessories.**

1 Anglo-Saxon **bronze sewing box.**

2 Pinball of knitted silk. The five following implements were all made to swing from a common head that was attached to the waist and known as a **chatelaine.**

3 Yard measure.

4 Needle case.

5 Folding scissors.

6 Pincushion made from two layers of metal with a fabric padding.

7 Thimble holder.

8 Etui, an ornamental case for sewing tools.

9 Emery cushion used for cleaning rust from pins and needles.

10 Pin-poppet, a lidded pincushion.

11 Tortoiseshell needle box.

12 Powder sprinkler made from a carved peach stone.

13 Yard measure, with wax at the bottom for waxing thread.

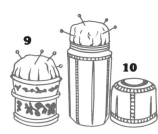

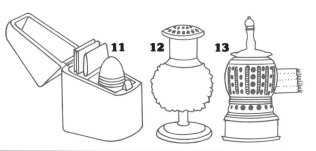

The tools shown on the right were clamped onto tabletops during use.

1 Sewing clamp made of bone and ivory; clamps were used to hold work at one end so that it could be stretched. This clamp has a pincushion on the top.

2 Thread-winding clamp.

3 Hemming bird; the fabric was clamped in the bird's beak so that it could be stretched taut for hemming.

4 Embroidery frame with clamp; the frame can be screwed to the table, leaving both hands free for the work.

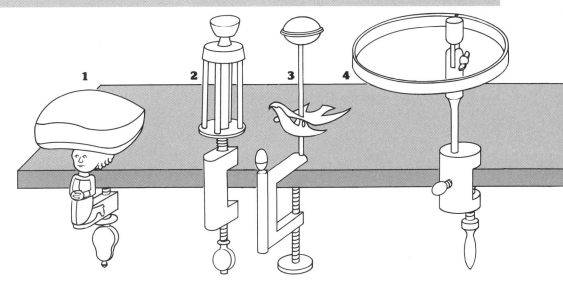

5 Tambour hook made of ivory. Tambour work was stitched in a chain of thread, made by hooking it through the fabric.

6 Stiletto with pearl handle.

7 Mellore, a steel point for use in gold work.

8 Broche for laying gold thread.

9,10 Thread winders.

11 Silk winder in a barrel to protect it from dirt.

12 Slate frame, a rectangular embroidery frame.

13 Tambour frame.

14 Oval embroidery frame.

15 Circular embroidery frame.

16 Embroidery frame on a stand so that it can be tilted to any angle.

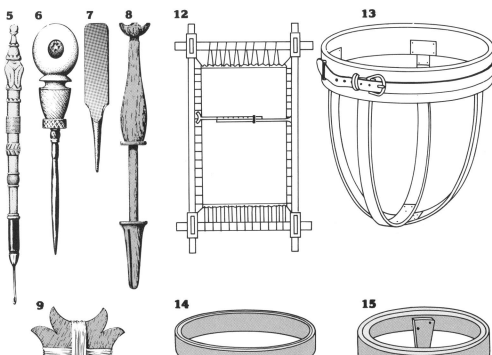

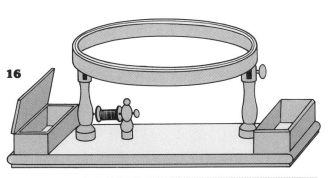

Sewing machines

Sewing machines are mechanical aids, powered either manually or by electricity, that perform the work of stitching fabrics. Modern machines have two threads, one above and one underneath the fabric; the upper thread is taken down through the fabric by the needle, and winds around the lower, or bobbin, thread to form a stitch.

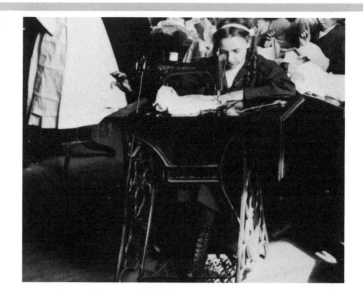

The photograph (right) was taken in 1905, and shows a girl using a treadle sewing machine. As the treadle is rocked back and forth, it drives the belt that moves the needle up and down.

The ancestor of the modern **sewing machine** is a design patented in 1790 by an English cabinetmaker, Thomas Saint. This machine was for chain-stitching leather with a single thread, but Saint never actually built his machine, and the first person to construct a sewing machine was a French tailor, Thimonnier. Even he did not really win acclaim, since his first production machines were destroyed by jealous tailors; when he finally managed to gain a patent for his invention, other practical sewing machines were already being marketed.

The **machine parts** shown in the illustration on the right are common to most modern sewing machines.
a   Take-up lever to carry the slack thread when the needle is lifted.
b   Needle clamp.
c   Feed; this moves the material along during stitching.
d   Needle.
e   Tension regulator for the top thread.
f   Stitch-length regulator.
g   Thread spool.
h   Bobbin tension-spring used when thread is wound onto a new bobbin.

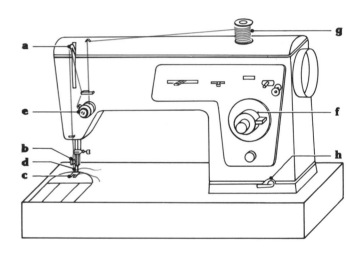

Needles fit into the **needle clamp** and carry the upper thread through the fabric.
1   Sharp-pointed needle.
2   Ball-pointed needle for knits.
3   Wedge-pointed needle for leather and vinyl.
4   Twin needle.
5   Treble needle.

Bobbins are the small spools that carry the bottom thread underneath the fabric.
6   Bobbin case.
7   Metal bobbin.
8   Plastic bobbin.

The two basic **stitching feet** are the straight-stitching foot and the swing needle; most stitch variations use these feet.
9   Straight-stitching foot.
10   Swing needle used for zigzag stitches.

Needle plates are supplied to fit the two basic stitching feet.
11   Straight-stitching plate.
12   Swing-needle plate.

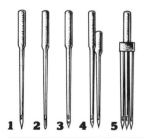

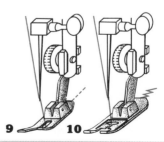
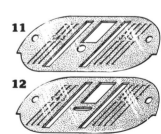

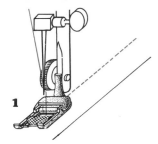

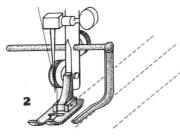

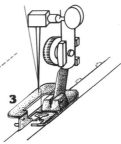

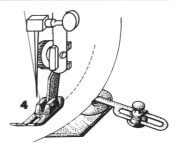

1 Roller foot is used when stitching two fabrics of different weight. The roller ensures that the top fabric feeds through the machine at the same rate as the bottom one.

2 Quilter guide bar is an adjustable extension to the machine foot. It is fixed to a set width, and can be moved along a guide line to produce even quilting channels.

3 Blind hemming guide holds the fabric piece and the folded hem in correct relation to each other while they are being stitched.

4 Seam gauge is adjusted to a specific distance from the needle. The fabric is butted up against the gauge to ensure that the stitching line is parallel to the fabric edge.

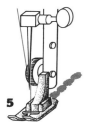

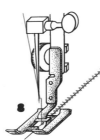

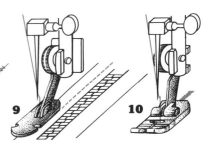

5 Embroidery foot has a groove cut out of the bottom so that thick blocks of solid embroidery can pass underneath it without jamming.
6 Overedge foot is used for binding stitches on the edge of fabric.

7 Narrow hemmer turns in a small fold of fabric which is then stitched by the machine as usual.

8 Cording foot allows for cord to be fed steadily into the foot and then makes zigzag stitches to secure it.
9 Zipper foot is a narrow foot that can be fitted to either side of the needle. Its narrowness prevents it from catching on the thick bulk of the zipper.

10 Buttonhole foot is made of transparent plastic so that the operator can gauge the exact place to begin and end the line of stitching.

11,12 Chainstitch attachments adapt the sewing machine so that the top thread only is required for stitching, and produce a continuous chain of stitches.

13,14 Stitching cams are guides that program the machine to produce stitches in predetermined patterns. Fancy designs and stitch combinations of many different kinds can be built into the cams.

Maintenance tools are usually provided with each sewing machine.
15,16 Screwdrivers in two different sizes.
17 Small brush for removing dust and dirt from the crevices of the machinery.
18 Oil applicator.

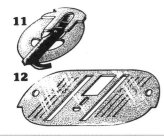

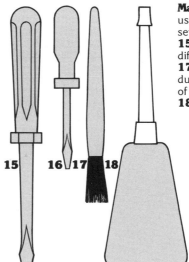

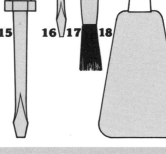

Decorative fabric work

Patchwork began as a way of reusing fabric scraps, quilting as a means of combining layers of fabric for warmth, but both soon developed into decorative arts with their own carefully planned designs. Appliqué has a long tradition of decorative use in Palestine and among American Indians; fabric collage is a more modern, abstract type of appliqué.

Shown (right) is a portion of patchwork skirt made from silk fabrics in different patterns and plain colors. The sections have been cut from diamond shaped templates and stitched together in a zigzag design.

The tools on the right are common to patchwork, quilting, appliqué and fabric collage, since all four techniques require the marking of the design, the cutting of the fabric, and some sewing.

1 **Pencil.**
2 **Steel rule.**
3 **Compasses.**
4 **Protractor.**
5 **French curve.**
6 **Scalpel.**
7 **Scissors.**
8 **Pins.**
9 **Pincushion.**
10 **Needles.**
11 **Thimble.**
12 **Seam ripper.**

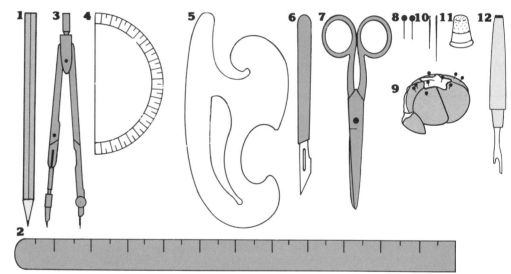

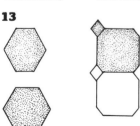

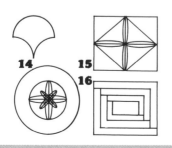

Templates are cutting guides for papers and fabric pieces.
13 **Templates** of the most popular patchwork shapes.
14 **Suffolk puff,** a circle of gathered fabric.
15 **Cathedral window,** an elaborately folded design.
16 **Log cabin,** a design made from fabric strips.

Patchwork consists of making a mosaic of fabric pieces joined with stitching.
a A piece of fabric is cut to the chosen shape. The edges are folded over a piece of paper slightly smaller than the fabric, and the two are lightly basted together.
b Two patches are joined by placing the fabric sides together and oversewing one straight edge. When every side of any fabric shape has been stitched to another shape, the tacking threads can be taken out and the paper removed.

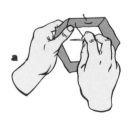

Illustrated on the right are examples of quilting, appliqué and fabric collage. The quilting is a piece of traditional white work, with curved shapes outlined in tiny quilting stitches. The appliqué is a complex shape cut from one fabric and used to provide a decorative border on a fabric of a different color, and the fabric collage illustrates the more unconventional and freer approach characteristic of this craft.

1 Small **quilting frame;** the fabric is basted to the woven strips on the front and back rods, and the rods are turned to tauten the fabric.
2 **Spare rods** in pairs, used to adapt the frame for longer pieces of fabric.

Quilting is the technique of making decorative stitched designs on a padded fabric ground.
a The padding material is stretched across a **frame.** The chosen background fabric is marked with the design to be quilted, and placed on top of the padding.
b The two layers are joined with small stitches, along the lines of the design. The stitching may be in the same color as the fabric, or chosen to contrast with it.

Appliqué means "applied," and the word describes the technique of applying small pieces of fabric to a larger background.
a The shape of the piece to be applied is cut out in fabric, and the edges are turned in and basted down to stop them fraying.
b The fabric shape is placed on the background and secured with stitching around the edges. This is repeated with each shape to be applied, and further shapes can be appliquéd to these in turn.

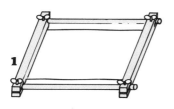

Fabric collage is an extension of appliqué, but it is more concerned with color and texture than with well-defined shapes.
a The pieces of fabric to be used for the collage are chosen, and either cut or torn to the required size.
b The fabrics are attached to a background, using stitching, glue or any other means to hold them securely. The fabrics may be folded, wrinkled, slashed or frayed in order to vary their textures, and they may be used with threads, beads, and pieces of wood, glass, plastic or metal.

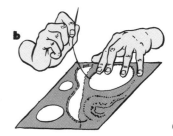

Metal thread embroidery

Metal thread embroidery has a long tradition of use for ecclesiastical and royal vestments, because of the richness of the materials used. Gold and silver is spun, woven or plaited into threads or stretched into wires, and these are used for the embroidery; extra care is required because of the delicacy of the threads, which are easily broken or tarnished.

The picture (right) is a detail from a painting of Queen Elizabeth l, and shows elaborate embroidery in gold and silver threads. Many of Elizabeth's dresses were encrusted with this kind of embroidery, often with the addition of precious stones.

Parfilage, or drizzling, was the craze among court ladies in the 18th century for unraveling and selling the gold from ornate embroideries.
1,2 Parfilage tools.
3 Scissors for clipping away surrounding threads.
4 Case for parfilage tools.

5,6,7 Needles in various shapes and sizes for the different types of thread.
8,9 Two **thimbles** used to protect the middle finger on each hand.
10 Mellore, a pointed tool used for laying gold thread.

11 Stiletto used for making the holes for the metal thread to pass through.
12 Embroidery scissors.
13 Embroidery frame used to keep the fabric taut so that the metal will not buckle or twist.

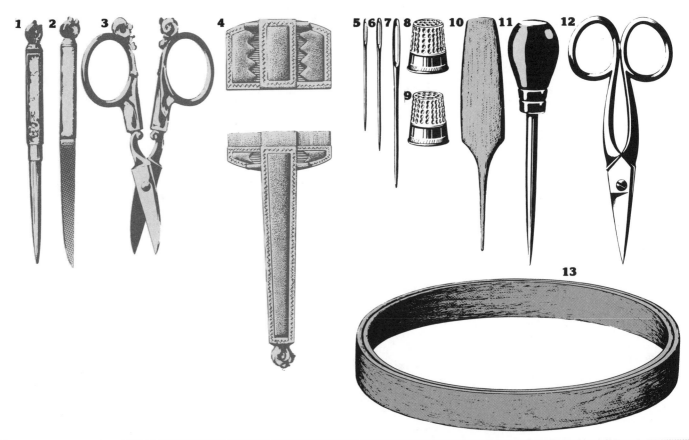

Metal thread is often couched onto the fabric so that it will not become worn by passing through the fabric too frequently.

a The fabric to be couched is marked out with the design, using a **soft pencil** so that the marks can later be erased.

b The metal thread is cut to the approximate length required, and holes are made with a **stiletto** at each end of the pencil line to be couched. The metal thread is laid along the line, and inserted gently into the holes at each end so that it is secured.

c The thread can be kept in place with a **lead block** so that it does not roll out of line, and a blending or contrasting thread is used to stitch through the fabric and over the metal thread, so that the thick thread is caught down onto the fabric.

d Burls, small twists of gold or silver, can be incorporated into the work by threading them onto the needle. **Burling irons** are used to pick up the burls so that their luster is not lost by handling them.

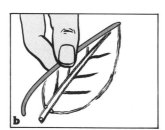
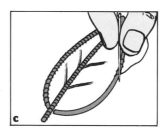
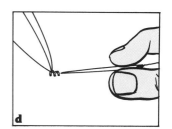

1 Thread clippers; these tiny clippers can be held in the hand while sewing, so that they are always handy when required.
2 Burling irons, pointed tweezers for lifting burls.
3 Thread bobbin.
4 Lead weight.

5 Measuring tape.
6 Small ruler.
7 Soft pencil for marking out the fabric.
8 Eraser.
9 Thumb tack for securing the fabric while working.

In order to protect the gold and silver threads from the air, which would cause them to tarnish, they are wrapped in **black tissue paper** and stored in **airtight tins.** The threads are handled as little as possible, as they are so fragile.

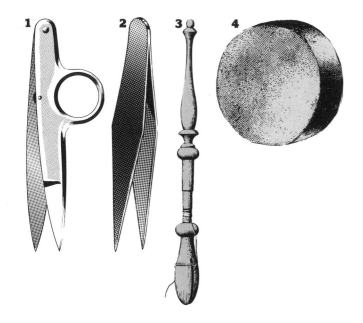
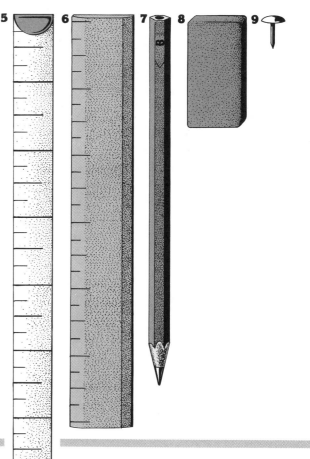

© DIAGRAM

Millinery

The making and finishing of hats has traditionally been divided into two crafts: hatting and millinery. Hatting is the craft of making men's hats, often including felting and scalding; millinery involves making, but more particularly decorating, women's hats, and tends to be a more gentle, ornamental craft.

The hats illustrated (right) were advertised in a shopping catalog at the turn of the century, and illustrate some of the styles of headgear that were popular at that time.

Milliner's tools include the following.
1 Measuring tape.
2 Sharp scissors for cutting card templates.
3 Wirecutters; wire is used to give shape and body to the hats.

4 Embroidery scissors for cutting fabric and decorations.
5 Hand mirror.
6 Dressmaker's pin.
7 Glass-headed pin.
8 Straw needle, a long, strong needle suitable for millinery.
9 Thimble.

10 Thumbtack, used for holding fabric temporarily in place.

Hatter's tools are illustrated (right).
1 Bow used for fluffing up fibers for felting.
2 Club used for planking, a beating to which the felt fibers are subjected after boiling and felting.
3 Runner-down used to smooth the hat over the block.
4 Tolliker used to flatten the hat brim.
5 Paddle with wires, used to raise a nap on the felt.
6 Hat iron.
7 Hat block.
8 Bell-crowned hat block.

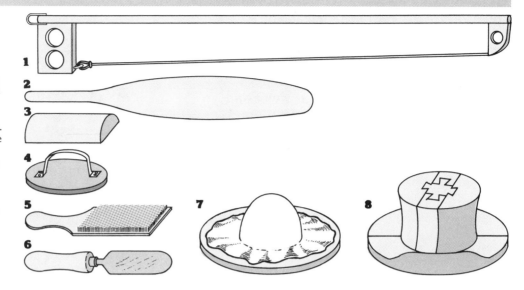

Additional **milliner's tools** are illustrated (below).
9 Spiral used for taking accurate head measurements.
10 Headband.
11 Brim roll made of fabric stuffed with sawdust.
12 Brim block, used with the brim roll for shaping hat brims.

13 Canvas dolly, a life-size head dummy.
14 Dome block.
15 Hat stretcher; the screw mechanism forces the two halves apart.
16 Kettle; steam is used to soften fabrics so that they can be shaped.

17 Iron used for pressing fabric before it is shaped.

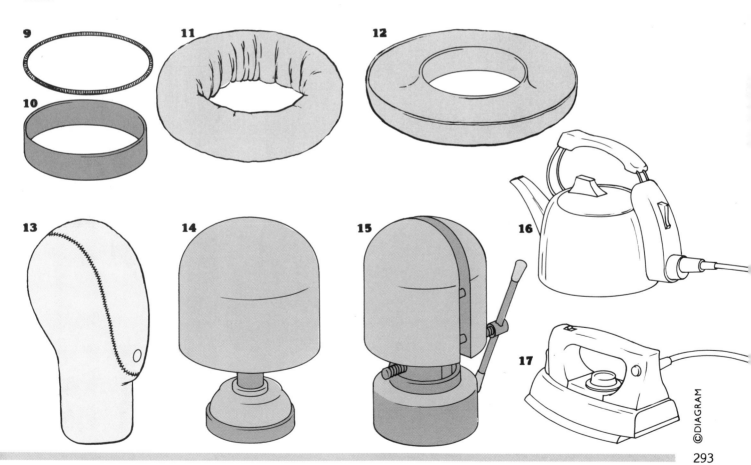

©DIAGRAM

Upholstery

Upholstery is the craft of attaching soft furnishing materials to the wooden frames of furniture, particularly chairs, sofas and footstools. Upholstery is a unique combination of skills, as the upholsterer ideally requires a knowledge of basic woodwork as well as an understanding of needlework and pattern-cutting.

This print from Diderot's "Encyclopedia of Industries" illustrates an upholsterer at work in the 18th century. The furnishings he is working on are typical of the lavish styles current in France at that time.

Upholstery makes use of many specialized tools, but other tools that are used for various crafts are also useful for upholstery, for instance pencils, rulers and other measuring equipment, pincers, chi els, pliers and screwdrivers.

1 Ripping chisel, with an angled blade for reaching into awkward corners.
2 Tack lifter.
3 Staple extractor.
4 Bevel rule.
5 Sash cramp, a holding device.

6 Mallet, used for driving the chisels.
7 Flat rasp.
8 Pincers with corrugated jaws; these are used to grip webbing and to stretch fabric.
9 Web strainer, used for stretching the webbing across chair seats.

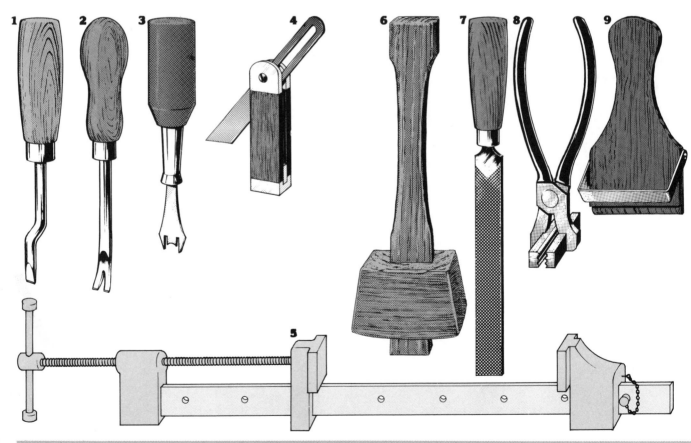

Trestles are used to rest the furniture on so that the required part of the frame is accessible. Trestles of various styles are illustrated (below and right); the double trestle (far right) is used to elevate entire pieces of furniture.

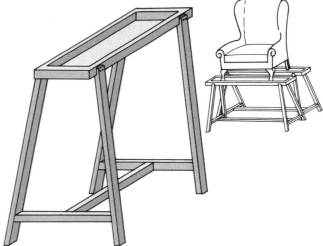

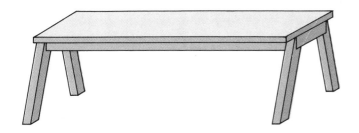

1 Bradawl, used for making screw holes in the wood.
2 Tack hammer.
3 Stud template, used to guide the positioning of studs so that they are evenly spaced.
4 Cabriole hammer, a small-headed hammer for studs.
5 Upholstery studs.

6 Trimming knife.
7 Upholsterer's skewer; these skewers are used to hold fabric and webbing in place while they are being measured and fitted.
8 Regulator, a long needle used to even out upholstery padding.

9 Mattress needle.
10 Spear-pointed needle.
11 Spring needle, a curved needle used for attaching upholstery springs.
12 Half-circular needle.
13 Brace and bit used to make holes for buttoning.

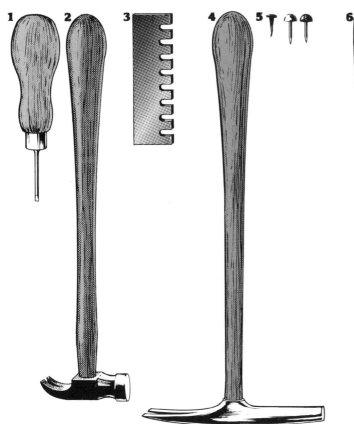

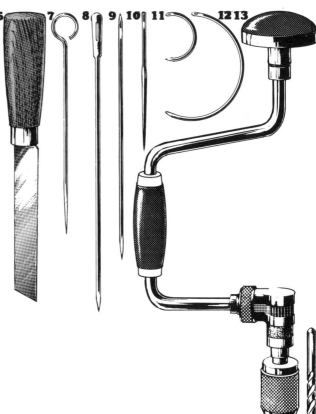

©DIAGRAM

18 Leatherwork

Leather clothing was probably first used by man in the Ice Age to protect his body and feet from the cold. Before the invention of metal tools, animal skins were scraped with sharp flints and stones. Later, man also learned the art of rubbing the hides with animal fats and oils in order to soften them. More sophisticated leather clothes and shoes, sometimes with stitching to hold them together, can be seen in contemporary depictions from the ancient world, and leather has been used for many centuries for making harnesses and saddles.

Leather, even when treated to clean and soften the hides, is a very tough material, and so the tools for working it need to be very sharp and strong and often require a certain amount of pressure in their use. Stitching leather presents particular problems, since the holes cannot be made with an ordinary needle in the way that fabric can be stitched. The stitch holes in leather are either made beforehand with special punches, or very strong needles are used and forced through the leather by applying pressure to their ends.

The revival of interest in leatherworking has led to the updating and development of the traditional tools, which have been improved by combining traditional styles with modern methods of shaping and tempering the metal. Today, tools are available in such a wide range of styles that every possible requirement for shaping or decorating leather is catered for.

The painting reproduced here is from the tomb of Tekhmire at Thebes, and shows leather craftsmen at work. Although the painting was executed over three thousand years ago, the tools are very similar to their modern counterparts.

Preparing and cutting

The leatherworker was once a key figure in every village; he had the specialized task of turning raw skins and hides into essential commodities—shoes, saddles, belts, bags and aprons. Tanning and curing processes are now largely chemical, but the craft of working with leather to produce attractive goods happily still survives.

The leather cutout shown (right) is the silhouette of an elk, and was made in the fifth century BC. The figure was found in the frozen tombs of Siberia; the ice had preserved the leather perfectly.

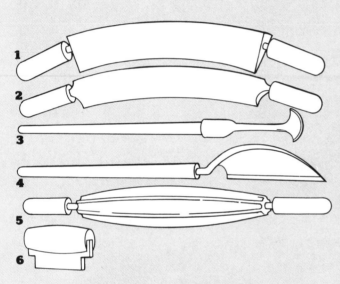

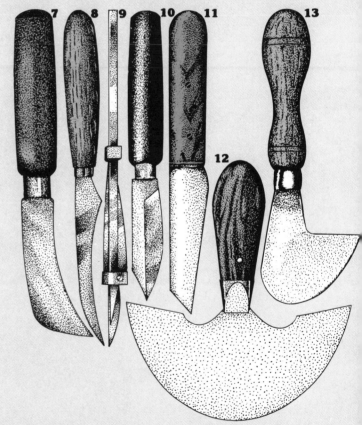

Leather needs to be tanned and cured in order to keep it soft and pliable. The hides are first soaked and scraped to remove the hair, fat, and any traces of flesh; they are then steeped in tannin, a chemical obtained from tree bark. The bark is stripped in the spring and ground up finely, then made up into the infusion used for soaking the hides. The hides remain in the **tanning vats** for anything up to a year, then the leather is washed, dried, and beaten thoroughly to make it soft and compact.

1 Fleshing knife for cleaning the raw hides. The tool is held in both hands and drawn down the flesh side of the hide over a curved surface.
2 Dehairing knife, used on the reverse of the hide.
3 Spud, a sharp tool for stripping the tanbark from the trees.
4 Skiver; this tool is for splitting hides and skins so that they can be handled easily.
5 Pin, a tool for removing the yellowish "bloom" from the grain side of the sheepskin and goatskin.
6 Slicker, used for burnishing the surface of skins.

Knives for leather vary widely in the shape and style of the blade. Each knife produces a particular stroke, and is adapted to meet specific leather-cutting requirements.
7 Hawkbill knife.
8 Curved clicker.
9 Gauge knife used for making cuts of an exact depth.
10 Sloyd knife.
11 Shoemaker's or **cobbler's knife.**
12 Round knife.
13 Single-head **saddler's knife.**

Leather-splitter (above) is used to split leather to a uniform thickness. The blades are adjustable to produce differing thicknesses of leather. As the leather is pulled through the blades, a piece is pared away from the top.

Cutting accessories enable the leatherworker to make accurate and safe cuts in the leather.

1 Steel square used when cutting right angles.
2 Cutting board made of nylon and rubber.
3 Zinc templates, used as guides when cutting curves or complex shapes.
4 Clamp for holding the leather while it is being pared.
5 Safety ruler, with a guard to protect the fingers against accidental slipping of the knife.
6 Steel ruler.

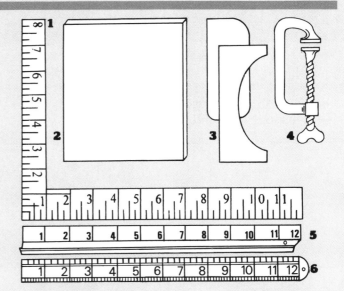

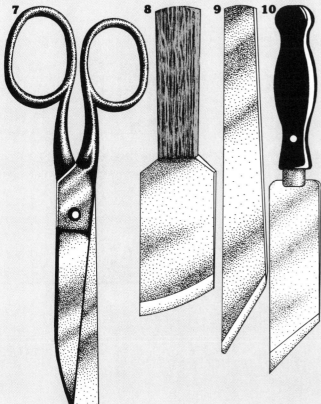

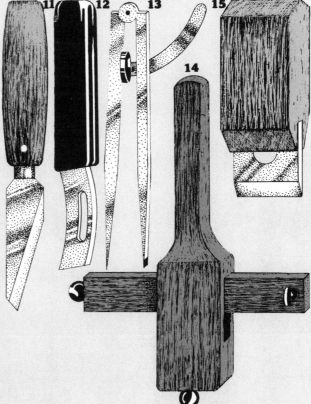

7 Leather shears with one straight-ended blade to ensure an accurate cut.
8 French-pattern paring knife used to thin the edges of leather pieces.
9 Swedish-pattern paring knife.
10 Skiving knife.
11 Bevel point skiver.

12 Skife; the hole in the tool is fitted with a razor blade, and pares an accurate width of leather from a cut edge.
13 Cutting dividers; one edge is sharpened to a cutting blade so that the tool can be used to cut circles.

14 Strap cutter, a tool used for cutting a strip of leather to a uniform width. The gauge of the blade is set and fixed, and when the tool is run down the side of a straight piece of leather it makes a parallel cut further in.

15 Home-made paring knife is made from a spoke-shave blade set in a wooden handle; this tool is used for paring down large areas of leather.

Leather decoration 1

Leathercarving is a craft that has become very popular in recent years. The leather for carving needs to be fairly thick, so that the knives will not cut right through it and so that there is some scope for modeling. All the tools used must be kept very sharp, otherwise they will not leave a clean impression on the surface.

The shield shown (right) is of cut and embossed leather, and was made in Italy in the 16th century. The technique used is that known as "cuir-bouilli," in which the leather is first boiled to soften it before being shaped.

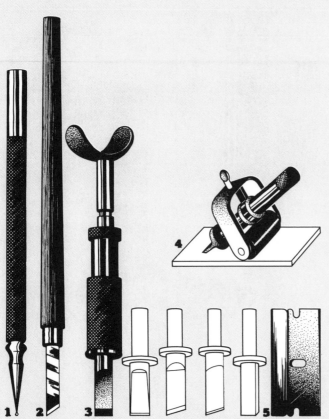
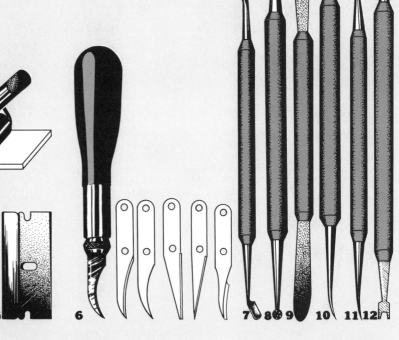

1 Tracer, a metal point used for transferring patterns or shapes onto the leather.
2 Incising knife with beveled blade.
3 Swivel knife with interchangeable blades; this is a very versatile leathercarving tool.

4 Swivel knife sharpener; the knife is screwed into the holder, which keeps it at the correct angle while it is run across the sharpening stone.
5 Razor blade for delicate cutting work.

6 Leathercarving knife with interchangeable blades. The different blades are used for cutting a variety of different strokes into the leather.

7,8,9,10,11,12 Modeling tools forged from stainless steel. These tools are used for pressing down and shaping outlines when carving patterns into leather; each head produces a particular mark on the leather surface.

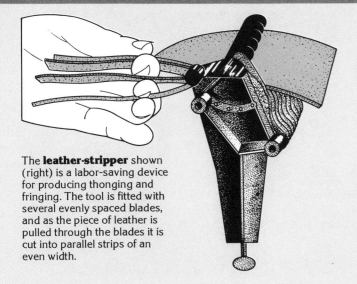

The **leather-stripper** shown (right) is a labor-saving device for producing thonging and fringing. The tool is fitted with several evenly spaced blades, and as the piece of leather is pulled through the blades it is cut into parallel strips of an even width.

A **turntable,** such as the one above, is a valuable accessory when leathercarving. The leather piece is placed on the top, and the turntable can be spun to present a new part of the work to the carving tool, so that the leather need not be picked up.

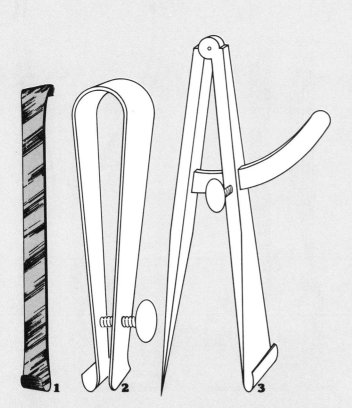

Racers or **races** are cutting tools with horseshoe-shaped cross-sections; the outside of the curve is sharpened so that it cuts a groove in the leather as the tool moves across the surface.
1 Double-ended racer.
2 Screw or **adjustable racer;** the straight edge can be used

as a guide at the side of the leather piece so that the line cut by the racer head will be parallel to the edge of the leather.
3 Compass racer, used for cutting grooves in the shape of a circle.

4 Gouge used for cutting channels in leather, either for decoration or as an aid to folding.
5 Adjustable gouge; this tool is capable of gouging grooves of various depths. The groove depth is altered by turning the guide ring on the handle.

6 Edge beveler or **edge shave** for rounding off and smoothing cut edges of leather.
7 Edge cutter, used to ensure that borders are cut accurately.

©DIAGRAM

301

Leather decoration 2

Punches are metal (or hard plastic) tools that are driven into the leather and leave either a cut or an indented shape when they are removed. Hammers and mallets are generally used with the punches in order to provide the necessary driving force. Punches may be used decoratively, or to produce holes for stitching, thonging, or fastenings.

The example of punched and stamped leatherwork illustrated (right) is a chair seat made from treated cowhide. The background of the pattern has been stamped all over with a repeat pattern to produce a regular texture.

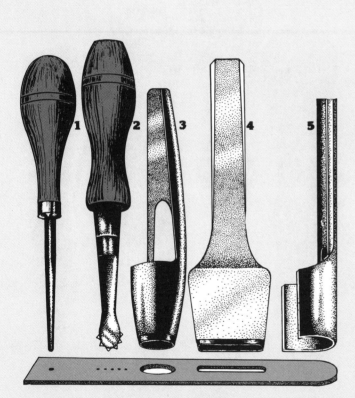

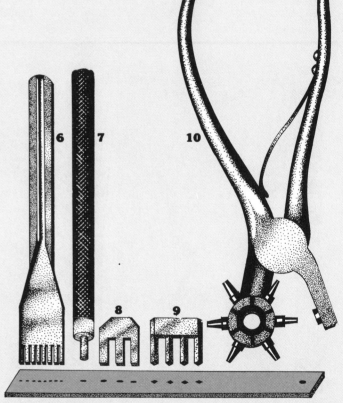

1 Fid awl used for enlarging punch holes.
2 Spacemaker; this tool makes indentations which are then pricked through with an awl.
3 Drive or **wad punch** for cutting small circular holes.

4 Bag or **crew punch,** used to cut elongated holes in the leather.
5 Strap end punch; this tool is used to shape the tongues of belts or the end of straps, and saves the trouble of cutting an accurate curve by hand.

6 Stitching punch or **pricking iron** with eight points, for making evenly spaced stitching holes.
7 Thonging chisel, a punch used for making lacing slits in leather.
8 Multiple-point thonging chisel, for making several slits simultaneously.

9 Diamond-point thonging chisel; this chisel produces slanted holes.
10 Revolving punch with six different-sized heads; each head punches a hole of a specific diameter. The punching is accomplished by squeezing the handles of the tool together.

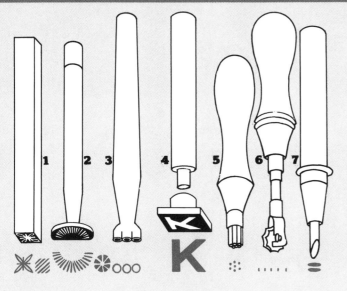

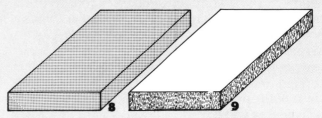

Stamp punches are used to impress decorative designs onto the leather surface.
1,2,3 Pattern stamps; these stamps may be bought ready-made, or may be created by the craftsman.
4 Alphabet stamp.
5 Stippler.
6 Embossing wheel.

7 Pyroelectric pen for burning patterns into the leather.
8 Rubber board for use with stamps and punches; the rubber protects the tool heads from damage.
9 Wooden end-grain block can be used instead of a rubber board.

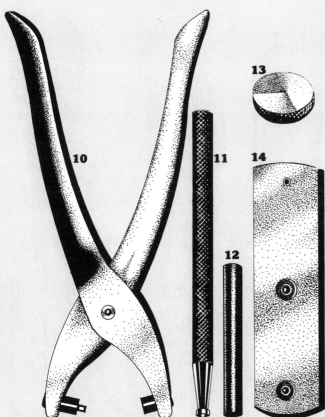

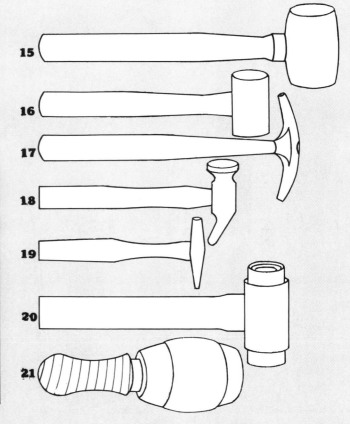

10 Eyelet pliers for setting metal eyelets into the leather.
11 Grommet setter.
12 Eyelet setter.
13 Anvil for use with eyelet and grommet setters.
14 Multiple anvil for setters of different sizes.

Hammers and mallets are used to strike punches, eyelet setters etc.
15 Rubber mallet.
16 Rawhide mallet.
17 Magnetic hammer stops metal fittings moving while they are being struck.
18 Shoemaker's hammer.
19 Riveting hammer.

20 Rawhide hammer.
21 Rawhide maul.

©DIAGRAM

Shaping, sewing, finishing

Leather can be shaped, stitched, glued, colored and dressed in an almost infinite variety of ways. Shaping can be achieved by folding, by hammering over a former, or by stitching several pieces of leather together. Dye can be applied to an entire article, or may be painted on in patterns, and smooth leather can be polished or waxed.

The print on the right illustrates some leather gloves that were made and sold at the turn of the century. Gloves are articles that are often made in fine leatherwork, and they present many challenges to the leatherworker because they require small, strong seams and very accurate shaping.

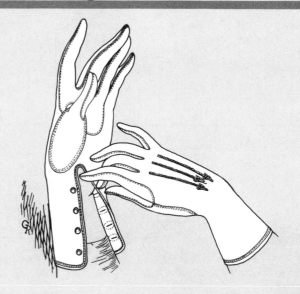

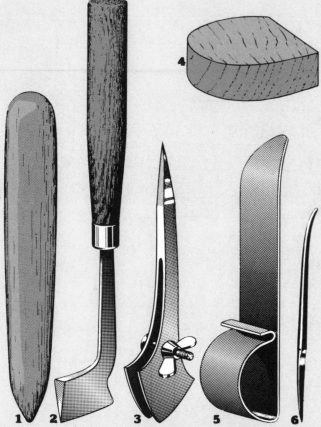
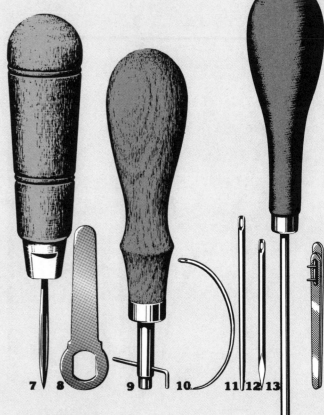

1 2 3 5 6 7 8 9 10 11 12 13

1 Bone folder used for making folds in leather.
2 Creaser for producing firm, neat creases.
3 Double creaser with adjusting screw so that the width between the creases can be altered.
4 Horseshoe-shaped **former** for making jewel-cases etc.

5 Bracelet bender used in shaping bracelets; the leather is hammered over the curved shape.
6 Curved sewing awl.
7 Harness awl, an awl with a chuck and wrench for fitting alternative heads.
8 Awl wrench.

9 Stitching awl used for placing stitch holes.
10 Curved leather needle.
11 Harness needle with blunt end.
12 Glover's needle.
13 Collar awl.
14 Lacing needle.

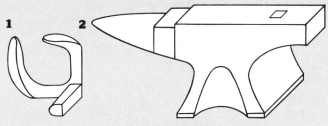

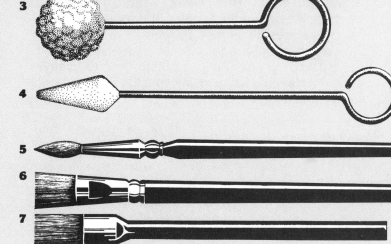

1 Last has multiple heads and is particularly useful for clinching nails in leather footwear.
2 Anvil is used as a base for hammering and shaping, and as a hard surface for eyelet and grommet setting.

Leather articles can be easily colored and dyed.
3 Wool dauber, a piece of sheepskin used for applying dye.
4 Hole dauber with pointed end for coloring the insides of punched holes.
5,6 Dye brushes.
7 Glue brush.

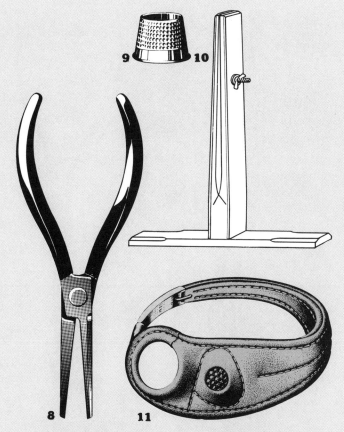

8 Lacing pliers, used to grip lacing so that it can be pulled tight.
9 Open-ended thimble with large indentations to take the thick needle heads.
10 Lacing pony; this tool holds pieces of leather while they are being stitched together.

11 Thimble palm used for pushing needles through the leather.
12 Wool for applying dyes, waxes and other dressings.
13 Shine brush for polishing up glossy finishes.

14 Edge slicker, used to smooth leather edges; the slicker is run down the cut surface.
15 Sole scraper, a tool for roughening leather surfaces (such as the soles of shoes) before they are cemented.

Saddlery and harnessmaking

Saddlery and harnessmaking are both very ancient crafts. The Romans used wheeled vehicles drawn by harnessed horses, and the Byzantines developed the saddle in the fourth century. Leather has almost always been used as the basic material, and distinctive tools have been devised to meet the specific requirements of the two crafts.

The print reproduced (right) depicts the inside of a saddler's workshop, and illustrates many of the tools used in the craft. The saddle tree being used in the print is very similar to those used by saddlers today.

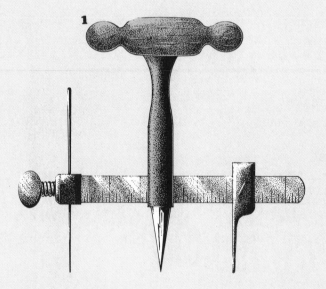

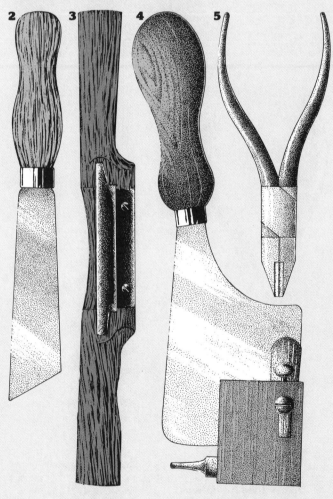

The saddler and harnessmaker, in addition to their specialized tools, also need many of the general leatherworking tools that have been illustrated on the previous pages—such tools as a paring knife, round knife, cutting gauge, edge trimmer, hole punches, pattern punches, racers, creasers, pricking iron, beveler, cutting board, hammers, and an anvil. All the various tools for cutting and shaping straps are mainly useful to the harnessmaker, and the many stitching tools will be required by the saddler and harnessmaker alike.

1 Washer cutter, a compass-like mechanism for cutting circles of leather.
2 Hand knife used for cutting and splicing.
3 Saddler's spokeshave for splitting and trimming the leather.
4 Plow or **plow gauge,** a tool for cutting straps and belts evenly by ensuring that the cut edges are parallel.
5 Cutting pliers.

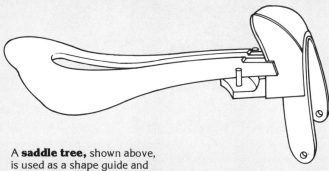

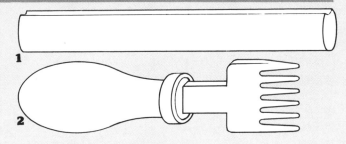

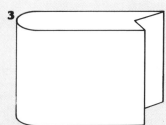

A **saddle tree,** shown above, is used as a shape guide and as a core for the finished saddle. The tree is covered with webbing and serge, and the pads of leather for the various parts of the saddle are stuffed and stitched onto the base as required.

1 Loop stick, used to form the leather hoops that hold straps in place.
2 Straining fork for stretching webbing or wet leather.
3 Rubber, a piece of hard wood or glass used for smoothing down leather or stitching.

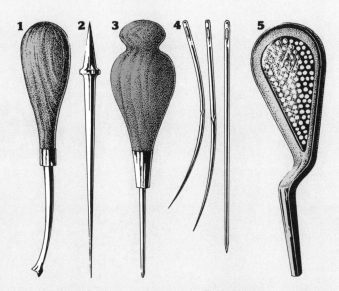

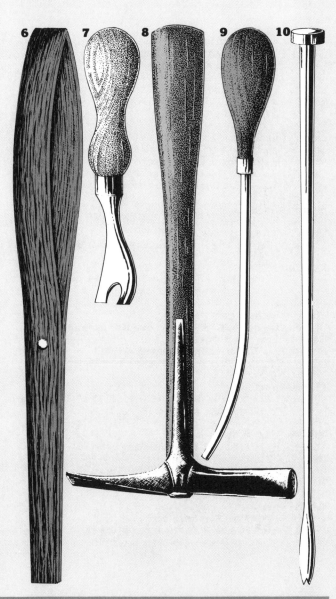

1 Checker, a small double creaser with parallel edges.
2 Seat awl used to regulate the stuffing in collars and saddles.
3 Sewing awl.
4 Harness needles.
5 Hand iron, a kind of heavy-duty thimble palm, used for driving the sturdy harness needles through the leather. The pointed end has a hole drilled to take the eye of the needle; this is used to apply pressure if there is not enough space available to use the broad part of the iron.

6 Clamp or **pair of clams;** the jaws hold the work while it is being stitched, and the clamp itself is gripped between the saddler's knees to hold it firm.
7 Nail claw is used to pull out the nails that temporarily hold the work together during the assembly and stitching.
  8 Saddler's hammer.
  9 Seat iron used for stuffing saddle pieces.
10 Collar rod, also used for stuffing.

Bibliography

General
Amman, Jost **The Book Of Trades** Dover
Diderot, D **Encyclopedia of Trades and Industry** Dover
Egbert, Virginia W **The Medieval Artist at Work** Princeton University Press
Feller and Tourret **L'Outil** Editeur
Flinders Petrie, W M **Tools and Weapons** Aris and Phillips
Griswold, R and K **The New Handicraft Processes and Projects** Van Nostrand Reinhold
Hickman, B **Japanese Crafts, Materials and Their Applications** Fine Books Oriental
Hommel, R P **China at Work** Doylestown Bucks Co
Reader's Digest **Things To Make And Do**
Salaman, R A **Dictionary of Tools** George Allen and Unwin

Writing and drawing ·
Fairbank, Alfred **A Handwriting Manual** Faber
Johnson, E **Writing and Illuminating** Pitman
Osley, A S **Calligraphy and Palaeography** Faber
Quick, John **Artists' and Illustrators' Encyclopedia** McGraw Hill
Whalley, Joyce I **Writing Implements and Accessories** David and Charles
Yee, Chiang **Chinese Calligraphy** Harvard University Press

Printing
Caza, M **Silk Screen** Van Nostrand
Chamberlain, W **Etching and Engraving** Thames and Hudson
Irving, W M **How Prints Look** Beacon
Moore, K H **How To Make Japanese Woodblock Prints** Acropolis Books
Ross and Ronald **The Complete Printmaker** Free Press

Making books
Johnson, E **Writing and Illuminating** Pitman
Lewis, A W **Basic Bookbinding** Dover
Middleton, Bernard **The Restoration of Leather Bindings** American Library Association

Painting
Hayes, Colin **Painting and Drawing Techniques and Materials** Phaidon
Sutherland, W G **Modern Signwriting** Sutherland

Pictures without paint
Hickman, Peggy **Silhouettes, A Living Art** David and Charles
Harbin, R **Secrets of Origami** Octopus
Hulbert, Anne **Victorian Arts Revived** Batsford
Portchmouth, John **All Kinds of Papercrafts** Studio Vista

Clay and pottery
McKenzie, Compton **The House of Coalport 1750-1950** Collins
Warring, Ron **The Amateur Potter** Pan Craft Books

Modeled and cast sculpture
Collins, Paul **Introducing Candlemaking** Batsford
Dawson, R **Starting with Sculpture** Studio Vista
Farnworth, Warren **Creative Work With Plaster** Batsford
Hauser, Christian **Art Foundry** Van Nostrand Reinhold

Carved sculpture
Dawson, R **Practical Carving** Studio Vista
Eliscu, Frank **Slate and Soft Stone Sculpture** Pitman
Meilach, Dona **Contemporary Stone Sculpture** George Allen and Unwin
Rich, Jack C **The Materials and Methods of Sculpture** Oxford University Press

Cabinetmaking
Blandford, Percy **Country Craft Tools** David and Charles
Mercer, H C **Ancient Carpenters' Tools** Horizon
Taubes, Frederic **Better Frames For Your Pictures** Thames and Hudson

Wood decoration
Child, P **The Craftsman Woodturner** Bell
Lincoln, W A **The Art and Practice of Marquetry** Thames and Hudson

Working with glass
Bernstein, Jack W **Stained Glasscraft** Collier Macmillan
Clarke and Feher **The Technique of Enamelling** Batsford
Haswell, J M **Mosaic** Thames and Hudson
Heddle, G M **Manual on Etching and Engraving Glass** Tiranti
Reyntiens, Patrick **The Technique of Stained Glass** Batsford
Savage, G **Glass and Glassware** Octopus

Fine metalwork
Branson, Oscar T **Indian Jewelry Making**
Choate, Sharr **Creative Casting** George Allen and Unwin
Untracht, Oppi **Metal Techniques for Craftsmen** Hale

Lapidary and beadmaking
Gemcraft Magazine

Preparing thread
Brown, Rachel **The Weaving, Spinning and Dyeing Book** Routledge and Kegan Paul
Leadbeater, E **Handspinning** Studio Vista

Weaving
Coffinet and Pianzola **Tapestry** Bonvent
Ling Roth, H **Studies in Primitive Looms** County Borough of Halifax
Tovey, John **The Technique of Weaving** Batsford
Wright, D **Complete Book of Baskets and Basketry** David and Charles

Knitting and knotting
McDonald, Joanna **Knitting** Burke's Pastime Series
Nottingham, P **Techniques of Bobbin Lacemaking** Batsford
Wright, Doreen **Bobbin Lacemaking** Bell

Needlework
Gostelow, Mary **Embroidery** Marshall Cavendish
Groves, Sylvia **The History of Needlework Tools and Accessories** David and Charles
Reader's Digest **Complete Guide to Sewing**
Whiting, Gertrude **Old Time Tools and Toys of Needlework** Dover

Leatherwork
Attwater, W A **Leathercraft** Batsford
Leathercrafters Supply Co Publications
Stohlman, Al **How To Carve Leather** Craftool

Acknowledgements

Abrasive Tools Ltd
Akron Tool Supply Co
Allcraft, Enamelaire Ltd
Amalgamated Tool Distributors Ltd
American Handicrafts
H W Anger and Son Ltd
Arnold and Walker
Claudius Ash, Sons and Co Ltd
E P Barrus Ltd
Benson Industries Ltd
The British Museum
British Oxygen Co
Brookstone Co Inc
Buck and Ryan Ltd
Burgon and Ball Ltd
CeKa Works Ltd
Cole Ceramic Laboratories
Albert Constantine and Son Inc
Charles Cooper (Hatton Garden) Ltd
Coronet Trading Co
Covington Engineering Corporation
Crafts Advisory Council
Crystalite Corporation
Deancraft Ceramic Supplies
Dryad
Ebersole Lapidary Supply Co
Emmerich (Berlon) Ltd
Entwistle, Thorpe and Co Ltd
Ferro (Great Britain) Ltd
Furnival Steel Co Ltd
Gemcraft Magazine
Gem Instruments Corporation
Gilman's Lapidary Equipment
GKN Fastener and Hardware Distributors Ltd
Greenham Tool Co Ltd
Beno J Gundlach Ltd
Hall and Ryan Ltd
L G Harris and Co Ltd
Hartley Reece and Co
James Hetley and Co Ltd
Highland Park Manufacturing
Hunter Penrose Ltd
George Ibberson
The Jacobs Manufacturing Co Ltd
C I Jenkinson and Son Ltd
Johnson Alridge Ltd
Johnson Matthey
A J Jubb Ltd
Keuffel and Esser Co
Kingsley North Inc
Knitmaster

C B Latham (Colours) Ltd
T N Lawrence and Son Ltd
Leathercrafters
Leather Journal
Lortone Fine Lapidary Equipment
A D McBurney
W J Meddings (Sales) Ltd
Minnesota Woodworkers Supply Co
Monument Tools Ltd
Nasco Arts and Crafts
Parry and Son (Tools) Ltd
Peugeot Outillage
George Pike Ltd
Podmore and Sons Ltd
Protofram Ltd
Proto Tool Division (International)
J W Ratcliffe and Sons (Engineers) Ltd
Rathbone Chesterman Ltd
Raytech Industries Ltd
Record Ridgway Tools Ltd
Tyrone R Roberts
George Rowney and Co Ltd
Russel Bookcrafts
The Salmon and Trout Association
Sandvik UK Ltd
Sculpture Associates Ltd
Sculpture House
Selectasine Silk Screens Ltd
The Shelburne Museum
Skilcrafts Division
Smith Francis Tools Ltd
Spear and Jackson (Tools) Ltd
SRS Diamond Tools Ltd
Stanley Tools Ltd
J Stead and Co Ltd
Swest Inc
Sykes-Pickavant Ltd
Tandy Leather Co
Taylor and Co Tools Ltd
Henry Taylor (Tools) Ltd
Taymar Ltd
Alec Tiranti Ltd
S Tyzack and Son Ltd (London)
University College, London
Vaughans (Hope Works) Ltd
The Vernon Park Museum, Stockport
The Victoria and Albert Museum
Westwood Ceramic Supply Co
Winsor and Newton Ltd
Woodcraft Supply Corporation

Index

Index

Index

Index

Picture Credits